"Every single American needs to read Michael Knowles's *Speechless*. I don't mean 'read it eventually.' I mean: stop what you're doing and pick up this book. We're running out of time to save our culture. We need to get smart and fight back now, and Michael spells out exactly how to do it!"

> —**Candace Owens,** bestselling author of *Blackout*, founder of BLEXIT, and host of *Candace*

"Michael Knowles is one of the most important conservative leaders of his generation. With characteristic wit and clarity, Michael explains how conservatives have continuously lost ground in the battle against political correctness despite decades of trying to stop it. *Speechless* is the most important book on free speech in decades—read it!"

> —**Senator Ted Cruz,** #1 bestselling author of *One Vote Away*

"Michael Knowles is a rare combination: the conservative who understands the roots of his opponents' thought, and the fighter who understands the necessity for tactical aggression. In *Speechless*, Knowles delivers a deeply necessary exposition on both."

> —**Ben Shapiro,** #1 bestselling author and host of *The Ben Shapiro Show*

"Michael Knowles not only lays out genuinely fresh and intelligent arguments in a persuasive style, but also shows real moral courage in breaking with the stale slogans of movement conservatism. This is more than a book, it is a sign of the times and needs to be widely read."

> —**Adrian Vermeule,** Ralph S. Tyler Professor of Law, Harvard Law School

"In *Speechless*, Michael Knowles sheds new light on the scourge of political correctness and 'cancel culture.' He perceives with keen insight the reasons conservatives have failed to thwart these destructive phenomena and offers helpful guidance on how to fight back. This book is a must-read for anyone who hopes to preserve our culture."

—**Mike Pompeo,** former U.S. secretary of state

"Michael Knowles's magnificent attack on political correctness in *Speechless* is like nothing you've ever read before. There's loads of fascinating history, such as the truth about 'Stonewall,' the source of one of JFK's most famous lines (Satan), and the story of Dr. John Money's sexual abuse of children based on his crackpot theories. While dismantling the Left's war on normality, Knowles also has some tough love for hapless right-wingers forfeiting our culture to the radical Left."

—**Ann Coulter,** political commentator and bestselling author of
¡*Adios, America!*

"Michael Knowles understands that we must take the radicals head on. In *Speechless*, he makes the compelling case that conservatives who cede territory or ignore the advance of adversaries do so at the peril of our nation. *Speechless* spells out how to fight and win."

—**Scott Walker,** president of Young America's Foundation and
former governor of Wisconsin

"Michael Knowles's powerful new book, *Speechless*, is a crucial milestone on the road to a revived conservatism in America. Knowles shows how Marxists like Gramsci and Marcuse created the woke cultural revolution with the aim of destroying the Western political and moral order. But Knowles's real target is contemporary 'conservatives' who've been hiding for decades behind feel-good slogans about freedom instead of rising to defend the actual beliefs that are the bedrock of our civilization."

—**Yoram Hazony,** bestselling author of *The Virtue of Nationalism* and chairman of the Edmund Burke Foundation

"This book is a howitzer in the fight against the totalitarians targeting both people and organizations for 'cancelation.' It explains in vivid detail the existential importance of this critical conflict."

—**Dan Bongino,** bestselling author and host of *The Dan Bongino Show*

"With *Speechless*, Michael Knowles proves himself a bold and intelligent iconoclast, reminding a wayward conservative movement that real freedom is freedom for the good, and that we must fight for the right to speak the truth, not merely to run our mouths."

—**Sohrab Ahmari,** author of *The Unbroken Thread: Discovering the Wisdom of Tradition in an Age of Chaos*

"With his signature eloquent bluntness, Michael Knowles delivers a knockout blow to leftists and a wake-up call to conservatives. Michael has lived the thesis of *Speechless* and issues a challenge to every patriot to stand up to the poison of political correctness by standing up for what we believe in. The Left will not just hate this book, they will fear it—especially if we heed Michael's clarion call."

—**Pete Hegseth,** bestselling author and Fox News host

"The answer is always more speech, not less. I believe that wholeheartedly, and for those of us on the left side of the political spectrum, *Speechless* is an important look at how the other side is thinking—or could come to think if Michael has his way. Though he and I disagree on much, including his take on the Left's use of 'vague' language, Black Lives Matter, and critical race theory, Michael's book is incisive, meticulously researched, and in-depth. I appreciate that he takes on those who share his own political ideology as well. If anything, *Speechless* will give you fodder for discussion with those you agree with and those you don't. And is there anything better than a good argument?"

—**Jessica Tarlov,** Democratic strategist, Fox News contributor, and head of research at Bustle

"If they can control the words we use, they can control the thoughts we think—that is Michael Knowles's disconcerting but compelling gravamen. Knowles analyzes a stratagem as old as Marxism, as contemporary as Facebook and Twitter, and as dangerous as any threat we have ever faced—and summons us to defeat it. A work of bravery."

> —**Peter Robinson,** Murdoch Distinguished Policy Fellow at the Hoover Institution and a former speechwriter for President Reagan

"Michael Knowles is a national treasure. He is witty, creative, and incredibly talented. Focusing on the new movement to shut us up and take away our fun, this book is a must-read by a true American. Buy this book and tell your friends."

> —**Charlie Kirk,** bestselling author and host of *The Charlie Kirk Show*

"Warning: this book is not politically correct. At a time when so many want to upend the system, Michael shows us exactly why the Founding Fathers got it right. *Speechless* teaches young conservatives how to work smarter, not harder, to win arguments and outwit their political opponents."

> —**Nikki Haley,** former governor of South Carolina and U.S. ambassador to the United Nations

"Michael Knowles has become one of America's most fearless and important political thinkers. In a time of unparalleled censorship, the fact that he put actual words in this book is proof of just that."

> —**Dave Rubin,** bestselling author and host of *The Dave Rubin Show*

"Michael Knowles, who is both sobering and funny, explains to readers just how dangerous 'political correctness' is. *Speechless* demonstrates that we're not dealing with mere polite euphemisms but rather a political agenda to stifle free thought through the strategic control of language. This book is a must-read for anyone wanting a diagnosis on how American culture and politics became so ill."

— **Andy Ngô,** journalist and bestselling author of *Unmasked*

"Knowles has written an insightful and gripping deconstruction of the mind-prison called political correctness. He doesn't just trace its origins, he reveals its destructive purposes. This is a must-read."

— **Andrew Klavan,** Edgar Award–winning and bestselling author and host of *The Andrew Klavan Show*

"Conservative complaints against 'political correctness' have become stale and visionless as many of the Right's own leaders play a game designed and dictated by the totalitarian Left. But we need not be so foolish, declares the rambunctious wit Michael J. Knowles in his dazzling new polemic. Readers: sharpen your pencils, as well as your minds, for between all your chuckles, gasps, and foot cramps (induced by serious toe-curling), Mr. Knowles will have you reaching for precise words in order to convey the precise meaning of your convictions."

— **Madeleine Kearns,** staff writer at *National Review* and contributor to *The Spectator*

"We are in a war for truth. Words matter, and Michael Knowles's *Speechless* nails how the Left has used political correctness to redefine not only acceptable speech but also reality."

— **Lisa Boothe,** Fox News contributor and host of *The Truth with Lisa Boothe*

"Never has a book about such an unpleasant topic—political correctness—been such a pleasure to read. Michael Knowles shows us that freedom and truth are necessarily related, that a society without standards is an illusion, and our liberties have limits. We must join the debate of today, then, on the terrain of truth, standards, and limits."

—**Ryan T. Anderson,** president of the Ethics and Public Policy
Center and author of *When Harry Became Sally: Responding
to the Transgender Moment*

"Knowles makes a compelling moral argument against the softness of Americans, right and left, whose deference to political correctness has helped create a culture in which bad ideas (and bad people) thrive. This book breaks away from the typical conservative talking points about the absoluteness of the First Amendment and posits a better solution to the political and social problems we face: good ideas represented by good speech."

—**Allie Beth Stuckey,** host of *Relatable*

Speechless

By the author of the satirical bestseller
Reasons to Vote for Democrats

SPEECHLESS

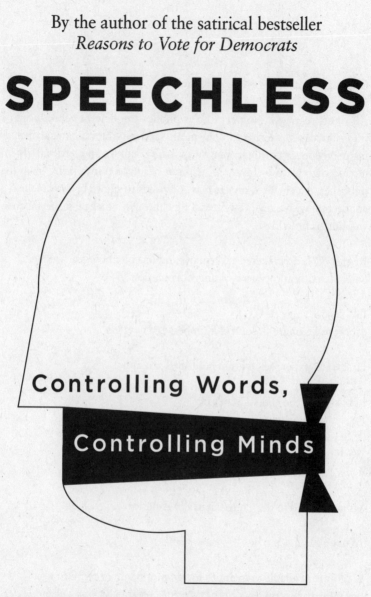

Controlling Words,

Controlling Minds

MICHAEL KNOWLES

Regnery Publishing
WASHINGTON, D.C.

Regnery® is a registered trademark and its colophon is a trademark of Salem Communications Holding Corporation

ISBN: 978-1-68451-335-2
Library of Congress Control Number: 2021933875

First trade paperback edition published 2022

Published in the United States by
Regnery Publishing
A division of Salem Media Group
Washington, D.C.
www.Regnery.com

Manufactured in the United States of America

10 9 8 7 6 5 4 3 2 1

Books are available in quantity for promotional or premium use. For information on discounts and terms, please visit our website: www.Regnery.com.

For Alissa, with love

CONTENTS

PREFACE

It is ironic that the author of a bestselling blank book should choose for his next subject language itself. But irony lies at the heart of political correctness. To call something "politically correct" is to acknowledge that it is not correct, at least by the standard of reality. A man in a dress is a man, but according to political correctness he is a "trans woman," a term with the same ironic structure. To call someone a "trans woman" is to acknowledge that he is not really a woman.

Moreover, few people who support "political correctness" invoke the phrase in earnest. More often they will do so with tongue in cheek, as if to acknowledge their own overreach. But though self-aware progressives may not always use the term with sincerity, they always seem to enforce the standards with severity.

My wordless bestseller took aim at the Left. Ironically, my second book spills more ink on the failures of the Right, which through decades of incompetence has permitted political correctness to invert our culture. The more conservatives attempt to fight political correctness, the worse the problem seems to get. The situation recalls Chesterton's distinction between progressives, whose business "is to go on making mistakes," and conservatives, who exist "to prevent mistakes from being corrected."[1]

Americans became aware of political correctness during the late 1980s and early 1990s, as debates over language roiled college campuses and corporate boardrooms. The speech standards had developed gradually since the early twentieth century with little notice from conservatives, who would spend the next several decades fighting against them in vain.

Conservatives have failed to thwart political correctness because most do not understand what it is. They have portrayed political correctness and its derivatives, including "wokeism" and "cancel culture," as "censorship," which we must oppose in the name of "liberty." These bumper sticker arguments reveal that conservatives understand as little about liberty and censorship as they do about political correctness.

Despite the vague complaints of many conservatives over the years, political correctness is not merely a synonym for "censorship," though the two concepts are related. Political correctness (PC) is a standard of speech and behavior along leftist ideological lines. It no doubt censors certain words and actions, but then so does chivalry. All societies embrace and enforce standards. Yet today this basic social fact seems to be lost on many conservatives. Ironically, the putative defenders of tradition have come to eschew standards altogether.

The social engineers who developed political correctness set out with the explicit goal of destroying traditional standards and establishing new standards of speech in their place. As politically correct orthodoxy has progressed, its proponents have often contradicted themselves. But though PC's positive claims may change by the hour, its attack on traditional mores remains constant.

Conservatives have reacted to the new standards in two ways. The more compliant among them have acquiesced to the radicals' demands, adopting politically correct language as a matter of convenience and, they believe, politeness. The slightly more stalwart conservatives have declined to accept the new jargon, but they have grounded their refusal in vague appeals to liberty and denunciations of censorship. Rather than making a substantive defense of the culture they claim to wish to conserve, these conservatives are left making limp defenses of "free speech" in the abstract, with nothing to say in practice.

Both conservative reactions advance the purpose of political correctness: the more compliant surrender, the more stalwart self-immolate. Either way, the traditional speech standards are abandoned. And since nature abhors a vacuum, the new standards take their place, in a process by which the latter category of conservative eventually transforms into the former.

Conservatives have wasted decades attempting to thwart political correctness through dime-store philosophizing over "free speech," progressively abandoning their substantive cultural inheritance for a misbegotten notion of liberty that can never exist in practice. They marvel at the supposed irony that leftists now advocate censorship while conservatives endorse the anything-goes approach to speech that liberals of a prior generation once disingenuously demanded. They fail to realize that they have fallen into PC's trap.

While these befuddled conservatives gawk, political correctness progresses apace, suppressing and even prohibiting words and ideas considered common sense for millennia. To stop it, conservatives must ditch the shallow slogans and take their opponents' arguments seriously. Contrary to center-right self-flattery, the leftist intellectuals who developed political correctness understand speech, censorship, and even liberty far better than the conservatives who have thus far opposed it. Politically correct radicals wield speech, censorship, and liberty in a war against our civilization. And none can doubt they are masters of these tools: they have thoroughly succeeded in reordering our words, thoughts, and culture.

Either conservatives will summon the courage to enforce traditional standards, or we will all succumb to the new rules. The choice between "free speech" and "censorship" is illusory—a false dichotomy from which political correctness has profited for a century. We will speak and act according to some set of standards or other, whether conservatives are willing to admit it or not. Political correctness has left us speechless, but the right to speak means nothing to those who have nothing to say.

Michael Knowles
January 18, 2021
Nashville, Tennessee

CHAPTER 1

THE WEST IN WONDERLAND

*"When I use a word," Humpty Dumpty said in rather
a scornful tone, "it means just what I choose
it to mean—neither more nor less."*

*"The question is," said Alice, "whether you can
make words mean so many different things."*

*"The question is," said Humpty Dumpty, "which is
to be master—that's all."*[1]

With that brief exchange in *Through the Looking-Glass*, Lewis Carroll prefigured political correctness, the war of words that would define our politics more than a century later. What does it matter whether we call someone who breaks the law to enter the country an "illegal alien" or an "undocumented immigrant"? What's the difference between a Christmas tree and a "holiday tree"? Doesn't global warming pose the same threat to our civilization regardless of whether or not we rename it "climate change" or, more recently, "the climate crisis"? Why quibble over semantics?

The difference may be semantic, but semantics matter. When people describe a distinction as "just semantics," they mean to dismiss it as trivial. But how many of those people know what the word "semantics" means? "Semantics," it turns out, means meaning itself. Semantics is the study of the meaning of words, which exist so that we can distinguish one thing from another. This process of discernment begins with our very first words. A baby cries out, "Mama!" to distinguish Mommy from Daddy. Today even that basic distinction falls afoul of politically correct orthodoxy, as we will come to see. What Humpty Dumpty understands and Alice fails to see is that words shape how we think; they color how we view the world.

Humpty Dumpty had clearly read his Aristotle, the ancient philosopher who defined man as a "political animal," more so than "any other gregarious animals" because man has the power of speech. Other beasts may have the ability to grunt or yell indications of their pleasure or pain, but only man has the power of speech "to set forth the expedient and inexpedient, and therefore likewise the just and the unjust."[2] Man alone can tell good from evil. The ability to articulate those distinctions "makes a family and a state." And both Humpty Dumpty and Aristotle understood that the relationship goes further: politics is speech. In statecraft, when speech fails, war ensues. If, in the words of the Prussian military theorist Carl von Clausewitz, "war is the continuation of politics by other means," speech is the practice of politics by ordinary means.[3]

Language changes naturally over time. A notable recent example is the word *literally*, which once meant the use of words in their most basic sense without recourse to metaphor but now also describes the use of words metaphorically, which is the opposite of literally. If that isn't confusing enough, the word *literal* refers to letters, which are symbols and therefore the opposite of literal, and the non-literal sense of *literal* goes back at least a century, to James Joyce's novel *Ulysses*—all of which is to say that the natural evolution of language is complicated.[4]

The politically correct perversion of language, on the other hand, is neither natural nor complicated. Political correctness is like a man attempting to give himself a nickname. The artifice and transparency of the act make it impossible. The nickname will never stick—unless the man has the power to enforce it.

Consider social scientists' newly invented, politically correct name for young criminals. There is nothing natural about calling a young criminal a "justice-involved youth," and the reason for the lexical change isn't complicated.[5] Leftist political activists wanted to spring bad kids from the clink, so they decided to rename the juvenile delinquents, who by definition had involved themselves with injustice, as "justice-involved" to make the public more amenable to their release. The unnatural jargon hasn't taken hold in popular culture, but it has stuck in higher education and administrative government because the activists and their allies control those institutions.

Since words matter so much, the definition of "political correctness" itself must matter. Differing definitions of political correctness agree that it involves rejecting certain language to better conform to some political orthodoxy. The *Oxford Dictionary of New Words*, for example, defined the term in 1997 as "conformity to a body of liberal or radical opinion on social matters, characterized by the advocacy of approved views and the rejection of language and behavior considered discriminatory or offensive."[6] These are all necessary features of political correctness, but they are not sufficient. Political correctness does not merely mask the harsh realities to which clear language refers; it actually contradicts the underlying meaning of words, thrusting culture through the looking glass.

Most people recognize that language plays a role in leftist ideology. But the relationship goes further than that. In *Nineteen Eighty-Four*, George Orwell describes the relationship between the politically correct lexicon Newspeak and the English socialist regime IngSoc. "Don't you see the whole aim of Newspeak is to narrow the range of thought?" asks a member of the totalitarian party. "The Revolution will be complete when the language is perfect. Newspeak is IngSoc and IngSoc is Newspeak."[7] The same might be said of political correctness and leftism. A man who believes he is a woman must at all times be called a "trans woman," or better still just a "woman," because leftist ideology demands a liberation so radical that a man can become a woman simply by saying so. Language does not merely reinforce the ideology but actually constitutes it.

Some defenders of political correctness have admitted that they use language to manipulate reality, but they maintain that their conservative opponents do the very same. The Oxford linguist Deborah Cameron made this accusation during the debates over political correctness that roiled the academy in the 1990s. According to Cameron, with the advent of political correctness, liberal "verbal hygienists" were simply pointing out "that the illusion of a common language depends on making everyone accept definitions which may be presented as neutral and universal, but which in fact represent the particular standpoint of straight white men from the most privileged social classes."[8] In other words, they declared value-neutral language a lie designed to enforce patriarchy and white supremacy.

Around the same time, the literary theorist Stanley Fish published *There's No Such Thing as Free Speech*, in which he denies the possibility of a "disinterested search for truth" and insists that traditional language is "no less politically invested" than politically correct jargon.[9] Even the conservative columnist Robert Kelner dismissed concerns over the new jargon in the early 1990s as "our phony war on political correctness." Conservatives manipulate language and culture too, he conceded, and that spin constitutes our own form of political correctness.

The critics have a point. Leftists are not alone in manipulating language for political ends. President John F. Kennedy, quoting the journalist Edward R. Murrow, famously commended Winston Churchill for having "mobilized the English language and sent it into battle" during the Second World War, and no one has ever accused Winston Churchill of being "politically correct," as Lady Astor could attest.[10] Statesmen and orators from Pericles to Donald Trump have wielded language to suit their purposes. No one considers Donald Trump "politically correct" either. What the critics miss is that the manner in which each side manipulates language differs.

The Right tends to manipulate language by using strong words to evoke clear images. Churchill promised, "We shall fight on the beaches, we shall fight on the landing grounds, we shall fight in the fields and in the streets, we shall fight in the hills; we shall never surrender."[11] Churchill didn't speak of "overseas contingency operations," as Barack Obama would decades later. He told the world he would "fight"—a clear, concise

Saxon word. Then he tells you exactly where he intends to fight, and then, in case you missed his point, he tells you he will "never surrender."

Donald Trump chose similarly blunt words, albeit perhaps less gracefully, when he announced his bid for president in 2015 by decrying illegal aliens, whom he accused of "bringing drugs," "bringing crime," and being "rapists." Even his caveat—that some, he assumed, were "good people"—relied on strong, simple speech to convey his meaning.[12] Whether or not you liked what Trump said, you knew what he meant.

Political correctness relies on euphemism, soft words used to sugar-coat harsh realities. We all use euphemisms some of the time as a matter of good manners. We refer to old women as "women of a certain age." We mourn those who have "passed away" rather than those who have died. In prior ages, a lady went to "powder her nose," and she still uses the "bathroom" or the "restroom" rather than the toilet.[13] We use euphemisms—literally, "well-speaking" or auspicious words—to be polite.[14]

In all those cases, the polite euphemism softens the reality it describes, but it doesn't contradict that reality. The old woman is indeed a woman of a certain age. The poetical "passing away" describes the spiritual fact of death. Women may indeed powder their noses after they've done whatever else they do in rooms that often include a bath and in which anyone might rest. Polite euphemisms soften the truth, but they do not lie.

Leftists tend to manipulate language by using vague terms and jargon not just to soften but to conceal and even contradict the realities to which they refer. Killing babies in the womb becomes "women's healthcare" and "reproductive rights," even though abortion results in precisely the opposite of health and reproduction. After a Muslim terror attack on a church in Sri Lanka, Hillary Clinton tweeted her support for "Easter worshippers," a bizarre moniker designed to hide the victims' Christian identity. In fact, the sole instance in which Hillary used clear language in 2016—when she referred to Americans who refused to support her as "deplorable" and "irredeemable"—proved to be the most disastrous moment of her campaign. Clinton had made a critical error for a radical politician: she told people what she really thought.

A blunt term such as "cripple" conveys a clear meaning. Less vivid synonyms such as "disabled" or "handicapped" retain that meaning while giving perhaps less offense. The politically correct "handi-capable" gives less offense still but at the expense of meaning: the euphemism means the opposite of the condition it describes.

Political correctness lies. The very phrase "political correctness" illustrates this intrinsic dishonesty, as "political correctness" is no more political than any other sort of speech, and it isn't correct. The phrase came into use as a way to categorize falsehoods that ideologues believed ought to be considered true for political purposes. Much politically correct jargon follows the formula of adding an unusual adjective or adverb to a noun or adjective. The late presidential speechwriter and conservative columnist William Safire described this form as the "adverbially premodified adjectival lexical unit," the description itself a play on PC jargon.[15] Around the time Safire described this form, comedians were also mocking it endlessly, translating terms like "short" into the politically correct–sounding "vertically challenged."

In this formula, the adjective or adverb usually serves to negate the noun or adjective it modifies. The term "politically correct" itself follows this politically correct formula by using an adverb to negate the adjective it precedes. That is, "correct" means true. But "politically correct" means not true. "Justice" means getting what one deserves without favor. The politically correct "social justice" is a form of injustice because it means getting what one does not deserve because one is favored. "Marriage" in every culture throughout history has meant the union of husbands and wives. "Same-sex marriage," however favorably one views the concept, is not marriage.

The history of "same-sex marriage" offers a telling glimpse into the ultimate purpose of political correctness: to achieve political ends without ever having to engage in electoral politics. One cannot really speak of a debate over same-sex marriage in the United States because there never was any debate. Before any such debate could take place, politically correct wordsmiths had redefined marriage to include monogamous same-sex unions and in so doing redefined the central question of the debate from nature to rights. The question "What is marriage?" passed quickly to "Who has the right to get married?" presupposing that the first issue had already been settled in the radicals' favor.

According to the view held by every society everywhere in history, marriage involves sexual difference. Some societies permit polygamy, some permit divorce, but all cultures have understood marriage as an institution of sexually different spouses oriented toward, though not necessarily requiring, the procreation and education of offspring. A good-faith debate over redefining marriage would first consider what marriage is and why everyone everywhere else in history has gotten it so wrong. But that debate might have stymied political "progress." The cultural revolutionaries found it far easier to redefine the terms according to the conclusions they hoped to reach. When conservatives acquiesced to the verbal trickery, the radicals won the debate before it had even begun.

Likewise the debate over whether "transgender" people should be able to use the bathroom of their choice came down not to argument but to the definition and redefinition of terms. This ostensibly frivolous question dominated American political discourse in the mid-2010s, and the debate continues even into this decade, despite the infinitesimally small number of people who actually suffer confusion over their biological sex—a condition known as "gender dysphoria" before radicals normalized the disorder.

On the one side, the politically correct insisted that men who believe themselves to be women must be permitted use of the women's bathroom. After all, those poor souls aren't really men but rather "trans women," entitled to use the facilities available to every other kind of woman. On the other side, sensible people observed that men are not in fact women, and if single-sex bathrooms are to exist at all, men must be barred from the ladies' room. The debate, such as it was, had little to do with bathrooms or rights or the small number of sexually confused people themselves. Rather, it came down to Alice's question "whether you can make words mean so many different things" and to Humpty Dumpty's politics: "which is to be master?"

Political correctness goes further than demanding fealty to a set of opinions. It promises to fundamentally transform the world. Political correctness contorts language in an attempt to remake reality along leftist lines. The *Washington Times* has described it as "the destructive manipulation of idealism to suit it for totalitarian purposes."[16] According to the premises of political correctness, a man can become a woman if only we all agree to call him "her." A baby will cease to be a baby if we all just agree to call him a "fetus" or better yet—since "fetus" means "offspring"— a "clump of cells" or a "product of pregnancy." As Hamlet declares when feigning madness, reality is nothing more than "words, words, words," and "there is nothing either good or bad but thinking makes it so."[17] According to political correctness, words do not describe reality; they constitute it.

CHAPTER 2

REDEFINING REALITY

The radical skepticism on which political correctness relies collapses under even the slightest scrutiny. Every freshman philosopher who ever declared, "There is no such thing as objective truth," must inevitably explain how he came to regard his own statement as objectively true. But logical rigor and consistency do not much matter when it comes to political correctness, which implicitly denies the possibility of both. Even taking this radical skepticism as just another well-intentioned lie—assuming, for example, that the politically correct know deep down that a man who believes himself to be a woman is not actually a woman, but they consider it good for that individual and for society to pretend that he is—means uncovering an even more radical premise at the heart of political correctness: the evil of truth and the goodness of lies.

Traditionally, our society has frowned on lying. We have believed that "the truth shall make you free." The politically correct invert this understanding. They believe that the truth about the man who thinks he's a woman will actively harm him. The truth about the baby will damage the mother who wants to rid herself of it. They consider the truth destructive and lies compassionate. For the politically correct, the lie that the man is a woman will free him from the shackles of biology. The lie that a baby isn't human or alive will free his mother from the undesired umbilical chain that imposes responsibility upon her. If language really does constitute reality, there isn't anything wrong with this sort of lying. If words can redefine reality, it isn't even lying at all.

So ambitious a goal as redefining reality has required broadening the political realm beyond its usual bounds. Consider the example of "handicapable." Until the past half century, politics was understood to concern public matters. Euphemisms for physical and mental handicaps would have fallen well outside the scope of politics. But political correctness blurs the distinction between the public and private spheres. Now "the personal is the political," as the feminists of the 1970s insisted. According to political correctness, nothing can be merely personal. Everything must become political, with one exception: politics.

Ironically, while political correctness politicizes everything from household chores to running shoes, it constricts the traditional realm of electoral politics. According to the politically correct, we may and indeed must parse the public significance of seemingly trivial personal choices, but no one may dare question—much less put to a vote—a man's right to the ladies' room, which the new standards enshrine as a fundamental right beyond the realm of legitimate debate. What begins with semantic quibbles ends with refashioning the entire political order.

Most historians of political correctness trace it to the early 1990s, when *New York Magazine* ran a front-page story on the phenomenon. Writers such as Dinesh D'Souza and Roger Kimball found PC flourishing in the campus debates of the 1980s and the battle over the Western canon. William Safire and leftist academic Ruth Perry traced it to the Chinese communist revolutionary Mao Tse-tung and his American acolytes in the 1960s.[1]

In fact, progressives' unnatural manipulation of language goes back further still. The spelling reformers of the early twentieth century tried to hasten society's march toward progress by erasing inefficient flourishes and vestiges of tradition from language. The Esperantists of the late nineteenth century sought to break down barriers to global communication and identity through the contrivance of a universal second language, ironically just at the moment when the world's traditional universal second language, Latin, fell out of favor among progressives, who derided it as "dead" even before they had succeeded in killing it. Despite progressives' best efforts, Esperanto never caught on, and few today speak the unnaturally simplistic language. (It should come as no surprise that one of the few people ever to speak Esperanto as a child is George Soros, the most infamous and influential leftist financier of our age.[2])

Political correctness has fared better at colonizing popular language, but people don't seem to like it any more than they did Esperanto. Polls conducted in 2015 by Fairleigh Dickinson University and the Pew Research Center found that most Americans count political correctness among the nation's most pressing problems.[3] According to a study by scholars Stephen Hawkins, Daniel Yudkin, Míriam Juan-Torres, and Tim Dixon, opponents of political correctness make up a silenced majority of Americans comprising every race, age, and sex.[4]

Donald Trump relied on this group in his 2016 campaign. "I think the big problem this country has is being politically correct," Trump told moderator Megyn Kelly in August of 2015.[5] "I've been challenged by so many people, and I don't, frankly, have time for total political correctness. And to be honest with you, this country doesn't have time either."[6] America faced urgent problems, and Americans couldn't waste their breath on elaborately choreographed semantic distortions.

Ironically, Trump's broadside against political correctness harkened back to the PC debates of the late twentieth century, when both conservative accommodators and leftist critics argued that the battle over verbal hygiene, while perhaps a noble cause, distracted from more substantive debates over serious issues.[7] Who cares if you call a poor black man "black" or "African-American" when neither moniker will help him to escape generational poverty? That argument held sway in the twentieth century when the aims of the campaign for political correctness seemed limited. But by the twenty-first century, political correctness seemed less a silly distraction than a significant threat to the political order. Even many leftists considered political correctness a waste of time in PC's early days. But that critique faded away as partisans across the political spectrum came to recognize the singular power of language to transform perception.

One sees evidence of this power in leftists' perpetual invective against "institutional racism," even as the Left controls virtually every influential institution in the country: the mainstream media, Hollywood, administrative government, higher education, lower education, and Big Technology, among others. If "institutional racism" really threatened the justice and harmony of our republic, whose fault would that be? The Left controls the institutions, and it wields them to enforce a rigid regime of politically correct speech that can destroy the reputations of any who dare to contradict it. A single unapproved word can cost a man his livelihood, and enforcement of this ideological orthodoxy begins long before he enters the workforce.

According to a 2019 poll conducted by Echelon Insights for the center-right Young America's Foundation, nearly half of students aged thirteen to twenty-two had "stopped [themselves] from sharing [their] ideas or opinions in class discussions" for fear of reprisal from the enforcers of political correctness. The students have every reason to fear punishment for contradicting leftist orthodoxy. During a lecture I gave for the Young America's Foundation in 2019 at California State University, Los Angeles, on the costs and dangers of illegal immigration, a professor declared that my very speech constituted "violence" against students and as such ought to be banned.[8] Curiously, not once in her censorious diatribe did she acknowledge that the audience and I, through our tax dollars, paid the salary that enabled her own public speech.

For the politically correct, conservative speech is violence, and leftist violence is speech—a new standard that took center stage during the tumultuous spring of 2020. As the Chinese coronavirus led to the widespread curtailment of political and economic rights throughout the United States, some conservatives peaceably demonstrated for an end to the lockdowns. Leftist politicians, public health "experts," and propagandists in the mainstream media castigated the pro-freedom protesters as "super spreaders" and even "serial killers," accusing them of inflicting violence on their fellow citizens simply by breathing.[9]

Yet when the death of George Floyd sparked widespread riots, looting, and arson in 2020, those same politicians and propagandists excused the violent gatherings as speech not only protected by the First Amendment but indispensable to containing the virus. "White supremacy is a lethal public health issue that predates and contributes to COVID-19," read an open letter signed by over 1,200 public health "experts." The self-styled experts implausibly celebrated leftist riots for curing the virus even as they condemned peaceful, conservative protests as "dangerous" to public health and, even worse by the light of the new standards, "mostly white."[10] The demagogues curtailed their opponents' freedom and invented new rights for themselves, not through the democratic process, but through the redefinition of words.

Conservatives never seem to fight back. They can't even seem to keep up. Just as soon as they learn the newly coined term or definition, the jargon mutates again. The fate of the word "retarded" highlights conservatives' slow response to the semantic crusade. Sometime around the early 2000s, the radical wordsmiths banned the word "retarded," which literally means "slow," for the softer euphemism "mentally challenged," a term on its face no less offensive than the word it replaced, only different. The change seemed arbitrary, bound by its own logic to change again at the whims of the speech police. But this constant flux is a feature, not a bug, of political correctness. As the Claremont Institute's Angelo Codevilla explains, "The point of PC is not and has never been merely about any of the items that it imposes, but about the imposition itself." For this reason, the British historian Paul Johnson defined political correctness as "liberal fascism."

Political correctness goes back much further than the people caught in its grip seem to understand. Most people trace the movement's origins to the popular culture of the 1990s or the campus curriculum debates of the 1980s or the radical revolts of the 1960s. No matter where people locate its origin, PC always seems new and aberrant, destined to collapse under the pressure of its own absurdity. In fact, political correctness goes back further still. It has not arisen through the delusions of "leftist loons" or the sensitivity of "snowflakes."

Political correctness is an insidious and influential political strategy developed by sophisticated thinkers and propagated over the course of a century by revolutionaries seeking to subvert our culture as well as by dupes who know not what they do. Even the most conscious opponent of political correctness struggles to avoid its euphemisms because the jargon shapes the society in which we move and therefore the way in which we think. As a fish forgets the water in which he swims, so we fail to recognize the subtler effects of political correctness on our culture.

Resistance against this hostile takeover of our language and culture will take more than haphazard polemics. It requires an accurate history of the movement and a coherent political philosophy to rebuff it, neither of which conservatives have managed to develop over the century since political correctness began. Gibes about "triggered snowflakes" followed by rote bumper-sticker slogans exalting "free speech" will not suffice to stem the revolutionary movement, which seeks to redefine reality and thereby transform the political order. Political correctness has always been a power grab. From PC's earliest days, its practitioners have cared about the meaning of words only as a means to an end. The question is how to be master—that's all.

CHAPTER 3

CULTURAL HEGEMONY

In 1848, Karl Marx and Friedrich Engels predicted the "inevitable" triumph of socialist revolution.[1] By 1929, as the Italian Communist Party founder Antonio Gramsci languished in prison, the revolution seemed decidedly evitable even to Marx's most fervent disciples. Marx had declared that the oppressed underclasses of Europe would quickly rise up and throw off the shackles of tradition and social order that held them in bondage. But it turned out the poor proles enjoyed their traditions. If the social order enslaved them, the slaves didn't seem to know or care.

Marx viewed man as a material rather than a metaphysical or hylomorphic being, and consequently he believed that material conditions define history and politics.[2] The machinery of the Industrial Revolution had formed the oppressed proletariat into a revolutionary force, and the inevitable unfolding of history would compel it to overthrow its oppressors.[3] But while Marx and Engels perceived the historic enormity of industrial exploitation, they failed to recognize a stronger, more pervasive force that inhibited revolution: culture.

Karl Marx died a failure in 1883. The revolution had not materialized. But two years after Marx's death, the first in a new generation of Marxists was born who would empower Marxism by redirecting its focus from economics to culture. The first of these "cultural Marxists" was the philosopher, critic, and Hungarian minister of culture Georg Lukács, who was soon eclipsed by the godfather of this new ideological movement: Antonio Gramsci, Marxist philosopher and communist politician.

In recent years, leftist activists have attempted to rewrite the history of this pivotal political movement, cultural Marxism, as a "conspiracy theory." The most ambitious revisionists have added the implausible charge of "anti-semitism" to the smear. Political operatives at the Southern Poverty Law Center (SPLC) launched a censorious campaign based on this canard as early as 2003. Bill Berkowitz, a leftist activist and freelance writer for the SPLC, claimed that the term cultural Marxism was "intended to conjure up xenophobic anxieties," in particular against "the Jews."[4] In May 2019, leftist activist and Al Jazeera columnist Paul Rosenberg took to the pages of Salon to indict "cultural Marxism" as "the grand unifying narrative for the hard, fascist, and neo-Nazi right," comparing the concept to the Protocols of the Elders of Zion, which served "to inspire Hitler and his Nazis."[5]

The concerted effort to make the phrase "cultural Marxism" taboo underscores the central strategy of political correctness: control the words, control the culture. And the strategy worked. By 2019, mainstream information channels accepted the new definition. Wikipedia, the most popular source for general knowledge on the internet, had redefined cultural Marxism as "an anti-semitic conspiracy theory which claims that the Frankfurt School is part of a continual academic and intellectual effort to undermine and destroy Western culture."[6] (When one investigates the phrase "conspiracy theory," which came into fashion in its present meaning during the late 1960s, one discovers leftists insisting that research into the origins of "conspiracy theory" itself constitutes a conspiracy theory.[7])

In an essay outlining the sudden leftist denial of a well-known intellectual movement, political scientist Paul Kengor reflected on the charge.

"An 'anti-semitic conspiracy theory'?" he asked. "That sounds like the very conspiracy-mongering that the anonymous writers are charging as conspiracy-mongering."[8] So it was, and the conspiracy-mongers didn't intend to let Professor Kengor off the hook just because he had figured out their game. Predictably, an alumnus of Kengor's college mailed a letter to the professor's bosses assailing him for uttering the forbidden phrase and demanding his dismissal.[9]

How can one even blame the author of that letter? He merely parroted the definition offered him by the mainstream media, which in turn parroted leftist activists, who for their part invented the smear out of whole cloth. This very process of cultural transformation exhibits what Gramsci called "cultural hegemony," later reformulated by the radical student activist Rudi Dutschke as "the long march through the institutions."[10] Leftists now have such sway over the culture that they can spread their lies on a whim. In smearing Kengor, the Left proved his point.

Radicals seek to silence any mention of "cultural Marxism" because that well-known intellectual movement undergirds, though it does not fully explain, the phenomenon of political correctness. They justify their censorship of the phrase and their attacks against those who dare utter it as a matter of public safety. The logic goes something like this: *A couple of deranged killers once also griped about cultural Marxism, so we must prevent word from getting out about that intellectual movement, which also does not exist.* The fearmongers never seem to show the same worry over the radicals who preach Marxism in T-shirts celebrating Che Guevara, who spilt an ocean of blood in its name.

In a November 13, 2018, piece in the *New York Times*, Yale professor Samuel Moyn offered the typical argument: "That 'cultural Marxism' is a crude slander, referring to something that does not exist, unfortunately does not mean actual people are not being set up to pay the price, as scapegoats to appease a rising sense of anger and anxiety." Moyn assailed the concept as "inseparable from" the "most noxious anti-Semitism" and "a dangerous lure in an increasingly unhinged moment."

But just a few paragraphs earlier in the very same piece, Moyn contradicted his own thesis. "Some Marxists, like the Italian philosopher Antonio Gramsci and his intellectual heirs, tried to understand how the class rule they criticized worked through cultural domination," he admitted.[11] In other words, cultural Marxism does exist, it has been around since the early twentieth century, and its most prominent progenitor was Italian, not Jewish. So much for "conspiracy theories" and "anti-semitism."

Among Mussolini's many sins and blunders, the least acknowledged and most significant may have been the dictator's decision to imprison Antonio Gramsci—not because Gramsci didn't deserve it, but because imprisonment afforded the communist agitator the time and focus to write his influential *Prison Notebooks*.

"For 20 years we must stop this brain from functioning," explained the prosecutor at Gramsci's trial in 1926.[12] With the hindsight of a century, one understands the prosecutor's fear and sense of urgency. But given the widespread recognition of Gramsci's genius, one fails to understand the fascist regime's decision to permit him a pen and paper in his cell. Rather than stop Gramsci's brain from functioning, Mussolini focused it so that it would resound throughout the ages.

Gramsci continues to exert his influence even today, particularly on university campuses and from there throughout the broader culture. A recently deceased founding member and president of the International Gramsci Society was Joseph Buttigieg, an influential professor of English at Notre Dame whose son, Pete, sought the Democratic Party nomination for president in 2020. That a putatively "moderate" presidential candidate could boast so radical an intellectual pedigree highlights the extent to which Gramsci's views have infiltrated the mainstream.

In 2011 the elder Buttigieg published the first and only critical edition of Gramsci's *Prison Notebooks* translated into English.[13] The journal entries give readers a glimpse into not merely the seeds of political correctness but also the justification for the denial and deceit practiced in its name, particularly in Gramsci's admiration of Niccolò Machiavelli, the prince of political immorality and founder of modern political science. The name

Machiavelli conjures different and contradictory images to different people. He defended principality; he supported republics. He encouraged deceit in public dealing; he demanded honesty about human nature. He was an active participant in the political intrigues of his time; he was a disinterested philosopher communing with the ancients.

Many more scholarly books have investigated Machiavelli's true character and aims. For our purposes it suffices to understand how Gramsci viewed the man and, through him, the relationship between political philosophy and politics—theory and practice. Gramsci read in Machiavelli "a 'philosophy of praxis' or a 'neo-humanism,' in that he does not recognize either immanent or transcendent elements (of the metaphysical kind) but only the *concrete action of men* who because of their own historical needs work on and transform reality" (emphasis mine).[14] For Gramsci, Machiavelli was no dispassionate political scientist but a man of action.

Gramsci, too, was a man of action—a practicing politician until his imprisonment—but he recognized that the revolution he sought could never take place without cultural upheaval. Gramsci believed that Marxists should aim to attain what he called "cultural hegemony," an early expression of Andrew Breitbart's famous dictum that "politics is downstream of culture." And the beating heart of culture is language.

In the little-read *Discourse or Dialogue about Our Language*, Machiavelli compares the infiltration of an opponent's language with the military tactics used by ancient Rome to control foreign territories and armies. By "cultural hegemony," Gramsci understood, as did Machiavelli, that society may be overcome not solely by force but also by internal subversion. A crafty revolutionary may find more success by transforming a society's traditions, institutions, and most of all its language than by picking a fight out in the open.

According to stereotype, the absentminded professor can tell you everything about his abstract theories, but he knows nothing of the practical world. Intellectuals, ideologues, and radicals may excite one another with their utopian visions, but their lack of common sense precludes them from persuading common people. No revolution can succeed if it opposes common sense. Therefore, the clever revolutionary must transform the common sense to accord with his vision.

So Gramsci undertook to change the common sense by infiltrating the social institutions that shape common sense. He differentiated between "wars of maneuver," in which the revolutionaries engage their opponents head on, and "wars of position," in which the aggressors defeat their adversaries by gaining positions of power within the established institutions. The latter strategy has come to be called the "long march through the institutions," a phrase "ubiquitously attributed" to Gramsci, in the words of Joseph Buttigieg, but in fact coined by Rudi Dutschke. For revolution to take hold, it does not suffice merely to control the means of production or even the levers of political power; it requires cultural hegemony—total domination of the prevailing institutions.

"Together with the problem of gaining political and economic power," explained Gramsci, "the proletariat must also face the problem of winning intellectual power. Just as it has thought to organize itself politically and economically, it must also think about organizing itself culturally." Gramsci understood that culture cultivates—at both the individual and societal level. "Culture . . . is organization, discipline of one's inner self, a coming to terms with one's own personality. It is the attainment of a higher awareness," he wrote.[15] Gramsci desired to create a new "higher awareness" for the oppressed proletariat because he deplored the "awareness" with which he found them.

Gramsci encountered the same dilemma his disciples face today: no matter how confident they are in the ability of their radical theories to improve the lot of the common man, the common man never seems to like those theories. In fact, the common man tends to enjoy his own customs, language, and way of life. This contentment must therefore constitute a "false consciousness" that cannot be overcome save by "raising awareness," a popular phrase derived from Gramsci. To raise the awareness of the people, to transform the common sense, one must subtly uproot and replant their culture. "Every revolution," he wrote, "has been preceded by an intense labor of criticism, by the diffusion of culture and the spread of ideas amongst the masses of men."[16] Thus the revolutionary must take up two goals simultaneously: to criticize and to educate.

A group of Marxist academics took up the task in the 1920s, first in Germany and later in the United States. Initially called the Institute for Marxism and later the Institute for Social Research, the group came to be known simply as the Frankfurt School, after the university that lent the scholars institutional credibility.[17] The Frankfurt School developed the social philosophy of Critical Theory, which over the past century has come to dominate not just college campuses in the United States but primary and secondary education as well. These educational institutions have offered an incubator to protect and nourish Critical Theory even after the fall of the Berlin Wall relegated orthodox Marxists to their own ash heap of history.

In the words of Martin Jay, the preeminent and sympathetic historian of the Frankfurt School, "The academy has become virtually the last refuge of critical thinking of the type epitomized by the Frankfurt School and the opportunities for its practical realization have virtually disappeared." Though Jay derides "the alarmist Right" for "its often hysterical campaign against the alleged specter of 'political correctness,'" he nonetheless acknowledges Critical Theory's "unexpectedly secure—perhaps ironically even . . . canonical—status as a central theoretical impulse in contemporary academic life."[18]

The double meaning of the word "critical" obscures Jay's assessment of academia. Critical thinking in the sense of objective analysis hardly exists on university campuses today. But the sort of thinking proposed by Critical Theory dominates. And just what is the theory? Simple: to criticize.

The Frankfurt School theorists varied in interest, approach, and even ideology. "What united them," according to Max Horkheimer, an influential early director of the Frankfurt School, "was the critical approach to existing society."[19] Some modern critics of Critical Theory portray the Frankfurt School as a monolithic movement with a substantive message, but this analysis fails to give the devils their due. Concrete systems may be criticized, as the critical theorists well knew. The Frankfurt School never left itself open to the sort of attack it leveled at others. The strength of Critical Theory came not from any philosophical coherence but rather from its position, in Jay's words, "as a gadfly on other systems."[20]

In an 1843 letter to the German philosopher Arnold Ruge, Marx called for "the ruthless criticism of all that exists."[21] Marx wanted to watch the world burn. While the Frankfurt School diverged from Marx in many ways, it remained faithful to this delight in destruction. According to Marx, the bulk of mankind was enslaved by economic circumstance. According to Gramsci and the Frankfurt School, culture was the culprit. But both Marxism and Critical Theory propose, in the words of Horkheimer, "to liberate human beings from the circumstances that enslave them," by which he meant Western civilization, though even that grand target fails to capture the enormity of their goal.[22] The Frankfurt School saw enslavement even beyond the bounds of society, in nature itself—a perception that helps to explain the group's obsession with sex.

Critical Theory entered the world through the unholy matrimony of Marx and Freud. At its most basic tactical level, the Frankfurt School, especially Erich Fromm, Max Horkheimer, and Herbert Marcuse, sought to reconcile sex and socialism. The Frankfurt School took its cues from Marx, who denied the classical conception of human nature as fixed and permanent.[23] Instead, he considered it to be socially constructed and therefore fluid. "The human essence is no abstraction inherent in each single individual," wrote Marx in *Theses on Feuerbach*. "In its reality it is the ensemble of the social relations."[24] From this understanding of human nature, or rather the lack thereof, Gramsci derived the necessity of cultural hegemony. Fromm, Marcuse, and other neo-Marxists deduced from it the revolutionary importance of sex.

No social relation influences the "human essence" more than sex, which sits at the center of every creation account. Uranus plows Gaia in the ancient Greek myths. The sacred prostitute Shamhat tames Enkidu's savage lust and civilizes him in *The Epic of Gilgamesh*. Within the first three chapters of Genesis, Eve tempts Adam, he succumbs, and God banishes mankind from paradise. If social relations hold the key to transforming the "human essence," sex holds the key to human relations.

Sex also plays a role in the construction and destruction of society's fundamental institution: the family. Culture-minded Marxists have long understood that any successful "march through the institutions" must overcome the family. Among the most imaginative and memorable of these deviants was Wilhelm Reich, an Austrian communist and disciple of Freud who carried his patients from the psychiatrist's couch to the bed. When those unprofessional relations produced children, Reich often forced his wives and mistresses to snuff them out with illegal abortions.[25]

In 1940, Reich published his bizarre, pseudoscientific treatise *The Function of the Orgasm*, which blamed chastity for illness, poverty, and war. Reich believed that the mystical energy "orgone" constituted the primary force of life and that "psychic health depends upon orgastic potency." He encouraged people to sit for extended periods of time in wooden boxes he called "orgone accumulators." Reich viewed the traditional family as society's "endemic illness," which he called "familitis."[26] He encouraged all manner of deviancy to destroy the family, just as his ideological heirs do today through the encouragement of often self-contradictory sexual theories and "gender identities," whose absurdity must be perpetually denied and concealed by the straight-faced enforcers of political correctness.

Wilhelm Reich may have been nuttier than a fruitcake, but his perverse theories found a large audience and flourished during the "free love" movement of the 1960s. Orgone accumulator contraptions gained popularity among literary celebrities such as J. D. Salinger, Saul Bellow, and Norman Mailer; and Woody Allen parodied them as the "orgasmatron" in his 1973 film, *Sleeper*.[27] Reich's ideas continue to impress prominent leftists, whose radicalism perhaps owes to cooking too long in their orgone accumulators. Less charming than the orgasmatron was Reich's fascination with "the elucidation and concrete realization of child and adolescent sexuality," a disturbing theme that has enthralled radicals of the far Left for decades. But this perverse obsession with child sexuality follows naturally from the cultural communists' premises: if man has no fixed nature, then the "human essence" derives from human relations, the most influential of which is sex, which must therefore be molded from the earliest stages of life.

The socialist senator and sometime presidential candidate Bernie Sanders expressed this once-prominent strain of leftist sexual thought in an infamous 1969 op-ed for the radical *Vermont Freeman*:

> In Vermont, at a state beach, a mother is reprimanded by Authority for allowing her 6-month-old daughter to go about without her diapers on. Now, if children go around naked, they are liable to see each other's sexual organs, and maybe even touch them. Terrible thing! If we bring children up like this it will probably ruin the whole pornography business, not to mention the large segment of the general economy which makes its money by playing on people's sexual frustrations. The Revolution is coming and it is a very beautiful revolution. It is beautiful because, in its deepest sense, it is quiet, gentle, and all-pervasive. It KNOWS.[28]

Sanders outgrew his perverted sexual rhetoric over time. By 2015, he disavowed the bizarre essays as "a dumb attempt at dark satire in an alternative publication."[29] In fact, he eschewed identity politics altogether, campaigning instead on the class conflict that defines classical Marxism. Sanders's career harkens back to the early Marxists of the nineteenth century, who sought to remake society through political revolution. Despite his dalliances with Reich's orgastic theories, Sanders stands for the class struggle of the Old Left. But as Bernie campaigned for president in 2016 and 2020, another force arose in the tradition of the twentieth-century cultural Marxists, who understood that class engendered weaker bonds of solidarity than culture and race. Black Lives Matter, a radical organization that formed in 2013 after the trial of George Zimmerman for the killing of Trayvon Martin, demonstrated the racial focus of the New Left.[30]

Both shades of red have endured into the twenty-first century. The socialist senator, some eccentric essays notwithstanding, has "been insanely consistent his whole life," as the podcaster Joe Rogan once observed, albeit with insufficient emphasis on the adverb.[31] Sanders's socialism has more in common with old-school labor warriors than with the cultural radicals who supplanted them during the 1960s.

Bernie reserved his ire not for "straight, white males" or "colonizers" but for "the millionaires and billionaires," though he dropped the millionaires from his invective after he became one in 2016.[32] Sanders took issue not with Bill Shakespeare, but with Bill Gates.[33]

Bernie's longstanding divergence from modern-day, mainstream leftists on immigration highlights the distinction.[34] Though Sanders brought his position more into line with the Democratic Party's pro-immigration policies during his presidential runs, particularly in 2020, the Vermont senator long opposed increased immigration because he felt it would harm American labor. "It does not make a lot of sense to me to bring hundreds of thousands of those workers into this country to work for minimum wage and compete with Americans' kids," he explained in 2013.[35]

Patrisse Cullors, co-founder of the Black Lives Matter movement, described herself and co-founder Alicia Garza as "trained Marxists."[36] The organization's third co-founder, Opal Tometi, has been more circumspect in her self-definition, though one may deduce Marxist sympathies from the several photographs of her smiling next to Venezuela's communist dictator Nicolás Maduro.[37] Cullors, Garza, and Tometi share Sanders's basic Marxist framework. But they didn't name their organization "Workers' Lives Matter" or "Proletarian Lives Matter." While Bernie focuses on wealth to fight a class war, BLM highlights race to wage a culture war.

Sanders's war is one of maneuver. He endeavors to change society by winning elections, which is why he spent a decade of his life running unsuccessfully for office before finally winning the mayoralty of Burlington by just ten votes. He then launched more unsuccessful bids, for governor and then Congress, before winning a seat in the House of Representatives and later the Senate, at which point he ran two unsuccessful campaigns for president. For all his radical rhetoric, Bernie confined his revolution to the traditional political realm.

Black Lives Matter has embraced a different strategy: a war of position. Though it behaves much like a political party, Black Lives Matter has not yet run a candidate for office. Instead, it has infiltrated the cultural institutions: Hollywood, corporate America, the mainstream media, technology, higher education, lower education, and various civic associations.

In mid-2020, Netflix and Amazon Prime began promoting "Black Lives Matter"–themed movies on their streaming platforms. Twitter changed its own Twitter bio to "#BlackLivesMatter" with the later addition of "#BlackTransLivesMatter," in case the former declaration did not suffice for the grievance-mongers.[38] Goodyear Tires encouraged employees to embrace BLM while banning them from suggesting that "all lives matter," that "blue lives matter," or that we ought to "make America great again."[39]

Universities, the incubators of BLM ideology, adorned their student-athletes' uniforms with the motto. Primary and secondary schools adopted it into their curricula with the *New York Times*'s anti-historical 1619 Project, which, over the objections of even left-wing academic historians, baselessly recast the American Revolution as a war to preserve slavery.

In June of 2020 even the Boy Scouts, once a bastion of traditional American values, announced the creation of a new "diversity" badge in partnership with Black Lives Matter.[40] To ascend the Boy Scouts' highest ranks a scout no longer need even be a boy, but he or she does need to recite the credo of self-described Marxists.[41]

BLM's cultural Marxist roots help to explain the organization's "queer" advocacy despite black Americans' traditional opposition to aberrant sexual behaviors. In the mid-2000s, just 21 to 25 percent of black Americans supported redefining marriage to include same-sex unions, a percentage far lower than among whites and Hispanics, and that difference persists to this day.[42]

Nevertheless, despite black Americans' relatively conservative views of sex, Black Lives Matter declares on its website, "We are self-reflexive and do the work required to dismantle cisgender privilege and uplift Black trans folk, especially Black trans women who continue to be disproportionately impacted by trans-antagonistic violence."[43] Fortunately very few "black trans women"—that is, black men who present themselves as women—are murdered each year, and when the killers are discovered, they usually turn out to be black themselves.[44] So why would an organization ostensibly dedicated to racial issues devote so much energy to sex?

Not only does Black Lives Matter "foster a queer-affirming network" and free itself "from the tight grip of heteronormative thinking," it seeks ultimately to "disrupt the Western-prescribed nuclear family structure."[45] Wilhelm Reich couldn't have put it better. On closer inspection, Black Lives Matter seems to use race merely as an instrument in the same project undertaken by culturally sensitive radicals all the way back to Antonio Gramsci.

Bernie has spent his career encouraging speech, particularly radical speech, as he did in his independent newspaper columns and fringe documentaries. After losing the Democratic presidential nomination in 2016, Bernie debated the merits of socialism with conservative senator Ted Cruz on CNN.[46] Sanders pursues direct confrontation with other ideas in the public square, confident that his views will prove the more persuasive.

The self-proclaimed Marxists of Black Lives Matter have taken the opposite approach, seeking instead to silence any and all who disagree with them. It should come as no surprise, therefore, that Bernie Sanders and Black Lives Matter have locked horns on the campaign trail. On several occasions during the 2016 and 2020 presidential cycles, Black

Lives Matter activists stormed the stage at Sanders campaign events and took his microphone away from him. Alongside similar leftist groups such as Antifa, they have shouted down speakers, demanded firings, and generally stifled speech on university campuses, in corporate boardrooms, and everywhere in between.

In their efforts to combat creeping political correctness, conservatives tend to agree with Sanders on the form of battle. The answer to bad speech, they insist, is more speech, following a line of thinking popularized by the liberal philosopher John Stuart Mill and Supreme Court Justice Louis Brandeis among others.[47] Whatever else one might say about Sanders, he has respected the traditional American political process, spreading his radical ideas on newspaper pages and the campaign trail.

Black Lives Matter and other more culturally minded radicals have taken a different tack. They have pursued their political goals outside of ordinary channels, disrupting campaign speeches and even extorting corporations and public figures.[48] The answer to bad speech, they believe, is censorship.

Which strategy has proved more effective? By 2020, after nearly four decades in political office without a single legislative achievement to show for it, Bernie Sanders once again lost the Democratic Party nomination for president, that year to Joe Biden, a self-styled "moderate" who nonetheless adopted many of the mottos and policy goals put forward by Black Lives Matter in his bid to ride the zeitgeist to victory. Sanders's political action accomplished little; the cultural hegemony achieved by Black Lives Matter and its fellow travelers transformed the country.

Like Sanders, conservatives have failed. They have failed to conserve our culture from the radicals' designs. They haven't even managed to conserve the ladies' room. More speech has delivered us more bad ideas, chief among them the censorship of traditional speech. The very word "censorship" sends a chill down the spines of most Americans, and yet, however distasteful it seems, the tactic appears to work.

No two people could disagree more on the subject of socialism than Ted Cruz and Bernie Sanders. But these seeming opposites have more in common than perhaps either of them would admit. They each respect the standards that set the boundaries of our political system. Both men may wish to change that system according to their political lights, but they undertake that task while respecting the established rules.

Black Lives Matter and like-minded cultural revolutionaries do not respect the rules. They recognize that established standards of speech and behavior will always impede their plans; indeed, the thwarting of such radicalism is the standards' very purpose. Contrary to conservatives' usual talking points, these radicals understand free speech far better than its supposed defenders.

From the 1920s through the 1970s, the radical rantings of the revolutionaries met derision and dismissal. The country was not yet ready for the "orgasmatron." By the second and third decades of the twenty-first century, however, those ideas had entered the mainstream. Eventually the radicals achieved cultural hegemony. Having realized much of Gramsci's, Reich's, and the Frankfurt School's visions, today's revolutionaries have only to enforce their new orthodoxy through a ruthless system of censorship—and thereby usher in our brave new world.

CHAPTER 4

STANDARDS AND PRACTICES

Radical theorists had not long pursued culture as their means to revolution before artists, the producers of culture, took notice. In the 1930s and '40s, two British novelists saw the coming cultural tyranny: George Orwell and Aldous Huxley. The phrases they coined have become bywords for the politically correct regime: "Newspeak," "Big Brother," "thoughtcrime," "doublethink," "memory hole," "brave new world."

While these artists did not predict the future, we may call them political prophets. As my friend Father George Rutler has observed, prophets "predict the future only in a derivative sense of cautioning about the consequences of denying the truth."[1] Orwell, Huxley, and other writers who sounded the alarm during this era had no need of a crystal ball because they saw the seeds of political correctness planted all around them.

In 1948, George Orwell wrote *Nineteen Eighty-Four*, a dystopian novel about a totalitarian government's use of thought control to maintain power. The inversion of the year in which he wrote prefigured the future inversion of standards that has come to pass, off the page. Orwell imagined a world under universal surveillance and perpetual historical revision. As his protagonist Winston Smith explains, "Every record has been destroyed or falsified, every book rewritten, every picture has been repainted, every statue and street building has been renamed, every date has been altered. And the process is continuing day by day and minute by minute. History has stopped. Nothing exists except an endless present in which the Party is always right."[2]

The Black Lives Matter riots of 2020, which targeted and destroyed countless historical monuments throughout the United States, put Winston's words into action. The rioters wrought their violence in the name of "social justice" and "woke" politics, new jargon for the same old scourge of political correctness. The rioters took their cues from the *New York Times*'s 1619 Project, which cast the United States as hopelessly unjust on the false premise that the Founding Fathers fought the American Revolution to preserve slavery.

Although academic historians from across the political spectrum refuted this central lie, the *Times* persisted, and the revisionist series went on to win the Pulitzer Prize.[3] The 1619 Project sought not to reexamine American history but to rewrite it as a pretext for re-founding the country. When the political philosopher Charles Kesler called the nationwide violence of 2020 the "1619 Project riots," the project's author Nikole Hannah-Jones welcomed the moniker as "an honor" and thanked him.[4]

Beyond historical revision, Orwell's regime also employs perpetual, arbitrary war and technology such as the "telescreen," an innovation that eerily prefigured our own ubiquitous broadcasting devices. But more than anything else, Big Brother's government relies on the control of language to maintain power. "Newspeak," the novel's most direct prophesy of political correctness, controls its subjects' minds by changing and limiting their lexicon. Through this curtailing of language, "thoughtcrime"—that is, dissent from party orthodoxy—becomes impossible.

"Don't you see that the whole aim of Newspeak is to narrow the range of thought?" explains Syme, the party apparatchik in charge of compiling the new dictionary. "In the end we shall make thoughtcrime literally impossible, because there will be no words in which to express it. . . . The Revolution will be complete when the language is perfect.

Newspeak is Ingsoc and Ingsoc is Newspeak."[5] The ruling Ingsoc regime, short for English socialism, considered language control no mere instrument of its power but rather the totality of it.[6]

Orwell's warnings about the dangers English socialism posed to language and free thought raise more questions than answers in light of the author's own political identity: Orwell himself was an English Socialist. "Every line of serious work that I have written since 1936 has been written, directly or indirectly, against totalitarianism and for democratic socialism, as I understand it," Orwell explained.[7] When conservatives invoke Orwell in their arguments against socialism, leftists point out Orwell's own confusing political views. The key to understanding how Orwell could inveigh against "Ingsoc" and Newspeak while simultaneously siding with the Ingsocs and the Newspeakers of his day lies in the final four words of his statement: "as I understand it."

Orwell deplored what he called "oligarchical collectivism," or totalitarianism. He admired Leon Trotsky and opposed Joseph Stalin, two Russian communists whose ideological differences their disciples love to overstate. (In practice, their differences boiled down to the exile of the former and his assassination at the hands of the latter.) Orwell longed for a socialism without collectivism or totalitarianism, as he explained to the anti-socialist liberal economist Friedrich Hayek.

"In the negative part of Professor Hayek's thesis there is a great deal of truth," Orwell admitted. "It cannot be said too often—at any rate, it is not being said nearly often enough—that collectivism is not inherently democratic, but, on the contrary, gives to a tyrannical minority such powers as the Spanish Inquisitors never dreamed of."[8] Stalin's purges shattered the illusions of many leftist intellectuals throughout the West, as the ex-communist Whittaker Chambers chronicled in his influential 1952 memoir, *Witness*. George Orwell supported socialism as he understood it. And even a genius such as he, like so many political naïfs who still today insist that "true socialism" has never been tried, did not understand it well.

A more incisive prophesy of our present politics came from the pen of Orwell's high school French teacher, Aldous Huxley. *Brave New*

World, written seventeen years before Orwell's *Nineteen Eighty-Four*, envisions a different type of dystopia. The title derives from the most famous line of Shakespeare's tragicomedy *The Tempest*, expressing innocent obliviousness to natural evil: "O wonder! How many goodly creatures are there here! How beauteous mankind is! O brave new world, that has such people in't."[9] In *Brave New World*, a tyrannical one-world government has wielded technology, ideology, and man's basest impulses to engineer a docile populace too distracted by sex and drugs to notice their own slavery within a rigid hierarchy.

Orwell envisioned a repressive state that deprives its people of pleasure. In *Nineteen Eighty-Four*, the gin, cigarettes, and coffee available to the public all taste foul. The people can't even find solace in sex, which constitutes no more than the people's "duty to the Party" after all undutiful sex is outlawed. Huxley foresaw a subtler oppression that would not deny but rather saturate the public with physical pleasure. The state encourages promiscuity, bans monogamy, and plies its people with "soma," a euphoric drug that causes pleasant hallucinations and obscures the reality of time.

Big Brother's three maxims in *Nineteen Eighty-Four* recall political correctness in their brazen dishonesty: "war is peace," "freedom is slavery," "ignorance is strength." But the moral code by which the regime maintains its rule bears a greater resemblance to puritanism than to postmodern perversity. It enforces the traditional virtues—chastity, temperance, diligence, patience, kindness, humility, and charity—albeit in a corrupted form.

Huxley's World State, on the other hand, maintains its power by exacerbating vice. Whereas Orwell's Big Brother rules by breaking his subjects' faith in their faculties of reason, as Winston learns when the regime tortures him into believing that two plus two make five, Huxley's World State holds power by exacerbating its subjects' vices so that they can never build or maintain the capacities and institutions necessary for self-rule.

This promotion of vice provides a subtler means to political power than quasi-puritanical suppression, and Huxley claimed that it made his dystopian vision more likely than that of his former student. Though Huxley considered *Nineteen Eighty-Four* "profoundly important," he found Big Brother's heavy-handedness unrealistic. "Whether in actual fact the policy of the boot-on-the-face can go on indefinitely seems doubtful," he explained. "My own belief is that the ruling oligarchy will find less arduous and wasteful ways of governing and of satisfying its lust for power, and these ways will resemble those which I described in *Brave New World.*"[10]

Though the opponents of political correctness invoke Orwell more often than they do any other author, Huxley understood more clearly the subtle method by which cultural revolutionaries would overthrow traditional society.

Political correctness has succeeded by its opponents' failure to appreciate subtlety. To invoke another mid–twentieth century novel, the new standard poses a "catch-22," a problem that denies any solution. It creates a trap, and just about every prominent opponent of political correctness has fallen for it. The trap lies in PC's dual character as at once a speech code and the antithesis of a moral code. The constantly churning jargon and taboo terms constitute a new speech code, as anyone who has ever been scolded for using an out-of-date epithet well understands. "Persons of color," for example, must never be called "colored persons"—at least according to this week's standards.

But the new speech code did not spring out of a vacuum. Rather, it developed specifically to undermine and overthrow existing norms. By inventing and enforcing new jargon, political correctness prohibits older terms and the moral attitudes they imply. For instance, the politically correct term "homeless" and the more recent and euphemistic "unhoused" necessarily displace the more traditional terms "bum" and "tramp."[11] In defining vagrants by their material circumstances, the terms "homeless" and "unhoused" deny that such people might bear any responsibility for their condition. The terms "bum" and "tramp" suggest that the vagrants' situation might be a consequence of their own choices and behavior, a possibility now deemed politically incorrect.

Many bums are junkies, a term that has long since given way to the politically correct formulation "addict" or the even more recent "person with a substance use disorder," as former president Barack Obama's drug czar once suggested.[12] Drunkards and druggies make poor choices and live with the consequences, but victims of the "disorder" or "disease" of drug use cannot be held responsible for their miserable state. By its speech codes, political correctness removes responsibility and therefore the possibility of any coherent moral code. Under political correctness, saying the right thing supplants doing the right thing.

Political correctness denies oddity. Civilization has traditionally considered it unusual for men to masquerade as women. Political correctness calls such men "transgender," a perfectly reasonable alternative to those who are "cisgender" and identify with their actual sex. "Homosexual" behavior is considered no more unusual than "heterosexuality," despite its relative rarity in society. In refusing to acknowledge any trait or behavior as deviating from the norm, political correctness denies any norms at all.

Beyond mainstreaming the unusual, this denial of established standards prohibits traditional moral opprobrium. The lexical shift from "bum" to "unhoused" necessarily implies a moral shift from ne'er-do-well to victim. It removes the stigma from living on the street and suggests that the sidewalk denizen bears no responsibility for his lodging or lack thereof.

The Christian religion on which our culture rests holds human nature to be fixed and immutable, and it views certain sexual behaviors with opprobrium, as do the other major theistic religions, Judaism and Islam. Political correctness overturns both views, denying the fixity of human nature and asserting the propriety of any sexual behavior with the exceptions, perhaps, of bestiality and pedophilia—though even that latter exception has begun to weaken, as California demonstrated in 2020 with the passage of a law that partially legalized pederasty.[13] Netflix's defense of the exploitative preteen twerking film *Cuties* underscored the same phenomenon the very same year.[14]

The old and new orders cannot coexist. The "ruthless criticism of all that exists" undertaken by Marx and his ideological heirs must be thorough. Only one moral and philosophical framework can win out in the end. And therein lies the trap.

Ever since cultural conservatives first sounded the alarm on political correctness in the 1980s, they have misunderstood the conflict as a battle between censorship and free speech. They marvel that the University of California, Berkeley, home to the Free Speech Movement of the mid-1960s, would become one of the campuses least hospitable to free speech by 2017, when lectures by conservative commentators elicited an eruption of leftist violence. The security costs for just one event with Ben Shapiro—a mild-mannered, Orthodox Jewish friend of mine—exceeded $600,000.[15]

Conservatives reacted, as they always have in the face of politically correct aggression, by doubling down on their support for "free speech." They began to describe themselves as "free speech purists" opposed to all forms of "censorship" and to the leftist "snowflakes" who seek "safe spaces" from harsh realities by refusing to engage in "the marketplace of ideas." They failed to see that this novel conception of "free speech," unfettered from all standards and norms, plays right into the politically correct censors' hands.

All societies in all places throughout all of human history have embraced and enforced standards of speech and behavior. Critics of political correctness have assailed it as a "new puritanism." In a sense it is, but that new puritanism didn't spring into existence out of thin air. It has replaced the old puritanism, which "purified" Anglicanism, which replaced Catholicism, which suppressed heresy, and so on and so on. Civilization cannot stand for nothing.

When the liberal scholar Stanley Fish declares "there's no such thing as free speech," he has a point. "'Free speech' is just the name we give to verbal behavior that serves the substantive agendas we wish to advance," he asserts. "We give our preferred verbal behaviors that name when we can, when we have the power to do so, because in the rhetoric of American life, the label 'free speech' is the one you want your favorites to wear."[16]

Plenty of speech has fallen outside the purview of the First Amendment over the course of American history, including libel, threats, sedition, fraud, obscenity, and "fighting words," among other categories.[17] Although many self-described conservatives today defend pornography on First Amendment grounds, a federal court sentenced a prominent pornographer to prison for obscenity as recently as 2008.[18] Even John Milton, perhaps the best known defender of free speech in the English language, explicitly endorsed censorship of certain ideas in his most famous treatise on the subject, *Areopagitica*.

"I mean not tolerated Popery," wrote Milton, by which he meant Catholicism, "and open superstition, which as it extirpates all religions and civil supremacies, so itself should be extirpated . . . that also which is impious or evil absolutely either against faith or manners no law can possibly permit, that intends not to unlaw itself."[19] Even liberals have their limits.

Milton wrote in 1644 as the English Civil War raged, in no small part over the role of Catholicism in the country. He defended free speech as a solution to the civil turmoil, but he considered certain speech beyond the bounds of acceptable discourse. Milton considered Catholicism a threat to the peace and order that permitted free speech in the first place.

Catholics, too, can understand the political dilemma posed by the practical limits of toleration. A later English Catholic, G. K. Chesterton, put the matter this way: "There is a thought that stops thought, and that is the only thought that ought to be stopped. That is the ultimate evil against which all religious authority was aimed."[20] Milton decried what he considered superstition; Chesterton, radical skepticism. Both saw the same problem: we can abuse our reason to undermine our reason; we can abuse speech to undermine speech.

"Free speech" carries a different meaning in America than it does in Western Europe or anywhere else in the world. The American Constitution and legal tradition offer broader protections for political speech, in particular, than do other nations. But the United States, like all nations, has standards of speech, and it has always enforced them.

In a self-governing republic, speech is politics, and politics is speech. As the realm of politics requires limits, so too must the realm of speech. By failing to acknowledge this practical reality, the so-called "free speech purists" give the game away to politically correct censors, whose immediate object is not even the establishment of new standards but merely the abolition of the old.

This clever strategy amounts to a "heads I win, tails you lose" coin toss. If the "free speech purists" follow their own logic only insofar as it does not threaten their traditional moral standards, they expose themselves as hypocrites and concede the argument. But if in an attempt at consistency they reject all speech codes, including those that aim to uphold traditional morality, then they forfeit the traditional standards that the radicals hoped to abolish in the first place. Either way, the radicals win.

Specificity holds the key to escaping this rigged semantic game. If "free speech" does not mean and has never meant that one may say literally whatever one pleases without consequence, then what precisely does it mean? Here again we may benefit by learning from our ideological opponents. Stanley Fish asserted, "Speech, in short, is never a value in and of itself but is always produced within the precincts of some assumed conception of the good to which it must yield in the event of conflict."[21] Political correctness has narrowed the range of thought, as Orwell's Syme predicts. But it has also overturned the conception of the good that public thought and speech aim to uphold.

Whereas our civilization has traditionally pursued justice—that is, giving to each what he deserves without favor—political correctness exalts "social justice," or giving to each what he does not deserve because he is favored. While our civilization traditionally esteemed accomplishment, political correctness rewards grievance and victimhood. Whereas our civilization traditionally cherished its cultural inheritance, political correctness maligns that inheritance and demands reparations.

Free speech cannot be an open plain, nor can it be a jungle; it must be a delicately manicured garden. As long as conservatives defend free speech as a neutral, natural state rather than as a substantive product of our culture's keenest insight and best traditions, we will lose. The radicals recognize that speech rests on an established conception of the good. By failing to recognize this, we are effectively mounting a retreat, leaving radicals to redefine the good and abolish what we call free speech itself.

CHAPTER 5

MAO GOES MAINSTREAM

olitical correctness, ironically, is neither correct nor strictly political, and its conception of the good is evil. But almost from the beginning, irony has defined "political correctness," inasmuch as it transforms words and phrases to make them mean their opposite. The term first entered the American lexicon through the Supreme Court's 1793 decision in *Chisholm v. Georgia*. Chief Justice John Marshall, referring to "sentiments and expressions" of an "inaccurate kind," wonders, "Is a toast asked? 'The United States,' instead of the 'People of the United States,' is the toast given. This is not politically correct."[1] Marshall meant the phrase sincerely: the toast got the political order of the country wrong.

This initial deployment of "politically correct" bears little if any relation to the phrase's current use. The relevant sense of the term did not appear for nearly a century and a half after Marshall's coinage. In 1935, the American writer and critic Joseph Wood Krutch accused "liberal turned radical" professors at Columbia University of disregarding "the importance of free discussion" and instead indoctrinating students in allegedly "correct opinions."[2]

Ralph Ellison's 1952 novel, *Invisible Man*, set in the 1930s, uses the concept of correctness in the same sardonic way. "In my opinion the speech was wild, hysterical, politically irresponsible and dangerous. . . . And worse than that, it was incorrect," declaims a member of the politically radical Brotherhood.[3] Ellison emphasizes this last term: "He pronounced 'incorrect' as though the term described the most heinous crime imaginable, and I stared at him open-mouthed, feeling a vague guilt."[4] By the 1930s, the fanatical insistence on "correctness" in politics had begun to take hold.

Vladimir Nabokov introduced the phrase "politically incorrect" in its present meaning in his 1947 novel *Bend Sinister* about an imaginary totalitarian regime. "Some organizations used to be pretty bad and are forbidden today," reports the state-controlled press, "but nevertheless it is better for a man to have belonged to a politically incorrect organization than not to have belonged to any organization at all."[5] Nabokov meant "politically incorrect" as we mean it today: that is, deviating from party orthodoxy.

Six years after the Russian Nabokov invoked the term, it made its way into Eastern European literature through Czesław Miłosz, who used the Polish phrase *poprawny politycznie*, which his translator Jane Zielonko rendered literally as "politically correct," in his novel *The Captive Mind*. "Still, a politically correct theme would not have saved him from the critics' attack had they wanted to apply orthodox criteria," wrote Miłosz in Zielonko's translation, "because he described the concentration camp as he personally had seen it, not as one was supposed to see it."[6] The author recognized a chasm between "political correctness" and reality.

All of these prophets of political correctness, from Orwell and Huxley to Nabokov and Miłosz, understood the power of language to shape politics. "If thought corrupts language, language can also corrupt thought," wrote Orwell in his essay "Politics and the English Language," which examines the relationship between linguistic perversion and political orthodoxy. "A bad usage can spread by tradition and imitation even among people who should and do know better."[7] Political correctness has succeeded because even its opponents fall victim to its allure.

Antifa, a left-wing terror group that rose to prominence in the United States during the Trump administration, exemplifies this relationship between word and deed. Antifa, short for "anti-fascist," perpetrates violence against mainstream conservative civilians and police officers to achieve its radical leftist political ends. Antifa members train in advanced battle tactics, don black uniforms, and arm themselves with knives, brass knuckles, bricks, high-powered lasers, and other weapons.[8] They target not fascists, but conservatives. The simple possession of a "Make America Great Again" hat suffices to get oneself labeled a "fascist" by Antifa.

Noting the similarities in tactics and even uniform between Mussolini's Blackshirts and Antifa's street warriors, many conservatives reveled in the irony. The so-called "anti-fascists," they argued, were actually fascists.[9] But they aren't fascists, and conservatives' giggling to the contrary demonstrates the PC trap.

Some Antifa members are anarchists; others are communists. All are very bad fellows. But they are not fascists. By describing them as such, conservatives have accepted the radicals' premise that fascism uniquely threatens the peace and body politic. As Orwell observed, "The word *Fascism* has now no meaning except in so far as it signifies 'something not desirable.'"[10] And that is precisely how the radicals want it.

Fascism once had a narrower definition. Benito Mussolini, the founder of fascism, defined the term with the help of the philosopher Giovanni Gentile in 1932. Fascism, according to Mussolini and Gentile, rejects individualism, economic liberalism, egalitarianism, pacifism, Christianity, and "Marxian socialism." It supports one entity above all others: the state.

"The keystone of the Fascist doctrine is its conception of the State, of its essence, its functions, and its aims. For Fascism the State is absolute, individuals and groups relative. Individuals and groups are admissible in so far as they come within the State. Instead of directing the game and guiding the material and moral progress of the community, the liberal State restricts its activities to recording results. The Fascist State is wide awake and has a will of its own. For this reason it can be described as 'ethical.'"[11]

Neither conservatives nor leftists in the twenty-first century meet the definition of fascism, which is an ideology unto itself. Yet the Left flings the term at the Right, and the Right foolishly hurls it right back at the Left, accepting "fascism" as the ultimate political evil, the very premise leftists sought to establish in the first place. Both sides excitedly condemn fascism, a phantom villain that died with Mussolini on the streets of Milan. Meanwhile, the extant evil of Marxian socialism, openly embraced by the Left's most influential activist groups and vast swaths of the Democrat Party, gets off the hook and spreads.

Political correctness thrives by turning opponents into unwitting supporters. It exhibits what the essayist Nassim Nicholas Taleb calls "anti-fragility," the quality of not merely resisting but actually becoming stronger through shock and challenge.[12] The more we argue against it, the more we accept its terms—its very substance—into our language, thought, and culture.

"The fight against bad English is not frivolous and is not the exclusive concern of professional writers," warned Orwell. We may resist political correctness and the radical ideology it carries, but effective resistance requires that we know what we are saying.

"You are not obliged to go to all this trouble," Orwell admits. "You can shirk it by simply throwing your mind open and letting the ready-made phrases come crowding in. They will construct your sentences for you—even think your thoughts for you . . . and at need they will perfect the important service of partially concealing your meaning even from yourself."[13] Political correctness transcends political parties and movements. It transforms the entire culture, and careless conservatives abet its advance just as much as the radicals who celebrate it.

Politically correct language infects the mind like a virus and spreads like a pandemic—so contagious, in fact, that its origins can be traced all the way across the world to China. Among the many plagues that

China has unleashed upon the world, from the Black Death in the fourteenth century to the Wuhan virus in the twenty-first, none has so crippled Western society as the idea of political correctness, which first entered radical circles through the translation into English of *Quotations from Chairman Mao Tse-tung*, better known as *Mao's Little Red Book*, in 1966.[14]

Neither the phrase "political correctness" nor any of its derivations appears in the famous communist tract. But the word "correct" appears 110 times. The translators preferred "correct" to "right," which they rarely used in the sense of "justified" or "acceptable," perhaps for fear of associating rightness with the Right.[15] Whatever the reason, the odd and persistent use of "correct" caught the attention of Western radicals, who adopted the phrase and the ideology it described.

Ruth Perry, a leftist professor and founder of MIT's "Women's Studies" program, credits the term to Mao in her essay "A Short History of the Term *Politically Correct*." Barbara Epstein, founding co-editor of the *New York Review of Books*, suggests the additional influence of "correct lineism," a Communist Party term, on the radicals who embraced "political correctness."[16] Though historians of the movement continue to debate the precise details of its spread, all agree that foreign communists bequeathed the notion to Western radicals, who popularized it.

Chairman Mao, like Antonio Gramsci and the intellectuals of the Frankfurt School, understood that cultural upheaval must precede political revolution. "In the world today all culture, all literature and art belong to definite classes and are geared to definite political lines," he declared in the *Little Red Book*. "There is in fact no such thing as art for art's sake, art that stands above classes, art that is detached from or independent of politics."[17] Mao's cynical and exploitative view of art may explain why his regime never produced a Michelangelo. But his understanding of politics helps to explain politically correct radicals' success in spreading their worldview and conservatives' incompetence at stopping it.

Many conservatives will recoil at the suggestion that all art and culture must be "political," as Mao and his followers in the West

declared. Do the paintings of Caravaggio or Rembrandt not delight leftists as well as conservatives? Can one not enjoy the poetry of Dante or
Shakespeare without sharing the political perspective of the poets themselves? Unless a present-day reader harbors some particularly strong
attachment to the Ghibelline faction of fourteenth-century Florence, one
struggles even to imagine how Dante's partisan views could affect appre-
ciation of his poem.

Mao's theory of art rankles conservatives because they hold a narrower view of politics than their radical opponents. While conservatives
tend to cherish some separation between public and private life as
necessary to self-government, the radicals recognize no such distinction. For them, "the personal is the political."[18] Precisely because separation between public and private life is necessary for republican
government, the revolutionaries must abolish this separation to further
their revolution.

The radicals have a point. Politics in its most basic sense does not
refer merely to "the government" or the various bureaucratic entities that
govern us, as right-wing ideologues often assume. Politics more broadly
means how we all get along together. It derives from the ancient Greek
word *polis*, which refers to the entire city-state. Conservatives may prefer
a broad private sphere, but such a private realm cannot exist without the
support of a stable public sphere in which citizens broadly agree on the
premises of the state.

In other words, the separation between public and private life
requires some measure of political consensus. Republicans and Democrats of yesteryear may have disagreed, for example, on immigration
policy, but they agreed that citizens have the right to determine who
enters their country. The two parties may have disagreed on tax rates
and trade deals, but both accepted the legitimacy of protecting property.
They may have favored different aspects of the national identity, but both
stood for "The Star-Spangled Banner."

Mao's radical admirers sought and continue to seek the collapse of
even those basic points of agreement. The distinction between past and

present holds the key to the communist leader's theory of art. He did not state as an eternal truth that "all culture, all literature and art belong to definite classes and are geared to definite political lines."[19] Rather, Mao grounded that assertion "in the world today." In the past, art may not have conformed to the contours of ideology. But Mao's revolution transformed all that: politics, art, and everything else. Now nothing can escape ideology. The "ruthless criticism of all that exists" spares no edifice.

Mao described the revolutionaries' purpose as ensuring "that literature and art fit well into the whole revolutionary machine as a component part, that they operate as powerful weapons for uniting and educating the people and for attacking and destroying the enemy."[20] A partial revolution would be no revolution at all; on the contrary, it would accept the very liberal premises the radicals sought to overturn. Totalitarian revolutions must be achieved in total; not so much as a painting or piece of music may be permitted to escape their influence.

The radicals' cultural revolution progressed as Mao predicted it would. He described his revolution as a "long march," at once "a manifesto," "a propaganda force," and "a seeding-machine" that would sow "many seeds which will sprout, leaf, blossom, and bear fruit, and will yield a harvest in the future."[21] The seeds planted in the early and mid-twentieth century have borne fruit, and conservatives took notice only after radicals had infiltrated every cultural institution.

Political correctness has advanced not in a short burst of advocacy, but rather in Dutschke's "long march through the institutions." Dutschke, who read Gramsci's ideology through Mao's tactics, shaped a generation of leftist activists.[22] A German student, interpreting Italian and Chinese admirers of a German philosopher, inspired a generation of American radicals.

And yet casual observers of political correctness may scoff at the very notion that one can trace the movement back more than two or three decades. Many leftists deny political correctness altogether. "Political Correctness: How the Right Invented a Phantom Enemy," read one representative headline from the left-wing British newspaper *The Guardian* in 2016.[23] "The truth about 'political correctness' is that it doesn't actually exist," insists *Vox*.[24] Countless other outlets parrot the same line. Four in five Americans may consider political correctness a national problem, but according to left-wing journalists, they fear an illusion.[25] The phrase "cultural Marxism" elicits not merely denial but invective, as in Wikipedia's assertion that "Cultural Marxism is a far-right, anti-semitic conspiracy theory."

But political correctness does exist, its most prominent advocates have described themselves as cultural Marxists, and its origins can be traced all the way back to Karl Marx himself, as we have discussed. Why and how would reasonable people deny these plain facts?

The answer lies in the essentially deceptive nature of translation. "*Traduttore, traditore*," goes an Italian idiom, which translates to "translator, traitor," though it sounds better in the original—proving the point. The expression captures the ultimate impossibility of translation. No matter how skillful the translator, any translation from one language into another transforms the text because the source and target languages differ in sound and culture. A Russian can get the gist of Shakespeare in translation; a Brit can get the gist of Dante. But a translation must always betray some aspect of the original because no two languages and no two cultures are identical.

Political correctness is itself a process of translation, betraying culture through language that reorders the culture's standards. As we have seen, politically correct wordsmiths pretend that the term "justice-involved person" is a synonym for "criminal." Both terms refer to the same people—that is, people caught committing crimes—but they imply entirely different moral frameworks. The translation distorts and betrays the original meaning.

Language changes naturally over time, but the shift from "criminal" to "justice-involved person" did not come about through natural linguistic development. Rather, leftist academics, political activists, and bureaucrats contrived the new term, and left-wing journalists parroted it.[26] The two terms reflect two different cultures: one in which people have moral agency, another in which they do not. Criminals break the law and deserve punishment. "Justice-involved persons" are passive characters; if active at all, they sound as though they pursue justice. And only a cruel society would punish someone for pursuing justice.

If culture worked precisely as the radicals would have it, this process of translation would remake the world, and that would be the end of it. But while new jargon may shift attitudes for a time, a countervailing force cuts against it: the "euphemism treadmill." Harvard psychologist Steven Pinker identified and named this concept in his 2003 book, *The Blank Slate*. "Linguists are familiar with the phenomenon, which may be called the euphemism treadmill," Pinker wrote. "People invent new words for emotionally charged referents, but soon the euphemism becomes tainted by association, and a new word must be found, which soon acquires its own connotations, and so on."[27] A pretty word can conceal a harsh fact for only so long; eventually, the harshness of the reality will pollute the beauty of the word.

The simplest example of the euphemism treadmill may be "simpleton," an offensive word by today's standards that was introduced into public discourse in 1846 by S. G. Howe, a well-intentioned physician who meant no disrespect.[28] Two years after coining "simpleton," Dr. Howe founded the Massachusetts School for Idiotic and Feeble-Minded Youth—not to be confused with nearby Harvard.[29] "Feeble-minded," from the Latin *flebilis*, "lamentable," was not an insult but rather a clinical descriptor for slow folk. When society deemed those terms too harsh, scientists replaced them with "moron," coined by psychologist Henry Goddard from the Greek word *moros*, "dull."[30] Other euphemisms such as "retarded" (from the Latin for "slow") and imbecile ("weak") in turn replaced "moron" and "idiot," and the process continues. No matter which term society chooses, the word inevitably attains a negative connotation because it refers to a condition that most people consider lamentable.

"The euphemism treadmill," Pinker explains, "shows that concepts, not words, are primary in people's minds. Give a concept a new name, and the name becomes colored by the concept; the concept does not become freshened by the name, at least not for long."[31] Pinker contends that reality reasserts itself in the end, which offers some consolation to conservatives. But does he place too much faith in the inevitable triumph of reason in human affairs?

Concepts may weigh more heavily in people's minds over time, but they cannot be dispositive. New jargon may be colored over time by the concept to which it refers, but it does not therefore follow that the concept derives no long-term benefit from the euphemism.

Consider, for example, the history of sodomy laws. The term "sodomite" conjures images of fire and brimstone from the Book of Genesis, while the word "homosexual" elicits no such reaction. For most of American history, sodomy has been illegal, though rarely prosecuted. In 1986, the Supreme Court upheld the constitutionality of sodomy laws in *Bowers v. Hardwick*.[32] Only in 2003, in *Lawrence v. Texas*, did the Court discover a theretofore hidden provision of the Constitution guaranteeing the right to those sexual acts, and it abolished by judicial fiat sodomy laws in the fourteen states that still maintained them.[33]

One may applaud the demise of sodomy laws while lamenting the anti-constitutional way in which the Court overturned them. But beyond applause and lamentation, one must marvel at the role language played in the repeal, which seems to have owed its success less to judicial activism than to shifting semantics.

Would the Supreme Court have invented this new right had "sodomy" remained the common term for homosexual acts? One cannot say for sure. But the homosexual appropriation of the rainbow and the term "gay"—respectively, a symbol of hope and a synonym for "happy"— seem to have helped the rebranding campaign. Perhaps hardwired prejudices against homosexuality will re-color the rainbow. Regardless, few people, if any, expect or desire the return of sodomy laws any time soon.

We are left with the tension of translation. The new words transform our understanding of the old concept, but not entirely. And as the old concepts shine through again, the strength of the new words weakens, and the euphemism treadmill shifts to yet another word. So the radicals must constantly create new words to stave off this coloring and continue to shift public opinion in their desired direction.

The euphemism treadmill underscores two other features of political correctness: irony and inconsistency. To continue with the previous example, consider the term "queer," which dates back to the sixteenth century and originally meant "strange." In the nineteenth century, the word became a slur for homosexuals, and this meaning persisted well into the twentieth century.[34] In 1968, the conservative journalist William F. Buckley Jr. memorably lost his temper and warned leftist public intellectual Gore Vidal, "Listen, you queer, stop calling me a crypto-Nazi, or I'll sock you in your God-damned face, and you'll stay plastered," much to the delight of Vidal, who at that point won the debate.[35]

Today the slur that delighted Vidal delights the practitioner of political correctness for a different reason. By the late twentieth century, homosexuals had appropriated the term for themselves and begun to use it with pride. But at the same time the older, derogatory sense persisted, at least for some people. So universities can dedicate whole departments to "queer studies," but when the conservative comedian Steven Crowder refers to a homosexual journalist who goes by the screen name "Gay Wonk" as a "queer," YouTube cuts off his income.[36]

Political correctness holds that the meaning of words differs depending on who utters them, the clearest example of this phenomenon being "the n-word." The "n-word" has two senses: one derogatory (hard "r"), another affectionate (soft "r"). Politeness has exorcised the former from common use; political correctness has simultaneously encouraged and banned the latter use, depending on the identity of the speaker. Black people may use the term all they like, notably in rap music, and proponents of political correctness will cheer them on for appropriating and redefining a slur. But white people may not sing along to those rap songs, or the PC police will condemn them for racism. According to the enforcers of political correctness, the meaning of the word changes not with semantic context but with the skin color of the speaker.

But these dictators of diction ignore even this rule when convenience calls. In 2020, a recording of the liberal comedian Jimmy Kimmel using "the n-word" while impersonating the rapper Snoop Dogg resurfaced. Kimmel, who in the early 2000s had darkened his skin to impersonate Oprah Winfrey and the basketball player Karl Malone on his politically incorrect television program *The Man Show*, faced no consequences.[37] At some point between *The Man Show* and *Jimmy Kimmel Live!*, the comedian had transformed his act to accord with political correctness. He had become the darling of liberal Hollywood and hosted the Emmys for the third time the very same year that his "n-word" tape leaked.[38]

Joy Behar, a liberal host at ABC, pulled out the proverbial shoe polish to dress as "a beautiful African woman" for a Halloween party in 1971.[39] But her career survived the resurfacing of that scandal in 2019. Meanwhile Megyn Kelly, a non-liberal host at NBC, lost her job over the mere suggestion that white fans of Diana Ross might darken their skin to resemble the singer for Halloween.[40] The propriety of certain racial speech and dress depended not on race but ideology. The rules did not set an equal standard but instead served as an excuse for politically convenient censorship.

While it may seem inconsistent, this cynical censorship—enforcing the rules only on some people and, even then, only some of the time—follows from the radicals' political premises. If nature is fixed and objective, then the identity of a speaker cannot change the meaning of words because the reality to which the words refer exists apart from the speaker; if nature is perfectible and evolves, the identity of a speaker can change the meaning of words because there is nothing separate and enduring to which words refer.

Woodrow Wilson, the most consciously progressive president in the history of the United States, explained the irreconcilable difference between these two political frameworks by way of scientific example. The Founding Fathers and framers of the Constitution, Wilson contended, established constitutional government because they lived under the sway of Isaac Newton, who believed that eternal and fixed laws governed nature. But now, Wilson explained, we live in the age of Charles Darwin, who has demonstrated that nature is never fixed but always "evolving," and therefore our politics must acknowledge this discovery, ditch the old fixed rules, and "evolve."[41]

Under Newton, politics must acknowledge the imperfectability of nature and strike a prudent balance of power. James Madison described this system and its logic in *Federalist* 51:

> What is government itself but the greatest of all reflections on human nature? If men were angels, no government would be necessary. If angels were to govern men, neither external nor internal controls on government would be necessary. In framing a government which is to be administered by men over men, the great difficulty lies in this: You must first enable the government to control the governed; and in the next place, oblige it to control itself.[42]

Under Darwin, this separation of powers and system of checks and balances could only hamper progress, which requires a great concentration of energy if we hope to "evolve."

Conservatives err when they try to oppose political correctness by following or refuting its purported rules. As on the improv comedy program *Whose Line Is It Anyway?*, the rules are made up, and the points don't matter. All that matters for proponents of political correctness is the imposition of the rules. A phrase might carry one meaning one day and the opposite the next. The meaning of the term "political correctness" itself developed by just such an ironic reversal.

According to Deborah Cameron, a feminist linguist who holds the Rupert Murdoch Professorship in Language and Communication at Oxford—how's that for irony?—the terms "politically correct" and "politically incorrect" began as self-effacing inside jokes among leftists. "They functioned on one hand to differentiate the new left from the orthodox old left," Cameron explains, "and on the other to satirise the ever-present tendency of 'politicos' to become over-earnest, humourless and rigidly prescriptive, poking fun at the notion that anyone could be (or would want to be) wholly 'correct.'"[43] In Cameron's telling, the term was ironic from the beginning.

Paul Berman, the liberal writer and historian of the 1960s radicals, disagrees. He believes that this self-effacing irony followed an initially earnest use of the term. "'Politically correct' was originally an approving phrase on the Leninist left to denote someone who steadfastly toed the party line," he contends. "Then it evolved into 'PC,' an ironic phrase among wised-up leftists to denote someone whose line-toeing fervor was too much to bear."[44] Doctrinaire leftists who consciously identified with foreign political movements used the term sincerely, but their ardor repelled their lukewarm intellectual heirs, particularly in the West.

Geoffrey Hughes, an historian of the English language, agrees. "In the totalitarian context of its communist and Maoist origins, *political correctness* had a serious doctrinaire sense," he admits. "Once it was borrowed into a democratic and liberal political milieu, it became an anomaly, an empty formula of conformity open to subversion."[45] In other words, the intrinsically skeptical character of modern, liberal democracy undermined the initial self-seriousness of political correctness. Totalitarians, for their many faults, tend to take ideas more seriously than liberals, who doubt the possibility of grasping absolute truth and therefore leave politics largely to the whims of the people rather than the integrity of ideas. For the liberal, "Fifty million Frenchmen can't be wrong."

Sophie Tucker coined that phrase, which summed up the liberal view, in her hit 1927 song contrasting gay Paris with more restrictive political regimes. "When they put on a show, and it's a hit,/ No one tries to censor it./ Fifty million Frenchmen can't be wrong!/ And when a book is selling at its best,/ It isn't stopped; it's not suppressed./ Fifty million Frenchmen can't be wrong!"[46] These lyrics took aim at the United States, which since its earliest days has been torn between liberal ideals and conservative practices—the Declaration of Independence and the Hays Code.

In the end, Sophie Tucker got her way. America has liberalized a great deal since the 1920s. A *laissez-faire* attitude reigns even on the right, as shown by the prominence of libertarianism in "conservative" circles throughout the late twentieth and early twenty-first centuries.

During the early days of political correctness, restrictiveness pervaded the entire political landscape, albeit with different expressions on the right and on the left.[47] The House Committee on Un-American Activities was neither liberal nor skeptical. It put forth a substantive moral vision of America and sought to smoke out commies wherever it could find them. William F. Buckley Jr., the urbane father of the postwar conservative movement, published a book-length defense of Joe McCarthy in 1954. But in the decades that followed, even most conservatives disavowed the moral certitude that characterized that era in favor of skeptical liberalism.

Irony and apathy tend to spread in skeptical, liberal societies, as anyone who has ever witnessed the French shrug can attest. While at one time popular entertainment inspired us with grand performances of beauty and precision, now dressed-down, grotesque burlesques make a mockery of those traditional standards. Marilyn Monroe and Ella Fitzgerald fade; Lena Dunham and Miley Cyrus shine. The enthusiastic comedy of Bob Hope loses favor, and the cynical irony of David Letterman replaces it.

Irony thrives in liberal and decadent societies because it permits the evasion of responsibility. One never need commit too much. The ironic utterance of a phrase or performance of an action allows one to conceal his true motives. He may mean what he says, or he may mean the opposite; in any case, no one can ever hold him to account.

A meme arose in 2019 to describe the application of this deceptive strategy to politics: the "irony bro," who evades criticism for his statements and actions by reciting the four-word incantation, "It's called irony, bro!"[48] Urban Dictionary, an online encyclopedia of slang, defines the "irony bro" as "someone who claims to enjoy something ironically or just for fun, while hiding the fact that they have genuine interest in the thing they claim to be enjoying ironically or mocking for the LOLZ." It cites "hipsters and internet edgelords" as examples of the phenomenon.[49]

In *Notes from the Underground*, Fyodor Dostoevsky described irony as "the last refuge of modest and chaste-souled people when the privacy of their soul is coarsely and intrusively invaded."[50] Pride, he observes, causes people to hide their intentions behind sarcasm, a form of verbal irony.

The Scottish philosopher Thomas Carlyle cast sarcasm in even darker terms. "Sarcasm I now see to be, in general, the language of the Devil," he confessed, "for which reason I have, long since, as good as renounced it."[51] Sarcasm, like the Devil, only accuses; it offers nothing positive.

Cultures on the rise know what they believe, and they possess the confidence to defend those beliefs; decadent societies retreat into irony and criticism. Medieval Europe repelled invaders and set out under the Cross of St. George to reconquer lost lands; decadent modern Europe opens its borders to those same hostile powers because it lost its faith long ago and now detests its own past triumphs.

Ironically, Mao's *Little Red Book* might have more directly influenced Western politics had decadence and irony not overtaken the radicals. Geoffrey Hughes observes the paradox that "political correctness increased in vogue in America precisely when hard-line Communism was waning." But one should not wonder at the coincidence. Communism demands confidence. A communist insurrection in America would require revolutionaries to risk imprisonment, ostracism, and death. Political correctness better suits an exhausted and decadent society. Euphemisms and vagueness go down easier than manifestos and war, and the radicals can always deny their subversive intentions by claiming irony.

But if the term "political correctness" arose as a tongue-in-cheek in-joke among leftists, what exactly was the punch line? If the New Left of the 1960s sought to distinguish itself from the dogmatic Old Left, how precisely did they differ? The radicals of the 1960s may have used the term to mock their forebears' rigidity and humorlessness, but the New Left fought just as earnestly as the Old to design and enforce new codes of speech and behavior for society. The veneer of irony merely helped to mask their radical aims. They attacked traditional dogmas as repressive and therefore illegitimate, but then they treated the inversion of the old standards with precisely the same dogmatism.

In the name of tolerance, the cultural revolutionaries toppled traditional standards and persecuted any who dared dissent. In the name of diversity, the radicals overthrew an old order and demanded adherence to the new one, ostracizing any who opposed them. Conservatives struggled to gain ground against the insurrection as left-wing irony bros constantly moved the goal posts. Heads they win, tails we lose.

Conservatives need not rely on convoluted theories of conspiratorial cabals to account for political correctness. The importation of Mao's writings into a decadent and critical culture accounts for the fact just fine. But while the radical foot soldier of the '60s generation may have stumbled unwittingly into this political framework, it took a heftier mind to give coherence to this politics of irony. Herbert Marcuse of Frankfurt School fame supplied just that with his articulation in 1965 of "repressive tolerance."

CHAPTER 6

THE TOLERANT LEFT

"If you think we're rallying now, you ain't seen nothing yet," warned Maxine Waters, the influential Democrat politician who has held elected office since the Ford administration. "Already you have members of your cabinet that have been booed out of restaurants, who have protesters taking up at their house, who sang, 'No peace, no sleep! No peace, no sleep!'" she reminded President Trump, while her supporters cheered.

Then came the call to arms. "If you see anybody from that cabinet in a restaurant, in a department store, at a gasoline station, you get out and you create a crowd! And you push back on them! And you tell them they're not welcome anymore, anywhere!"[1] Democrats did as they were told. A few months after Waters's war cry, Democrats mobbed Transportation Secretary Elaine Chao and her husband, Senate Majority Leader Mitch McConnell, at a restaurant in Louisville, Kentucky.[2] Around that same time, another group of left-wing activists swarmed Texas senator Ted Cruz and his wife, Heidi, at a restaurant in Washington, D.C., and still another group vandalized the home of conservative cable news host Tucker Carlson.[3]

Rather than condemn Waters's radical rhetoric, Democrat leadership amplified it. "You cannot be civil with a political party that wants to destroy what you stand for, what you care about," declared Hillary Clinton. But Hillary's first four words would have sufficed to convey her point: "You cannot be civil."[4] Either civility extends to one's political adversaries, who by definition seek to destroy what their opponents stand for and care about, or else it has no purpose at all. Civility, which derives from the Latin *civilis*, "relating to citizens," preserves polite and peaceful relations among citizens with divergent interests and opinions.[5] To reject civility is to reject self-government.

So much for "the tolerant Left." That phrase has become a punch line, first among conservatives, who accuse the Left of hypocrisy for praising tolerance while censoring dissent, but later also among liberals, who deem conservatives "intolerant" and therefore undeserving of tolerance. Both sides have a point. The Left is intolerant, but the Right oversimplifies and consequently misunderstands what tolerance means.

When opponents of "cancel culture" demand that we "cancel cancel culture," they do not contradict themselves. Neither did Chesterton when he observed that "there is a thought that stops thought" and that "that is the only thought that ought to be stopped."[6] Similarly, leftists observe that there is a tolerance that undermines tolerance, and that sort of tolerance must not be tolerated. Tolerance means the bearing of hardship, an intrinsically limited concept, as man can only bear so much before he breaks his ability to bear anything at all. During the 1960s, left-wing radicals recognized that tolerance must always have limits, and so they set out not to destroy tolerance but to shift and even invert its bounds.

Herbert Marcuse, the scholar who developed Critical Theory at the Frankfurt School in the 1930s, returned to prominence in the 1960s through his subversive books *One-Dimensional Man* and *A Critique of Pure Tolerance*, which earned him the title "Father of the New Left."[7] During the intervening decades, Marcuse had prepared reports on Nazi Germany for the U.S. government, first in the Office of War Information and later at the Office of Strategic Services, the precursor to the Central

Intelligence Agency.[8] In 1945, Marcuse continued his intelligence work for the government at the State Department as head of its Central European bureau.[9] At first glance, the government's employment of a prominent Marxist during World War II might suggest some sort of conspiracy until one remembers that the United States officially allied in that war with Joseph Stalin, the most powerful communist on earth, to defeat the Nazis. War and politics make for strange bedfellows.

But why did the government continue to employ Marcuse for seven years after the war ended? We now know the State Department employed many communists during those years, most notably Alger Hiss, who helped found the United Nations before his conviction five years later for perjury in regard to an earlier, expired charge of espionage on behalf of the Soviets.[10]

Whether subversion, incompetence, or some other motive prompted the government to employ Marcuse for so long after the war, in 1952 the Marxist philosopher turned his attention back to academia. Over the next two decades, some of the most elite universities in the country welcomed Marcuse. He taught first at Columbia, then Harvard, next Brandeis, and finally the University of California, San Diego, where taxpayers funded his blistering critiques of America and the insurrections they incited.[11]

In his 1964 work *One-Dimensional Man*, Marcuse castigated the United States as a "totalitarian" society that repressed the "authenticity" and "liberation" of the individual through mass media and technology.[12] Marcuse may have overstated his case, but conservatives understand as well as anyone the insidious political effects of mass media and technology, particularly today as the handful of corporations that control both segments of society censor and ostracize anyone to the right of Hillary Clinton. One sometimes wonders whether the frequent inscrutability of Marcuse's prose owes more to the quirks of his native German tongue or to the perversity of his ideological ends. In any case, when Marcuse does manage to make his meaning clear, he often makes keen observations, offensive though they may be to traditional American sensibilities.

Therein lies the genius of Critical Theory: everything that exists is susceptible to criticism. The cultural vandal undertakes "the ruthless criticism of all that exists" more easily than the conservative cultivates and builds. But if American society fails to live up to its allegedly liberal, pluralistic, tolerant ideals, what ought to replace it? Marcuse offered an answer: "repressive tolerance."

"The realization of the objective of tolerance would call for intolerance toward prevailing policies, attitudes, opinions, and the extension of tolerance to policies, attitudes, and opinions which are outlawed and suppressed," Marcuse explained in 1965.[13] In other words, toleration for me, but not for thee. Though conservatives both then and now tend to regard tolerance as an abstract, eternal, and boundless ideal, Marcuse and the radicals he inspired recognized tolerance as a contextual, bounded concept.

From one vantage, no institution in history has rivaled the tolerance of the Catholic Church, which welcomes men of every race, sex, language, labor, and class. From another perspective, no institution has ever been so intolerant as the Church, which launched a millennium of inquisitions and crusades to quash heresy. Milton's encomium to free speech, *Areopagitica*, preaches tolerance for all points of view—so long as they're Protestant. No regime, no matter how tolerant, can tolerate everything.

"Today tolerance appears again as what it was in its origins, at the beginning of the modern period—a partisan goal, a subversive liberating notion and practice," wrote Marcuse. "Conversely, what is proclaimed and practiced as tolerance today, is in many of its most effective manifestations serving the cause of oppression." The Father of the New Left considered tolerance a value-neutral tool that could be harnessed for good or for ill. Just as, in Marcuse's mind, the capitalist system exploits tolerance to stamp out individuality and oppress the masses, radicals could wield tolerance as a weapon of liberation to tear down the system.

The "totalitarian" democracy of the United States, Marcuse complained, had destroyed critical thought and obliterated "the difference between true and false, information and indoctrination, right and wrong."[14] Here Marcuse conceals the radicalism of his proposal behind euphemism, but hints of his partisan ends creep out. What precisely distinguishes "information" from "indoctrination"? Both words simply mean teaching.[15] The former entered English in the early fourteenth century with the meaning "to train or instruct in some specific object"; the latter appeared in the 1620s with the meaning "to teach."[16] Marcuse simply considers some teaching good—namely, his own—and other teaching bad. Rather than discerning between truth and falsehood or right and wrong as those terms have traditionally been understood, Marcuse appears more concerned with the distinction between "politically correct" and "politically incorrect."

Pure tolerance would permit all views into the public square and allow people to make up their own minds. But according to Marcuse, the people, having been educated—or rather "indoctrinated"—in the "propaganda" of America's "totalitarian" society, lack the liberty of mind to distinguish between true and false ideas. "To enable them to become autonomous, to find by themselves what is true and what is false for man in the existing society," he asserts, "they would have to be freed from the prevailing indoctrination (which is no longer recognized as indoctrination)."

Since the allegedly oppressive traditional society has already slanted the people so far in the direction of falsehood, Marcuse insists that "the trend would have to be reversed: they would have to get information slanted in the opposite direction" through "undemocratic means," as the deluded masses cannot understand their own oppression.[17] In the name of objectivity and free thought, he proposes control and propaganda.

Marcuse justifies his censorship in the name of "liberation." Unlike classical liberalism, which defines liberty as the absence of coercion, and also contrary to Christianity, which defines liberty as the rejection of sin, Marcuse defines "liberation" as a matter of history. "Freedom is liberation," he explains, "a specific historical process in theory and practice, and as such it has its right and wrong, its truth and falsehood."[18]

When progressives refer to "the right side of history" or claim that "the arc of the moral universe bends toward justice," they are invoking the same alleged historical process. The Coen Brothers pilloried this conception of history and Herbert Marcuse himself in their 2016 comedy, *Hail, Caesar!* George Clooney's tailor-made character, movie star Baird Whitlock, spends an evening with a secret communist study group led by Professor Marcuse, who indoctrinates him in his theories. When Whitlock returns to the film studio, he gushes to his boss about the radical professor.

"These guys are pretty interesting," Whitlock tells the studio chief, Eddie Mannix. "They've actually figured out the laws that dictate . . . everything! History! Sociology! Politics! Morality! Everything! It's all in a book called *Kapital*—with a 'K.'"

"Is that right?" asks a visibly irritated Mannix.

"Yeah," Whitlock goes on, "you're not going to believe this. These guys even figured out what's going on here at the Studio." He explains, "We may tell ourselves that we're creating something of artistic value or there's some sort of spiritual dimension to the picture business. But, what it really is, is this fat cat, Nick Skank, out in New York, running this factory, serving up these lollipops to the, what they used to call the bread and circuses for the—" at which point Mannix pulls Whitlock from his chair, smacks him across the face, and reminds him that the so-called "fat cat" founded their feasts.[19]

Marcuse's highfalutin historical sense and pretentious prose seduced countless midcentury dimwits like Baird Whitlock. The turgid prose dulled readers' senses, but eventually he came to his point: censor conservatives. "Liberating tolerance, then, would mean intolerance against movements from the Right and toleration of movements from the Left," Marcuse concluded.[20] Conservative speech, by inhibiting liberation and oppressing the masses, constitutes violence and must not be tolerated.

Twenty-first century leftists have embraced Marcuse's argument and use it to justify kicking conservatives off of college campuses and out of corporate boardrooms. These fragile radicals claim that conservative speech makes them feel "unsafe," which is why they need ever-expanding "safe spaces" barred to conservatives.

The most excitable radicals claim that conservative speech not only makes them feel unsafe but even physically harms them. In 2017, Lisa Feldman Barrett proclaimed in the *New York Times* that, while sticks and stones may break our bones, words can also hurt us. "Scientifically speaking," she warned, "it's not that simple. Words can have a powerful effect on your nervous system. Certain types of adversity, even those involving no physical contact, can make you sick, alter your brain—even kill neurons—and shorten your life."[21]

Barrett, like Marx and his acolytes before her, invokes "science" to suggest that one may not reasonably disagree with her. We may quibble over politics or philosophy, she implies, but "science" is a settled matter.[22] One wonders how long the *New York Times* would remain in print under a Republican administration should Barrett's proposed banning of noxious language pass into law. Perhaps for that reason, most mainstream leftist censorship advocates have offered more modest arguments for curtailing conservative speech.

During the campus uprisings of 2017 and 2018, left-wing opinion columnists invoked the most banal cliché in the censorship toolkit: that no one has the right to yell "Fire!" in a crowded theater. The line derives from the 1919 Supreme Court case *Schenck v. United States*, in which the justices unanimously upheld convictions under the Espionage Act of 1917 for distributing flyers opposing the draft in World War I. One suspects the Left might hesitate to invoke this principle if they understood the political context in which it arose.

Justice Oliver Wendell Holmes defended the Court's abridgment of free speech on the grounds that the flyers created a "clear and present danger" by hampering the government's efforts to recruit soldiers for the war. "The most stringent protection of free speech," the justice insisted, "would not protect a man falsely shouting fire in a theatre and causing a panic."[23] But Holmes appears to have changed his mind later that year when he dissented in *Abrams v. United States*, arguing that the distribution of flyers opposing the government's interference in the Russian Revolution did not violate the Espionage Act. And in 1969, the Court partially overturned the *Schenck* decision in *Brandenburg v. Ohio*.[24] Nevertheless, the lazy phrase has persisted in our discourse.

Herbert Marcuse himself invoked the phrase, writing, "The traditional criterion of clear and present danger seems no longer adequate to a stage where the whole society is in the situation of the theater audience when somebody cries: 'fire.'"[25] Taking Holmes's logic to an extreme and dubious conclusion, Marcuse invoked the general deviation of society from his ideal to justify permanent censorship. The country was in crisis, according to Marcuse, and we simply did not have time to inquire too closely into the details. Urgency demanded we act.

Marcuse's political heirs seem to embrace this line of argument more and more closely each year. Citing the supposed "scientific consensus" regarding changes in the weather, the socialist politician Alexandria Ocasio-Cortez predicts a dozen years remain till Armageddon and thereby justifies the fundamental reordering of society.[26] The 2,700-page Affordable Care Act, better known as Obamacare, might cause millions of Americans to lose their physicians and upend whole industries, but who has time to read it when the need is so urgent? "We have to pass the bill" immediately, Nancy Pelosi explained, "so that you can find out what is in it."[27]

Marcuse employed the same scare tactics. He redefined "clear and present danger" to mean whatever he disliked, much as twenty-first century leftists do when they classify constitutionally protected gun ownership as a "public health crisis" or the predictions of fickle meteorological models as a "national emergency." Rather than admit the enormity of his plan to reorder society, Marcuse pretended social circumstances had so shifted that his radical proposals actually fit within the American legal tradition.

Any remedy for society's urgent ills "must begin with stopping the words and images which feed this [false] consciousness," prescribed Marcuse, invoking a concept that would figure more fully into political correctness in the ensuing decades. "To be sure, this is censorship, even precensorship, but openly directed against the more or less hidden censorship that permeates the free media."[28] Conservatives often dismiss the claim that there already exists a hidden conservative censorship, which radicals simply seek to overturn. But here again the radical professor understands language and standards better than the conservatives who presume to refute him.

Marcuse's observation that words and images shape consciousness requires no explanation. If they didn't, why would anyone care about the politically correct attempt to redefine them? But his claim that hidden censorship permeates even ostensibly free media merits consideration as well. Today vulgar language and sexually explicit images pervade television and film. But for years industry codes and even government regulations banned such expression. And public advocacy of communism or socialism could ostracize a man and even land him in the clink, as Mr. Schenck learned the hard way.

Until the Supreme Court's landmark decision in *Texas v. Johnson*, which created or recognized, according to one's point of view, the constitutional right to burn the American flag, the law could prohibit desecration of venerated objects. Now courts hold that the First Amendment protects flag-burning.[29] And yet in 2019, an Iowa judge sentenced thirty-year-old Adolfo Martinez to fifteen years in prison for the "hate crime" of stealing and burning a rainbow flag, which symbolizes colorful sexual desires.[30] So in fact, the government still outlaws desecration of venerated objects; it's just that the objects of veneration are different.

"Previously neutral, value-free, formal aspects of learning and teaching now become, on their own grounds and in their own right, political,"—a process Marcuse encouraged as "radical criticism throughout" and "intellectual subversion."[31] In the past, though partisans disagreed on much, all waved the same American flag, which symbolized the nation founded on the belief that "all men are created equal and endowed by their Creator with certain unalienable rights."[32] Today the American flag has become a partisan symbol. Left-wing athletes and even elected Democrats disrespect the star-spangled banner; conservative politicians hug and kiss it on the campaign trail.[33] Where once schoolchildren learned the arguments that our Founding Fathers set forth at the constitutional convention, today they study the subversive calumny of the 1619 Project.[34]

While heretofore-innocuous objects become politicized, previously political objects exit the public square. The burning of an American flag, once condemned by all, now constitutes legitimate political speech; moral opprobrium for aberrant sexual acts, once almost universally held, now suggests a ménage of "phobias" unfit for civilized society. Our prejudices have not disappeared; they have merely changed.

Our prejudice regarding the word "prejudice" illustrates this shift. Today the term connotes injustice and irrationality, but until recently the word meant no more than a received opinion, the sentiments and instincts that pass through a culture without the aid of philosophic and scientific abstraction. Prejudices shape all cultures at all times whether the acculturated admit it or not, and coherent conservatives once celebrated that fact.

The Enlightenment of the seventeenth and eighteenth centuries established a common prejudice against prejudice, which the conservative philosopher Edmund Burke mocked in his *Reflections on the Revolution in France*:

> I am bold enough to confess, that we are generally men of untaught feelings; that instead of casting away all our old prejudices, we cherish them to a very considerable degree, and, to take more shame to ourselves, we cherish them because they are prejudices; and the longer they have lasted, and the more generally they have prevailed, the more we cherish them. We are afraid to put men to live and trade each on his own private stock of reason; because we suspect that this stock in each man is small, and that the individuals would do better to avail themselves of the general bank and capital of nations, and of ages.[35]

Men are not walking, talking syllogisms. Only a fool would attempt to translate every impulse, passion, and preference he feels into the cold language of reason. Those radicals who vanquish their natural prejudices simply clear a space for new prejudices, a political reality Marcuse well understood. His description of prejudice reads as a mirror image of Burke's; he decries exactly what the Irish statesman celebrated:

> The avenues of entrance are closed to the meaning of words and ideas other than the established one—established by the publicity of the powers that be, and verified in their practices. Other words can be spoken and heard, other ideas can be expressed, but, at the massive scale of the conservative majority (outside such enclaves as the intelligentsia), they are immediately "evaluated" (i.e. automatically understood) in terms of the public language—a language which determines "a priori" the direction in which the thought process moves. Thus the process of reflection ends where it started: in the given conditions and relations.[36]

Ironically, Marcuse's lament makes a fine argument *for* just prejudice, if only conservatives could bring themselves to take it seriously. The conservative prejudices and established institutions of Marcuse's day inoculated society against the poisonous ideology that he and his fellow-travelers peddled. Since then, however, radicals have succeeded at shifting those prejudices through a war of position that gave them control of every established institution.

Consider the case of court-packing. In 1937, President Franklin Roosevelt, frustrated that the Supreme Court continued to strike down many of his unconstitutional New Deal laws, attempted to increase the number of justices on the Court, thereby supplying reliable judicial votes to ram his schemes through. The American people opposed the plan, Congress never took it up, and FDR's scheme fizzled.[37]

In 2020, however, court-packing lost much of its fetor. Democratic legislators and even presidential candidates embraced the proposal. They went so far as to redefine the term by conflating the constitutionally mandated appointment of justices with the partisan addition of new justices to the bench.[38] In the 1930s, the traditional American deference to legal norms prevailed. But by 2020, after decades of radical infiltration of the established institutions, conservatives could no longer rely on the old constitutional prejudices. Rather than ending "where it started," the "process of reflection" Marcuse described led to an open debate.

The outright reversal of prejudice regarding our national flag illustrates where that open debate inevitably leads. In a body politic where only subversives have the stones to stir hearts and make substantive claims, open debate will be won by the subversives. My friend Ben Shapiro rightly notes that "facts don't care about your feelings," but we must add to that observation that politics cares greatly about our feelings, as the demagogic Left well knows. Conservatives have refused even to state simple facts for fear of the politically correct lynch mob, retreating instead to arcane encomia on the right to free speech.

The radicals have gained ground in our society by making substantive claims to advance an amoral agenda and then whipping their followers into a frenzy to defend them. When leftists contrived a fictional constitutional right to abortion in 1973, they not only invented a new form of jurisprudence wholly divorced from the text of the Constitution; they also asserted the positive goodness of murdering a million babies each year. They then hypnotized their acolytes into defending the slaughter as the essence of freedom. Conservatives' attempts to reverse this onslaught through compromise and cautious appeals to federalism have failed just as surely as an umbrella against a tsunami. When leftists railroaded right-wing judicial nominees, conservatives acquiesced and nominated more liberal jurists, who reaffirmed the "right" to abortion. When leftists warned the public that conservative judges might outlaw abortion by overturning *Roe*, conservatives countered that any such reversal would do no more than return the butchery debate to the states.

Conservatives have approached the issue of immigration in much the same way. Over the past half century, more than 60 million immigrants have entered the United States, constituting the largest mass migration in recorded history.[39] Polls consistently show that most Americans want to reduce overall immigration. A 2018 survey conducted by Harvard's Center for American Political Studies and Harris Poll found that a full 81 percent of voters want to reduce not just illegal but also legal immigration, and 63 percent of voters want to cut it by at least half.[40]

Yet even President Trump, the most hardline anti-immigration president in generations, restrained his rhetoric to call only for the reduction of illegal immigration. "I want people to come into our country in the largest numbers ever," he declared, "but they have to come in legally." Conservatives quibble over procedure, but they largely leave the substantive issues alone, even when the public largely agrees with their beliefs. Such is the cultural pull of political correctness. In the end, many, if not most, conservatives concede legal abortion and mass migration. They simply advocate a different mechanism for achieving the same left-wing end. "Thus the process of reflection ends where it started: in the given conditions and relations," just as Marcuse lamented in the relatively conservative culture of his age. One suspects the radical philosopher would smile at that line today.

Tolerance necessarily has limits. The radicals of the 1960s understood this fact and set about to move the boundaries of our tolerance in what they considered a more favorable direction. For decades, conservatives have attempted to rebuff the radicals by denying the intrinsic limitations of tolerance, thus permitting leftists to shift the range of acceptable discourse, known sometimes as the "Overton window," ever leftward.

No less a liberal than John Locke, in his *Letter Concerning Toleration*, admitted limits on tolerance. Locke begins by praising toleration as "the chief characteristic mark of the true Church . . . so agreeable to the Gospel of Jesus Christ." But soon enough, like his elder contemporary Milton, Locke questions whether Catholics ought to be afforded that same toleration. "That Church can have no right to be tolerated by the magistrate which is constituted upon such a bottom that all those who enter into it do thereby *ipso facto* deliver themselves up to the protection and service of another prince," Locke clarifies, referring one presumes to the pope. Much like twenty-first century Democrats, Locke was willing to tolerate Catholics only if the dogma lived not so loudly within them.

But beyond Catholics, the great philosopher of toleration reserved his most trenchant intolerance for atheists. "Those are not at all to be tolerated who deny the being of a God," Locke declared. For starters, "promises, covenants, and oaths, which are the bonds of human society, can have no hold upon an atheist," who rejects the moral order. "The taking away of God, though but even in thought, dissolves all" that one might cherish in society, and the atheists have none but themselves to blame, since "those that by their atheism undermine and destroy all religion, can have no pretense of religion whereupon to challenge the privilege of a toleration."[41] Our notions of tolerance rely upon Christianity; one cannot coherently demand the former while rejecting the latter.

Conservatives who invoke the high-minded tolerance of Locke with respect to our most radical opponents would benefit from actually reading the liberal philosopher. The atheism Locke decried has now combined with an overt hatred of our civilization, and the radicals who embody both have enlisted our culture's unique concept of tolerance as an instrument for its own destruction. Hence the split personality of political correctness, which, in the name of tolerance for "marginalized" people, enforces a rigid code of speech and behavior intolerant of dissent.

CHAPTER 7

NOTHING PERSONAL

The televangelist and sometime presidential candidate Pat Robertson once colorfully described feminism as "a socialist, anti-family political movement that encourages women to leave their husbands, kill their children, practice witchcraft, destroy capitalism and become lesbians."[1] His comment shocked liberal sensibilities, though Robertson's foes have encountered the same difficulty Bertrand Russell found when he attempted to refute the ontological argument for the existence of God— namely, that "it is easier to feel convinced that it must be fallacious than it is to find out precisely where the fallacy lies."[2] Feminists of the mid-to-late-twentieth century may not have flown around on broomsticks, but they nevertheless inflicted a curse on the culture in the form of political correctness.

Leftist academics contrived the intellectual framework for political correctness in the 1920s and '30s. Novelists around the world prophesied the political effects of PC in the 1930s, '40s, and '50s. Student radicals, armed with the writings of Mao and Marcuse, took up the cause in the 1960s. And in the 1970s, feminists helped political correctness break into mainstream public discourse.

"A man cannot be politically correct and a chauvinist too," averred the feminist activist Toni Cade in her 1970 anthology, *The Black Woman*.[3] Nabokov may have coined "politically incorrect" in print, but Ruth Perry identifies Cade's remark as the first instance of "politically correct" in its present meaning.[4] Sexual politics powered the expansion of political correctness beyond niche ideological circles and into the broader public sphere during the ensuing decade.[5] Feminists sought to overthrow a culture they decried as patriarchal by making language fickle, which itself required a fundamental restructuring of the political order.

Complacent conservatives have long dismissed fears of a war between the sexes on the grounds that everyone is sleeping with the enemy. They make a fine point as pertains to wars of maneuver, but they neglect, to risk a lurid image, wars of position. Though feminists' most barbarous bastardizations of language have never caught on in the culture, their infiltration of private realms secured them a platform from which to enforce even the most unpopular politically correct contrivances.

The radical feminist Carol Hanisch launched the attack in 1970 with the publication of her essay "The Personal Is Political."[6] Hanisch had already garnered some notoriety two years earlier by protesting beauty queens at the 1968 Miss America Pageant in Atlantic City. She and her fellow travelers set up a "freedom trash can" and encouraged women passing by to throw away their bras, girdles, and other putative symbols of oppression.[7] Critics called the dowdy libbers daft and jealous, and Hanisch wrote her essay in response to those criticisms.

For years, Hanisch explained, radical feminists had met in groups to whine about their lives over apple pie and ice cream, and this ritual had given people the wrong idea that feminism amounted more to group therapy than politics. Hanisch did not disavow the therapeutic aspect of these gabfests, but she insisted that "these analytical sessions are a form of political action." Therapy in a certain sense is politics. "One of the first things we discover in these groups," Hanisch wrote, "is that personal problems are political problems." Individuals could not fix the systemic injustice, as Hanisch saw it, and so the women needed to organize politically to solve their personal problems.[8]

The politico-therapy sessions sought to effect political change by "raising consciousness." The feminist Kathie Sarachild, whom Hanisch credited with getting her essay published, adopted the concept from the Old Left and put it into practice. Sarachild recalled the moment she first encountered "consciousness-raising," during a meeting of the New York Radical Women:

> One woman in the group, Ann Forer, spoke up: "I think we have a lot more to do just in the area of raising our consciousness," she said. "Raising consciousness?" I wondered what she meant by that. I'd never heard it applied to women before. "I've only begun thinking about women as an oppressed group," she continued, "and each day, I'm learning more about it—my consciousness gets higher."[9]

Forer had never considered herself oppressed until feminists put the notion in her head, and their regular whine and cheese soirées made her progressively more miserable—a process she celebrated as an awakening from the slumber of her oppressive serenity.

"Consciousness-raising" derives from the Marxist concept of "false consciousness," a phrase that Friedrich Engels coined in an 1893 letter to the communist historian Franz Mehring.[10] Gramsci, Marcuse, and countless other Marxist intellectuals in and out of the Frankfurt School have relied on the concept to explain why the oppressed masses seem so much better adjusted than the theorists who write about them. The radicals think they understand the little guy better than he understands himself, and they intend to convince him of his own misery.

Wendy Doniger, a feminist professor at the University of Chicago, took the notion of false consciousness to an absurd extreme in 2008 when she declared in *Newsweek* that Republican vice presidential candidate Sarah Palin's "greatest hypocrisy is in her pretense that she is a woman."[11] Palin, a former beauty queen, possesses decidedly feminine features. No one has ever mistaken her for a man. But Doniger considers Palin so deluded by "the patriarchy" and so ignorant of the gnostic feminist faith that she has actually surrendered her biological sex.

In 2020, the *New York Times*'s Nikole Hannah-Jones explained "false consciousness" in the racial realm. "There is a difference between being politically black and being racially black," she tweeted. "I am not defending anyone but we all know this and should stop pretending that we don't."[12]

In fact, Hannah-Jones was defending someone. Earlier that day, Democrat presidential candidate Joe Biden had appeared on a popular radio program and informed the audience, "If you have a problem figuring out whether you're for me or Trump, then you ain't black."[13] One presumes not even doddering Joe Biden believed a man might lose the melanin in his skin upon the mere consideration of voting for a Republican. He knew that the open-minded voter of African extraction would retain his hue. But according to the presidential candidate, on a deeper, metaphysical level that man would abandon his blackness, which Biden, Hannah-Jones, and the rest of the radicals believe has more to do with political "consciousness" than color.

Back in 1970, Carol Hanisch translated Sarachild's vision of consciousness-raising into a political plan of action. She explained the explicitly Marxist character of the endeavor in a 2006 introduction to her essay. Whereas earlier feminist activism had "used spiritual, psychological, metaphysical, and pseudo-historical explanations for women's oppression," Hanisch preferred "a real, materialist analysis . . . in the Marxist materialist . . . sense." In the essay itself, Hanisch refers admiringly to "Marx, Lenin, Engels, Mao, and Ho [Chi Minh]," the communist dictator of Vietnam who had died in office a year before she wrote it.[14] Like Gramsci before her, she recognized that cultural upheaval must predate political revolution. American culture cherished the separation between public and private spheres on which republican government rests, so she set out to destroy that distinction.

John Locke, the liberal English philosopher who helped to shape the American Founding, insisted on a separation between private and public—that is, between the familial and the general or, in Carol Hanisch's words, the personal and the political. He began his *Second Treatise of Government* by declaring, "The Power of a Magistrate over a Subject, may be distinguished from that of a Father over his Children, a Master over his Servant, a Husband over his Wife, and a Lord over his Slave."[15] As one might suspect, Locke's penultimate example rankled feminists, who deplored the notion that a husband might lawfully lord over his wife. Whereas Locke sought to circumscribe the scope of government and its interference with the family, feminists feared the patriarchal family more than they did the state.

Ironically, in their ideology the "Second Wave" feminists of the 1970s aligned more closely with throne-and-altar conservatives whose monarchal philosophy the liberal Locke sought to supplant. In *Patriarcha: A Defense of the Natural Power of Kings against the Unnatural Liberty of the People*, Sir Robert Filmer defended the political legitimacy of monarchs on the personal grounds that kings are the fathers of their people.[16] Present-day feminists might require a fainting couch should they discover that they hold more in common with the author of *Patriarcha* than with the father of liberalism, but their radical foremothers—or fore-aunts, more likely—had their reasons for rejecting limited, liberal statecraft.

Locke's distinction between the public and the private protected home life from the intrusions of work and politics, but women remained stuck at home regardless of who ruled. Though Locke's emphasis on the rights of the individual no doubt shaped the entitled tone of feminism more than Filmer's focus on reverence and humility, feminists took the more conservative tack and eschewed the liberal protections of private life in order to transform the personal as well as the political.

When the personal becomes the political, everything gets politicized—with the ironic exception of politics, which actually becomes depoliticized. Today every facet of our culture has taken on a political aspect, from sneakers to sports leagues to fast food chicken sandwiches. How a family structures household chores, whether a wife adopts her husband's surname, who gets to use the home office—all these formerly private matters come to denote a political perspective. Yet at the same time, citizens have ceded more and more political control to bureaucrats, experts, and judges. The politicization of everything has robbed the people of basic political rights.

The issues of contraception and abortion shed light on this counterintuitive process. In 1965, the Supreme Court "discovered" in the Constitution a theretofore-unnoticed general right to privacy, which it announced in *Griswold v. Connecticut*. Where precisely the judges had found this right, no one could quite say. Justice William O. Douglas, writing for the Court, claimed, "Specific guarantees in the Bill of Rights have penumbras, formed by emanations from those guarantees that help give them life and substance. Various guarantees create zones of privacy."[17] If any reader can translate the justice's gobbledygook into English, please write to the publisher. The dictionary tells us that penumbras are partial shadows, and emanations are "effluence."[18] The U.S. Constitution contains neither, but these elusive penumbras and emanations returned in *Roe v. Wade* to establish a "fundamental right" to abortion as a consequence of the similarly secret general right to privacy.[19]

Feminists hailed both Supreme Court decisions, but these personal victories came at great cost to political liberty. Before *Griswold* and *Roe*, the people possessed the right to decide for themselves, through their elected legislators, the degree to which they would tolerate contraception and abortion. The people could amend the laws over time. More licentious generations might expand them, chaster generations might restrict them. In *Griswold* and *Roe*, the Court stole that more fundamental political right from the people. Nine unelected lawyers decided those questions for every American in perpetuity.

The late Justice Antonin Scalia lamented the power grab decades later in *Obergefell*, which redefined marriage. "It is not of special importance to me what the law says about marriage," explained Scalia in his dissent. "It is of overwhelming importance, however, who it is that rules me. Today's decree says that my Ruler, and the Ruler of 320 million Americans coast-to-coast, is a majority of the nine lawyers on the Supreme Court."[20] What masquerades as an expansion of liberty actually restricts political rights. The personal appeals offered on behalf of inventing constitutional guarantees to contraception, abortion, and redefined marriage—"my body, my choice," "love is love," and so forth—extort through emotional blackmail the once-cherished rights of self-government.

"The personal is the political" cuts two ways: private life becomes political, and political life becomes personal. Carol Hanisch embraced both transformations. "This is not to deny that these sessions have at least two aspects that are therapeutic. I prefer to call even this aspect 'political therapy' as opposed to personal therapy," she wrote. "It seems to me the whole country needs that kind of political therapy."[21] Politics has never been for the faint of heart, but therapy treats disorders. If Hanisch believed our political system requires therapy, the disorder she hoped to treat was constitutional government.

Progressives of an earlier era had already weakened constitutional government by taking many political decisions out of the hands of the people and their representatives and putting them into the hands of bureaucrats and the administrative state. These earlier progressives considered constitutional government outdated, a relic of Newton's universal laws unsuited to the modern Darwinian world of perpetual evolution. The Second Wave feminists of the 1970s took even more power from the people and handed it to judges as well as to more bureaucrats. But the most powerful tool in the feminist arsenal operated off the bench and outside the bureaucracy. These women, or "wimmin," as the more doctrinaire gals styled themselves, warped minds by changing language.

In 1985—a bygone, halcyon era when the *New York Times* still retained at least the pretense of sense and humor—the Gray Lady suggested the term "woperdaughter" as a politically correct substitute for "woman," which gave offense for its reliance on the word "man," and "wo-person," which gave offense for its reliance on the word "son."[22] The paper mocked humorless feminists—forgive the superfluity—who opted for "wimmin," "womyn," and "womin" to avoid the dread three-letter word.

Amid all the ridiculous misspellings, one might almost forget that "man" is a gender-neutral term, referring not just to members of the male sex but also to humanity as a whole. No less an authority on the English language than the King James Bible uses the word in this way: "So God created man in his own image, in the image of God created he him; male and female created he them."[23]

Feminists set out to abolish the separation between personal and political life, and nothing can be more personal than the words that form one's thought and speech. The feminist linguist Deborah Cameron explains the strategy. "Meaning works by contrast: the words you choose acquire force from an implicit comparison with the ones you could have chosen, but did not," she observes. "By coining alternatives to traditional usage, therefore, the radicals have effectively *politicised all the terms*."[24] The mere existence of politically correct jargon, ridiculous though it may be, charges traditional language with heightened political significance.

"Wimmin" never quite caught on. But other politically correct feminist formulations have taken hold. The coinage of "chairwoman" and "chairperson" unseated the traditional, gender-neutral "chairman" because of its perceived political incorrectness. Often "chairpersons" go by the bizarre abbreviation "chair," as though they were pieces of furniture rather than the people who sit on them. Now to refer to oneself as a person rather than a seat connotes a political worldview.

Christopher Hitchens, a left-wing opponent of political correctness, observed, "The real tendency of PC is not to inculcate respect for the marvelous variety of humanity but to reduce each group into subgroups and finally to atoms, so that everyone is on their guard against everyone else."[25] Political correctness breaks the unconscious bonds and traditions that protect private life from the intrusions of ideological engineering.

Rather than dismissing this semantic engineering and retreating to stale platitudes about a neutral or de-politicized world, conservatives ought to admit that the feminists have a point. They recognize that traditional language and behavior prop up a traditional moral standard, which they seek to overthrow. They manipulate language in order to transform the consciousness of women who, they believe, unwittingly uphold wicked and false ideas about sex in particular and human nature in general. The Second Wave feminists understood that culture can never be neutral. So they undertook to rewrite the terms of engagement.

Lazy liberals of the Left and Right parrot slogans about the "marketplace of ideas" without ever taking seriously the radicals' complaint that someone sets and enforces the rules of the market. They don't even inquire into the provenance of that phrase, which entered the American mind in 1953 through a concurring opinion written by the infamous sophist William O. Douglas in *United States v. Rumely*.[26] Here again one sees the trap of political correctness, which posits a false dichotomy between accepting radical new standards or abandoning standards altogether. Either way, political correctness achieves its purpose of overthrowing traditional society.

Simone de Beauvoir, the famous French feminist and strumpet of Jean-Paul Sartre, acknowledged the strategy. "Language is inherited from a masculine society and contains many male prejudices," she wrote. "Women simply have to steal the instrument; they don't have to break it or try *a priori* to make it something totally different. Steal it and use it for their own good."[27] Beauvoir erred in her bleak assessment of traditional society's prejudices, which benefit both men and women in different ways, but she understood far better than benighted liberals on both sides of the aisle that language and culture necessarily carry prejudices, and those natural preferences and revulsions will dictate the boundaries of any society's marketplace of ideas.

According to traditional prejudices, men hold the door, pick up the tab, take out the trash, and bring home the bacon. Second Wave feminists sought to dismantle those prejudices, not because they didn't benefit women, but because they implied the reality of sexual difference. The traditional view held that men and women complement one another and belong together; the Second Wave feminists believed that "a woman needs a man like a fish needs a bicycle."[28] Their language reflects their largely successful efforts to break the traditional bonds between men and women—or rather "wimmin," who have nothing at all to do with men.

There can be no neutral term between "women" and "wimmin" that leaves open the question of whether or not women relate to men. The words carry entire worldviews, and the term that dominates will reflect society's prejudice. To seek neutrality is to misunderstand the tussle entirely.

The clear-eyed Simone de Beauvoir tried to explain this hard fact to Betty Friedan, a radical feminist in her own right, whose book *The Feminine Mystique* sparked Second Wave feminism in America. During a dialogue that Friedan recorded and published in her collection *It Changed My Life*, Beauvoir declared, "No woman should be authorized to stay at home to raise her children. Society should be totally different. Women should not have that choice, precisely because if there is such a choice, too many women will make that one." Then, to make sure Friedan had understood the enormity of her point, she added, "It is a way of forcing women in a certain direction."

Friedan objected to Beauvoir's rigidity. "I follow the argument," she responded, "but politically at the moment I don't agree with it. . . . There is such a tradition of individual freedom in America that I would never say that every woman must put her child in a child-care center." One cannot quite tell from Friedan's comments whether she rejected Beauvoir's argument as wrong in itself or merely on the practical grounds that it would fall on deaf ears, given America's more conservative views of sex and liberty. Friedan may have felt that America was not yet ready for such radicalism. Perhaps she was not ready for it herself.

Regardless, Beauvoir had no patience for Friedan's naiveté. "But that's not how we see it," she continued. "We see it as part of a global reform of society which would not accept that old segregation between man and woman, the home and the outside world." In other words, Beauvoir would not accept the distinction between the personal and the political, and Beauvoir's view won the day. "As long as the family and the myth of the family and the myth of maternity and the maternal instinct are not destroyed," she concluded, "women will still be oppressed."[29]

Political correctness seeks to destroy the social order for the purpose of liberation. Radicals from Beauvoir to Black Lives Matter, which undertakes to "dismantle the Western-prescribed nuclear family," have found in that fundamental political institution the most persistent font of oppression.[30] So they set out to destroy the family as well as "the myth of the family." When Beauvoir used strange phrases such as "the myth of the family" and "the myth of maternity," she did not mean to imply that family and motherhood do not exist. Rather she was taking aim at the veneration our culture affords to motherhood and the family. She objected to the social prejudice that cherishes the family and honors mothers for raising their children. Beauvoir, the jilted common-law wife of a notorious philanderer, considered the family intrinsically oppressive but all too attractive to women suffering from a false consciousness in a patriarchal society.

The word "mothering" entered the English language sometime in the early fifteenth century, more than half a millennium before "parenting" began to replace it.[31] References to a child's "parent or guardian" have almost entirely supplanted references to mothers and fathers in official documents and even polite conversation, much as the sterile terms "partner" and "significant other" have replaced "husband" and "wife" in a society that shuns normativity. Liberals may argue that "parenting" offers a neutral alternative to an outdated, sexist term. But that neutrality is illusory, as "parenting" carries just as many social implications as the traditional word it supplanted.

"Motherhood" implies that women have a special role in raising a child, a role for which they are better suited than men. "Parenting" suggests that no particular distinction exists between mothers and fathers—or men and women, for that matter. A culture that talks about "mothering" and "fathering" will more likely preserve the family than one that preaches "parenting," which might be undertaken by single women, single men, same-sex couples, mixed-sex throuples, or a commune.

In 1991, John Taylor wrote a *New York Magazine* cover story, "Are You Politically Correct?" which signaled the arrival of political correctness as a major cultural phenomenon. Taylor warned, "To the politically correct, *everything* is political."[32] He was right, but the politically correct have a point. Public life is by definition political, and even the institutions that define our private life exist and develop with the aid and assent of our politics. We fail to recognize the political nature of most things because we take them for granted as the given facts of our society, a cultural inheritance beyond the scope of conscious tinkering and debate. If we tried to reason through the political significance of every action we undertook, we would hardly be able to get out of bed in the morning.

When a man holds a door for a woman, he unconsciously makes many political statements, just as the politically correct contend. He implies that women are physically weaker than men. He suggests that men have some responsibility to protect and cherish women. He assumes that men and women complement one another. But he doesn't think about any of that. He gives no thought to holding the door. His mother or father taught him it's polite, and so he does it. Political correctness undertakes a process of criticism—the "ruthless criticism of all that exists," in Marx's words—to "raise consciousness" and make people aware of the political meaning behind their reflexive, traditional behaviors. It is an exhausting, tedious process, and people tire of it eventually. But the radicals must break down traditional culture before they can rebuild it after their own fashion.

Politically correct radicals have concentrated much of their focus on sex because sex is the fundamental distinction within man. Other differences—race, height, weight, and so forth—pale in comparison to sex, which rests at the basis of human self-understanding, from Gilgamesh to the Greek myths to Genesis. The dismantling of our sexual self-understanding that took hold through Second Wave feminism would reach fruition decades later in transgender ideology, but in the meantime political correctness took a detour back through the universities, by then more "politicized" than ever.

After Taylor observed that "to the politically correct, *everything is political*," he continued, "[a]nd nothing is more political, in their view, than the humanities, where much of the recent controversy has been centered."[33] The humanities explore what it means to be human, preserving civilization's greatest triumphs and insights from generation to generation. Having established a beachhead in human sexuality, politically correct radicals next moved to redefine our civilization and our very selves through a new style of teaching: the school of resentment.

CHAPTER 8

THE SCHOOL OF RESENTMENT

Professor Harold Bloom's research assistant entered his office in distress. "Harold, I'm rather stunned," she began, shaking her head. "I've just gone to my undergraduate seminar in American Studies. We just had a lecture on Walt Whitman. The professor spent the entire two hours explaining to us that Walt Whitman was a racist."

Bloom, the legendary liberal literary critic and defender of the Western canon, recounted the story the following year. "In the face of that, my dear, I almost lose my capacity for outrage, shock, or indignation," he told his interviewer. "Walt Whitman a racist? It is simply lunatic."[1]

Had history taken a different course, radical academics might have exalted the homosexual and religious skeptic Whitman as a progressive hero. But Whitman loved his country. He began the second edition of *Leaves of Grass* by declaring, "The United States themselves are essentially the greatest poem."[2] He earned the title "America's poet," and so American Studies professors have to hate him.

Virtually all the pseudo-academic disciplines that developed out of Critical Theory valorize their subjects. "Black Studies" exalts black people, "Women's Studies" venerates women, and "Queer Studies" casts a sympathetic light on homosexuals. The exceptions are "Whiteness Studies" and "American Studies," which exist to deconstruct and denigrate white people and America, respectively.

In fact, all the other "critical studies" denigrate America too. The nominal concern for one putative victim group or another serves merely as a lens through which to focus the broader project of criticizing America in particular and Western civilization more generally. Harold Bloom dubbed this pedagogical brood of vipers "the School of Resentment."

Before Critical Theory conquered the academy, readers approached texts in search of wisdom. Now radical ideologues have driven the humility, curiosity, and love required for learning out of the classroom. They have replaced the traditional approach to teaching with a resentful attitude derived from Critical Theory that castigates authors and texts according to modern ideologies. This form of "analysis" often ignores the meaning of the text, instead imposing on it whatever faddish notion strikes the reader's fancy. Not even the superlative works of William Shakespeare can withstand the academic obsession with an author's race and sex.

In 2016, a group of undergraduate barbarians petitioned Yale to "decolonize" its English department by lifting a requirement that students study Shakespeare and Chaucer, among other writers, in the university's Major English Poets course. "It is unacceptable that a Yale student considering studying English literature might read only white male authors," reads the petition.[3] The English Department offered countless classes on non-white non-male authors. But the possibility that an English major might focus more on Shakespeare's sonnets than slam poetry proved too much for the cultural revolutionaries, who demanded the right to earn an English degree without ever once reading the Bard.

Major English Poets included white male authors because the major English poets are white and male. In what world would the presence of English poets in a course on English poetry constitute "colonization"? Colonization means the sending in of settlers to establish political control over a territory. In the case of Yale's English department, the only colonizers are the student radicals themselves, whose political goal of cultural hegemony impels them to march on the established institutions and seize the means of cultivation.

One doubts that the student radicals would protest a course on Major Zulu Poets because the curriculum comprised too many black male authors. In the School of Resentment, only the West must be "deconstructed." New forms of literary analysis arose to dismiss the West's great intellectual discoveries as self-serving, socially contrived, and historically contingent. Deconstruction, poststructuralism, postmodernism, and many other pretentious academic movements proliferated throughout the academy during the 1960s, '70s, and '80s, all to the same political purpose. They sought to undermine the philosophical and cultural basis of Western civilization.

In 1976, the French philosopher Jacques Derrida summed up the maddening technique of deconstruction in six words: "There is nothing outside the text."[4] Derrida's critics and admirers have long debated the precise meaning of his cryptic statement, translated from the French ("*il n'y a pas de hors-texte*").[5] Since rehashing these debates threatens even greater danger to brain cells than does his philosophy, the safest way to understand Derrida's meaning is by observing the consequences of his writing on the Western mind, now atrophied by generations of arglebargle to the point of denying objective truth itself.

No one denies that social and historical context can help a reader to interpret a text. But the deconstructionists' obsession with context to the exclusion of absolute truth and objective knowledge has had the ironic effect of depriving great works of their proper context. The puerile focus of the "decolonizers" on Shakespeare's genetics and genitals obscures the objective beauty of his poetry and the profundity of his observations about human nature. The radicals revel in castigating the Bard for his stereotypical portrayal of Shylock as a greedy Jew in *The Merchant of Venice*, but they never get around to praising his profound description of "the quality of mercy" that "droppeth as the gentle rain from heaven upon the place beneath" and "becomes the throned monarch better than his crown" as "an attribute to God himself."[6]

The radicals have no mercy on the West, which they unjustly blame for all the sins of mankind. But while conservatives mock the illogic of their theories, we might also acknowledge the perfect logic of their tactics. Shakespeare's works and the King James Bible have shaped the English-speaking peoples more than any other texts. A cursory glance at the Gettysburg Address or Lincoln's Second Inaugural reveals the extent to which those great works educated America's greatest orator, Abraham Lincoln. Shakespeare and the KJV in no small part wrought the Western mind.

The cultural revolutionaries forced the Bible out of schools the decade before the School of Resentment began to poison American education. In 1963, in *Abington School District v. Schempp*, the Supreme Court "discovered" a theretofore-hidden constitutional ban on biblical education in public schools.[7] With the Bible thus vanquished, the radicals next set their sights on Shakespeare and the other great writers of the Western Canon. They portrayed their campaign as an effort to expand the curriculum—to make it more open, liberal, and inclusive. But curricula cannot expand. There are only so many hours in the day, and students can only study so much in a semester. Every minute spent on one writer or work means a minute away from another.

The revolutionaries did not seek to expand the curriculum but rather to change it. They sought to remove focus from the great authors of the Western tradition in favor of newer and lesser writers selected along narrow ideological lines. Here again conservatives have all too often fallen into the trap laid before them, responding to the cultural massacre with lame, liberal platitudes praising "choice." Perhaps universities need not require that English majors read Shakespeare, they whimper, just so long as they have the choice.

These meek concessions miss the point, just as do popular slogans distinguishing between "education" and "indoctrination." Education by its very nature is coercive. University students may choose to study the lyrics of Cardi B rather than the works of Shakespeare but once they have made that decision, free choice gives way to assignments, exams, and the threat of low grades.[8]

Does anyone believe that the radicals intend to leave the future of their ideological education program up to the free choice of students? Just as student demands in the 1960s for "free speech" led to the establishment of new, politically correct speech codes, so too campaigns to "expand" curricula in the 1970s led over the ensuing decades to the establishment of "diversity" requirements in course selection and even mandatory "training sessions" in politically correct ideology.[9]

"Choice" will not suffice to save the Western mind. Dithering conservatives must make choices themselves. Not only must they defend the cultural tradition that the revolutionaries ruthlessly and relentlessly criticize, but they must also actively oppose the radical curricula that those revolutionaries are installing in its place. Not only should universities teach classes on Shakespeare, but they should not offer courses on Cardi B or Underwater Basket Weaving or Lesbian Dance Theory, all of which have actually appeared in recent years at American universities.[10] Such courses need not actively oppose the Western tradition to effect the radicals' goals. Whether subversive or merely frivolous, these courses waste students' time and keep them away from the great works that made the great culture now fading before our very eyes.

Conservatives consider these radicals barbarians, but in many ways they understand culture better than we do. Rather than learning from leftists such as Gramsci and Marcuse, conservatives have dismissed them as kooks. But Marcuse was right to observe that tolerance necessarily involves limits, even if the limits he sought to impose repel all reasonable people. Gramsci offered keen insight into cultural hegemony, even as he tried to wrest it for the radicals.

The revolutionaries understand the importance of language to culture, hence their focus on literary criticism within the university and on politically correct speech among the broader public. Once entrenched, these "critical studies" expanded their scope into virtually every academic discipline, from history to hard science.

Leonard Jeffries, the founding chairman of the Black Studies department at the City College of New York, provides a typically absurd glimpse into this sort of pseudo-scholarship. Beginning in 1972 and continuing throughout his two-decade tenure in the classrooms of CUNY, Jeffries expounded on his theory that Africans constitute a superior race of "sun people," in contrast to whites, who make up the inferior race of "ice people."[11] The black "sun people," he explained, possess "core spiritual values," unlike the materialistic "ice people," who objectify everything they see—most notably the "sun people," through slavery—because "the ecology of the cave is different than the ecology of the riverbank."[12] Readers who have followed the argument thus far might consider seeing a psychologist.

In the summer of 2020 television personality Nick Cannon regurgitated Jeffries's theories for a new generation. During an episode of his podcast *Cannon's Class*, the actor argued that "melanated people" possess compassion and souls, unlike white people, who "are actually closer to animals" and "are actually the true savages" because they lack "the power of the sun." This pigment deficiency means that "the only way that they can act is evil," he explained. "They have to rob, steal, rape, kill . . . in order to survive."[13] Jeffries couldn't have said it better himself.

After decades of spouting this bilious nonsense, Jeffries crossed a line on July 20, 1991, during a two-hour-long speech at the Empire State Black Arts and Culture Festival in which he blamed "rich Jews" for controlling Hollywood and financing the trans-Atlantic slave trade. The *New York Times* and the *Washington Post* both rightly denounced him.[14] But what took so long? As the *Post* reported at the time, "Jeffries' race-baiting harangues have been a familiar part of CUNY life for years, [and] this has not prevented him from gaining both tenure and the chairmanship of his department, not to mention a following at City College as, in the *Times'* description, 'a popular, flamboyant lecturer.'"[15] Jeffries festered at City College for two decades on the grounds that his dismissal would threaten "academic freedom."

Both conservatives and radicals exalt "academic freedom," much as they do "free speech" and "tolerance." But like free speech and tolerance, in practice academic freedom only ever seems to cut one way. Respect for "academic freedom" kept Leonard Jeffries employed for decades spewing barmy fantasies about "sun people," ensoulment, and the ancient Egyptians. But "academic freedom" didn't keep conservative professor Peter Berkowitz employed at Harvard, or Carol Swain at Vanderbilt, or even the occasionally-vaguely-conservative liberal Erika Christakis at Yale.[16]

In 2007, Columbia University invited Iranian president Mahmoud Ahmadinejad to lecture in New York. Columbia defended its invitation to Ahmadinejad, who at the time was actively killing U.S. servicemen in Iraq, on the grounds of "academic freedom." Protests took place around the campus, and Columbia's president opened the lecture by listing the Islamic leader's crimes, but still the university permitted the international terrorist to address a full auditorium, interrupted only by the applause of Ahmadinejad's supporters in the room.[17] Ahmadinejad spent his lecture denying the existence of homosexuals in Iran and the historicity of the Holocaust.[18]

A decade later, when the Columbia University College Republicans invited the right-wing British activist Tommy Robinson to give a speech on the pitfalls of mass Islamic migration, the lecture met tougher resistance. Protesters stormed the lecture hall and shouted down the speaker. University officers barred attendees from entering the room. More protesters outside banged on the door so that the audience that had managed to enter could not hear.[19] And Robinson himself was not even physically present; instead, he addressed the group by video conference after the U.S. State Department, at the insistence of left-wing British legislators, refused to grant the speaker a visa to enter the country.[20] If only Robinson had been an Islamic terrorist rather than a conservative critic of Islamic terror, perhaps he would have been afforded the "academic freedom" to give his lecture.

Conservatives may condemn this sort of censorship and castigate leftists as hypocrites for abandoning their own avowed devotion to "academic freedom" when it suits their ideological ends, but the radicals understand the true nature of this slogan far better than their present-day conservative critics. Pure "academic freedom," like pure "free speech" and "tolerance," has never existed, nor can it. The ancient Athenians killed Socrates for corrupting the youth.[21] The Catholic Church, which invented the university in the Middle Ages, exerted significant control over the boundaries of academic discourse, most notably in the case of Galileo Galilei.[22]

The modern notion of academic freedom began after the Protestant Revolution with the founding of the University of Leiden in 1575. Yet even the University of Leiden refused to grant absolute academic freedom, and the Protestant Synod of Dort in 1618 restricted this liberty even further in its efforts to stifle the spread of the Arminian heresy. In the eighteenth century a handful of German universities attempted to establish relative academic freedom once again, but Napoleon reversed those efforts when he rose to power in the early nineteenth century.[23]

In 1636, the Great and General Court of the Massachusetts Bay Colony founded the College at Newtowne, later renamed Harvard, but not with any notion of "academic freedom." Rather, the Court established Harvard to rid Newtowne, later renamed Cambridge, of the antinomian heresy promoted by Anne Hutchinson, who was banished from the colony and later killed by Siwanoy Indians in New York.[24]

Even into the twentieth century, the most ardent defenders of "academic freedom" insisted on limitations to that freedom. In 1940, the American Association of University Professors issued its "Statement on Academic Freedom and Tenure," which reiterated similar professions made in 1915 and 1925. The AAUP endorsed the right of teachers to "freedom in the classroom in discussing their subject," but in the very same sentence it cautioned that educators "should be careful not to introduce into their teaching controversial matter which has no relation to their subject" and later instructed them to "exercise appropriate restraint."[25] The broadest defense of academic freedom in modern history barred controversy and demanded restraint.

Conservatives once understood the silliness of the "academic freedom" slogan. William F. Buckley Jr. launched both his career and the postwar conservative movement with a book inveighing against "academic freedom," which he dismissed as a "hoax." Twenty-first century conservatives may remember the book's title, *God and Man at Yale*, but few seem to recall its subtitle, *The Superstitions of "Academic Freedom."* All universities must have a mission, Buckley argued, so educators must structure their lectures toward advancing that mission and leave sermons that contradict it out of the classroom.

Buckley attacked universities for justifying their godless and collectivist curricula on the basis of academic freedom over the objections of parents and alumni. "In the last analysis," Buckley concluded, "academic freedom must mean the freedom of men and women to supervise the educational activities and aims of the schools they oversee and support." While Buckley encouraged alumni to withhold donations until universities encouraged Christian morality and free-market economics, present-day conservatives relegate themselves to making piddling pleas for "intellectual diversity" in the hope that radicals don't run them off campus altogether.[26]

Buckley's intellectual heirs have flipped his stance on "academic freedom," which WFB's own magazine has recently defended in the very manner its founder mocked.[27] Buckley, like Milton and Locke, has come to serve as a byword for ideas he never espoused and even denounced. But Buckley had it right. Universities educate, which means they necessarily encourage certain ideas and discourage others. Neutrality is an illusion.

The more things change, the more they stay the same. Harvard continues to fight heresy today just as vigorously as it did in the seventeenth century. But today political correctness rather than congregational Protestantism defines the university's orthodoxy. Benighted conservatives bewail this state of affairs, but education must have boundaries. Contrary to the popular and meaningless mantra that educators ought to "teach students how to think, not what to think," education necessarily teaches certain facts to the exclusion or outright contradiction of others. The slogan actually disproves itself, as it tells people what to think about education.

When a teacher informs his students that two plus two make four rather than five, he teaches them what to think; the students' grasp of basic arithmetic, in turn, teaches them how to think about more complex problems. The principle extends beyond mathematics. When a teacher in ethics or religion tells his students that it is wrong to steal or that it is wrong to commit murder, he teaches them what to think, and these lessons teach students how to think about other moral issues.

So when a leftist instructor teaches that it is right to murder through abortion, when he teaches that it is right to steal through confiscatory public policy or even outright looting, he too teaches his students what to think, and this perverse moral education likewise shapes how they think about other questions—at grave cost to society.

If conservatives hope to regain the political and cultural ground they have ceded over the past century, they must extricate themselves from the trap laid for them by radicals, who have convinced conservatives to abandon all standards and substantive claims for an abstract ideal of openness that has never existed in practice. We cannot rest easy in the belief that the good, the true, and the beautiful will necessarily win out in the "free marketplace of ideas" when the radicals regulate the market to subsidize the wicked, the false, and the ugly.

The *New York Times* exemplified this ideological market distortion in 2020 when it set out to rewrite the history of the United States through the 1619 Project. The project, which took its name from the year in which the first slave ship arrived at the shores of Virginia, aimed "to reframe the country's history by placing the consequences of slavery and the contributions of black Americans at the very center of our national narrative."[28] To lead the ambitious project, the *Times* tapped the left-wing journalist Nikole Hannah-Jones, who based her series of essays on a lie.

"Conveniently left out of our founding mythology," Hannah-Jones wrote, "is the fact that one of the primary reasons the colonists decided to declare their independence from Britain was because they wanted to protect the institution of slavery."[29] Hannah-Jones, who majored in history and "African-American Studies," may have overheard this canard as she steeped in the School of Resentment during her undergraduate years, but the claim has no basis in reality. Hanlon's razor impels us never to attribute to malice that which is adequately explained by stupidity. But whether through dishonesty or ignorance, the 1619 Project began with a lie.[30]

Not even left-wing historians could abide the deceit. Princeton historian Sean Wilentz drafted a letter, signed by academic historians from around the country, and sent it to the editors and publisher of the *Times*.[31] The historians established their leftist credentials by beginning the letter with praise for the project. "We applaud all efforts to address the enduring centrality of slavery and racism to our history," they professed. "Raising profound, unsettling questions about slavery and the nation's past and present, as The 1619 Project does, is a praiseworthy and urgent public service," they continued. But finally they came to their objection: the Project got the central facts wrong.

"These errors, which concern major events, cannot be described as interpretation or 'framing,'" the historians explained. "They are matters of verifiable fact, which are the foundation of both honest scholarship and honest journalism."[32] If the naive historians were looking for either, they had come to the wrong place, but they nevertheless offered their correction, which merits quotation at length:

> On the American Revolution, pivotal to any account of our history, the project asserts that the founders declared the colonies' independence of Britain "in order to ensure slavery would continue." This is not true. If supportable, the allegation would be astounding—yet every statement offered by the project to validate it is false. Some of the other material in the

project is distorted, including the claim that "for the most part," black Americans have fought their freedom struggles "alone."

Still other material is misleading. The project criticizes Abraham Lincoln's views on racial equality but ignores his conviction that the Declaration of Independence proclaimed universal equality, for blacks as well as whites, a view he upheld repeatedly against powerful white supremacists who opposed him. The project also ignores Lincoln's agreement with Frederick Douglass that the Constitution was, in Douglass's words, "a GLORIOUS LIBERTY DOCUMENT." Instead, the project asserts that the United States was founded on racial slavery, an argument rejected by a majority of abolitionists and proclaimed by champions of slavery like John C. Calhoun.[33]

The historians' critique reads like an usher at Ford's Theatre asking, "Other than that, Mrs. Lincoln, how did you enjoy the play?" The entire 1619 Project hinges on the premise that our forebears founded the country to defend slavery. When the historians refuted that claim, the thesis fell apart. The *Times* persisted in error for a full seven months before "clarifying" its central claim to read, "One of the primary reasons *some of* the colonists decided to declare their independence from Britain was because they wanted to protect the institution of slavery" a change that succeeded neither in admitting fault nor in salvaging the thesis (emphasis mine).[34]

But the *Times* never needed to prove the thesis, only to popularize it, which the outlet spent a fortune doing. In the fall of 2019, the *Times* secretly spent three million dollars on just three Facebook ads promoting the project and an unknown amount more after that. While Facebook requires the buyers of "ads about social issues, elections, or politics" to make information about audience reach and ad spend available to the public—a requirement the *New York Times* demanded and praised—the *Times* itself skirted those rules by presenting their false, highly ideological, revisionist history as objective journalism.[35]

Within a year, the Pulitzer Center on Crisis Reporting had translated the project into a curriculum with lesson plans and reading guides, which promptly entered more than 3,500 classrooms around the country.[36] The academic historians had complained that the project's lies "suggest a displacement of historical understanding by ideology," but that was the point from the very beginning.[37] The 1619 Project did not attempt to recover some hidden truth or refute some long-told lie but rather to "reframe" American history itself.

When did America begin? The first permanent English settlers arrived at Jamestown in 1607. The first slave ship landed at Point Comfort in 1619. The Pilgrims first set foot on Plymouth Rock in 1620. An unknown soldier fired the shot heard round the world in 1775. The Continental Congress approved the Declaration of Independence in 1776. In 1789, the Constitution became the law of the land. In 1865, Abraham Lincoln won the Civil War and with it "a new birth of freedom."[38] In 1964, Lyndon Johnson signed the Civil Rights Act, which the politically incorrect historian Christopher Caldwell has called America's second constitution.[39]

For much of our history, Americans traced their roots to Plymouth rather than Jamestown, even though the Mayflower sailed more than a decade after the southern settlers reached Virginia. The Pilgrims' religious zeal, work ethic, and focus on the family better "framed" the national spirit than the all-male Jamestown settlers' hapless quest for wealth, which ended in starvation and even cannibalism before mail-order brides arrived to repopulate the colony.[40]

Many Americans find their Founding in 1776, glossing over the century and a half of English settlement that preceded the signing of the Declaration. Now radicals have attempted to re-found the Founding in 1619, ignoring every virtue in American history to focus solely on the sin of slavery. Their first try failed on the facts, but in the long run they may yet succeed, as fact succumbs to framing.

Conservatives have attempted to refute the 1619 Project on almost exclusively factual grounds. Here again they have refused to learn from their radical opponents, who understand that attitude trumps even facts in the narration of history. If conservatives will not listen to their opponents, they might at least read their own philosophers, such as Edmund Burke, who observed, "In history a great volume is unrolled for our instruction, drawing the materials of future wisdom from the past errors and infirmities of mankind." All well and good, but what happens when ideologues abuse that great volume for their own political ends? "It may, in the perversion, serve for a magazine, furnishing offensive and defensive weapons . . . and supplying the means of keeping alive, or reviving, dissensions and animosities, and adding fuel to civil fury," wrote Burke, whose comments could serve as a review of the 1619 Project.[41]

Facts matter, but the same set of facts can evoke any number of different attitudes. The radical activist Howard Zinn played fast and loose with the facts in his notorious polemic *A People's History of the United States*, but his lies have caused less damage than his attitude, which recast America as a dark and devilish morass rather than a shining city upon a hill. He highlighted our nation's vices and ignored her virtues. According to Zinn, America exists authentically only in her sins.

Two national narratives have emerged from this great, unrolled volume of history. The conservative version affirms America's basic goodness and acknowledges her shortcomings with humility—both the national humility of our forefathers, who considered themselves sinners in the hands of an angry God, and also the personal humility expected of heirs to a great fortune given us by those selfsame forefathers. The "politically correct" history of the United States differs from the conservative version not so much in the facts it acknowledges as in its attitude toward the nation. The politically correct narrative approaches our national scandals with wrath and pride, delightedly condemning our ancestors and boasting of the radicals' own righteousness. Conservatives tend to arm themselves with facts in the battle against leftist "feelings." Facts matter, but feelings dictate where those facts find themselves in the historical narrative.

Political correctness shows us history through the lens of resentment, rewriting standards and speech codes for the benefit of allegedly aggrieved minority groups. But despite these proletarian pretensions, minorities themselves rarely promote PC. More often, white leftists feign indignation on behalf of the groups they believe ought to be offended. Howard Zinn was a straight, white male. The same goes for Herbert Marcuse and even the swarthier Antonio Gramsci.

The identitarian tenor of politically correct language and history would seem likely to divide Americans along racial and sexual lines, with ethnic minorities, women, and "queers" embracing PC and straight white males opposing it. Ryu Spaeth, for example, described the "average anti-PC crusader" in the *New Republic* as "straight, white, male, conservative."[42] But this picture, like political correctness itself, runs counter to reality. The majority of Americans hate political correctness, and minorities hate it most of all.[43] According to "Hidden Tribes: A Study of America's Polarized Landscape" by scholars Stephen Hawkins, Daniel Yudkin, Míriam Juan-Torres, and Tim Dixon, a full 80 percent of Americans believe that "political correctness is a problem in our country."

Contrary to Spaeth's popular misconception, Hawkins and his colleagues found that whites are less likely than the average American to oppose political correctness. Asians, Hispanics, and American Indians all reject PC at higher rates than whites. These rates reach as high as 82 percent among Asians, 87 percent among Hispanics, and 88 percent among Indians—feather, not dot, to use a politically incorrect distinction—while just 79 percent of whites take issue with the new lingo.[44] Only blacks oppose PC at lower rates than whites, and still three-quarters of black Americans consider political correctness a problem.

Support for political correctness does not even break down as a battle between the old and the young. Respondents aged twenty-four to twenty-nine have the greatest affection for PC, and still 74 percent of them dislike it. Political correctness is even less popular among those under the age of twenty-four, 79 percent of whom oppose it. The radicals have not managed to win over a single age group, and they seem to have lost support between the Millennial and "Zoomer" generations.

Most people in every single allegedly oppressed group for whom the politically correct purport to speak oppose political correctness. Neither race, nor income, nor education, nor age significantly divides Americans on the issue. Instead, as the name would suggest, support for political correctness breaks down along political lines.

All but 3 percent of "devoted conservatives" oppose political correctness. Most traditional liberals feel the same way. Political correctness enjoys majority support among just one group—progressive activists—a fact that undermines PC's pretensions to be the voice of oppressed minorities: progressive activists are the whitest, richest, most highly educated group in the country.[45]

Political correctness masquerades as the *cri de cœur* of long-aggrieved racial and sexual minorities. In reality, Professor Jeffries's idiotic ramblings aside, white elites have always stood at the vanguard of political correctness. They set out to upend society from its most rarified perch, the university campus. And in the 1980s, despite the movement's unpopularity, the campuses capitulated.

CHAPTER 9

CAMPUS CODES AND COERCION

The university campus gave birth to political correctness, and with characteristic ingratitude political correctness killed its alma mater. Colleges across the country nursed neo-Marxism, Critical Theory, deconstruction, postmodernism, and all the other radical analyses that would come to constitute what we know as political correctness. Universities gave these movements the means to transmit their radical ideas to an entire generation of elites who could import them into corporate boardrooms and the halls of government. But to put those ideas into practice, political correctness had to destroy the institution that gave it life.

Political correctness is an anti-standard standard, a negative device designed to overthrow traditional mores and institutions. So paradoxically, political correctness must both preserve the university and destroy it in order to succeed. Only the university campus, one of the West's defining institutions, could provide the safe haven from reality necessary to nurture the ruthless criticism of all that exists; but the practice of those ideas dismantles that very institution.

Long before "trigger warnings" and "safe spaces," university campuses offered a respite from the dangers of the real world. But radicals needed a pretext for overhauling campus policy regarding speech and behavior, so they implausibly portrayed universities as perilous hotbeds of racism and rape. Violence did occasionally break out on campuses, particularly during the 1960s, but in those cases the radicals themselves committed the assaults.

In 1969, rifle-wielding student activists stormed and occupied Willard Straight Hall at Cornell University, evicting parents who had been visiting their children for the weekend.[1] The students demanded the creation of an "Africana Studies" department. The armed occupiers justified the takeover as a response to reports of a burning cross the previous night outside of the Wari black women's cooperative on campus.

But the cross-burning appears to have been a hoax. Ithaca police never tracked down the elusive cross-burners, and they suspected Afro-American Society (AAS) members of setting the blaze themselves to justify further protests—a thesis that one AAS member later seems to have confirmed. Stephen Goodwin, a Cornell student who served as treasurer of the Afro-American Society, called the cross-burning "a set-up." The Society had contrived the hoax, according to Goodwin, "to bring more media and more attention to the whole thing."[2] Whatever really transpired that night, racial hate hoaxes of the sort Goodwin described would proliferate in the ensuing decades as student radicals, bereft of any real grievance, invented imaginary oppression.

The actor Jussie Smollett turned in a poor performance in 2019 when he hired two Nigerian body-builders to don red Trump hats, punch him in the face, and gently lay a noose around his neck in the dead of night while shouting, "This is MAGA country!" in the middle of Chicago, a city governed exclusively by Democrats since 1931.[3] When the truth came out, everyone from President Trump to the left-wing comedian Dave Chappelle mocked Smollett.[4] But similar hoaxes happen often, most notably on college campuses.

In 2016, three black students accused Ohio bakery owner Allyn Gibson of racially profiling Oberlin College students. Oberlin faculty, staff, and administrators organized protests. The university canceled its contracts with Gibson's Food Mart. In reality, Gibson had caught the students stealing liquor from the store, a crime the ringleader later admitted. Fortunately the Oberlin story had a happy ending: an Ohio jury awarded the owners $44 million dollars in punitive and compensatory damages in its defamation case against the college.[5]

On the very same day the Oberlin students slandered Allyn Gibson as a bigot, Bowling Green State student Eleesha Long fabricated an attack by rock-hurling white Trump supporters. Long struggled to keep her story straight, and cell phone records later revealed she wasn't even present at the site of the alleged attack. The only evidence of racism or violence investigators found was a trove of text messages that Long had sent to her boyfriend disparaging whites and wishing death upon Trump supporters. "I hope they all get AIDS," she wrote.[6]

In 2017, a black student activist left a racist threat on her own car at St. Olaf College in Minnesota.[7] That same year, five black Air Force Academy cadets wrote racial slurs on their own doors.[8] The following November, Fynn Arthur, a black student at Goucher College in Maryland, wrote, "I'm gonna kill all niggers," in a dormitory bathroom.[9] The list of similar incidents in recent years could fill not just its own chapter but a full book.

When police discovered the true source of the threatening graffiti, Arthur confessed to having scrawled the threat as well as a backward swastika and the dorm room numbers of black students, including himself. He blamed his "bottled up anger" for motivating him to commit the crime.[10] Whatever the source of his anger, it could not have been racial bigotry on campus, so lacking that he had to invent it. Stranger still, Arthur's mugshot reveals that he hardly even looks black. He may have black ancestors, but Arthur appears to be white, making even more preposterous the notion that skinheads might target him for attack.[11]

Lest one conclude that race plays the decisive factor in these hoaxes, the many false claims of rape that have bedeviled college campuses in recent years as well bear recounting. Left-wing activists have popularized the claim that one in five women will be raped during their undergraduate years.[12] Some radicals inflate the statistic to one in four.[13] If those numbers were true, women would face greater danger on the picturesque green of Harvard Yard than they do in the back alleys of Botswana.

No reasonable person could believe those statistics, least of all the purported victims, many of whom "had not realized they had been raped" until left-wing activists informed them of their victimhood.[14] The origin of the "one in five" statistic lies in a thirteen-question survey designed by the social scientist Mary Koss for Kent State University students in 1976. The first twelve questions addressed various sexual acts with different degrees of ambiguity. The thirteenth asked bluntly, "Have you ever been raped?" According to Koss, many respondents got the last question wrong.

Koss then revised and re-administered the survey to six thousand university students across thirty-two campuses in the United States. She determined that 27 percent of respondents—more than one in four—had suffered rape since the age of fourteen. But only 55 percent of those clinically classified victims agreed with Koss's assessment.[15]

A more recent survey by the Association of American Universities arrived at the one-in-four statistic through the explicit use of political correctness: the social scientists administering the survey simply redefined the terms. The surveyors found that 11 percent of female undergraduate respondents had suffered rape or sodomy according to the legal definitions of those terms, but that number soared to 23 percent when measured by the vaguer category of "sexual assault," which might include any unwanted "grabbing, groping or rubbing against the other in a sexual way, even if the touching is over the other's clothes."[16] But this broad definition robs the statistic of all meaning. One cannot compare an unwanted pinch—however unpleasant, immoral, and even illegal—to rape.

Still, even discarding the dubious "one in four" statistic, the survey's finding that 11 percent of female undergraduates had suffered rape or sodomy still sounds implausibly high. A closer look at the data reveals why. Just half of those 11 percent of respondents reported that any force was involved in their encounter. The other half report being too drunk to give consent according to the law, a circumstance that raises a problem for the statisticians: sexual encounters and drinking go hand in hand on campus.

Drunken undergraduates often get frisky. Depending on the circumstances, the law or a social scientist with an agenda might classify an ostensibly consensual sexual encounter as rape, even if neither party involved agreed with that assessment. A crime might well have taken place. One party or even both might consider the encounter coercive even absent physical force. The structure of the survey means one simply cannot know.

Still, even counting none of the drunken encounters as rape, 5.5 percent is a staggering statistic. Is one of every eighteen girls really raped during her time in college? Probably not, as even the AAU researchers admit. Fewer than one in five students asked to take the survey agreed to do so. Hundreds of thousands of students chose not to participate, which likely accounts for a "non-response bias," as researchers find that students who have been assaulted are more likely to take the survey in the first place.[17]

These methodological issues and others explain the discrepancy between the "one in four" or "one in five" statistics and data gathered by the Justice Department over the past several decades, which show that female college students are significantly less likely to be raped or sexually assaulted than non-student women of the same age.[18] The DOJ found a victimization rate of 7.6 among 1,000 non-students and 6.1 among 1,000 students. In both cases, the Justice Department data show victimization rates more than an order of magnitude lower than the ideological surveys suggest.[19]

Harvard is not more dangerous for women than Botswana. It isn't more dangerous for women than the surrounding neighborhoods of

Boston. In fact, it is much safer, as everyone knows intuitively. Yet the popular fantasy of epidemic campus rape persists, encouraged by regular, high-profile hoaxes.

In 2016, a female student at Austin Peay State University in Tennessee reported a sexual assault. She refused to provide a description of the suspect, changed her story, and later admitted she had fabricated the incident.[20] That same year, an undergraduate woman at Clemson University in South Carolina falsely claimed to have been abducted and sexually assaulted. The next year, in 2017, a female undergraduate at the nearby College of Charleston accused her classmate of sexual assault after a night of drinking. A jury took just twenty-eight minutes to acquit the young man when the case made it to trial, but by that point the college had already labeled the accused man a rapist and thrown him out of school.[21]

Also in 2017, a twenty-one-year-old Michigan student claimed to have been raped by a stranger while walking to her car. When police investigated, she refused a physical examination and changed virtually every detail of her account as the story began to unravel. At one point she named a suspect, who presented investigators with text messages in which the accuser had accused another man at a different location of committing the same rape. Police later charged her with filing a false report.[22]

In 2014, *Rolling Stone* magazine alleged in a lengthy article that members of the Phi Kappa Psi fraternity at the University of Virginia had gang-raped an undergraduate identified only as "Jackie" during an initiation ritual. The thinly sourced story offered no evidence for its shocking claims beyond the yarn-spinning of an anonymous accuser. Her fable fell apart, and *Rolling Stone* retracted the story in its entirety the following year, to the great surprise of gullible fools who imagine college campuses teeming with predators and rapists.[23]

Though college rape hoaxes have multiplied in recent years, the phenomenon goes back much further. In 2006, a stripper named Crystal Gail Mangum alleged that members of the Duke lacrosse team had raped her. Prosecutor Mike Nifong suppressed evidence, the case fell apart, and all charges were dropped the following year. Nifong was later disbarred, and Mangum ended up in prison after murdering her boyfriend.[24] But justice came too late for the lacrosse players, whose education and reputations had been destroyed for a lie.

Even the halcyon days of the early 1990s, before political correctness had run its poisonous course, saw their fair share of rape hoaxes at colleges including George Washington University and Princeton, where the accuser Mindy Brickman eventually recanted her claims in the *Daily Princetonian* and admitted never even having met the man she falsely accused.[25]

One suspects some psychological issues deranged these hoaxers. But psychology cannot explain why these incidents seem to have become more frequent and elaborate in recent years, dominating the mainstream media and our "national conversation," as ideologues euphemistically dub the cacophony. The relative safety and racial harmony enjoyed on college campuses ought to be a cause for celebration, particularly among self-styled social justice warriors. Why would students fabricate stories of violence at their most cherished institutions?

The "Reverend" Jesse Jackson shouted the answer on January 15, 1987, as he led some five hundred student activists in a march down Palm Drive on Stanford University's campus. "Hey hey! Ho ho! Western Civ has got to go," chanted the radicals.[26] The marchers were referring specifically to Stanford's introductory humanities program, known as "Western Culture," but that narrow protest betrayed broader aims.

Progressives have long had a parasitic, even parricidal, relationship with the university, which incubates their ideology, supplies them with sinecures, and furnishes the expertise and social scientific data necessary to their administrative state. But universities more than any edifice save perhaps cathedrals symbolize the Western culture that the radicals seek to subvert. The revolutionaries cannot afford to burn campuses to the ground, as they often do churches, so instead they empty universities of the traditional culture they represent and transmit.[27]

A year after Jackson's stunt, Stanford appointed a task force to decide whether or not to revamp the Western Culture curriculum. Barry M. Katz, a Stanford historian and member of that committee, saw an irreconcilable conflict of visions. "The existing course requirement asserts that we have a common culture and it asserts that it can be defined by a bit of reading in the great works," he explained. "This has been an affront to a large number of students and faculty, to women and members of minority groups."[28] In reality, ideology more than race or sex united the politically correct reformers. But even taking the radicals at their word, how had Western civilization affronted racial minorities and women?

Contrary to popular propaganda, not only did the West not invent "racism" and "sexism," but it has uniquely eschewed both. Unlike closed and tribal cultures everywhere else on earth, Western civilization has welcomed and integrated new peoples to enjoy and contribute to its superior cultural achievements.

The very same year Stanford and other universities debated heaving-ho Western Culture, the Nobel Prize–winning novelist Saul Bellow infamously challenged the politically correct curriculum reformers. "Who is the Tolstoy of the Zulus?" he asked them. "The Proust of the Papuans? I'd be happy to read them."[29] The radicals wailed and gnashed their teeth, but none has refuted his point.

The race-hustling writer Ta-Nehisi Coates quoted Bellow with indignation in his second autobiography, *Between The World And Me*. "Tolstoy was 'white,' and so Tolstoy 'mattered,' like everything else that was white 'mattered,'" wrote Coates. "And this view of things was connected to the fear that passed through the generations, to the sense of dispossession. We were black, beyond the visible spectrum, beyond civilization. Our history was inferior because we were inferior, which is to say our bodies were inferior."[30]

But Tolstoy does not matter because he was white; he matters because he wrote *War and Peace*. He wrote *Anna Karenina* and countless other stories that plumb the depths of human nature and hold a mirror to mankind. Plenty of white people do not matter in the slightest to the advancement of knowledge—for example, the many frivolous whites who admire Coates's work. But Coates's radical materialism prevents him from recognizing the metaphysical character of Tolstoy's greatness. For Coates, only matter matters.

But even as a matter of matter, the perpetually aggrieved Coates reveals at best his ignorance and at worst his cynically selective indignation. The Russian Tolstoy looms large in the Western tradition, but not nearly so large as the African Saint Augustine. Three Berbers ascended to the papacy within the first five centuries of the Church, which since the fifth century has venerated Saint Moses the Black, among other non-white Christians.

Later in *Between The World and Me*, Coates recalls the sports journalist Ralph Wiley's famous rejoinder to Bellow. "Tolstoy is the Tolstoy of the Zulus," admonishes Wiley, "unless you find a profit in fencing off universal properties of mankind into exclusive tribal ownership."[31] Coates and Wiley are right that reading Tolstoy edifies readers regardless of their race. But Tolstoy was no Zulu, and the "universal" mind of "mankind" did not educate him. A specific culture—loosely Western, specifically Russian—produced Tolstoy. That same culture has generously opened its books, classrooms, and ports of entry to the rest of the world.

Ta-Nehisi Coates's own career disproves his thesis. In 2015, Coates's prosaic whining won him the National Book Award and a MacArthur "Genius Grant" worth half a million dollars.[32] Establishment elites cannot get enough of his grousing. Despite possessing a "black body"—the singularly oppressed flesh that Coates never ceases to lament—today the young author of two memoirs enjoys far greater acclaim than Bellow and perhaps, in some circles, even Tolstoy.

The radicals at Stanford contended that Western Culture affronts women and minorities. In fact, no civilization in history has shown women and minorities greater respect. But radicals exploited that singular deference to undermine the civilization itself. They pressured the university to drop the course, arguing with a straight face against the "Eurocentricity" of European culture.[33] Stanford caved.

In 1988, the administration abandoned Western Culture for "Civilization, Ideas, and Values," or "CIV." Bureaucrats never can resist an acronym. The old Western Culture curriculum, among the most popular and successful courses in the university's century-long history, included fifteen required books, eighteen strongly recommended texts, and other works of literature and philosophy broadly considered "monuments of Western thought."[34] The new CIV course traded some of those great books for "emerging scholarship in gender, race and ethnic studies."[35] In other words, Stanford embraced the School of Resentment.

These academic debates over history, literature, and language reverberated far beyond the campus walls. Education Secretary William Bennett deplored the curriculum change as "a proposal to drop the West."[36] In 1987, the same year Jackson led his march against Western Civ, the philosopher Allan Bloom published *The Closing of the American Mind*, an unexpected bestseller that tracked the decay of the modern university. Bloom subtitled his book, *How Higher Education Has Failed Democracy and Impoverished the Souls of Today's Students*. Despite the dry subject and ponderous subtitle, the book sold over a million copies.[37] The public understood that something in the nation's psyche had snapped.

Bloom saw in the new campus culture the central paradox of political correctness: the pursuit of "openness" had closed people's minds. "Openness—and the relativism that makes it the only plausible stance in the face of various claims to truth and various ways of life and kinds of human beings—is the great insight of our times. The true believer is the real danger," Bloom wrote. Whereas in the past American education had aimed at excellence, scholarship, and the cultivation of the knowledge and virtues necessary to liberty—that is, the liberal arts—by the mid-to-late-twentieth century it valued "openness" above all else.

Allan Bloom understood the radicals to believe that "the study of history and of culture teaches that all the world was mad in the past; men always thought they were right, and that led to wars, persecutions, slavery, xenophobia, racism, and chauvinism." We must therefore liberate ourselves, not only from false opinion, but from opinion itself. As Bloom saw it, the reformers' "point is not to correct the mistakes and really be right; rather it is not to think you are right at all."[38] The American mind had become so open that its brain had fallen out.

A handful of conservative intellectuals such as Bloom and Bennett put up a fight, but most right-wingers rolled over, if they paid attention to the academic controversy at all. Conservatives continued to write the same checks to send their children to the same schools despite the collapse in educational quality. So the students lost a few weeks of Socrates to read Shulamith Firestone—not ideal, the parents shrugged, but nothing to lose sleep over.[39] The new culture of "openness" may waste students' time, they reasoned, but when devising curricula one would rather be too open than too closed.

Once again conservatives fell for the trap. The radicals did indeed want to "open" the curriculum, but only to close it again on terms more favorable to their political ends. Just as with "free speech" and "tolerance," perfect openness cannot exist. Boundaries must constrain free speech if only to protect speech, as in the case of laws against sedition or rules against the heckler's veto. Tolerance cannot tolerate intolerance. And openness cannot leave itself open to closed-mindedness. In Bloom's words, the education of openness "is open to all kinds of men, all kinds of life-styles, all ideologies. There is no enemy other than the man who is not open to everything."[40] But no man really can be open to everything—least of all the reformers. Education requires judgment, and popularity contests do not determine truth. Pedagogy is neither an open nor a democratic process.

When one decides that two plus two equals four, he closes off his mind from the possibility that two plus two might equal five. One may read the King James Bible and agree, "O Lord, our Lord, how excellent is thy name in all the earth!" Or one may read Hamlet's rewriting of that psalm and agree that the earth and sky appear "no other thing than a foul and pestilent congregation of vapors."[41] Each vision precludes the other. Even Hamlet's assertion, when feigning madness, that his reading amounted to no more than "words, words, words"—a forerunner of the genuinely mad, politically correct radicals' relativism—constitutes a judgment. Radical openness collapses into the claim that no meaning exists at all, and therefore it excludes the possibility that any meaning does exist.

"When there are no shared goals or vision of the public good, is the social contract any longer possible?" Bloom asked. But the radicals do share a goal: the ruthless criticism of all that exists. They lack a vision of the public good, but they have a clear sense of the public evil. Oppressive tradition impedes progress, so to open itself to the future, society must close itself off from its past.

Political correctness advances by redefinition. Americans cherish free speech, tolerance, open minds, and liberty. Rather than turn people against those values, the radicals turned the concepts inside out. They launched a "Free Speech Movement" to overturn traditional standards by appealing to the nation's reverence for free speech, after which they inaugurated a new era of censorship to enforce their new standards. They preached tolerance until their ideas had entered the public discourse, at which point they demanded repression for their ideological foes. They demanded educators open curricula to new, resentful theories of race, sex, and citizenship, at which point they closed the American mind to its own culture. All of these perversions and inversions took place at the university, our secular culture's intellectual and spiritual center. So it comes as no surprise that the university's mission also came to be redefined.

Liberal education long predates modern liberalism and even classical liberalism. It traces its roots back to ancient Greece, where it cultivated in citizens the habits, knowledge, and skills that befit free men. In medieval Europe, university students studied grammar, rhetoric, logic, geometry, arithmetic, music, and astronomy. These seven subjects did not train pupils for any particular jobs. The liberal arts served a loftier goal: the liberal arts trained men to be free.

The Marxist concept of "false consciousness," popularized by the Second Wave feminists of the 1970s, may have proven perverse in practice, but it began with a true principle: men must be forced to be free. We come into this world helpless slaves to our appetites. If we persist in thoughtless pursuit of our lusts and desires, we descend into licentiousness; if we educate ourselves and tame our appetites through training in virtue, we attain liberty. A free politics requires free people. But free people reject the radicals' politics. So the radicals redefined liberal education.

The reformers began by conflating licentiousness, the permission to do as one pleases, with liberty, which is the right to do what one ought. Today few appreciate the difference between these polar opposites, but the men who built our country considered the distinction essential to self-government. The Rhode Island Charter of 1663 proclaimed that residents might "freely, and fully have and enjoy his and their own judgments, and conscience in matters of religious concernments. . . . they behaving themselves peaceably and quietly and not using this liberty to licentiousness and profaneness." The New York Constitution of 1777 insisted, "Liberty of conscience, hereby granted, shall not be so construed as to excuse acts of licentiousness. . . ."[42] Licentiousness threatens liberty, which explains why the Founding Fathers spoke with such force on the need to suppress vice and encourage virtue.

"Virtue or morality is a necessary spring of popular government," declared George Washington in his farewell address.[43] Benjamin Franklin observed, "Only a virtuous people are capable of freedom. As nations become more corrupt and vicious, they have more need of masters."[44] Thomas Jefferson, our nation's third president and, more important in his eyes, the founder of the University of Virginia, warned, "Without virtue, happiness cannot be. This then is the scope of all academical emulation."[45] Jefferson took education seriously. Unfortunately the academy forgot his wise admonition, and by the latter half of the twentieth century the radicals had succeeded at replacing standards of virtue with a culture of licentiousness masquerading as liberty in the name of openness.

But the university did not remain "open" for long. The inclusion of critical race theory on reading lists soon led to mandatory "diversity" trainings for faculty, staff, and students. The relaxation of social and sexual mores gave rise to campus tribunals that empowered professors and deans to scrutinize students' most intimate encounters and convict them of crimes as grave as rape without due process. The collapse of standards in language and composition led quickly to new speech codes along the radicals' ideological lines.

Recent years have shown how quickly "openness" can transform into repression. In 2017, an applicant to Stanford composed his personal statement by writing the phrase "#BlackLivesMatter" one hundred times.[46] In saner eras such repetitious exercises were reserved for dunces to chalk on the blackboard after school. By the twenty-first century they gained students admittance into prestigious universities. But just a few years later, Kansas State University attempted to expel a student for making a joke on Twitter that contradicted the politically correct narrative about George Floyd and the Black Lives Matter movement, though ultimately the law prohibited the university from expelling the student for his tweet.[47]

No sooner had the radicals abolished traditional standards of speech and behavior than they began to demand new codes to replace them. In 1988, the University of Michigan adopted a new policy on speech that prohibited "any behavior, verbal or physical, that stigmatizes or victimizes an individual on the basis of race, ethnicity, religion, sex, sexual orientation, creed . . . and that . . . creates an intimidating, hostile, or demeaning environment for educational pursuits, employment or participation in University sponsored extra-curricular activities."[48] The broad, new code appeared to run afoul of the First Amendment, but inaction posed legal risks for the university as well.

The previous year, a flier had appeared on campus declaring "open season" on black students, whom it referred to as "saucer lips, porch monkeys, and jigaboos." Investigators never determined who distributed the offensive fliers. Bigots may well have orchestrated the stunt, though the prevalence of racial hoaxes on campus forces one to consider the possibility that "anti-racist" activists themselves perpetrated the offense.

Regardless, the student-led United Coalition against Racism threatened the university with a class-action civil rights suit "for not maintaining or creating a non-racist, non-violent atmosphere" on campus. The administration acquiesced to the students' demands.[49]

A federal district court ultimately overturned the speech code on the grounds that "the terms of the policy were so vague that its enforcement would violate the due process clause."[50] Students had not referred to any objective standard or established tradition to determine whether or not the speech they wanted to forbid "stigmatized" or "victimized" anyone on the basis of race, ethnicity, religion, sex, sexual orientation, or creed. If a Muslim student quotes the Qur'an, which asks, "What, of all creation will you go to (fornicate with) the males, leaving aside those whom Allah has created for you as your mates[?] Nay, you are a people that has transgressed all limits," and instructs, "Punish both of those among you who are guilty of [sodomy]," does he thereby victimize or stigmatize homosexuals on the basis of their sexual orientation?[51] If the Muslim student faces criticism or punishment for quoting the Qur'an, has he been victimized or stigmatized on the basis of his religion?

The University of Michigan speech code overstepped the bounds set by the Constitution and the American legal tradition. But it does not therefore follow that the Constitution prohibits all limits on speech. In 1942, the Supreme Court ruled unanimously to uphold a New Hampshire law that prohibited "any offensive, derisive or annoying word to anyone who is lawfully in any street or public space . . . or to call him by an offensive or derisive name." Justice Frank Murphy, writing for the Court, explained, "There are certain well defined and narrowly limited classes of speech, the prevention and punishment of which have never been thought to raise any Constitutional problem." Justice Murphy cited lewd, obscene, and libelous language as well as "fighting words" as examples of speech outside the purview and protection of the First Amendment.[52]

As we have already discussed, limitations on certain types of speech can be traced back to the earliest days of our republic. Some of those unprotected categories appear broad and vague, such as New Hampshire's ban on "annoying" address or the nation's longstanding suppression of "obscenity," which evades precise definition though we all "know it when we see it," to borrow Justice Potter's famous phrase.[53] Conservatives and libertarians overstate their case when they argue that all limitations on speech are unconstitutional. But worse, they misunderstand political reality and fall into the same utopian idealism of which they accuse their left-wing opponents.

Nature abhors a vacuum, and no society will long tolerate the total absence of standards. Unless conservatives summon the courage to enforce our own standards of speech, vague encomia to "free speech" will accomplish nothing more than to delay the inevitable establishment of the radicals' politically correct standards. The University of Michigan proved this point when, decades after the district court struck down their speech code, the school established a new "bias response team" to serve the same function.

Administrators tasked the team with investigating campus incidents that could give offense on the basis of race, sex, sexual preference, or religion. Speech First, a free speech advocacy group, sued the school on First Amendment grounds. A U.S. district court ruled in favor of the university, but the Sixth Circuit Court of Appeals later reversed this ruling and found that the Bias Response Team "acts by way of implicit threat of punishment and intimidation to quell speech." The school disbanded the team and settled with Speech First. But no sooner had university administrators retired the team than they established a new "campus climate support team" to "support students, faculty or staff" who claimed to have been offended.[54] Once again, the defense of "free speech" in the abstract rather than through the practical tradition of free speech circumscribed by standards seems only to have delayed the politically correct radicals' victory.

The Michigan speech code and the New Hampshire Offensive Conduct law that the Supreme Court upheld in 1942 both outlawed broad swaths of speech. But the New Hampshire law was not vague; it followed long and widely held standards. The Michigan speech code was vague because it attempted to establish a new standard on politically correct lines. The issue could not be settled by the frivolous debate over whether one may have standards at all; it came down instead to the substantive question of what the standards said.

Sex offers the clearest view of how the debate over standards has proceeded on campus. Until the mid-twentieth century, universities enforced strict guidelines regulating how the sexes socialized on campus. Coeducation barely existed at American universities before the 1960s, and where it did administrators took pains to make sure the co-eds remained focused on their studies rather than more titillating activities.

Of her freshman year in 1969, Harvard graduate Carol Sternhell recalls, "My memory was that boys were only allowed up in the rooms on Sundays—with the door open and three feet on the floor at all times." But the social rules extended far beyond the dorm room. "We had curfews: we had to sign out in the evenings . . . if we got in late we were in big trouble. Men still had to wear jackets and ties to dinner in the Freshman Union."

By Sternhell's sophomore year, women were living unofficially with their boyfriends. By junior year, whole dorms had gone co-ed. Her classmate Helen Snively observes, "Virginity and parietals were all falling apart, and no sweet dean from Fay House was going to prevent it." If the cultural revolution seems sudden from the vantage of history, it felt all the more so to the students living through it. "A change of values and morality, of politics, of possibilities, and of our most fundamental beliefs about ourselves," reflects Sternhell, "overnight!"[55] The Age of Aquarius had dawned, but its promise of free love and nonconformity would soon collapse into a new set of rules just as rigid as the standards it replaced.

In 1991, Antioch College in Ohio issued a new sexual assault–prevention policy at the behest of the "Womyn of Antioch," a student activist group whose ideological leanings one need not explain. The school required verbal consent from both parties—the bourgeois university assumed only two participants in any such encounter—"each and every time there is sexual activity," at "each new level of sexual activity," with judgment perfectly unimpaired by alcohol, drugs, or "mental health conditions," among other intoxicants, paired with the use of "safer sex practices," regardless of "the type of sexual activity that occurs, the props/toys/tools that are used, the number of persons involved, the gender(s) or gender expressions of persons involved."[56] Ideologues in the Antioch administration had achieved the impossible: they had made sex boring.

Worse, they had made sex dangerous by issuing guidelines that were virtually impossible to satisfy. Nothing kills the mood quite like requesting and providing explicit, clinical consent at each "new level" of sexual activity, whatever that means. Moreover, undergraduate liaisons involve impaired judgment almost by definition. (If wanton young women had sound judgment, they would demand a ring.) Antioch had defined practically all sexual activity as rape. Students had only to rely on the caprices of university administrators and undergraduate lovers, who could label them rapists at a whim.

The animated sitcom *South Park* satirized such policies in 2015 when it depicted "PC Principal" walking down the hallway of his politically correct fraternity collecting sexual consent forms from the brothers. "Rise and shine, guys!" yells PC Principal. "If you scored last night, I'll need your consent forms!" When he notices that one of his charges performed a particularly lurid sexual act, he corrects him. "Whoa, Barker . . . there's a different release form, bro."[57]

Antioch College shuttered its doors in 2008. But a similarly draconian consent code lives on at Gettysburg College, which requires "continuing and active" verbal consent for all sexual activity from "patting" and "hugging" to more invasive interactions.[58] Countless other colleges have adopted comparable policies. These sexual guidelines bear mentioning not because students have some right to sexual pleasure that colleges have violated. Students have no such right, and conservatives would not likely take umbrage at the violation even if they did. Rather, the policies merit reflection because they show the necessity and inevitability of standards. The sheer breadth of Antioch's sex code might have scandalized the most prudish prig in Victorian England.

The fantasy of higher education as an anarchic orgy in which freewheeling intellectuals and liberated students attain knowledge by doing as they please ignores the university's millennium-long history as an ordered institution dedicated to the pursuit of truth by the light of particular premises. Worse yet, it ignores the present reality of the university, which has methodically replaced every old rule it "deconstructed" with the new rigidities of political correctness.

During the latter half of the twentieth century, radical ideologues took over the universities, sometimes by force. They dismantled the norms and traditions that had fostered Western education with a campaign of withering criticism and wholly critical "studies" that weakened the moral resolve of educators—the very people who ought to have known better—and transformed the university into a free-for-all. The radicals then turned their critical eye on the university itself, which they portrayed as a hotbed of racial bigotry and rape. This dishonest depiction gave the radicals pretext to complete their takeover by installing rigid new rules more favorable to their political agenda. Meanwhile, gullible conservatives adopted the radicals' shallow, tactical, and temporary *laissez-faire* rhetoric as their *raison d'être*, abandoning the moral clarity and confidence necessary to oppose the new standard of political correctness. By the time the Berlin Wall crumbled at the turn of the 1990s and a new cultural cold war burst out into the open, the politically correct belligerents had accumulated every advantage.

CHAPTER 10

THE NEW COLD WAR

In the spring of 1991, the troubled University of Michigan invited President George H. W. Bush to address the students at commencement. The United States had just won the Cold War. The Berlin Wall had crumbled, and the Soviet Union would officially dissolve later that year. Freedom had defeated tyranny. And while the triumphant president of the United States spoke, a group of student radicals tried to shout him down.

The interruption played right into Bush's hand, as he had accepted the invitation precisely to address such stunts. "The power to create also rests on other freedoms, especially the freedom, and I think about that right now, to think and speak one's mind," the president began. The crowd, already annoyed with the protesters' shouting, roared with applause. "I had this written into the speech, and I didn't even know these guys were going to be here," Bush joked. Then he got to the heart of the matter.

"Ironically, on the 200th anniversary of our Bill of Rights, we find free speech under assault throughout the United States, including on some college campuses," Bush warned. "The notion of political correctness has ignited controversy across the land, and although the movement arises from the laudable desire to sweep away the debris of racism and sexism and hatred, it replaces old prejudice with new ones." The president continued in his characteristically conciliatory tone, even as he detailed the dire consequences of political correctness.

"It declares certain topics off limits, certain expression off limits, even certain gestures off limits," he explained to a cheering crowd. "What began as a crusade for civility has soured into a cause of conflict and even censorship."[1] Bush recognized the growing problem, but he misunderstood how it started.

Political correctness did not begin as a crusade for civility; it began as a political campaign to upend Western society. Its instigators viewed our culture as unjust and oppressive, and they undertook to remake that culture by forbidding traditional perspectives and enforcing the fashionable views of leftist ideologues. The new standard took the name of political correctness, a variation of an earlier communist slogan.

Bush decried this "bullying" as "outrageous" and "not worthy of a great nation grounded in the values of tolerance and respect."[2] But the proponents of political correctness do not consider our nation great. They condemn it as bigoted from the very beginning, and they seek to reset the boundaries of the nation's tolerance and the objects of her respect. Bush called his audience to "optimism," to the hope and conviction that "people can join in common cause without having to surrender their identities."[3] But political correctness takes as its common cause the destruction of the very culture Bush invoked, and to achieve that end it makes idols out of subsidiary identities.

"The freedom to speak one's mind—that may be the most fundamental and deeply revered of all our liberties," Bush declared. "Americans, to debate, to say what we think—because, you see, it separates good ideas from bad. It defines and cultivates the diversity upon which our national greatness rests."[4] Beneath many layers of dubious platitudes lay the philosophical insights of *Areopagitica* and the *Letter Concerning Toleration*. But while Milton and Locke had the insight and integrity to admit the necessary limits of free speech and tolerance, Bush extolled the virtues of free speech in the abstract, which he defended with vague appeals to "diversity."

How the process of separating good ideas from bad—that is, discrimination—could at the same time cultivate "diversity," Bush never quite explained. But fatuous bromides distinguish most political speech, particularly in the case of "kindler, gentler" conservatives such as George Bush.[5] The president's mere mention of the term elevated the debate over political correctness to the national level.

Most conservatives followed Bush's example, criticizing the Left for having the audacity to engage in political advocacy on campus at all rather than refuting the leftists' political stances themselves. The same year President Bush gave his commencement address, the conservative lawyer Robert Kelner published a column in the *Wall Street Journal* chastising his fellow right-wingers for waging "our phony war on political correctness."[6] Kelner had first encountered the term as an undergraduate at Princeton and used it to make "fun of the fact that the open-minded liberals were actually the most closed-minded people on campus."[7] In response to politically correct intolerance, conservatives presented themselves as the true stewards of tolerance and liberality. But conservatives' minds were not entirely "open" either.

"We sought—and still seek—ascendancy," Kelner reminded the Right.[8] If conservatives attacked the Left simply for having opinions and imparting them to others, right-wingers would forfeit the right to convey or even hold ideas of their own. Kelner believed conservatives needed to articulate a substantive vision for the culture rather than simply criticize the Left's rhetorical strategy.

Less than a year later, Kelner got his wish when President Bush's presidential primary rival Pat Buchanan gave his famous—or infamous, depending on your perspective—"culture war" speech at the 1992 Republican National Convention. "My friends, we must take back our cities, and take back our culture, and take back our country," the vanquished challenger instructed the delegates. Buchanan, though effusive in his endorsement of Bush, struck a distinctly more contentious tone than did the incumbent. Buchanan inveighed against "radical feminism . . . abortion on demand, a litmus test for the Supreme Court, homosexual rights, discrimination against religious schools, women in combat units," and countless other politically correct idols.[9]

Today even many conservatives might object to Buchanan's inclusion of "homosexual rights" on the list—so thoroughly have the radicals succeeded in manipulating language—but it bears remembering that the term did not refer to the granting of political rights to homosexuals, who already enjoyed them. No one denied homosexuals' right to vote or to due process, for example. Rather, Buchanan opposed the recognition of a new political victim group with special privileges created through judicial fiat, entailing the curtailment of other, long-cherished rights, most notably in the realm of religion. It seems no coincidence that Buchanan sandwiched the term between "the Supreme Court," which would rewrite the Constitution in the ensuing decades to create those new group rights, and "discrimination against religious schools," which followed as the inevitable consequence.

Buchanan never uttered the phrase "political correctness," but he described in detail the battle lines of the new culture war. President Bush took a different tack. He spent most of his acceptance speech on foreign policy: the demise of the Soviet Union, war in El Salvador, free elections in Nicaragua, Saddam Hussein's invasion of Kuwait, the role of the U.S. military in securing global trade, and the opportunity to transform "faraway places" into democracies "more and more like America."

He offered an odd, unsolicited denial that he harbored "prejudice and anti-Semitism," but otherwise avoided cultural matters almost entirely. Even when Bush bragged about passing the Americans with Disabilities Act, he focused exclusively on the economic rather than the cultural dimension of that law, which he bragged had brought "43 million people into the economic mainstream."[10] The defining philosophical struggle of the twentieth century had come to an end. Freedom had defeated tyranny. The Christian West had toppled the godless Soviet empire. And as millions of Americans and billions of other people around

the world grappled to understand the meaning of it all, the best the leader
of the Free World could muster was the prospect of making more money.

George Bush grasped the gravity of the moment. "The world is in
transition, and we are feeling that transition in our homes," he observed.
But Bush failed to grasp what the moment meant. "The defining challenge of the nineties," he opined, "is to win the economic competition,
to win the peace. We must be a military superpower, an economic superpower, and an export superpower."[11] Military, economic, and export
might matter no doubt, but what of cultural power? George H. W. Bush
had no interest in articulating a coherent, conservative cultural agenda
because he represented the liberal, establishment wing of the Republican
Party. He ran against Reagan in 1980 and coined the term "voodoo
economics."[12] He supported legal abortion before Reagan tapped him
to be his running mate. Bush supported the party platform and served
as a loyal vice president to Reagan, but his views on cultural questions,
which he sought to project overseas, aligned more closely with the liberal
establishment than with the conservative movement dedicated to preserving traditional American culture at home.

Bush accused his opponent Bill Clinton and the Democrats of looking
"inward" while he and the Republicans promised "to look forward, to
open new markets, prepare our people to compete," and otherwise to
project American hegemony abroad.[13] Both Clinton and Buchanan understood that the end of the Cold War meant an intensifying of the cultural
battle at home. Bush showed no interest in re-litigating the cultural fights
of the 1960s and '70s; he mistakenly thought America's leadership of a
"new world order" would paper over those domestic differences.

In a speech to a joint session of Congress the year before, Bush had
announced the advent of a "new era, freer from the threat of terror,
stronger in the pursuit of justice and more secure in the quest for peace—
an era in which the nations of the world, east and west, north and south,
can prosper and live in harmony."[14] Although the president may have
quibbled with his liberal opponents on the particulars, he espoused an
essentially progressive view of history.

Around that same time, the neoconservative political scientist Francis Fukuyama declared that the fall of the Berlin Wall heralded "not just the end of the Cold War, or the passing of a particular period of post-war history, but the end of history as such: that is, the end point of mankind's ideological evolution and the universalization of Western liberal democracy as the final form of human government."[15] A decade later, in a violent rejection of Fukuyama's "final" form of government, Muslim terrorists would launch the deadliest terror attack in American history. In the meantime, the radical social upheaval that had begun decades earlier and which threatened many tenets of Western liberal democracy continued apace, now known explicitly by the name "political correctness." Despite the optimism of the internationalists, history had continued.

The culture war might have turned out differently had the acerbic Buchanan or some more clubbable, culturally minded conservative clinched the Republican nomination in 1992. Instead the moderate, progressive George Bush ran against the moderate, progressive Bill Clinton and lost. At the crucial moment following the fall of Soviet communism, the ostensibly conservative political party offered only lip service in opposition to political correctness, despite a popular groundswell against the new standards growing among the unelected public.

The backlash against political correctness permeated pop culture and even reached the Great White Way, a nickname Broadway will doubtless one day eschew in the name of racial justice. In 1992, Pulitzer Prize and Tony Award–winning playwright David Mamet thrust political correctness center stage. Mamet's *Oleanna* opens with John, a university professor, on the phone with his wife discussing the house he plans to purchase to mark the tenure he soon expects to achieve. Across from him sits Carol, his failing feminist student. Their subsequent conversation veers from the pedagogical to the personal, as Carol explains how little she understands of the class, and John offers her an A if she agrees to start the class anew and try to understand.

By their next meeting, Carol has filed a vague complaint with John's tenure committee, and he has asked to see her to find out why and persuade her to retract it. A student group has convinced Carol to file the complaint, which accuses him of "sexism" and "elitism." As she leaves, John reaches out to stop her. By their third and final meeting, Carol has secretly accused John of rape for touching her as she left his office. He has lost his bid for tenure and will soon lose his job and his house. But she offers to rescind her complaint and rescue what remains of his reputation if he agrees to ban certain books from his curriculum. "Here is a list of books, which we . . ." she begins, referring to her activist group, "which we find questionable." The list includes John's own book.

"Get the fuck out of my office," John responds. "You're *dangerous*, you're *wrong* and it's my *job* . . . to say no to you. That's my job. You are absolutely right. You want to ban my book? Go to *hell*, and they can do whatever they want to me." Just then, with theatrical precision, the phone rings, and John's lawyer Jerry informs him of the rape accusation.

"Under the statute. I am told. It was battery," she insists. "And attempted rape. That's right."[16] It sounds preposterous, but she may indeed have been right, at least if her fictional school resembled Swarthmore College, which in 1991 defined rape as "a spectrum of incidents and behaviors ranging from crimes legally defined as rape to verbal harassment and inappropriate innuendo."[17]

John then reaches his breaking point.

The play ends with John viciously beating Carol as he yells, "You vicious little bitch. You think you can come in here with your political correctness and destroy my life?" As the lights fade, she looks at him and says, "Yes. That's right." Then again, to herself, she mutters, "Yes. That's right."[18] The ending offers catharsis after ninety minutes of injustice. And yet the politically correct student gets the last laugh. John may not have committed any of the offenses Carol claimed, but by the end she has taunted him into becoming the monster she described to the tenure committee.

As Carol lies bruised and bloodied on the floor of his office, she seems satisfied to show John she was right all along. More importantly, she delights in dispelling her own doubts. She repeats the line to herself as if to prove that neither her activist student group nor her ideological indoctrination has fooled her. John's blows remove any reservations she may have harbored. Political correctness was right, and Carol was right to use it to destroy John's life.[19]

Mamet portrays the subtlety of the trap set by political correctness. John saw only two options: betray his life's work or become a brute. Opponents of political correctness have fallen for this same false dichotomy for decades, as when in 2017 a conservative student activist donned a diaper and sucked a pacifier in a playpen to protest "safe spaces" during a "free speech week" demonstration at Kent State University in Ohio.[20] In depicting the degrading influence of political correctness, he degraded himself.

Leftists mocked conservatives for the Pyrrhic victory of wearing diapers to "own the libs." The student activist may have made the radicals look foolish—but not so foolish as he made himself. Ironically, the conservative student's protest achieved the very end for which radicals had set up the "safe spaces" in the first place: to undermine traditional academic standards by privileging emotion over reason on campus and weakening scholarly rigor.

In 2016, the right-wing Proud Boys began to describe themselves as "Western chauvinists" to counter a pervasive, politically correct narrative that blamed the West for all the world's ills. But "chauvinism" is by definition excessive. The term, which refers to an outsize love of one's country, comes from the legendary French soldier Nicolas Chauvin, who enlisted at age eighteen and was horrifically disfigured by seventeen wounds. Napoleon himself presented Chauvin with the Sabre of Honor, and the soldier's ceaseless devotion to Napoleon is said to have earned him widespread derision in France after the Bourbon Restoration.

Gavin McInnes, the conservative comedian and Proud Boys founder, no doubt suggested the name with tongue in cheek. But while it contradicts the radicals' explicit premise that Western civilization is evil, the descriptor unwittingly grants them their secondary premise: that the West's defenders must be excessive and unreasonable. Political correctness wins either way.

A third option exists. The Proud Boys need not be "Western chauvinists," allowing unmoored emotion to drive their patriotism in the same way politically correct radicals let unmoored emotion drive their hatred of their own country. Reason, tradition, and filial piety all serve as a proper grounding for love of country, particularly when that country is the United States. The conservative performance artist at Kent State needed neither diaper nor pacifier to protest "safe spaces." Instead, he could have ignored the politically correct speech code and stuck to the old standard. John did not need to beat Carol. From the very first outburst at their first office meeting, he could have refused to change her failing grade and politely asked her to leave.

Proponents of political correctness insist that their new speech codes make society more polite, reasonable, and civilized. When opponents of political correctness protest the new standards by behaving in impolite, unreasonable, and uncivilized ways, they give the radicals precisely what they want. Were the Proud Boys simply to defend the West, were the conservative Kent State student merely to disregard "safe spaces," were John to have dismissed Carol, all might still have faced retribution from the politically correct enforcers, but they would not have granted them their premise or helped the radicals to gain ground.

The scholarly setting of *Oleanna* may suggest that the campus battles of the late 1980s inspired the play. In fact, Mamet took his inspiration from a larger drama: the Supreme Court confirmation hearings of Clarence Thomas, in which political correctness nearly did destroy a man's life and succeeded in further degrading the American political process.[21]

In 1991, President George H. W. Bush nominated appeals court judge Clarence Thomas to replace the outgoing justice, Thurgood Marshall. Both were black, but the similarities between Thomas and Marshall ran only skin-deep. The two judges held diametrically opposed views of the Constitution. Marshall advocated judicial activism and considered the Constitution a "living document" that empowers judges to push the nation toward progress even if that means ignoring or contradicting the plain text and meaning of the framers.[22] Thomas held the then-minority opinion that the Constitution is a legal text that lacks organs and arteries but has meaning, which can be known through judicious study of what its words meant when it was ratified.

White House chief of staff John Sununu had predicted a "knock-down, drag-out, bloody-knuckles, grass-roots fight" from the beginning, since President Bush had promised to nominate a "true conservative."[23] Senate Democrats had assassinated the character of Judge Robert Bork just four years earlier, coining in the process a new verb for those sorts of scurrilous attacks, and the conservative Clarence Thomas expected much the same treatment. The Left opposed Thomas for his judicial philosophy and hostility to their most cherished rulings, notably *Roe v. Wade*. But whereas Ted Kennedy focused on Judge Bork's philosophy to disparage his character and insinuate that he was unfit for the Court, Senate Democrats took a more personal approach in their attacks on Clarence Thomas.

Bush nominated Thomas on July 1, 1991, and the confirmation hearings went off without a hitch.[24] A full three months passed, and the Senate was preparing to confirm Judge Thomas when, on October 6, the Democrat-run Judiciary Committee leaked accusations from Thomas's former colleague Anita Hill that the judge had sexually harassed her while the two worked at the Department of Education and later the Equal Employment Opportunity Commission. The FBI had already investigated the allegations, and the Judiciary Committee, led by Joe Biden, had dismissed them. Even at first glance, it strains credulity that Hill would have followed Thomas to the EEOC had he sexually harassed her at the Education Department. But common sense was no match for political correctness, and Biden reopened the hearings.[25]

Less than a week after the allegations leaked, the Judiciary Committee called Anita Hill to testify. Hill alleged that Thomas had discussed pornographic films, a performer dubbed "Long Dong Silver," and his own skill in the sack while she worked with him at the Education Department in 1981. She also claimed that after she had followed Thomas to the EEOC in 1982, he once looked at a can of soda on his desk and asked,

"Who has put pubic hair on my Coke?"[26] A couple of witnesses corrobo-rated Hill's statements to Senate staffers, but neither testified.

Several witnesses refuted Hill and defended Thomas. J. C. Alvarez, who had worked for Thomas at the EEOC, testified that Thomas "demanded professionalism and performance" and that the judge would not have tolerated "the slightest hint of impropriety, and everyone knew it."[27] She then made a politically incorrect inference that undercut the charges. "Women who have really been harassed would agree, if the alle-gations were true, you put as much distance as you can between yourself and that other person," Alvarez observed. But what if Hill needed the job? The suggestion was silly, according to Alvarez. "You don't follow them to the next job—especially if you are a black female Yale Law School gradu-ate. Let's face it," she leveled, "out in the corporate sector, companies are fighting for women with those kinds of credentials." Despite ample oppor-tunity for professional success elsewhere, Hill had stuck with Thomas.

Alvarez believed that professional opportunity impelled Hill to tes-tify in 1991. She called Hill "the Rosa Parks of sexual harassment," seeking "speaking engagements," book contracts, and movie deals. Two other former EEOC employees joined Alvarez in defending Thomas. Nancy Fitch, Thomas's special assistant historian, testified definitively, "I know he did no such thing." Phyllis Berry-Myers, another special assistant to Thomas, described him as "respectful, demanding of excel-lence in our work, cordial, professional, interested in our lives and our career ambitions." She also flipped the charges, accusing Hill of desiring a more-than-professional relationship with Thomas, rather than the other way around.

Phone records revealed that Hill and Thomas spoke, saw one another, and even dined together on multiple occasions after she left the EEOC. Still, Senate Democrats pursued the allegations until Clarence Thomas turned the leftists' politically correct script against them. To end the hearings, Thomas played the race card.

On October 11, 1991, more than one hundred days after his nomina-tion to the Court, Judge Thomas delivered his final statement to the judiciary committee, denying "unequivocally" and "uncategorically . . . each and every single allegation." He denounced the hearings and the leaks as "a travesty" and "disgusting." Then he ended them with a diatribe none could refute. "This is a circus. It's a national disgrace. And from my standpoint as a black American, as far as I'm concerned, it is a high-tech lynching for uppity blacks who in any way deign to think for themselves," he inveighed, "to do for themselves, to have different ideas, and it is a message that unless you kowtow to an old order, this is what will happen to you."[28] Joe Biden, presiding over the committee, dropped his head to his papers the moment Thomas mentioned the loaded word. But in case any senator hadn't gotten the point, Thomas continued. "This is what will happen to you: you will be lynched, destroyed, caricatured by a committee of the U.S. Senate rather than hung from a tree."[29] The Senate voted to confirm Judge Thomas four days later.

Democrats did not really care about Clarence Thomas's sex life. The party of John F. Kennedy had long taken a loose view of sexual morality, which they flaunted by nominating Bill Clinton for president the following year. Rather, the Democrats exploited—some might say contrived—the Anita Hill controversy because they detested Thomas's judicial philosophy, which threatened some of their most cherished achievements which had passed into law on the Supreme Court bench rather than the floor of Congress and the Resolute Desk.

Exploiting sex scandals for political gain has a long history in America. The practice goes all the way back to the Founding Fathers and Alexander Hamilton's extramarital affair with Maria Reynolds, which his political opponents used against him in 1797.[30] Had the Anita Hill hearings focused on an ordinary affair, they would merit little mention in American political history. A "sex scandal" did not upend Clarence Thomas's confirmation process. Given all of the hubbub, one almost forgets that Hill never claimed to have engaged in any sexual act with Thomas. Rather, Hill claimed Thomas had committed the vague offense of "sexual harassment," a term coined less than two decades before. The Anita Hill hearings transformed American politics not through their use of sex as a political cudgel but through the new sexual standards by which Thomas was judged.

Anita Hill had no evidence to support her claims beyond statements from a couple of colleagues, who were contradicted by numerous other women who had worked for Thomas. Hill's telephone records and employment history undermined her suggestion that Thomas had victimized her, and multiple colleagues called her a liar. Thomas never raped, molested, or even engaged in a consensual sexual relationship with Hill, nor did she ever suggest he did.

The cultural revolution of the 1960s had done away with the old sexual standards, but free love quickly gave way to a new sexual ethics along politically correct lines. At the same time, the radicals succeeded at undermining due process, the presumption of innocence, and equality before the law in favor of politically correct standards that would give rise to campus tribunals and maxims such as "believe all women," which suggests that women cannot lie and that men ought not defend themselves.

The Clarence Thomas confirmation hearings represented a conflict between these old and new standards. Thomas made it through in the end, but only by turning the politically correct obsession with race against the radicals. While conservatives won that battle, they lost the war, particularly on the judiciary, which enshrined the new standards of political correctness in constitutional law the following year.

In 1992, the Supreme Court delivered its most radical decision since George Washington established the court in 1789. *Planned Parenthood v. Casey* upheld the alleged constitutional right to abortion, which the Court had invented nineteen years earlier in *Roe v. Wade*. Sandra Day O'Connor, Anthony Kennedy, and David Souter—all Reagan or Bush appointees—wrote the majority opinion upholding that fictional right.

The Court found that abortion fell among the "matters, involving the most intimate and personal choices a person may make in a lifetime, choices central to personal dignity and autonomy" that "are central to the liberty protected by the Fourteenth Amendment."[31] But the conception of abortion as a personal matter misses the entire point of the debate, which asks whether the law may prohibit the killing of babies in the womb. Abortion is a political, not just a personal matter because it involves the right to end an innocent human life and even the right to outlaw that particular type of murder. Only by radically redefining standards of justice can abortion transform from a political to a personal matter, and the radicals achieved precisely that redefinition when they declared that "the personal is political," which the Courts then codified into constitutional law.

But the Court did not stop at abolishing the right of the people to pass their own laws regarding abortion. The judiciary took this elevation of the personal over the political further by declaring the right of the individual to redefine reality itself. "At the heart of liberty," wrote Justice Kennedy, "is the right to define one's own concept of existence, of meaning, of the universe, and of the mystery of human life."[32] Kennedy—along with Justices O'Connor and Souter, who signed onto this nonsense—appears to have mistaken the Supreme Court of the United States for a freshman-year philosophy class or a smoky, undergrad bull session, but his sophomoric slam poetry enshrined in jurisprudence a radical subjectivism that would accelerate the erosion of traditional standards.

The justices' frivolous philosophical musings never made any sense. No one has the right to define his own "concept of existence, of meaning, of the universe" or "of the mystery of human life." One may believe that the moon is made of green cheese, but academic standards bar that fanciful notion from biology classrooms, at least for now. One may believe that red traffic lights mean "go," but police officers have every right to insist on their own concept of the light's meaning and to give the driver a ticket. One may believe that babies are human beings, but our regime rejects that view in favor of its own "concept of existence." In fact, the justices did just that only one sentence prior to the infamous "sweet mystery of life" passage when they declared that the Fourteenth Amendment somehow confers a right to abortion.

The triumvirate persisted, undeterred by their own illogic. "Beliefs about these matters could not define the attributes of personhood were they formed under compulsion of the State," the justices concluded without even attempting to defend that preposterous assertion. In both *Planned Parenthood v. Casey* and *Roe v. Wade*, the state did compel belief about these matters. In both decisions, the Court prohibited as a matter of law the proposition that babies in the womb are human beings entitled to protection from murder.

Furthermore, the truth of an assertion does not depend upon its voluntary acceptance. Just because the state compels a particular belief, it does not necessarily follow that the belief is false. The state compels schoolchildren to believe that two plus two make four. It even compels them to accept unprovable axioms, such as the equivalence of A plus B and B plus A. Such beliefs are mathematically true whether the state compels belief in them or not. The state imposes on citizens the principle that murder is wrong, but that principle would be morally true whether the state enforced murder laws or not. The method by which one comes to understand reality does not change reality itself.

One doubts that the justices gave much thought to the rigor of their arguments—particularly in the case of Anthony Kennedy, who contradicted his own illogic almost a quarter-century later in *Obergefell v. Hodges*, which established a constitutional right to "same-sex marriage" by redefining marriage from the bench. "The nature of marriage is that, through its enduring bond, two persons together can find other freedoms, such as expression, intimacy, and spirituality," Kennedy wrote. The justice never quite explained how "intimacy" and "spirituality" constitute "freedoms," and his long-married colleague Justice Antonin Scalia mocked the notion that marriage expands such freedoms in his dissent. "Who ever thought that intimacy and spirituality (whatever that means) were freedoms?" asked Scalia. "And if intimacy is, one would think Freedom of Intimacy is abridged rather than expanded by marriage. Ask the nearest hippie." Expression is sure enough a freedom, Scalia admitted, but he disagreed with the notion that marriage expands that freedom. "Anyone in a long-lasting marriage will attest that that happy state constricts, rather than expands, what one can prudently say."[33] Scalia dispelled the Court's opinion with humor because Kennedy's argument was a joke.

The cultural consequences of Kennedy's illogic are not so funny. The highest court in the land now regularly invokes this illogic to dismantle long-cherished principles and institutions and reorder society according to political correctness and the corrupted vision of reality that it sets forth.

Kennedy wielded the power of the state to impose a novel and unpopular belief about the fundamental political and personal institution of marriage. He distracted readers from his redefinition of marriage as involving "two persons" rather than a man and a woman—or more precisely, given the historical practice of polygamy, husbands and wives—with gobbledygook about intimacy and spirituality. And in the name of freedom, he substituted his own novel repressive standard for the old.

America entered the 1990s as the victor in a Cold War that had pitted Western freedom against communist tyranny. The conservative coalition that won the Cold War "fused" traditionalists and religious conservatives, who opposed the Soviet Union's atheism and iconoclasm, with economic libertarians, who opposed the USSR's collectivism, and foreign policy hawks, who opposed the Kremlin's imperial ambitions. Opposition to the Russkies united all three divergent legs of the fusionist stool, and they rallied under the banner of freedom as they understood it.

The priorities of the economic libertarians came to dominate the coalition, as they were least offensive to the other members. Libertarians and foreign policy hawks often reject Christianity, traditionalists care little for foreign invention, but everyone can enjoy a nice tax cut. As the Cold War ended, inattention to cultural matters and the complacent embrace of "freedom" as a bumper sticker slogan rather than a particular political tradition gave politically correct radicals the advantage in the new cold war raging at home.

Conservatives fell victim to their own success. Paeans to freedom in the abstract would not suffice to stem the tide of leftist censorship overtaking society. Ebullient conservatives cheered a "new world order" that they mistakenly believed would favor their goals. Little did they know that their political sloganeering and cultural negligence would lead first to social chaos and then to a creeping order fundamentally opposed to the world they wished to conserve.

CHAPTER 11

TRADING TABOOS

Politically correct people portray themselves as empathic stalwarts of etiquette and manners. They insist that political correctness is just another term for politeness. Yet these same people often engage in crasser and more vulgar speech and behavior than their allegedly boorish, politically incorrect countrymen. Ironically profanity, not politeness, marks the rise of political correctness.

Practitioners of PC demand we all use faddish jargon when discussing race, sex, geography, and even science so as not to give offense. But then those demure dictators of diction talk like sailors on television, in print, and in the public square during topless "slut walks," bawdy "pride parades," and marches featuring "pussy hats." During the politically correct 1990s, cultural gatekeepers relaxed standards of decency, culminating at the end of the decade in Mark Harmon's uttering the word "shit" for the first time on network television during an episode of *Chicago Hope*. The animated series *South Park* later parodied this watershed moment by mentioning "shit" 162 times in a single episode, with an additional 38 written instances of the word, bringing the total number of mentions to an even 200.

The *South Park* episode, titled "It Hits the Fan," made particular use of profanity in a program already known for coarse language. But while it mocked both *Chicago Hope* for making much ado about very nearly nothing and network departments of Standards and Practices for their often incoherent rules, *South Park* did not dismiss the dangers of vulgarity outright. On the contrary, *South Park* imagined that the spread and normalization of curse words brought a literal curse on society—the Black Death, causing South Park's denizens to vomit up their intestines and die.

In *South Park*'s vision of the vulgar future, tasteless studio chiefs eventually replace all words on television with "shit," inadvertently summoning an evil dragon named Geldon, whom only a magical rune stone belonging to the mystical order of Standards and Practices can slay. As usual, *South Park* makes fun of everyone, satisfying neither the conservatives who would uphold traditional standards nor the radicals for whom four-letter words function as commas.

Just two decades after "It Hits The Fan" aired, the premise seems quaint. That particular four-letter word appears wholesome compared to the other obscenities permitted on the airwaves. In 2003, Comedy Central aired Richard Pryor's "I Ain't Dead Yet, Motherfucker" special.[1] That same year, Bono bellowed the phrase "fucking brilliant" during a network broadcast of the Golden Globe Awards.[2] Five years later, the ever-radical actress Jane Fonda broke the last linguistic taboo by uttering the word "cunt" on the *Today Show* during an interview with Meredith Vieira.[3]

From the vantage of twenty years, the premise of *South Park*'s "It Hits The Fan" does not just seem dated; it feels wrong. Today it is leftists, not conservatives, who rush to censor speech they find offensive. How did the world turn so rapidly upside down?

Dishonesty from both conservatives and radicals accounts for the confusion. Conservatives who today claim the mantle of "free speech absolutism" conveniently forget the Hays Code and the House Committee on Un-American Activities. Perhaps they never read George Washington's *Rules of Civility*. Maybe they think chivalry is not only dead but never even lived. Whatever the reason, these right-wing libertines erase a bygone, halcyon era when conservatives had standards and defended them.

Likewise, leftists who conflate political correctness with politeness hide how impolitely they have behaved since "the Left" was born during the French Revolution. In 1789, the National Assembly divided delegates by seating conservative supporters of the king to the assembly-president's right and radical supporters of the Revolution to the president's left. The Baron de Gauville explains how the division happened. "We began to recognize each other," he recalls. "Those who were loyal to religion and the king took up positions to the right of the chair so as to avoid the shouts, oaths, and indecencies that enjoyed free rein in the opposing camp."[4] The Left remains indecent to this day, even encouraging potty mouths among children for the sake of their political crusades.[5]

Historically, conservatives have been neither "free speech purists" nor the sole censors of offensive speech, and leftists have been neither purely "liberal" nor the only speech police. Like all people at all times, both camps recognize taboos, which differ according to their respective views of the world. Light up a cigarette or, worse, a cigar at an outdoor cafe, and watch leftists recoil in horror. After decades of public-service campaigns to "raise awareness" about the dangers of tobacco, the American crop has become politically incorrect. Since New York City mayor Mike Bloomberg banned indoor smoking in 2002 and then outdoor smoking in 2011, the bans have spread throughout the nation and the world.[6] For the Left, tobacco has become taboo.

Yet at the same time, wacky tobacky has entered the mainstream. In 1996, California became the first state to legalize medical marijuana, and over the ensuing two decades most other U.S. states followed suit.[7] In 2012, Colorado and Washington legalized recreational use of the Devil's lettuce, and multiple states have passed measures of varying ambition to legalize sin spinach every year since. Conservatives have tended, at least until recently, to consider marijuana taboo, but the Left has deemed it politically correct.

Polynesians did not invent taboos, but they coined the term and introduced it into our language.[8] The British explorer James Cook first heard the word on a trip to Tonga in 1777. "When a thing is forbidden to be eaten, or made use of, they say that it is taboo," wrote Cook, though the meaning extends beyond mere dietary restrictions. Cook described it as "a word of an extensive signification."[9]

Cook's friend Omai, whom he met in Tahiti and who later gained fame as the second Polynesian to visit Europe, described the subtler complexity of *taboo*. For instance, "if the king should happen to go into a house belonging to a subject, that house would be *taboo*, and could never more be inhabited by the owner." This standard made royal visits something of a double-edged sword. To avoid evicting too many of his subjects, the king established particular houses along travel routes for his reception. Veneration as well as repulsion marked *taboo*, and the two could blur together, as in the case of human sacrifices, known as *tangata taboo*. The prohibitions of *taboo* pertained to the regal as well as the common, the sacred as well as the profane.

Taboos served practical as well as mystical purposes. Cook relates a story he heard from Omai about Old Toobou, who "presided over the *taboo*; that is . . . he and his deputies had the inspection of all the produce of the island, taking care that each individual should cultivate and plant his quota, and directing what should, and what should not, be eaten."[10] President Franklin Roosevelt enacted an identical policy centuries later, albeit with less spiritual flourish and constitutional authority, when he signed the Agricultural Adjustment Act of 1933, which regulated how much food farmers could grow. Roosevelt's quotas aimed at lowering crop production and keeping agricultural commodity prices stable—a more elaborate formulation of Old Toobou's *taboo*, which sought to regulate the Polynesian economy and protect the people against famine.

All cultures have taboos. Whole books of the Bible delineate the foods, behavior, and words forbidden to the Jews. The Third Commandment, not to "take the name of the Lord thy God in vain" holds particular resonance for observant Jews, who refrain even from spelling the Lord's name, usually rendering it "G-d." Christians have many taboos of their own. For millennia, Catholics have refrained from eating meat on Fridays. From 1898 until at least 1979, the Protestants of Elmore City, Oklahoma, banned public dancing, as Kevin Bacon informed the world in *Footloose*.

Taboos make clear what a culture worships and what it abhors. They set a culture apart and bind it together. As the Jewish writer Ahad Ha'am once observed, "More than the Jewish people have kept Shabbat, Shabbat has kept the Jews."[11] Taboos differ among groups and even within groups as they take on new identities.

In 1972, George Carlin uttered the "seven words you can never say on television": shit, piss, fuck, cunt, cocksucker, motherfucker, and tits.[12] Today, those words have all made it on air, and most have become commonplace.[13] Now there remains just one unutterable word in American English: "the n-word."

The "n-word" wasn't always "the n-word." It once was simply and offensively "nigger," a racial slur for black Americans. Epithets abound for all races: white "crackers," Italian "guineas," Irish "micks," Hispanic "spics," Asian "gooks," and so on. But unlike other racial epithets, the "n-word" may not be said aloud. There is no Irish "m-word" or Asian "g-word." But there is an n-word, and one had better not say it even in the context of condemnation.

The "n-word" became "the n-word" during the criminal trial of O. J. Simpson, the double murderer who evaded justice by exploiting the debates over race and political correctness that raged during the 1990s. Simpson's "dream team" of defense lawyers, which included Johnnie Cochran, Alan Dershowitz, Robert Shapiro, and Robert Kardashian, sought to introduce as evidence several instances in which Mark Fuhrman, one of the first investigators at the crime scene, was said to have used the "n-word." Christopher Darden, the black deputy district attorney prosecuting the case, decried the Simpson team's stunt. "If you allow Mr. Cochran to use this word and play the race card," warned Darden, "the direction and focus of the case changes: it is a race case now."[14] And so it was.

At one point, as Cochran defended Simpson's interracial marriage to Nicole Brown, the double murderer theatrically wiped tears from his eyes. One suspects Simpson welled up less for the woman he had slain than for his ineptitude at hiding the evidence.

Judge Lance Ito lamented, "This is the one remaining unresolved problem of our society, and for those of us who grew up in the '60s and had hoped this was going to go away, it's a big disappointment."[15] Judge Ito seemed to have missed some of the other social problems plaguing American society in the '90s—AIDS, crack, nuclear proliferation, and the hole in the ozone layer, to name just a few—but he understood that racial tensions still lingered, offering ample opportunity for cynics and radicals to achieve their professional and political ends.

"It's the filthiest, dirtiest, nastiest word in the English language," Darden impressed upon the judge. "There's a mountain of evidence pointing to this man's guilt, but when you mention that word to this jury, or any African-American, it blinds people. It'll blind the jury. It'll blind the truth. They won't be able to discern what's true and what's not," he explained.[16] The case, tried in the wake of the racially charged Rodney King trial, hinged less on Simpson's guilt than on the racial resentments that O. J.'s "dream team" inflamed. The strategy worked.

History has vindicated Darden and the prosecutors on every charge. In 2006, Simpson "hypothetically" confessed to murdering his wife and her friend Ron Goldman during an interview to promote his book about the murders, *If I Did It*. Although the jury acquitted O. J. in the criminal trial, another jury found him financially liable in the civil trial, and the book passed to the Goldman family, who renamed it *If I Did It: Confessions of the Killer*.

But beyond Simpson's guilt, subsequent events also confirmed Darden's insights on race relations and the "n-word." Mark Fuhrman's alleged racism did prejudice the jury, which ignored Simpson's obvious guilt. Moreover, if Darden's description of the "n-word" seemed hyperbolic in the mid-'90s, it soon came to be regarded just as he had described it: as "the filthiest, dirtiest, nastiest word in the English language."

When the *New York Times* reported on the trial in 1995, the Gray Lady wrote plainly, "Detective Fuhrman is said to have used the word 'nigger.'" The *Times* used the term "n-word" only when quoting Christopher Darden.[17] A quarter-century later, the paper almost exclusively uses the euphemism when describing the taboo term. The word has taken on the same sort of sacred terror that prevented the ancient Israelites from uttering the Holy Name.

No one denies the ugliness of the "n-word" or suggests its inclusion in polite society. But the elevation of racial over religious and cultural taboos reflects a reordering of social priorities that redounds to the benefit, not of black Americans or any other racial group, but of leftist radicals. By emphasizing the physical to the exclusion of the metaphysical, as Ta-Nehisi Coates does when he waxes poetic over "black bodies" rather than black souls or whole black people, the radicals reorder cultural priorities and invert society. This inversion extends far beyond racial, sexual, and scatological swear words. By changing taboos, radicals reorient the entire moral order, up to and especially the deadliest of the seven deadly sins.

"Pride goeth before destruction," and political correctness before a fall. On June 28, 1970, a group of homosexual activists staged the first "pride parade" in New York to mark the anniversary of the "Stonewall Riots," which had occurred after police raided an illegal, mafia-run bar that catered to gay clientele in Greenwich Village.[18] Politically correct whitewashing has presented the raid as an attack by bigoted cops on a sexual minority, but the real story depicts a less gay image of Stonewall Inn.

In 1966, the notorious Genovese crime family bought the "straight" Stonewall Inn restaurant and converted it into a gay bar, as they had other establishments, hoping to profit by protecting then-illicit public homosexual behavior. During the renovation, the mafia neglected to install a fire exit, running water behind the bar to wash glasses, or clean, functioning toilets. The Genovese family proprietors not only gouged gay customers on watered-down drinks sold without a liquor license in a dingy, dangerous ambiance; they also blackmailed the bar's wealthiest clients.[19] Sexual politics aside, the police had every right and reason to shut down Stonewall.

But within a year, the Stonewall raid and the subsequent riots had attained a mythic status and become the basis for the first pride parade. During the 1970s and '80s, gay pride parades maintained a narrow, political focus on overturning laws that suppressed homosexual behavior in public. By the 1990s, the parades had expanded considerably in scope, diversity, and duration.[20] Pride parades, discrete events held on particular days, morphed into pride weeks and even pride months. The '90s saw the mainstreaming not just of alternative sexual preferences but of pride itself as a leftist virtue.

From a public relations perspective, pride poses some problems. It is not just one of the seven deadly sins but in fact the deadliest of the sins. Saints Thomas Aquinas and Gregory the Great held pride to be "the queen of vices."[21] A politically incorrect friend once observed that today it has become "the vice of queens." But pride as a political movement has extended far beyond sexual rights.

If homosexuals sought mere acceptance for their preferences or behaviors, why organize under the banner of the deadliest sin, pride? Why not organize a "Gay Acceptance Month" or "Gay Non-Judgment Month"? Even some lesser sin might suffice: "Gay Wrath Month," perhaps, or "Gay Gluttony Month." Greed, sloth, envy, even lust—any would offer a more palatable basis for acceptance than pride.

As with all politically correct revisions, it helps to recall the word's original definition before examining how radicals have redefined it. Pride is the excessive love of one's own excellence. We sometimes use "pride" as an imprecise synonym for other concepts, as when Lee Greenwood sings that he is "proud to be an American" when he really means that he loves his country—an admirable quality more akin to filial piety than to hubris. Love of country can become excessive, at which point patriotism transforms into chauvinism or jingoism. But pride is another matter altogether.

Pride insists on our own perfection just the way we are. Our culture already teems with the politics of pride. Social ills seem always to stem from others—from "society"—never from ourselves. But the utopian Left believes we can overcome society, progressing toward and ultimately reaching perfection, if only we give the radicals just a little more time, power, and money. Whittaker Chambers pointed out that communism was not a novel ideology. "It is not new," wrote Chambers. "It is, in fact, man's second oldest faith. Its promise was whispered in the first days of the Creation under the Tree of the Knowledge of Good and Evil: 'Ye shall be as gods.'" Chambers called communism "the great alternative faith of mankind . . . the vision of Man without God."[22] It comes as no surprise, then, that adherents of that alternative faith should make pride, the original sin of mankind, their paramount virtue.

In 1963, John F. Kennedy showed the world that Chambers's description of communism might apply to leftism more broadly. During an address to the Irish parliament, the president invoked the socialist playwright George Bernard Shaw. Kennedy frequently quoted great and popular writers, but because he rarely took the time to read those writers, he often got the quotes wrong. "George Bernard Shaw . . . summed up an approach to life," the president recalled, "other people, he said, 'see things and say, Why? But I dream things that never were, and I say, Why not?'" For once Kennedy quoted a line of literature more or less correctly, but by failing to understand its context he unwittingly cast his views in a sinister light.

The line comes from Shaw's play *In the Beginning: B.C. 4004*, the first of his five-play *Back to Methuselah* cycle. Specifically, it comes from the mouth of the Serpent tempting Eve in the Garden of Eden. "I tell you I am very subtle," the Serpent begins. "When you and Adam talk, I hear you say 'Why?' Always 'Why?' You see things; and you say 'Why?' But I dream things that never were; and I say 'Why not?'"[23] Kennedy hoped to inspire his audience with a line Shaw put in the mouth of the Devil, a question that the playwright imagined had caused the fall of man.

Robert F. Kennedy picked up the line from his brother and repeated it during his own ill-fated presidential run in 1968, and Edward Kennedy quoted it at Robert's funeral.[24] Countless liberals and leftists have recited the line since. To their credit, most people who have invoked the line as an inspiration likely have no idea of its origins, and even those who do understand its context may mean perfectly well.

The Christian writer G. K. Chesterton took just such a charitable view of his friend George Bernard Shaw. "If, for instance, I had to describe with fairness the character of Mr. Bernard Shaw, I could not express myself more exactly than by saying that he has a heroically large and generous heart," wrote Chesterton, "but not a heart in the right place. And this is so of the typical society of our time."[25] The radicals who have transformed our society and inverted our standards of decency may have had the best of intentions. But the road to Hell is paved with good intentions.

When Barack Obama ran for president in 2008, he promised that his election would be "the moment when the rise of the oceans began to slow and our planet began to heal."[26] He began that promise by claiming to "face this challenge with profound humility and knowledge of my own limitations, but. . ."—apparently unaware that what followed would negate everything he had previously said.

The inheritors of Obama's progressive tradition have also inherited his hubris. In 2019, socialist politician Alexandria Ocasio-Cortez warned the public, "We're, like, the world is going to end in 12 years if we don't address climate change," specifically by adopting her $93 trillion Green New Deal proposal.[27] In 2018, the chairman of the Democratic National Committee called AOC "the future of our party."[28] High praise, but Ocasio-Cortez had even higher ambitions: to become the future of the world, which only her schemes could save from total destruction.

The utopia described by Chambers, Shaw, and American progressive politicians does not exist. Though many people believe the word "utopia" means an ideal place, it actually means "nowhere," deriving from the Greek *ou* ("not") and *topos* ("place").[29] Saint Thomas More coined the term in 1516 as the title of his book about an imaginary island with the perfect political system, which has led many to conflate utopia with *eutopia*, or "good place."[30]

Pride has a personal dimension—the sort, for example, that has prompted Barack Obama to write a ceaseless stream of memoirs beginning at the age of thirty-four.[31] But it also has a political dimension, according to which human beings can overcome the imperfections of the world and even human nature through our own efforts and ingenuity. Conservatives take a humbler view of politics; we accept the fallenness of man.

The conservative political philosopher Michael Oakeshott summed up this more modest approach. "To be conservative, then, is to prefer the familiar to the unknown, to prefer the tried to the untried, fact to mystery, the actual to the possible, the limited to the unbounded, the near to the distant, the sufficient to the superabundant, the convenient to the perfect," Oakeshott explained, before arriving at his punchline: conservatives prefer "present laughter to utopian bliss."[32] Conservatives see a great deal of good in the imperfect world, which we cautiously hope to improve, always remembering that our own nature partakes of that imperfection, while leftists rage at the fallen world, which they seek to replace with the paradise that they feel we all deserve and that they believe they can effect through their own subtlety and cleverness.

"Pride parades" may have entered the American mind as specifically homosexual affairs, but today leftists of all sexual stripes attend them. The defining feature is no longer sexual preference but leftism, which approaches politics from a position of pride. Political humility puts conservatives at a disadvantage when it comes to showboating. (A "humility parade" would seem self-defeating.) Conservatives' public virtues, such as they are, flow from their political humility; radicals' political vices stem from their penchant for pride.

Traditional society discouraged the seven deadly sins, which in addition to pride include envy, wrath, sloth, greed, gluttony, and lust. But over the past century, radicals have established an inverse standard that recognizes those sins as virtues. Astute political observers saw the change happening in real time.

In 1948, Winston Churchill described socialism as "the philosophy of failure, the creed of ignorance, and the gospel of envy."[33] He, like

Whittaker Chambers, recognized socialism as the alternative religion of mankind, an anti-gospel that promoted the worship of lies over truth and exalted sin over virtue. Pope Leo XIII, like many pontiffs throughout the ages, condemned socialists, whom he charged with "stealing the very Gospel itself to deceive more easily the unwary."[34] The gospel of radical leftism—call it any name you like—trades the virtue of charity for the sin of envy.

According to the radicals' new standard, it is greedy to keep one's own property but charitable to covet and steal the possessions of another, a perfect inversion of the old standards of justice. People often confuse envy and greed, but while the Left exalts both, there is a difference. Greed is the excessive desire for acquisition; envy is pain at another's good fortune. The greedy want something for themselves; the envious merely want others not to have it.

When leftists clamor for "the rich" to "pay their fair share," they exhibit the latter sin, which they would make a virtue. In 2016, the top 3 percent of U.S. taxpayers paid the majority of all income taxes received by the government. The top 1 percent paid more than the bottom 90 percent combined. The top 50 percent paid 97 percent of total individual income taxes.[35] How much do the fair-sharers want "the rich" to pay: 98 percent? 100 percent? No proportion could ever suffice, as the radicals desire less to acquire than to deprive.

Hillary Clinton, perhaps the most enduring left-wing fixture of our age, expressed her fellow travelers' affinity for wrath in 2018 when she declared, "You cannot be civil with a political party that wants to destroy what you stand for."[36] Despite her impressive academic credentials—or perhaps because of them—Hillary seemed not to understand the meaning of civility, the formal politeness that exists to mediate relations between citizens with divergent interests and views in a body politic. But Clinton was not alone in her incivility.

After the establishment media declared Joe Biden the winner of the 2020 presidential election, before a single state certified the vote, prominent leftists called for the creation of enemy lists to punish anyone who had in any way supported President Donald Trump. Alexandria Ocasio-Cortez asked, "Is anyone archiving these Trump sycophants for when they try to downplay or deny their complicity in the future?"[37] AOC left vague her reasoning as to why Trump supporters would want to "downplay or deny their complicity in the future," but CNN's Jake Tapper made her meaning clearer. "I truly sympathize with those dealing with losing—it's not easy," Tapper began with characteristic condescension, "but at a certain point one has to think not only about what's best for the nation (peaceful transfer of power) but how any future employers might see your character defined during adversity."[38] Were Tapper more forthright, he might have spoken with the bluntness of the mobster who simultaneously warns and threatens, "That's a nice business you've got there. Sure would be a shame if something happened to it."

Still, Tapper only alluded to the consequences leftists had in mind for conservatives. The "Trump Accountability Project," which arose around the same time, put the radicals' plan in explicit terms. "Remember what they did," the website's headline read. "We must never forget those who helped further the Trump agenda. We should welcome in our fellow Americans with whom we differ politically. But," the avengers began before contradicting their conciliatory opening, "we should *never* forget those who, when faced with a decision, chose to put their money, their time, and their reputations behind" supporting the Trump administration, which the Accountability Project accused of various crimes, exaggerated and imagined. The Project's members promised to punish any and all people who had "elected him," "staffed his government," "served him," "funded him," "supported him," or "represented him."[39] In other words, they sought revenge on anyone in any way associated with Donald Trump, and they flaunted their wrath as a virtue.

But wreaking vengeance can be exhausting, a consequence that may explain why leftists have cast the virtue of "hard work" as a vice. In the wake of the 2020 BLM riots, the Smithsonian Institution published a politically correct guide for "talking about race" and specifically "being antiracist."[40] The guide decried "aspects and assumptions" of "white culture" that "have been normalized over time and are now considered standard practices in the United States." Among the many evils white people had foisted on the world, according to the Smithsonian, were "self-reliance," "be[ing] polite," and "hard work."[41] The politically correct author of the guide appears not to have asked any racial minorities about his theory that hard work is a specifically white trait. One imagines the suggestion might have resulted in a broken nose.

In 2010, House Speaker Nancy Pelosi struggled to sell Barack Obama's healthcare plan to the American people. She infamously insisted, "We have to pass the bill so we can find out what is in it."[42] She made only one strong argument for the law, after the fact, and the case she made revealed her party's inversion of traditional standards with respect to work: she sold Obamacare on sloth.

In 2013, Pelosi celebrated Obamacare's success at freeing Americans from the burden of work. "It helped us honor our promise of life, liberty, and pursuit of happiness to the American people. Life—a healthier life—liberty to pursue happiness, individual happiness because they could not, they wouldn't be job-locked, stay in a job because someone in the family had preexisting medical condition or that they did themselves," she babbled, in contravention of basic grammar.[43] Traditional standards recognized dignity in duty and honest labor; to the politically correct, work constitutes an indignity to be rectified.

And just what did Pelosi propose people do with Obamacare's gift of free time? "You could be a photographer or writer," she suggested, echoing points she had made for the law during the debates over its passage. "We see it as an entrepreneurial bill," Pelosi explained, "a bill that says to someone, if you want to be creative and be a musician or whatever, you can leave your work, focus on your talent, your skill, your passion, your aspirations because you will have healthcare."[44] But despite the Left's artistic pretensions, the muses favor few; most would-be artists fail because their passion and aspirations dwarf their talent and skill.

Dilettantes who approach the arts "or whatever" with a lackadaisical attitude will accomplish as much as layabouts in every other field. Pelosi and her comrades misunderstand not only work and art but also entre-preneurship, which entails financial risk. Remove the risk, and the gov-ernment will subsidize and encourage waste by establishing a sinecure for the talentless and, worse, the lazy.

Where the old standards honored hard work, the politically correct order castigates success as the unjust consequence of "privilege." Ironically, grievance and victimhood become the most valuable privilege, providing excuses for failure and the grounds for demands for special treatment. Both leftist critiques of the "American dream" and conservative defenses of social mobility, each based on its side's cherished statistics, miss the more fundamental transformation: radicals have replaced the virtue of diligence with the sin of sloth in the pantheon of public values.

Greed crosses partisan lines, but the same vaunted "studies" that liberals so often invoke reveal the Left to be greedier than the Right.[45] Even the *New York Times* has admitted that Republican counties give more to charity than those under Democrat control.[46] Bernie Sanders and Elizabeth Warren, the two most radical candidates of the 2020 presidential primaries, may rail against the "millionaires and billion-aires" who allegedly refuse to "pay their fair share," but for decades both millionaire politicians have refused to give much of anything to charity themselves.[47] Bernie has made his stinginess a point of pride. In 1981, the Vermont socialist told the *New York Times*, "I don't believe in chari-ties," preferring instead a government-takeover of almsgiving.[48]

Unlike Sanders, traditional society does not consider charity a dirty word. Christianity counts charity among the three theological virtues, next to hope and faith. "Now there remain faith, hope, and charity, these three," wrote Saint Paul in his first epistle to the Corinthians, "but the greatest of these is charity."[49]

In rejecting charity, the inveterate socialist Sanders was simply fol-lowing his ideological lights. Whittaker Chambers recounts in *Witness* the experience of encountering a beggar in New York's Bowery neighbor-hood while walking with his communist comrade Harry Freeman. "A shivering derelict came up to us and asked for a handout," Chambers recalled. "Harry glanced past him, which was the proper Communist attitude. Communists hold that to give alms is to dull the revolutionary spirit of the masses." When Chambers gave the beggar some coins, Freeman remonstrated with him. "You must not think about them," urged Freeman, moved by pity himself. Despite his natural sympathy, Chambers understood that "from the Communist position, he was right and I was wrong."[50] The old standards impelled Chambers to answer the beggar's plea, but the new standards put the good of "humanity" before the needs of any individual human.

The radicals may not feed the hungry, but they always seem to feed themselves. While traditional standards demand temperance, political correctness encourages indulgence and gluttony. Social scientific studies confirm this observation, as *Psychology Today* admitted in 2019 that "people with conservative political attitudes tend to have better health than their liberal counterparts because the former place greater value on personal responsibility."[51]

Conservatives come in all shapes and sizes, but they tend to acknowledge health and moderation as worthy goals, while politically correct radicals in recent years have peddled "body positivity" and "fat pride."[52] The "fat acceptance movement," like so many other radical identity campaigns, began during the late 1960s.[53] Every polite person eschews mocking the appearance of others or belittling them for their physical deficiencies. But the "fat acceptance movement" went further, affirming the positive good of unhealthy habits and even encouraging them. In 1967, five hundred fat fetishists gathered in Central Park to rally for gluttony. As the *New York Times* reported at the time, "Short fat people, tall fat people, and dozens of slim people who said they wished they were fat, gathered in Central Park yesterday afternoon to celebrate human obesity."[54] The fat-tivists sought far more than courtesy; they demanded the inversion of standards of beauty and behavior.

Beyond the particular issue of food, radicals reject temperance and moderation by definition. The word "radical" itself derives from the Latin *radix* meaning "root." They seek complete social change by

uprooting traditional society, and that ambitious aim precludes moderation. By arousing the people's appetites and convincing them to follow
their stomachs and lower organs rather than their hearts and brains,
radicals numb the rational and spirited parts of the soul to ease social
transformation. Hence the radicals' obsession with sex.

In addition to Pride Month, the leftist liturgical calendar reserves
another month for "LGBT history." And it should come as no surprise
that a full sixth of the year centers on sexual preference. The radicals
wield lust and sex as political tools because they know that sex sells. Pop
culture chalks the Left's embrace of the Sexual Revolution and "sex
positivity" up to their hipness and makes conservatives out to be
fuddy-duddies.

A cursory glance at relative birthrates in the United States dispels
that notion, as data from the General Social Survey confirm that conservatives have many more children than liberals—41 percent more, to be
precise.[55] Conservative Catholics have litters of children, according to
astute caricaturists, whereas the stereotypical leftist has only dating apps
and cats. Both conservatives and radicals enjoy sex and recognize its
potency, but while conservatives turn sex toward procreation, leftists
wield it as a weapon.

Ubiquitous pornography, "hookup culture," subsidized contraception, and abortion on demand combine to keep people out of their senses,
enslaved to their appetites, and focused on their most primal desires
while the activists reshape politics and culture. These allurements attract
more than just liberals. Conservatives fall prey to these temptations from
time to time as well. It is not hypocritical for one whose faith begins with
the fall of man to sin and stumble, and even if it were, François de La
Rochefoucauld reminds us that "hypocrisy is the tribute vice pays to
virtue."[56] Politically correct radicals have committed a greater offense
than hypocrisy: they have redefined vice as virtue and virtue as vice.

While radicals recast these seven deadly sins as the seven virtues
of political correctness, dithering conservatives have convinced themselves that they could avoid moral debate altogether by appealing to

libertinism masquerading as libertarianism that denies the inevitability of taboos. But taboos define every culture. They delineate what a society venerates and what it abhors. Cultural revolutionaries acknowledged this fact and transformed taboos toward their political ends. Meanwhile conservatives stood by unable, and often unwilling, to impede the inversion. With the new, secular standard safely ensconced, the radicals became more brazen in their attacks on the old moral code and the religion that sustained it. As silly as it may sound, politically correct progressives declared war on Christmas.

CHAPTER 12

THE WAR ON CHRISTMAS

The war on Christmas dates back to America's earliest days, though ironically the sides on which the belligerents once appeared have flipped. On Christmas Day 1621, Governor William Bradford marked the birth of our Lord with puritanical austerity. He forbade celebrations, demanded that his constituents tend their crops as on a regular workday, and confiscated toys and games from the residents who refused to work on Christmas Day. Bradford's policy recalls H. L. Mencken's famous description of Puritanism as "the haunting fear that someone, some-where, may be happy."[1]

The liturgically allergic Pilgrims of Plymouth Colony considered Christmas celebrations popish and pagan, and they observed the day by putting their Protestant work ethic to use in the fields, though Bradford did permit an exception for the Plymouth residents who desired to spend the day in prayer. "On the day called Christmas-day, the Governor called them out to work, as was used, but the most of this new company excused themselves and said it went against their consciences to work on the day," Bradford explains in his third-person history *On Plymouth Plantation*, "so the Governor told them that if they made it a matter of conscience, he would spare them until they were better informed." But when the Governor and his diligent co-congregationalists returned from work for lunch and found the conscientious objectors "in the street at play openly . . . he went to them, and took away their implements, and told them that it was against his conscience, that they should play and others work."[2] Bradford had no problem giving Plymouth's more religiously relaxed residents a day off for Christmas, but they had better not have any fun.

The Puritans in America outlawed Christmas celebrations for a full four decades, until 1681, and tradition continued to discourage observance of the holiday even after the repeal of laws that officially prohibited festivities. The Reverend Cotton Mather followed in his forefathers' footsteps when he complained in 1712 that "the Feast of Christ's Nativity is spent in Reveling, Dicing, Carding, Masking, and in all Licentious Liberty, for the most part, as tho' it were some Heathen Feast, of Ceres, or Bacchus."[3] But like his forebears, Mather was willing to permit reverent observance of the holiday.

New Englanders' opposition to Christmas festivities continued to relax throughout the eighteenth century until Massachusetts recognized Christmas Day as a public holiday in 1856.[4] President Ulysses S. Grant abolished any remaining stigma around the day fourteen years later, in 1870, when he signed legislation making Christmas a federal holiday alongside New Year's Day, the Fourth of July, and Thanksgiving.[5] In the opening engagement of the American war on Christmas, Santa had defeated Scrooge.

While today's progressives wage war on Christmas in the name of secularism, the Puritans attacked Christmas for the opposite reason. Bradford, Mather, and all the other Puritans objected to Christmas festivities because they considered them insufficiently pious. With the possible exception of John Knox, the founder of Presbyterianism who condemned all church festivals, no leading Protestant advocated the total abolition of Christmas.[6]

As the English pamphleteer Philip Stubbs complained in 1583, "The true celebration of the Feast of Christmas is to meditate (and as it were to ruminate) upon the incarnation of the birth of Jesus Christ, not only that time, but all the times and days of our life, and to show ourselves thankful to his Majesty for the same." But the proper way to celebrate Christmas in theory never seemed to translate into practice. "Who is ignorant," asked Stubbs, "that more mischief is that time committed than in all the year besides? What masking and mumming, whereby robbery, whoredom, murder, and what not is committed? What dicing and carding, what eating and drinking, what banqueting and feasting is then used more than in all the year besides?" According to Stubbs, such impious observances dishonored God and impoverished all of Christendom.[7]

Half a century later, the Puritan polemicist William Prynne lamented that, for the most part, his fellow Englishmen spent "the Christmas season, with other solemn festivals, in amorous, mixed, voluptuous, un-Christian, that I say not pagan dancing to God's and Christ's dishonor."[8] These Puritans attacked Christmas in order to defend Christ against the perceived corruptions of papists and pagans, between whom the reformers did not differentiate.

In the centuries following the Protestant Revolution, the celebration of the Nativity on December 25 became the subject of anti-Catholic polemics, which charged that the Church had selected the date because it coincided with various pagan feasts, including celebrations of Saturn, the Unconquered Sun, and Mithras. History, however, does not back up the polemicists' claims. The *Chronography of 354* offers the earliest mention of any pagan celebration on December 25. But the calendar also mentions Christmas on that day; thus, no evidence exists to suggest that the pagan festivals predated Christian celebration of the Nativity.[9]

Saturnalia, established centuries before the Incarnation, does not quite coincide with Christmas. The Romans originally celebrated Saturn on December 17, and even the feast's expansion to an entire week took the festivities only up through December 23. Moreover, no early Christian source mentions any connection between Christmas and the pagan feasts.[10] In fact, the dating of Christ's birth appears to derive not from the date of any pagan feast, but rather from the date of his death.

Around the turn of the third century, Tertullian dated the Crucifixion to March 25.[11] Other early Christian writers, notably Saint Hippolytus of Rome, stated that the world itself had been created on March 25, a perfect link between Creator and creation.[12] Given the ancient belief that a divine life comprised an exact number of years, Christ's conception would have occurred on the same date precisely nine months before Christmas.[13] The anonymous fourth-century Christian work *On Solstices and Equinoxes* defends this view, as does Saint Augustine, who wrote in his treatise *On the Trinity*, "For He is believed to have been conceived on the 25th of March, upon which day also he suffered; so the womb of the Virgin, in which he was conceived, where no one of mortals was begotten, corresponds to the new grave in which he was buried...."[14]

This theory regarding the dating of Christmas also helps to explain the discrepancy between the West and the East, where Christians celebrate the Nativity on January 6. The fourth-century Greek bishop Epiphanius of Salamis dated Christ's conception at April 6, precisely nine months before Eastern Christmas celebrations.[15]

The claim that pagan feasts account for the date of Christmas does not hold up to historical scrutiny. As Pope Benedict XVI explained at the turn of the twenty-first century, these old theories regarding Roman gods "can no longer be sustained. The decisive factor was the connection of creation and Cross, of creation and Christ's conception."[16] Still, given the debauchery that often accompanied Christmas, one may forgive the Puritans' mistaken belief in the holiday's pagan origins.

As Puritanism declined and transformed throughout the Anglosphere, Christmas came back into fashion during the eighteenth and nineteenth centuries. But by the turn of the twentieth century, a new critique of Christmas took shape. During the first stage of the war on Christmas, Puritans took issue with the debauchery that they saw accompanying the celebrations. The second phase of anti-Christmas sentiment involved objections to the commercialization of the holiday. Greedy capitalists were selling toys to rapacious children and their indulgent parents, all of whom seemed to care more for sentimental depictions of

Santa Claus than for the real Redeemer, whose Nativity provided the neglected "reason for the season."

C. S. Lewis laid out the battle lines of this second stage in his 1954 essay "Xmas and Christmas: A Lost Chapter from Herodotus." Lewis affects the voice of an ancient Greek historian, invoking the real figures of Herodotus and Hecataeus to describe the imaginary northern island of Niatirb, or "Britain" spelled backwards. In mid-winter the Niatirbians celebrate a strange festival called Exmas, for which they spend fifty days preparing in the "Exmas Rush" by sending cards that recipients immediately throw out, buying gifts beyond their means, and so glutting themselves on food and drink that they are exhausted by Exmas Day and barely move the day after.

But on the same day, a small sect of Niatirbians celebrate a separate feast called "Crissmas," which involves doing the opposite of the Exmas enthusiasts. Observers of Crissmas eschew the madness of the marketplace, rise early on Crissmas Day, and travel to temples to observe a sacred feast involving "a fair woman with a new-born Child," the details of which mystery the author declines to repeat.

Given the diametric difference between the two feasts, Lewis's historian suggests changing the date of Crissmas, to which a priest responds, "It is not lawful, O stranger, for us to change the date of Crissmas, but would that Zeus would put it into the minds of the Niatirbians to keep Exmas at some other time or not to keep it at all." The priest rejoices "that men should make merry at Crissmas," but unfortunately "in Exmas there is no merriment left." Lewis's perplexed historian asks why Niatirbians would endure the miserable market rituals of Exmas, to which the priest bluntly replies, "It is, O Stranger, a racket."[17]

By the middle of the twentieth century, many religious conservatives considered the Christmas industry a racket, and that critique persists to this day. Although during the latter decades of that century and the early years of the new millennium, economics-obsessed conservatives throughout the United States and Britain became reflexive defenders of big business, free trade at all costs, and "capitalism"—a term popularized by

Karl Marx—a deeper strain in the conservative tradition has always taken a more skeptical view of industrialization and the "invisible hand" of the free market, a quasi-religious concept in itself that often fails to live up to the promises of its priests and acolytes.[18]

The twentieth-century critique and the earlier complaints of the Puritans, though they differed in focus, shared one essential quality: the impulse to defend Christmas against corruption. Governor Bradford opposed Christmas celebrations because he considered such festivities an affront to Christ himself. C. S. Lewis deplored the practice of sending Christmas cards, buying expensive presents, and gorging oneself at holiday dinners because he believed those rituals distracted from the spiritual significance of the Nativity. At every stage of the war on Christmas before the late twentieth century, all combatants shared the same basic standard. Puritan and merry-maker alike espoused Christianity; their disagreement concerned how properly to observe the birth of Christ.

The most recent and familiar phase of the war on Christmas, which arose during the 1980s and '90s and continues to this day, falls along fundamentally different battle lines. On one side, both the religious and commercial observers of Christmas, as well as the great majority of people who fall somewhere between the two poles, defend public recognition of the holiday. On the other side, ideologues seek to drive Christmas out of the public square, and they justify this cultural upheaval according to the politically correct values of secularism, "inclusion," and "diversity."

The aggressors in this new attack on Christmas have pursued two contradictory strategies. First they deny that any such war exists. The left-wing Americans United for Separation of Church and State regularly decries "the Religious Right's phony 'War on Christmas,'" which the organization calls "bogus."[19] Then, no sooner does one detail decades of anti-Christmas activism than the politically correct campaigners change their tune from denial to dismissal.

Pulitzer Prize–winning *Washington Post* columnist Colbert King exemplified this shifting of the goalposts in a 2017 piece titled, "I Don't Care about 'Merry Christmas.'" Setting aside the unlikelihood that King would dedicate his national newspaper column to a topic about which he did not care, one at least appreciates the liberal author's admission that the war on Christmas exists, even if he dismisses the conflict as "cynically manufactured."[20] King's choice of words reveals his own cynical strategy. He does not deny the campaign to replace "Christmas" with generic terms such as "holidays," nor does he deny that liberals have led the charge to change the words—a campaign he credits to "respect for the sensibilities of others." Rather, King insists that the semantic switch doesn't matter.[21] But four decades of consistent anti-Christmas activism suggests the distinction matters quite a lot to politically correct radicals.

The first skirmish in this latest phase of the war on Christmas took place during the early 1980s in Pawtucket, Rhode Island, which since 1943 had erected an annual Christmas display in the city's shopping district. The display included a Christmas tree, a Santa Claus house, a small village comprising four houses and a church, a group of carolers, a spray of reindeer, a clown, a dancing elephant, a robot, a teddy bear, a banner that read "Season's Greeting," and a crèche. A dozen or so of these elements acknowledged one of the most important holidays in Christendom, and only one of them included Christ. But that was one too many for Pawtucket resident Daniel Donnelly, who demanded the city remove the baby Jesus. When the city refused, he sued Pawtucket with the help of the equally radical and ironically named American Civil Liberties Union.

The District Court of Rhode Island ruled that the Establishment Clause of the First Amendment prohibited the city from displaying the crèche, and the First Circuit Court of Appeals affirmed the district court's ruling. The city persisted in defending the Nativity scene, and the case made its way to the Supreme Court on October 4, 1983. Another Christmas passed with the plaster baby's fate in limbo until the following March 5, when the Court ruled in a 5–4 decision to overturn the lower courts' rulings and preserve Pawtucket's right to portray the birth of Christ at Christmas.[22]

The Court majority gave conservatives an immediate victory in this new front of the war on Christmas, but the narrow ruling set the stage for more litigation in the years to come. Just one vote had prevented the federal government from banishing Christ from Christmas, and the Court only ruled in Jesus' favor because it found "legitimate secular purposes" in Pawtucket's display of the crèche as well as "insufficient evidence to establish that the inclusion of the creche is a purposeful or surreptitious effort to express some kind of subtle governmental advocacy of a particular religious message."[23] The Son of God could remain, but only on the grounds that he was not a religious figure.

Conservatives won the case, but the arguments by which they won undermined their broader cultural objectives. Pawtucket argued, and the Court agreed, that the crèche was secular and therefore did not violate the Establishment Clause.

In fact, Pawtucket had every right to display the crèche even if the city admitted its intrinsically religious character. Even the establishment of a state church in Rhode Island might not violate the Establishment Clause, which historically prohibited only the federal government from making any "law respecting an establishment of religion, or prohibiting the free exercise thereof."[24]

Although secularists invoke the "separation of church and state," a slogan they paraphrase from an 1802 letter by Thomas Jefferson to the Danbury Baptist Association in Connecticut, neither the phrase nor the sentiment it now represents appears anywhere in the Constitution.[25] We can know with certainty that the Establishment Clause did not prohibit states from establishing churches because at the time of the ratification of the First Amendment several states maintained their established churches. New Hampshire did not disestablish its church until 1817, Connecticut kept its congregational establishment until the following year, and Massachusetts funded its state church until 1833, four and a half decades after it ratified the U.S. Constitution.[26]

The city of Pawtucket and the Supreme Court majority fell into a trap that has permitted political correctness to advance for decades and cost conservatives the culture. Pawtucket, the Court, and conservatives broadly have accepted the radicals' premise that secular liberalism is somehow a neutral battleground on which to play politics. In reality, that premise gives away the game and the country to the politically correct Left.

There will never be a firm "wall of separation between church and state," *pace* Jefferson, because all laws invoke a moral order, and any moral order relies upon religious tenets. "Cult" and "culture" derive from the same root word; what a culture prohibits and encourages reveals what that culture worships. Contrary to Jefferson's more eccentric rationalist musings, church and state have proven inseparable in all societies throughout history. Jefferson himself made this point explicit in the Declaration of Independence, which posits that "all men are created equal" and "endowed by their Creator with certain unalienable Rights," including "life, liberty, and the pursuit of happiness."[27] Jefferson may have demurred from choosing favorites among Congregationalists, Quakers, and Catholics, but he justified the American Revolution on a specific understanding of his Creator, without whom the country could not exist.

When Jefferson fails to prove the secularists' case, they often turn to John Adams, who they claim once wrote that "the Government of the United States of America is not, in any sense, founded on the Christian religion."[28] In fact, Adams did not write that phrase, though he did affix his name to it. The American diplomat and Jeffersonian republican Joel Barlow authored those words in the Treaty of Tripoli, which Adams signed in 1796.[29] For centuries Muslim pirates had preyed on Western sailors off the Barbary coast, stealing their cargoes and selling the survivors into slavery.[30] According to William Eaton, the American Consul General to Tunis, "The Christians who would be on good terms with [the Muslims] must fight well or pay well." The fledgling United States did not look forward to either option, and the pirates' ultimatum may explain America's eagerness to deny the nation's Christian founding in the treaty.[31]

When they were not attempting to placate Muslim pirates, our Founding Fathers spoke more favorably of Christianity and its role in American public life. Whatever he signed onto in the Treaty of Tripoli,

John Adams considered America to be a Christian nation. In an 1813 letter to Jefferson, Adams affirmed, "The general principles, on which the Fathers achieved independence, were the only Principles in which that beautiful Assembly of young Gentlemen could Unite. . . . And what were these general Principles? I answer, the general Principles of Christianity, in which all these Sects were United." He believed "the general Principles of Christianity" to be "as eternal and immutable, as the Existence and Attributes of God," and considered the "Principles of Liberty" that England's Christian heritage had fostered to be "as unalterable as human Nature and our terrestrial, mundane System."[32] Adams did not forward his correspondence with Jefferson to the Barbary pirates.

John Jay, another Founding Father and the first chief justice of the Supreme Court, put the nation's Christian founding in even starker terms. "Providence has given to our people the choice of their rulers," he wrote in 1816, "and it is the duty, as well as the privilege and interest of our Christian nation, to select and prefer Christians for their rulers."[33] Had the ACLU existed at the Founding, it no doubt would have taken the chief justice to court.

In 1979, Bob Dylan observed, "[I]t may be the devil or it may be the Lord/ But you're gonna have to serve somebody."[34] There can be no perfectly "liberated" or neutral political ground: all regimes have some sort of religious vision.

The ensuing two decades witnessed the replacement of America's native religion with the anti-religion of secularism, a gradual change to which even many conservatives acquiesced thanks to their shallow and mistaken understanding of law, liberty, and the nation's founding. After the Supreme Court's establishment of secularism as the *sine qua non* of municipal Christmas displays in *Lynch v. Donnelly*, radicals pressed the principle of the ruling to its logical conclusion and attempted to rid the public square of all specifically Christmastime cheer.

At some point during the 1990s, the Capitol Hill Christmas Tree in Washington, D.C., became a "holiday tree." As with so many politically correct sleights of semantics, no one can quite pinpoint when or how the name was changed. *Washington Post* reporter Petula Dvorak blamed Paul Pincus, a Capitol Hill landscaper, whom she quotes as saying, "I'm Jewish, and this is a holiday tree."[35] By Pincus's logic, as Dvorak relates it, a Hanukkah menorah would suddenly transform into a "holiday candelabra" the moment a Methodist walked by it. The Hindu festival of *Holi* would become "the holiday paintball game" should a Muslim happen to stumble upon it. But even if the presence of additional observers had the power to secularize religious and cultural symbols, the politically correct never seem to target non-Western signs and traditions.

Pincus himself denied that any change occurred during the '90s, insisting that as far back as the 1960s people referred to Capitol Hill's conifer simply as "the tree."[36] Regardless of how the name was changed, no neologism could change its Christmas character. For what purpose was "the tree" brought to the Capitol? Which holiday did the "holiday tree" celebrate?

Controversy did not accompany the change from "Christmas tree" to "holiday tree" in the 1990s, but debate did ensue upon House speaker Dennis Hastert's decision to restore the tree's proper name in 2005.[37] Hemal Jhaveri, writing for the DCist, typified the tone of the time. "Leave it to our Capitol City to make politics out of the holiday season," she complained. "Apparently political correctness now goes as far as Christmas trees or should I say holiday trees?" Jhaveri's mocking tone may resonate with readers of all political stripes, but one cannot immediately tell which aspect of the controversy she finds ridiculous, and the ambiguity persists throughout the piece.

"Regardless of any of these naming controversies, haven't we gone over the deep end as far as the trees are concerned?" she asks. Indeed we have, but the writer refuses to name which side of the debate pushed us over the edge. "These names mean very little to me," she insists. "I think the only difference between a 'Holiday,' 'Christmas,' or 'National' tree probably would be the size of the trunk, the types of needles, or the strands of lights," she suggests. Jhaveri declares that the "real truth" and "deeper meaning of the season" involve not the Incarnation but the vaguer wish of "peace on earth, good will to men" before exhorting her readers to "leave the bickering for the Christmas dinner table when the relatives visit."[38] In other words: stop making such a big deal about Christmas, conservatives, and just call it a "holiday tree."

For decades, politically correct cultural revolutionaries have evaded the task of justifying their radical plans by asking concerned conservatives, "Who cares?" The radicals care, or else they wouldn't spend so much time and energy attempting to overturn long-standing traditions. If the politically correct re-namers really believe that these semantic distinctions between Christmas and "holiday" trees mean nothing, then why not keep the traditional and precise term? The politically correct wordsmiths are the aggressing party in the cultural war, and they have the gall to call the rest of us obstreperous because we refuse to acquiesce to their inversions of our culture. The radicals know full well the power of apparently minor semantic shifts to transform culture; that is why they tried to banish Christmas trees from public squares around the country.

In 2005, when Dennis Hastert restored the Capitol's Christmas tree, the city of Boston moved in the opposite direction, renaming its own giant spruce a "holiday tree." Thomas Menino, Boston's mayor at the time, actually opposed the change. But the activists protected their plan from democratic backlash with a typically progressive strategy: they effected the change through bureaucratic tinkering, thereby insulating it from political debate. Boston's Department of Parks and Recreation, rather than the city's mayor, wrought the change, and there was nothing any elected official could do about it.

Philip Powell, a member of Harvard's Christian fellowship, expressed exasperation at the city's decision. "The 'holiday tree' really is ridiculous," he observed. "This is the Christmas season, and December 25 is Christmas, not some general feel-good day of celebration."[39] Powell must not have consulted Hemal Jhaveri, the Supreme Court majority that decided Lynch v. Donnelly, or the politically correct activists who sought to rid the public square of Christmas trees. According to them, December 25 is indeed a general, feel-good day of celebration. As the Court explained in *Lynch*, it is the holiday's secularism that makes it fit for the public square.

That very same year, major corporations joined the radical politicians in attempting to erase Christmas from Christmastime. Companies including Walmart, Target, Sears, Lowe's, and Best Buy, among others—some of the largest retailers in the country—avoided the word "Christmas" in their seasonal marketing materials. Some of the corporate giants corrected course in response to boycott threats from the American Family Association (AFA) and the Catholic League for Religious and Civil Rights, but many companies persisted in their secularizing program.[40]

In 2008, the AFA criticized Home Depot for avoiding the term "Christmas" in favor of the generic word "holiday," particularly as the company continued to mention Hanukkah, suggesting a double standard whereby only Christian holidays go unnamed.[41] Although the left-wing "fact-checking" website Snopes ruled the AFA's claim "false" because Home Depot had not entirely eliminated references to Christmas on its website, the home improvement retailer admitted to downplaying the holiday and promised to restore Christmas to its former prominence.[42]

As conservatives fought back against the concerted political campaign to diminish the importance of Christmas to Christmastime, politically correct activists modified their tactics. Rather than erase Christmas altogether, they would instead mention Christmas as just one Christmastime holiday among many. The clothing retailer The Gap adopted this approach in 2009, when one of its advertisements declared, "Go Christmas! Go Hannukah! Go Kwanzaa! Go Solstice!" and suggested customers celebrate "whatever holiday you Wanna-kah."[43] Americans were free to celebrate Christmas, but multiculturalism and "inclusion" demanded they not celebrate it exclusively.

But is Christmas really just one holiday among many? According to Gallup polling, a full 93 percent of Americans reported celebrating Christmas in 2019, down slightly from the 96 percent who celebrated Christmas in 1994, but more or less consistent with historical levels.[44] By comparison, just 1.8 percent of Americans describe their religion as "Jewish," and an additional 0.4 percent consider themselves irreligious Jews, meaning that a whopping 97.8 percent of Americans have no religious or cultural connection to Hanukkah whatsoever.[45] Moreover, Jews who do celebrate Hanukkah consider it a minor holiday compared to major feasts such as Passover, Rosh Hashanah, Yom Kippur, and Sukkot.[46]

A similar percentage of Americans celebrate Kwanzaa, an ideological holiday invented by Maulana Karenga, né Ronald Everett, in 1966. At the time Karenga was serving as chairman of the Black Studies department at California State University, Long Beach, and he created the holiday as a vehicle to promote black nationalism and socialism, both of which he enshrined among Kwanzaa's "seven principles," along with other then-fashionable ideological ends.[47]

Five years later, Karenga was forced to celebrate Kwanzaa inside a prison cell after his criminal conviction for imprisoning and torturing two women.[48] Deborah Jones, one of Karenga's victims, described being "whipped with an electrical cord and beaten with a karate baton after being ordered to remove" her clothes.[49] Gail Davis, another victim, endured a hot soldering iron in her mouth and on her face before Karenga placed detergent and running hoses in the women's mouths and hit them on the head with a toaster.[50] Perhaps the unsavory association helps to explain why Kwanzaa never took off.

Likewise, though cultural excesses might suggest otherwise, less than 0.3 percent of Americans identify as "pagan," raising doubts as to whether The Gap really needed to include "Solstice" among seasonal holidays on par with Christmas.[51] But without the unobserved pagan feast, the minor Jewish holiday, and the socialist contrivance, all that remains to celebrate in December is Christmas, which the politically correct cannot permit. So by the 2010s, the cultural revolutionaries had returned to unnamed "holidays" as their substitute term.

The controversy persists to this day. In 2019, Wisconsin's newly elected Democrat governor Tony Evers restyled his state's Capitol Christmas tree a "holiday tree." Republicans in the State Assembly quickly passed a resolution to reinstate the tree's proper title, after which lawmakers from both parties spent half an hour arguing over what to call the evergreen.

Democrat state representative Jonathan Brostoff accused his Republican colleagues of "trying to politicize a tree," even though it was his own party's politicization of the tree that had kicked off the debate. Republican representative Scott Krug observed his Democrat colleagues' obsession with semantic befuddlement. "Call the thing what it is," he demanded. "It's a Christmas tree, it's a Christmas tree, it's a Christmas tree!"[52]

It is indeed a Christmas tree, but it holds more than tinsel and ornaments. A Christmas tree in a state building or public square stands for Christianity's special role in a society. A Christmas tree reminds people that different religions are different and make different claims about nature and politics. A Christmas tree resists the religion of scientific liberalism with which politically correct radicals hope to replace our culture's traditional faith.

Governor Evers made this agenda explicit in a letter to students and educators in which he expressed his excitement "to announce the 2019 Capitol Holiday Tree theme is 'Celebrate Science.'"[53] Just as Christmas trees celebrate Christ, politically correct "holiday trees" celebrate secularism, which often masquerades under the moniker of "science."

Science properly understood means knowledge; the word derives from the Latin verb *scire* ("to know").[54] In the modern era, the term has taken on the specific meaning of knowledge about the physical world ascertained through methodical, material inquiry. But Evers, who believes that men can become women and denies that babies are human, does not mean science in either of these senses.[55] When Evers and his fellow secularists invoke "science," they are referring to the fatalist faith popular among leftists for more than a century. According to this faith, the "science of history" will unfold along a progressive path whether we place ourselves on "the right side" of it or not.

Conservatives sometimes refer to this perversion of science as "scientism," but it is better understood as a secular religion, a sort of anti-religious religion much as political correctness is an anti-standard standard. Political correctness works to destroy traditional standards of speech and behavior, and it succeeds both when it coerces some people to adopt the new code and when it convinces others to disavow standards entirely; either response overthrows the old order. Scientism works in a similar way to discredit traditional religious and ethical considerations as legitimate in public discourse. Whether or not people accept all of the secularists' barmy notions about sex and life matters little; if scientism simply convinces people to reject "religion" per se, it will have achieved the radicals' ends.

For decades conservatives have indulged the radicals' premises on both fronts, eschewing traditional standards as "illiberal" and traditional modes of moral discourse as "unscientific." Is it any wonder that "conservatives" who aspire to behave like scientistic liberals should fail to conserve their culture from the revolutionary plans of politically correct radicals? These caponized conservatives accept the premises of their opponents and, unlike our Founding Fathers and every other great statesman in history before or since, steadfastly refuse to assert their professed views of the world for fear of being wrongly called fascists or fools.

As recently as the early 2000s, the triumphs of political correctness seemed superficial and even frivolous. Social relations coarsened, language decayed, and reason retreated from the public square, but these changes provoked bemusement more than panic among most casual observers. Yet the sometimes-subtle perversions that political correctness wrought in standards, speech, and thought threatened to overturn our most basic self-understanding in the early 2010s.

Second Wave feminists first thrust political correctness into the public eye during the 1970s. Over the ensuing decades, their allegedly modest claims and demands metastasized throughout the body politic. Then, as the twentieth century gave way to the twenty-first, what had at first appeared as a battle of the sexes devolved into a battle for the sexes, and radicals began to deny the most basic distinction in human nature.

CHAPTER 13

THE BATTLE FOR THE SEXES

M en are not women. For most of human history, those four words would not have raised an eyebrow. On April 11, 2019, they raised a mob to assault your author.[1] This account has thus far eschewed the first-person singular pronoun. But I played a minor role in this particular phase of PC's advance, and as the battle for the sexes largely hinges on personal pronouns, I will avoid the singular first no longer.

Two conservative student groups, the Young America's Foundation and the College Republicans, invited me to give a lecture on campus at the University of Missouri–Kansas City in the spring of 2019. The students hoped that I would expound upon my controversial thesis that men are not women. For months a YAF speaking tour had taken me to at least a dozen schools to give speeches on innocuous topics that nonetheless raised the hackles of politically correct students, known to some uncharitable and incisive observers as "snowflakes."

At another campus on the tour, I suggested that "speech is not violence."[2] At yet another school, I defended the notion that "babies are people."[3] Both statements elicited condemnations from politically correct radicals, but no obvious truth drew the activists' ire quite like my assertion at UMKC that "men are not women." The moment I opened my mouth, the left-wing protesters in the audience started to scream. A video recording of the speech fails to capture the intensity of their shrieks because my podium microphone fed directly into the cameras, but in the room the wails overpowered my microphone, and most audience members could not hear the speech.

Deliberately obtuse agitators sometimes argue that a true defender of free speech would defend these interruptions. If a public speaker has a right to address his audience, they argue, so too do hecklers have the right to drown him out with their own speech. In fact these interruptions amount to a heckler's veto. According to its legal definition, the "heckler's veto" describes the government's unconstitutional prohibition of certain speech for fear that it might incite a violent reaction.[4] In colloquial use, the term refers to any incident in which hecklers use their speech to drown out that of another.[5] Just as Chesterton called for stopping "the thought that stops thought," so too American defenders of free speech have long called for stopping speech that stops the American free speech tradition.

The hecklers came to the auditorium prepared, but the speaker showed up better prepared. While the screechers tried to make me lose my train of thought with improvised shrieks, I simply read verbatim from my prepared remarks, which I had fortunately printed and brought with me to the event. The audience in the room may not have heard my speech, but millions of people on the internet did, and after fifteen minutes or so of shouting to no avail, the radicals ran out of breath and stood up to leave the lecture.

But before the banshees exited the hall, one of them snuck behind the stage to open a fire door, at which point a mask-clad activist ran in and sprayed me with an odiferous concoction from a Super Soaker. Just a drop or two hit my face before the stream trailed off. As I turned toward the water gun–wielding assailant, I saw why: a Kansas City police officer stationed behind the fire door had kneed the punk to the ground within just seconds of his entrance, before I'd even noticed that someone had tried to attack me.

The foolish squirt gunner struggled against the cops for the better part of a minute or two before he learned that his plastic toy, with whatever liquid he had left in it, was no match for an officer's taser gun. I stared at the young man, trying to figure out why someone would risk arrest to commit an act of violence over the observation that men are not women. He stared back at me with a look of pain on his face—the cops were, after all, attempting to subdue him with a taser—and also shock, as though he had never imagined he would face consequences for his actions.

After the police hauled the angry young man away, I used what little time remained to wrap up the speech and answer some questions from the audience. Before I left the auditorium, an event organizer informed me that it smelled as though the water gun concoction had included bleach. Police tested the fluid, and it turned out to have been a non-toxic combination of household chemicals designed to appear more dangerous than it was. The mixture stained my blazer, but fortunately we all made it out unscathed.

The following morning, I was pleased to read a public apology from the university's chancellor, Mauli Agrawal. That pleasure faded, however, when I realized that the chancellor had directed his apology not to the assaulted speaker but rather to the hysterical students. He was apologizing for having permitted my speech in the first place. "A student group brought a speaker to campus," Chancellor Agrawal began, "a speaker whose professed opinions do not align with our commitment to diversity and inclusion and our goal of providing a welcoming environment to all people, particularly to our LGBT community."[6] One can only imagine the surprise of tax- and tuition-paying parents upon learning that the biological difference between men and women did "not align with" the university's values and "commitments."

Agrawal went on to downplay the danger posed by the sprayed substance and affirm the university's commitment to "diversity, equity, and inclusion," the distorted trinitarian formula of political correctness. He then explained that "as a taxpayer-funded public university, UMKC is also required by law to strictly enforce the First Amendment right to free speech for all."[7] Agrawal's explanation was less a defense of civil rights than a plea for forgiveness from the mob. And he concluded by calling me a bigot.

"We continue to urge everyone in our UMKC community, and the broader community, to stay true to our values in the face of provocation," Agrawal averred, "and to respond to bias and intolerance with reason and courage; to hardened attitudes with open minds and honest questions; to false statement with calm, fact-based challenges."[8] The understanding that men are not women was once common sense; by the late 2010s, it constituted "provocation," "bias," "intolerance," "hardened attitudes," and a "false statement."

Four years earlier my friend Ben Shapiro faced similar treatment for pointing out the same facts about the same issue. During a panel discussion of Bruce Jenner's public transformation into Caitlyn on Dr. Drew Pinsky's *HLN* television program, Ben asked, "Why are we mainstreaming delusion?" When Ben responded to a point that his fellow panelist, Zoey (né Robert) Tur, had tried to make regarding genetics by inquiring into Tur's own chromosomes, the muscular transsexual grabbed Shapiro by the neck and threatened, "You cut that out now, or you'll go home in an ambulance."[9]

To give the gender-bending ideologues some credit, with the exception of eccentric radicals who insist upon the existence of the "biologically female penis," most sexual revolutionaries acknowledge the biological distinction between men and women.[10] Rather than begin with the outright denial of biology, the radicals have invented a new category, gender, which they insist may differ from one's sex but nonetheless describes one's "sexual identity."

The word "gender" dates back to the early fourteenth century, when it referred to kinds and classes of people and things. By the end of that century, it acquired a primarily grammatical use, referring to male and female nouns, pronouns, and adjectives.[11] For example, *la pizza* is a feminine noun in Italian, and *il gelato* is masculine, and neither fact implies that the slice or ice cream has genitals for toppings. "Gender" retained this grammatical sense almost exclusively for the next six centuries, until 1963, when feminists began to use the word, according to the Oxford English Dictionary, as "a euphemism for the sex of a human being, often intended to emphasize the social and cultural, as opposed to the biological, distinctions between the sexes."[12] Sex, they claimed, may be innate, but gender was "socially constructed." And what society had constructed, society could "deconstruct" as well.

The Second Wave feminists who embraced the sex-gender dichotomy sought to "liberate" women from the alleged bonds of family, children, and housework. Women may possess some different body parts and even the exclusive ability to bear children, but the feminists of the "Second Wave" denied that those biological facts in any way implied what women ought to do with those body parts. The sex-gender distinction offered sexual sophists the pseudo-scientific jargon they required to have their ideological cake and eat it too.

Dr. John Money helped to give a scientific patina to "gender theory" in the mid-twentieth century with his work in the broader field of "sexology." (Money preferred the crasser "fuckology" to describe his area of expertise.[13]) Dr. Money believed that, while nature determined biological sex and nurture forged one's "gender identity," the latter completely dominated the former. Sadly, Money had the opportunity to test his hypothesis on a human subject in 1965, with tragic results for both his victim and society.

On August 22, 1965, Janet Reimer gave birth to twin boys, Bruce and Brian, in Winnetoba, Canada. From the moment Janet and her husband Ron brought the boys home, they noticed that the babies had trouble urinating, leading six months later to a diagnosis of phimosis, a condition in which the foreskin impedes normal penile function. The doctors recommended circumcision as a simple fix for the problem, and Dr. Jean-Marie Huot performed the procedure on Bruce the following month. But Huot did not perform a conventional circumcision, instead opting for electro-cauterization, which went awry and burned Bruce's penis beyond recognition. After the debacle, the Reimers declined circumcision for Brian, whose phimosis soon disappeared on its own.

Early the following year, the distraught parents watched a news report about developments in the field of "gender identity" on a Canadian television station. The reporters interviewed Dr. John Money of Johns Hopkins University, and the Reimers made plans to visit in the hopes of giving their mutilated son some semblance of a normal life. Money told the Reimers that he could not fix the poor boy's genitals, but he could mutilate the child even further to make him look like a little girl. Since sex did not determine "gender," according to Money, Bruce could live a normal life as "Brenda," blissfully unaware of his masculine birth so long as his parents kept the secret.

The prospect of studying the development of identical twins, each raised with a different "gender identity," offered the perfect test of Money's theories. But Bruce, now Brenda, never felt like a girl. "Brenda's interests are strongly masculine," wrote clinician Joan Nebbs in a report on Brenda's psychological state during childhood. "She has marvelous plans for building tree houses, go-carts with CB radios, model gas airplanes." Moreover, the child had "strong fears that something has been done to her genital organs" and worse yet "some suicidal thoughts."[14]

Money's psychological interventions might better be called psychopathic. During regular "treatment" sessions, Money instructed the boys to simulate sex, with Brian performing the male role and Bruce the female. The sexologist believed that "erotosexual rehearsal play in childhood" led to healthy "gender identity" as an adult.[15] Money made the brothers pantomime all manner of sexual positions, strip, and inspect one another's genitals while he observed and occasionally photographed the performance.[16]

Even years later, Bruce could not recall the therapy sessions without crying, and Brian felt tortured and bewildered by the memory. "It's very hard to—I don't understand why to this day we were forced to do that," Brian wondered. Money's public defense of pederasty may shed some light on the abusive experiments. "If I were to see the case of a boy aged ten or eleven who's intensely erotically attracted toward a man in his twenties or thirties, if the relationship is totally mutual, and the bonding is genuinely totally mutual," Money once mused, "then I would not call it pathological in any way."[17] Only in a thoroughly perverse culture could a man who mutilates children, defends pedophilia, and photographs young brothers simulating sex on his orders claim the authority to determine what is and is not pathological.

After Brenda threatened suicide in his preteen years, the Reimers came clean about the discrepancy between his natural sex and his coerced "sexual identity," at which point he underwent surgery to reconstruct his male genitals, adopted the name "David," and lived the rest of his life as a man. But neither Brian nor David ever recovered from the physical and psychological torture Money had inflicted upon them in the name of "science" and "gender identity" theory. Brian developed schizophrenia and took an overdose of drugs to end his life at the age of thirty-six.[18] After three prior suicide attempts, David followed suit two years later when he sawed off a shotgun, drove to a parking lot, and put a final end to his misery.

The radicals who peddle gender ideology as compassionate never seem to mention the Reimers. They insist that only by indulging delusion can we show compassion for the estimated 0.005 percent of the population who suffer confusion over their sex.[19] This fantastical strategy appears to have spread sexual confusion as a social contagion, particularly among young people, whose rates of gender dysphoria have risen dramatically in recent years.[20]

The indulgence of delusion has also failed to improve rates of anxiety, depression, and suicide among people already suffering from gender dysphoria. That failure prompted Dr. Paul McHugh to stop "sex-reassignment surgery" at Johns Hopkins University, which had pioneered the procedure during the 1960s as part of broader research into sex and gender.

In the 1970s the university began to compare the outcomes of gender-confused people who had undergone the surgery with those who had not. "Most of the surgically treated patients described themselves as 'satisfied' by the results," explains McHugh, "but their subsequent psycho-social adjustments were not better than those who didn't have the surgery. And so we stopped doing sex-reassignment surgery." McHugh believes that "producing a 'satisfied' but still troubled patient is an inadequate reason for surgically amputating normal organs."[21] Any responsible physician or disinterested scientist would have to agree. But gender ideologues had other plans, scientific method be damned.

John Money gussied up his experiments and theories with technical-sounding jargon, a perennial instrument of political correctness, but beneath his scientific pretensions lay a political radical and a pervert. He sacrificed lives, not on the lab table of scientific inquiry, but on the altar of a false religion and repulsive moral code. Money believed himself to be blazing a trail in an unexplored academic field. In fact, he had stumbled blindly into an ancient heresy regarding the relationship between body and soul at a time when society had lost the philosophical sophistication to discuss such matters.

Paul McHugh has shed light on this philosophical and religious dispute by comparing gender dysphoria to other body-dysmorphic conditions such as anorexia and bulimia. "With the transgendered, the disordered assumption is that the individual differs from what seems given in nature—namely one's maleness or femaleness," he explains. "Other kinds of disordered assumptions are held by those who suffer from anorexia and bulimia nervosa, where the assumption that departs from physical reality is the belief by the dangerously thin that they are overweight." The anorexic's subjective belief in his obesity, no matter how sincerely held, does not make him fat. Regardless of his personal views, the anorexic is too thin.

McHugh has observed that "a solipsistic argument" often accompanies these dysmorphic delusions. The sufferers' feelings about their "gender" or weight exist only in their minds, and society cannot question them, even if their subjective sense contradicts observable reality.[22] This radical subjectivism at the heart of intersectionality, woke ideology, and gender theory abolishes the possibility of disinterested debate by recasting any disagreement with people who can claim to suffer as "erasing their lived experience." Descartes inaugurated this philosophy when he declared, "I think; therefore, I am"; politically correct radicals perfected it by asserting, "I suffer; therefore, I am."[23]

When a gender ideologue claims that a man is truly a woman trapped inside a male body, he implies that one's "true self" has nothing to do with one's body. The self, according to this conception, is purely metaphysical; the physical world has no bearing on it at all. A man may possess all the bodily attributes of a man, down to his very chromosomes, but if he feels "on some deeper level" like a woman then in fact he is a woman according to gender ideology.

To its credit, this ideology rejects the shallow materialism that became fashionable during the twentieth century. "New atheists" such as Christopher Hitchens and Richard Dawkins, prominent in the mid-2000s, may have been the last gasp of that sophomoric materialist philosophy. Even the liberal vanguard no longer insists that all our loves, hopes, joys, and everything else that matters most to us in life are illusory. Instead, by the 2010s, the pendulum had swung in the opposite direction. Matter no longer mattered at all. The physical world became the illusion; the realm of ideas, preference, and desire constituted the ultimate reality.

The allegedly scientific discoveries of gender ideology constitute no more than the latest iteration of gnostic dualism, an ancient heresy that has cropped up in the West every few centuries. It first arose in the first century after Christ, flourished during the fourth century as Manichaeism, and enjoyed a revival between the twelfth and fourteenth centuries under the name of Albigensianism.[24] In all its forms, gnosticism asserts the evil of the physical world, the good of the spiritual world, and the necessity of secret knowledge for salvation. The term derives from the ancient Greek word for knowledge, which may explain why this heresy has appealed from its inception to self-styled intellectuals.

Gnosticism and materialism offer opposite explanations of the world, and these opposites pose a problem for anyone attempting to understand the history of political correctness because PC's proponents have at different times embraced one and the other worldview. The old-school Marxists from whose lingo PC gets its name were devout materialists; the gender ideologues who now enforce political correctness are thoroughgoing gnostics. How could political correctness attract and encompass both contradictory views?

The same question might be asked regarding homosexual and transgender activism. Political correctness lumps those two categories together under the ever-expanding initialism that begins with "LGBT," but transgenderism and the gay rights movement start from opposite premises. According to the latter, innate sexual desires constitute an immutable "orientation," which no one ought to suppress. In Lady Gaga's words, "Don't hide yourself in regret./ Just love yourself and you're set./ I'm on the right track, baby./ I was born this way!"[25] Some men feel sexual attraction to other men, as do some women for other women, and there isn't anything they can do to change that, so society ought to let them pursue those sexual desires without opprobrium.

But this opinion requires belief in the objective reality of sex, which transgenderism denies. If man and woman do not exist as real sexual categories—if "gender" is a mere "social construct"—then the logic behind "gay rights" falls apart. Conversely, if men really are men, and women really are women, and men cannot become women by simply declaring that they are, then the logic behind "transgenderism" collapses. Yet political correctness demands that we hold both contradictory views at the same time.

The same contradiction crops up between feminism, which portrays men as oppressors hindering women's liberation, and transgenderism, which empowers men to redefine femininity and even to become women themselves. During the 1970s, proponents of political correctness took the side of the feminists. By the 2010s, politically correct radicals began to condemn feminists such as J. K. Rowling who refuse to embrace gender ideology, castigating them as "trans-exclusive radical feminists" or simply "TERFs."[26]

Since political correctness first entered the public consciousness, conservatives have reveled in pointing out these sorts of inconsistencies, as if demonstrating the illogic of political correctness would suffice to vanquish it. Instead, the radicals march on undeterred. Confused conservatives have failed to understand this persistence because they continue to view political correctness as a coherent political vision rather than an instrument for destroying traditional standards and culture.

Sometimes political correctness speaks the language of radical individualism, and other times it demands collectivism, but it always seeks to disrupt the family, federalism, and other traditional political institutions. Sometimes the radicals embrace the materialism that reduces man to a meat puppet, at other times they shun physical reality altogether, but they always reject hylomorphism—that is, the traditional view that man comprises both body and soul and that we cannot be reduced to one or the other.[27]

This traditional understanding of body and soul derives from Christianity and from ancient pagan thinkers such as Aristotle, whom Saint Thomas Aquinas is said to have "baptized" through his writings.[28] The terms "conservative," "traditional," and "Christian" may not be synonymous, but they overlap substantially in the same way that terms such as "radical," "politically correct," "secular," and "leftist" relate to one another. So it should come as no surprise that G. K. Chesterton, writing in the early twentieth century, observed the same contradictory attacks on the Church as we see levied upon our political tradition, by broadly the same sort of people.

Chesterton observed that it seemed "as if any stick was good enough to beat Christianity with," and he wondered "what again could this astonishing thing be like which people are so anxious to contradict, that in doing so they did not mind contradicting themselves." He saw critics attack Christianity both for the loneliness of the cloister and for encouraging large families, for misogyny and for attracting mostly women, for despising Jews and for being too Jewish, for the asceticism of the sackcloth as well as for the pomp and circumstance of the Holy Mass.[29]

The politically correct levy the same dishonest and self-contradictory attacks upon traditional standards. They attack conservatives for demeaning and caricaturing women, then they attack conservatives for refusing to believe that a smear of lipstick and a pair of stilettos can turn a man into a woman. The radicals are determined to upend society, and they will avail themselves of any instrument to bring about that end.

Transgenderism became a national political battle in February of 2016, when the liberal city council of Charlotte, North Carolina, passed an ordinance that banned discrimination on the basis of "gender" and "gender identity" in public restrooms and changing rooms, erasing an earlier provision permitting separate facilities for men and women.[30] In effect, the statute abolished the right of women and girls to undress and use the bathroom away from the prying eyes of men. If a little girl walked into a changing room at a public pool to put on her bathing suit, and a grown man followed her in, the young girl's father would have no legal recourse to stop him so long as the fellow following the daughter declared himself a woman.

The following month, the North Carolina state legislature responded by passing the Public Facilities Privacy and Security Act, better known as HB2, which defined sex according to the traditional, objective, and biological standard, overturning Charlotte's reframing of sexual issues as matters of "gender" or "gender identity" and thereby also overturning the city's bathroom bill.[31] Republican governor Pat McCrory signed HB2 into law on March 23.[32]

Two months later, the federal government, under the direction of President Barack Obama, sued North Carolina to protect the right of men to use the ladies' room.[33] In addition, the Office for Civil Rights in Obama's Department of Education issued a "dear colleague" letter threatening to withhold federal funds from school districts and colleges that did not permit men to use the women's bathroom.[34]

In 2017, President Trump reversed Obama's gender-bending agenda.[35] But a year earlier, Trump had taken a more liberal stance on the issue on the campaign trail, criticizing North Carolina for defending single-sex bathrooms and urging the state to "leave it the way it is." Referring to HB2, Trump observed in characteristically vague terms,

"North Carolina did something that was very strong, and they're paying a big price, and there's a lot of problems." He had a point. Since McCrory signed the bill into law, major companies and educational institutions threatened boycotts of the state on the grounds that the government "discriminated" against men who believed themselves to be women.

"There have been very few complaints the way it is," Trump reminded his audience. "People go, they use the bathroom that they feel is appropriate. There has been so little trouble. And the problem with what happened in North Carolina is the strife and economic punishment that they're taking."[36] Ironically, the man who launched his campaign as an antidote to political correctness had embraced the politically correct stance on an issue as fundamental as the difference between the sexes, and the cultural warrior justified his submission on purely economic grounds.

Trump's primary opponent Ted Cruz hammered him on the issue, accusing the New York billionaire of "embracing the PC police."[37] Indeed he had, albeit unwittingly. Trump's career in business rather than politics likely accounted for his unfamiliarity with the nuances of that particular public policy debate, and his justification of transgender restroom rules on the grounds that there had been "very few complaints" demonstrated a deeply conservative instinct for prudence over ideological purity. Nevertheless, Trump had gotten the issue wrong, and as he became more familiar with the premises at play in the laws and legal battles, he reversed his stance and told men to stay out of the ladies' room.

Trump's initial reaction resonates with many reasonable people. After all, how many people in the country actually suffer from this rare psychological disorder? And how many of those people have made a nuisance of themselves in the wrong public restroom? How has an issue that affects so few people come to dominate our national political discourse? Who cares?

The Left cares, or else it wouldn't invest so much time, money, and effort into the issue. Conservatives did not instigate the fight; leftist politicians in Charlotte did. When conservatives in the state legislature resisted the abolition of single-sex restrooms, leftists in the Obama administration elevated the local dispute to the federal level. As a personal matter, the bathroom rules affected only a small number of people. But as a political matter, the issue threatened nearly everything, from our loftiest conceptions of science, freedom of association, and federalism all the way down to the nature of the family and even sexual difference. If political correctness could abolish the most fundamental distinction in human nature, then nothing could escape its transformational reach.

By the end of the 2010s, the new gender ideology had progressed beyond bathrooms to libraries and classrooms, where it sought to pervert children's understanding of sex and sexuality. Rosy Clark, a teacher at Brooklyn's taxpayer funded PS 58 preschool, taught her four-year-old students that "everybody has the right to choose their own gender by listening to their own heart and mind," according to a classroom email obtained by the *New York Post*. "Everyone gets to choose if they are a boy or a girl or both or neither or something else," Clark explained, "and no one gets to choose for them."[38] Many young children might rejoice at the chance to identify as Superman or Wonder Woman, but their inevitable failure to fly or melt steel with a glance can only lead to confusion and disappointment. Education once existed to correct delusions and disordered desires; through political correctness, it has come to encourage those fantasies and destructive appetites.

Outside of the classroom, sexual revolutionaries sought to shape the next generation with "Drag Queen Story Hour," a program in which transvestites read, sing, and dance for children in public libraries. While one might expect to find such exhibitions in New York and San Francisco, the program quickly expanded beyond America's usual bastions of debauchery to Florida, Washington State, South Carolina, Texas, and even the United Kingdom. The drag queens don tight dresses, teach the toddlers to twerk, and indoctrinate them into a politically correct sexual ethic diametrically opposed to the old standards.[39] A Drag Queen Story Hour event in Houston featured Tatiana Mala Nina (né Alberto Garza), a thirty-two-year-old sex offender convicted a decade earlier of molesting an eight-year-old boy.[40]

Some conservatives who have acquiesced to the new sexual definitions simply fail to understand their far-reaching consequences. They may not enjoy the teaching of gender ideology in preschools or Drag Queen Story Hour performances in public libraries, but they invoke the "live and let live" language of libertarianism because they feel they have bigger fish to fry.

Another group of self-styled right-wingers, however, has not merely tolerated these sorts of displays but embraced and exalted them. David French, a center-right writer and lawyer who once admirably opposed the Obama administration's attempts to let men into the ladies' room, even went so far as to describe Drag Queen Story Hour as "one of the blessings of liberty."[41] One can almost hear the Founding Fathers turning in their graves. Whatever Gouverneur Morris had in mind when he wrote the preamble to the Constitution, it is doubtful that he envisioned twerking for toddlers among the "blessings of liberty" that the new government sought to secure.

The confused conservatives who defend Drag Queen Story Hour as the necessary consequence of free government fall into the classic trap of political correctness: they believe that if they reject the radicals' new public standards, they must reject all public standards. If the government can ban drag shows in public libraries, they seem to suggest, then what's to stop it from outlawing Sunday Mass or Monday Night Football? According to them, liberty requires that we permit everyone to do just about anything he pleases.

At a basic factual level, these would-be libertarians fail to acknowledge the history of the American government, which has never counted drag performances among the natural rights it was designed to protect. In fact, for most of the nineteenth century, dozens of cities outlawed cross-dressing altogether. Some cities—including San Francisco, of all places—kept these laws on the books until the late twentieth century.[42] But worst of all, these accommodating conservatives misunderstand the nature of liberty in the American regime by failing to recognize the distinction between liberty and license so important to the Founders' conception of republican government.

The preamble to the Constitution offers important insight into how liberty relates to the constitutional project. The framers, writing as "we, the people," articulate six reasons for establishing the government: "to form a more perfect Union, establish Justice, insure domestic Tranquility, provide for the common defense, promote the general Welfare, and secure the Blessings of Liberty to ourselves and our Posterity."[43] Though many readers on both the left and right have read this final purpose simply as "liberty," the actual goal is the blessings derived from liberty. According to the Constitution, liberty plays a key role in the regime, but that role is instrumental rather than an end in itself.

James Madison explains this instrumentality in *The Federalist*. "Justice is the end of government," wrote Madison. "It is the end of civil society. It has ever been and ever will be pursued until it be obtained, or until liberty be lost in the pursuit."[44] Civil society requires liberty, but it seeks justice. And just who defines justice? The present-day "conservative" defenders of Drag Queen Story Hour seem to suggest that no one has the right to define justice. What one man calls justice another might consider injustice. Therefore, they insist, we must throw up our hands and hold our tongues, lest the radicals prohibit the rituals and institutions that we ourselves cherish.

Never mind that the radicals already suppress traditional behaviors and organizations while promoting their own, as they demonstrated without a hint of shame during the coronavirus lockdowns of 2020, when leftist politicians shut down churches while allowing marijuana dispensaries to remain open and encouraging "mostly peaceful" riots by their fellow travelers. Even on its face, the argument makes no sense. If people cannot discern between good and bad, then free government is not possible, as all government requires a conception of truth and justice. Our forebears understood that our moral intuition, rational faculties, and received opinion bearing the wisdom of the ages allow us to pursue justice and establish a society ordered toward human flourishing. If we cannot count on our conscience and reason—and on the wisdom of our forebears—we cannot claim the ability to govern ourselves.

Politically correct radicals seek to suppress and ultimately transform our moral intuitions, deny our rational faculties, and erase the wisdom of the ages. They dismiss the traditional moral order as outmoded at best and evil at worst. They decry "objective, rational linear thinking" as a nefarious aspect of "whiteness" and then, ironically, malign received wisdom as irrational prejudice.[45] They have undertaken this task with patience and persistence, progressively chipping away at our norms and traditions until even so heinous a violation as the sexual abuse of children is considered normal.

During the 1970s, John Money hid his exploitation of the Reimer twins in therapy sessions behind closed doors and in carefully worded scientific papers. By the late 2010s, gender ideologues paraded their abuse of children on television and in the back of seedy bars. Not only have the abusers not faced punishment, but major cultural institutions have actually cheered them on.[46]

"Sashaying Their Way through Youth," read the headline of one *New York Times* article detailing the rise of "drag kids" in 2019.[47] The *Times* focused much of its report on Desmond Napoles, a young boy whose mother Wendy began dressing him in drag and trotting him out to gay pride parades at the tender age of eight.[48] Wendy Napoles claims to have discovered Desmond's deeply held desire to wear drag after the "theatrical" child began dancing to a Katy Perry song at a shopping mall food court.[49]

"Other moms are soccer moms," Wendy explains. "They take their kids to practice, to games, they cheer for their kids. That's how I see myself with drag." In 2018, Mrs. Napoles dragged her eleven-year-old son to 3 Dollar Bill, a gay bar in Brooklyn, where perverts threw crumpled cash at the little boy as though he were a stripper.[50] If traditional standards still governed society, Desmond's abusive mother would lose custody of her son and likely wind up in prison. In our politically correct culture, Hollywood produces feature-length films celebrating "drag kids," and the only people who risk ostracism and punishment are the onlookers who criticize the abuse.[51]

Sheer indignation ought to impel conservatives to oppose these new sexual standards and to articulate an alternative vision. But if even "drag kids" cannot spur them to action, complacent conservatives must at least recognize that inaction is a sort of action too. If PS 58 in Brooklyn teaches that "everyone gets to choose if they are a boy or a girl or both or neither or something else, and no one gets to choose for them," then the school cannot teach that boys are boys and girls are girls.[52] It cannot even permit that point of view, which the new ideology condemns as bigoted and intolerant.

If we accept this ideology, then the first chapter of Genesis, which states that "God created man in his own image, in the image of God created he him; male and female created he them" must be struck from polite discourse.[53] Christians, Jews, and Muslims—even atheists and agnostics with a modicum of common sense—must renounce their beliefs inasmuch as they contradict the established liberal faith and its politically correct orthodoxies. Scientists must deny physical and biological reality. If our public institutions declare that men can be women, and women men, then it must consider all contradictory views false. If we affirm gender ideology, we renounce our traditional understanding of sex.

Society cannot simultaneously embrace both contradictory views, as anyone who has ever fallen afoul of the pronoun police well knows. If John understands that Caitlyn (né Bruce) Jenner is a man, and his friend Jane considers Jenner a woman, then John and Jane can hardly converse. He will refer to "him," and she to "her," and no matter how likeminded John and Jane once were, they will now speak different languages, reflecting fundamentally different visions of the world that Jane may not have noticed as subtle semantic contrivances reshaped her mind, and all the while John kept mum.

Even the most hard-nosed scientist must eventually acquiesce to the delusions of political correctness. He may not care about the culture, but the culture cares about him. During the first two decades of the twenty-first century, the high priests of this new orthodoxy began to intrude as never before into the realm of science. The radicals made increasingly strident, frequent, and false scientific claims to justify their political ends. In service of this ideology, scientists denied basic biology. During the coronavirus lockdowns of 2020, the trend accelerated. "Science" became a synonym for "social justice," and scientists seemed to serve the caprices of radical politicians above all else.

CHAPTER 14

LOCKING DOWN DISSENT

ab coats do not confer special immunity from politics. The experts at the *New England Journal of Medicine* demonstrated this scientific fact in late 2020 when they declared, "Sex designations on birth certificates offer no clinical utility, and they can be harmful for intersex and transgender people."[1] It does not take a doctorate to know that sexual difference matters a great deal in medicine. The wokest obstetrician in the world will struggle to treat a "trans-woman."

These "experts" lend credibility to the politically correct regime, not by furnishing it with facts, but by redefining scientific terms to better accord with the dictates of progress. Gender ideology offers perhaps the clearest example of science's perversion by political correctness, but scientific disciplines as far afield as epidemiology and meteorology have succumbed to radical redefinition as well, as the World Health Organization demonstrated during the coronavirus epidemic of 2020.

While leftist politicians promoted a policy of lockdowns to fight the virus, some conservatives proposed an alternative strategy: herd immunity. Lockdowns entailed shuttering businesses, prohibiting social gatherings, and curtailing civil liberties. Many conservatives considered this sort of treatment more dangerous than the disease, particularly given the dearth of evidence that lockdowns offered any advantage over less severe measures.[2] Better to institute prudent precautions to protect those most vulnerable to the virus, these conservatives argued, while pursuing a broader strategy of attaining herd immunity, which the World Health Organization had defined as "the indirect protection from an infectious disease that happens when a population is immune either through vaccination or immunity developed through previous infection." The WHO validated the role of herd immunity in suppressing the coronavirus by noting in the spring of 2020 that "the threshold for establishing herd immunity for COVID-19 is not yet clear."[3]

But calls for more modest regulations in pursuit of herd immunity threatened the radicals' plans for cultural transformation, which benefited from the massive transfer of wealth and power brought about by the lockdowns. So by late November, the World Health Organization simply changed the definition of the key medical term. Herd immunity, the WHO now insisted, "is a concept used for vaccination, in which a population can be protected from a certain virus if a threshold of vaccination is reached." Not only did the WHO erase its references to infection; it went further to claim that "herd immunity is achieved by protecting people from a virus, not by exposing them to it."[4] The public health organization neglected to mention what groundbreaking discovery had led them to redefine the long-standing epidemiological concept because the shift had been semantic, rather than scientific.

Conservative skeptics of these "experts" noted the change, and the WHO failed to muster any scientific explanation to justify it. So in the final days of 2020, the World Health Organization un-discovered its new conception of herd immunity, which it redefined once more as "the indirect protection from an infectious disease that happens when a population is immune either through vaccination or immunity developed through previous infection." But this time the public health organization included political advice, noting that "WHO supports achieving 'herd immunity' through vaccination" and that "herd immunity against

COVID-19 should be achieved by protecting people through vaccination, not by exposing them to the pathogen that causes the disease."[5]

The word "should" reveals much about the relationship between science and political correctness. The WHO had attempted to enshrine its new, politically correct definition of herd immunity as scientific fact and therefore beyond the realm of legitimate political debate. When that transparent effort failed, the WHO admitted the true meaning of the term but nonetheless encouraged compliance with draconian lockdowns that would endure at least until most of the population had received the vaccine, whether herd immunity had been achieved or not. The "scientific" reasoning changed, but the political endgame always remained the same.

Left-wing politicians defended their draconian lockdown policies and suppression of conservative dissent for several months by appealing to the supposedly nonpartisan experts, according to whom "science" demanded the closure of churches and businesses as well as the suspension of civil rights. But as May rolled around, leftists themselves began to break the lockdown—along with glass storefronts—over alleged police brutality in the death of George Floyd. Black Lives Matter, an explicitly Marxist organization, led the riots, which soon spread throughout the country and even into Europe.[6]

Suddenly, the politicians lost interest in "public health." Many left-wing politicians encouraged the riots, even as they excoriated conservatives for protesting the lockdowns. Some liberal politicians even joined in the protests themselves.[7] For months, politicians had prohibited Americans from holding funerals for their loved ones, many of whom had to perish alone because of the public health policies. Yet those same politicians permitted thousands of mourners and activists to attend Floyd's funeral, pandemic or not.[8]

The political circumstances of a career criminal's death entitled him to a quasi–state funeral, attended and addressed by future president Joe Biden.[9] Meanwhile, cynical politicians prohibited any fanfare for countless ordinary Americans, whose deaths lacked political significance in their eyes. Liberal politicians castigated conservatives for peacefully protesting the lockdowns, but they encouraged nationwide riots and looting in the name of social justice.[10]

If the administrative state functioned as progressives promised, non-partisan "scientific experts" would have chided the hypocritical politicians and reminded everyone left, right, and center to stay home for the good of public health. Instead, in early June, more than 1,200 health care "experts" signed a letter that simultaneously condemned conservative protests and endorsed BLM riots.[11] Inexpert observers might observe that viruses spread just as quickly through liberal gatherings as through conservative ones, but the experts contested this common sense:

> On April 30, heavily armed and predominantly white protesters entered the State Capitol building in Lansing, Michigan, protesting stay-home orders and calls for widespread public masking to prevent the spread of COVID-19. Infectious disease physicians and public health officials publicly condemned these actions and privately mourned the widening rift between leaders in science and a subset of the communities that they serve. As of May 30, we are witnessing continuing demonstrations in response to ongoing, pervasive, and lethal institutional racism set off by the killings of George Floyd and Breonna Taylor, among many other Black lives taken by police. A public health response to these demonstrations is also warranted, but this message must be wholly different from the response to white protesters resisting stay-home orders.[12]

More than 120 words into their letter, the scientists had not made a single scientific claim. Instead, they asserted the political point that black leftists ought to enjoy greater civil liberty than white conservatives. They even implied black racial superiority through the persistent capitalization of "Black" and lowercasing of "white." The rest of the letter parroted similar politically correct claptrap.

In the entire 990-word letter, the scientists made only one "scientific" argument. "White supremacy is a lethal public health issue that predates and contributes to COVID-19," they claimed.[13] Leaving aside the supposed medical consequences of "white supremacy," the social fact that "whites" uniquely may be castigated on the basis of their race would seem to contradict America's alleged "white supremacy."

The scientists exploited their academic credentials to make their unrelated political claims appear "scientific" and therefore beyond the realm of legitimate debate—a tactic employed not just by the quacks who signed the letter but even by the most respected scientists in the country.

In the early days of the epidemic, Dr. Anthony Fauci had one clear message for the public: stop wearing masks. "There's no reason to be walking around with a mask," he insisted in March 2020. "When you're in the middle of an outbreak, wearing a mask might make people feel a little bit better, and it might even block a droplet, but it's not providing the perfect protection that people think it is." Further, according to Fauci, masking did not just fail to stop the spread of the virus; it actively damaged public health.

"Often, there are unintended consequences," he warned. "People keep fiddling with the mask, and they keep touching their face."[14] Fauci had led the National Institute of Allergy and Infectious Diseases since 1984.[15] He had worked with the broader National Institutes of Health for more than fifty years and advised every U.S. president since Ronald Reagan. In 2008, President George W. Bush awarded him the Medal of Freedom, the nation's highest civilian honor. According to the Institute for Scientific Information, from 1983–2002 Dr. Fauci was the thirteenth-most-cited scientist in the world across all disciplines among nearly three million authors.[16] When Dr. Fauci told the nation not to wear masks, the people listened.

Democratic congressman Eric Swalwell parroted Fauci's line, as did Surgeon General Jerome Adams, who dispensed the medical advice with greatest urgency. "Seriously people—STOP BUYING MASKS!" Adams insisted. "They are NOT effective in preventing general public from catching #Coronavirus, but if healthcare providers can't get them to care for sick patients, it puts them and our communities at risk!"[17]

Then a month later, they all changed their minds. On April 3, the Surgeon General recommended "wearing cloth face coverings in public settings where other social distancing measures are difficult to maintain (grocery stores, pharmacies, etc.) especially in areas of significant community-based transmission." He defended his change of heart as "data driven" and promised to "continue to update our response and guidance based on the data."[18]

Swalwell too reversed course, as did Dr. Fauci. "There should be universal wearing of masks," Fauci told ABC News.[19] But the "science" and "data" that Fauci and the others invoked to justify their reversal had not changed much over the intervening weeks. Indeed, the CDC had published a paper in May declaring that fourteen randomized controlled trials of cloth masks "did not support a substantial effect on transmission" of viruses, and even many months later studies raised serious doubts about the efficacy of masks in preventing coronavirus infection.[20] We may leave it to other books to debate the medical merits of the 2020 public health response. It suffices for our purposes to understand the politics.

Although public health experts such as Dr. Fauci insisted that ever-changing "data" prompted the cloth mask flip-flop, he later admitted in an interview with the *Washington Post* that the source of the change lay in political rather than scientific considerations. "Back then the critical issue was to save the masks for the people who really needed them because it was felt that there was a shortage of masks," he admitted.[21] In other words, the public health officials believed masks did offer protection against the virus. Fauci had lied when he told the public in March that there was "no reason to be walking around with a mask." Fauci just felt that certain people—namely, his colleagues in the medical field—deserved more protection against the virus than others, so he discouraged the use of masks until he knew they could secure enough supplies for hospital workers.

Fauci defended his misdirection on masks primarily on the grounds that it freed up more protective equipment for hospital workers—a political rather than scientific consideration. He misrepresented what he believed to be the scientific facts in order to effect his preferred political ends. And all the while, he denied that politics influenced his advice.

"For goodness sakes, I've never had any political ideology that I've made public!" the exasperated epidemiologist told *Daily Show* host Trevor Noah in September. "I'm really just talking to you about public health. When I'm telling you 'wear a mask,' 'keep social distancing,' 'avoid crowds,' 'wash your hands,' 'do things outdoors more than indoors,' there's nothing political about that," he insisted. "That's a public health message that we know works."[22] With that guarantee, Dr. Fauci revealed that he knew even less about politics than he did about masks.

By definition "public health" involves both science and politics. The word "public" means "political," as politics is simply the way we all get along together in public rather than private life.[23] Fauci receives his paycheck from a governmental agency; he has reported to politicians up to and including the president of the United States. His job entails mandating how hundreds of millions of people behave, all the way down to the minutiae of how they dress and celebrate holidays. Few people in American history have ever possessed such political power.

But Fauci shares the progressive understanding of politics, which trades democratic deliberation for scientific expertise and redefines political decision-making as "science." According to this view, citizens no longer have the right to debate eternal questions and persuade their fellow countrymen. Instead, "science" has progressed to the point that "data" and "expertise" can solve those stubborn problems once and for all. The "scientists" know what "works."

But in order for something to "work," it must have a purpose. A lawnmower "works" when it cuts grass. A lock "works" when it prevents intruders from getting in. Neither can "work" unless someone first determines that we ought to cut the grass or keep out intruders. Likewise, public policy can only "work" when it achieves predetermined goals. According to the old constitutional standard, we the people have the right and responsibility to determine those goals through deliberation and persuasion. According to the new progressive standard, we the people have the obligation to defer to "scientific experts," who dictate not merely how to achieve specific policy goals but often which goals to pursue in the first place.

When CNN asked Democratic Senate candidate Jon Ossoff to articulate his vision for public health in December of 2020, he robotically replied, "I think we should follow the expertise of public health experts."[24] To Ossoff's credit, he took the progressive approach to its logical conclusion and even admitted that he himself had nothing to add to the discussion beyond regurgitating the whims of technocrats in lab coats. "Politicians need to recognize the limits of our own knowledge and wisdom," he demanded. "Epidemiologists who dedicate their careers and their training to studying the spread of infectious disease are qualified to advise us on the correct mitigation procedures, and the problem we've had all year is that politicians have been suppressing and ignoring public health advice." Never mind that politicians had already outsourced public policy to the whims of epidemiologists for a full nine months at that point. "It's time to trust the experts," Ossoff concluded.[25]

But which experts do we trust, and what sort of expertise should they possess? Ossoff advocated that we "trust" epidemiologists, and even then only those epidemiologists who supported draconian lockdown measures. But experts exist in every field. One imagines 2020 would have played out rather differently had politicians deferred to economic or military experts rather than epidemiological experts, and the country might well have been the better for it. Pandemics do not put other political concerns on pause. While America followed the advice of public health experts, the nation's international adversaries took advantage for economic and military gain.[26]

Experts in public health, national security, and economics, to say nothing of constitutional law, criminal justice, political philosophy, and any other number of fields may all have disagreed with one another over how to handle the pandemic. We elect politicians to consider all of these various concerns and to exercise their judgment in forming public policy among competing priorities. Politicians are supposed to be expert at politics. We the people express our trust in these experts at the ballot box, and when they fail us, we put our trust in other politicians.

The United States has endured countless epidemics, from smallpox in the seventeenth and eighteenth centuries to cholera in the nineteenth century to the Spanish and Hong Kong flus in the twentieth century.[27] Not one of those epidemics prompted politicians to shut down the country as they did for the Chinese coronavirus, even though that virus was by no means the most virulent the country had ever faced. The nature of death and disease have not changed between then and now. But the standards by which people judge death, disease, and politics have changed, and this new standard demands deference to progressive technocrats, whose words carry the authority of science itself.

The Left's abuse of scientific credentials to effect political ends long predates the coronavirus pandemic, going back at least to the earliest days of "global warming," then known as "global cooling." "Get a good grip on your long johns, cold weather haters—the worst may be yet to come," warned the *Washington Post* in a front-page report titled "Colder Winters Held Dawn of New Ice Age" on January 11, 1970. "That's the long-long-range weather forecast being given out by 'climatologists,' the people who study very long-term world weather trends."[28] The *Post* saw fit to surround the word "climatologists" in quotation marks because so few readers would have recognized the emerging field in the 1970s. Half a century later, as "climatologists" have exerted more and more influence in public life, that particular breed of expert may enjoy greater recognition than any other, reflecting a shift not merely in scientific research but also in politics.

"Science: Another Ice Age?" asked *Time* magazine on November 13, 1972.[29] *Newsweek* covered "the cooling world" on April 28, 1975.[30] Other outlets joined the frenzy. Global warming alarmists sometimes dismiss the "global cooling" scare as a media contrivance at odds with the scientific views at the time.[31] But one need only read *Newsweek's* reporting on the subject to dismiss the dismissal. Quoting several prominent scientists, the National Oceanic and Atmospheric Administration, and National Academy of Sciences, *Newsweek* painted a bleak picture of earth's future. "Meteorologists disagree about the cause and extent of the cooling trend, as well as over its specific impact on local weather conditions," the magazine admitted. "But they are almost unanimous in the view that the trend will reduce agricultural productivity for the rest of the century. If the climatic change is as profound as some of the pessimists fear, the resulting famines could be catastrophic."[32] Four decades later, malnourishment hit an all-time low even as the world population doubled.[33]

The mistaken scientists made political demands along with their scientific predictions. "Climatologists are pessimistic that political leaders will take any positive action to compensate for the climatic change, or even to allay its effects," *Newsweek* reported. The scientists proposed "stockpiling food" and "introducing the variables of climatic uncertainty into economic projections of future food supplies" as well as more ambitious solutions such as "melting the arctic ice cap by covering it with black soot," which would have proved an awkward fix decades later when scientists reversed their judgment and identified melting ice caps themselves as an irrefutable harbinger of the end times.[34]

Fortunately, citizens of the 1970s had the good sense to ignore the scientists' hysterical warnings, which sometimes differed over cause but always foretold the same effects: famine and death. In addition to predictions of apocalyptically inclement weather, scientists of that era warned that "overpopulation" would strain the earth's resources and cause mass starvation. The Stanford biologist Paul Ehrlich began his 1968 book, *The Population Bomb*, by declaring, "The battle to feed all of humanity is over. In the 1970s and 1980s hundreds of millions of people will starve to death in spite of any crash programs embarked upon now." Lest any optimists hold out hope that agricultural advances might solve the impending famines, Ehrlich continued, "At this late date nothing can prevent a substantial increase in the world death rate." The dead-certain scientific expert explained that mankind had only one hope to preserve life: stop it from occurring in the first place.

"We must have population control at home, hopefully through changes in our value system, but by compulsion if voluntary methods fail," Ehrlich demanded, decrying "the cancer of population growth," which he insisted "must be cut out."[35] As a rule, people who describe newborn babies as a "cancer" tend to have a distorted vision of the world. But prominent leftists, whose vision had already been similarly distorted, lapped up Ehrlich's expertise. Johnny Carson invited him on *The Tonight Show*, after which *The Population Bomb* shot up the bestseller lists.[36]

India's leftist prime minister Indira Gandhi enforced policies that required sterilization in order to access water, electricity, ration cards, and medical care.[37] Communist China embraced the "one-child policy," which led to upwards of 100 million forced abortions and sterilizations.[38] Despite these atrocities, the world population continued to grow, but world hunger declined.[39]

Ehrlich had been perfectly wrong. Not only had his doomsday prophecy failed to materialize, but the greatest cause of mass death in the subsequent decades was the coerced abortions that his book spurred. Yet Ehrlich never paid a price for his fatally false predictions. He continued to teach at Stanford.[40] Prestigious institutions continued to laud him with honors.[41] And Ehrlich remained unrepentant, never failing to warn of "overpopulation" as he continued his crusade against human life.[42]

Leftist radicals made use of Ehrlich in their zeal to promote contraception and abortion, both of which undermined the old moral standards, but their agenda never depended upon the accuracy of his scientific views. The expert turned out to be scientifically wrong, but he was always politically correct. Left-wing billionaires such as Bill Gates, Warren Buffett, Oprah Winfrey, George Soros, and Mike Bloomberg continue to promote fears of "overpopulation," describing the imaginary scourge as the world's most pressing problem during a secret meeting that leaked to the press in 2009.[43]

As the irrefutable scientific fact of global cooling morphed into the irrefutable scientific fact of global warming during the 1980s and '90s, left-wing politicians incorporated Ehrlich's Malthusian musings into their new doomsday theory. In his 1992 book *Earth in the Balance*, Senator Al Gore asserted, "No goal is more crucial to healing the global environment than stabilizing human population."[44]

In 1997, Vice President Gore repeated this claim during a White House conference on global warming. While industrialized nations had "stabilized" their birth rates, Gore contended, through contraceptives and abortion, poorer countries in Africa and Asia had continued to have babies at unacceptably high rates. So Gore proposed a "Global Marshall Plan" to kill those poor brown babies in the womb through abortion and to prevent their conception in the first place by subsidizing contraceptives in poor countries.[45]

Al Gore continued to promote population control into the 2010s. During a speech to a New York audience in 2011, Gore disguised his advocacy of aborting African babies as "fertility management" and "educating and empowering girls and women," but even the liberal *Los Angeles Times* admitted that these euphemisms served only to make the "touchy topic" of population control more palatable.[46]

In 2019, during his second bid for president, Democratic Senator Bernie Sanders called for similar measures in poor countries. "Empowering women and educating everyone on the need to curb population growth seems a reasonable campaign to enact," claimed an audience member at CNN's climate change town hall. "Would you be courageous enough to discuss this issue and make it a key feature of a plan to address climate catastrophe?" she asked, introducing a new degree of hysteria to the allegedly scientific issue that began as "global cooling" before reversing into "global warming," then morphing into "climate change," and finally attaining the dramatic epithet "catastrophe."[47]

"The answer is yes," affirmed Bernie, who had already endorsed the Green New Deal (GND), a $93 trillion proposal by socialist politician Alexandria Ocasio-Cortez to upend American society in the name of saving the planet.[48] Ocasio-Cortez used apocalyptic environmental theories to justify the legislation, but her plan extended far beyond environmental measures.

In a Green New Deal fact sheet, AOC explained that the GND would guarantee the right to "a job with a family-sustaining wage, family and medical leave, vacations, and retirement security," "high-quality education, including higher education and trade schools," "healthy food," "high-quality health care," "safe-affordable, adequate housing," and "economic security for all who are unable or *unwilling* to work" (emphasis mine).[49] The freshman congressman soon removed the outline from her website, recognizing perhaps that a guaranteed income for deadbeats might not play in Peoria.[50]

But the formal House resolution on the Green New Deal did not significantly depart from the deleted FAQ page. It preserved universal entitlements to "high-quality health care," "affordable, safe, and adequate housing," and "economic security," as well as revolutionary plans to upgrade "all existing buildings in the United States." It promised "to promote justice and equity by stopping current, preventing future, and repairing historic oppression of indigenous peoples, communities of color, migrant communities, deindustrialized communities, depopulated rural communities, the poor, low-income workers, women, the elderly, the unhoused," and other allegedly aggrieved groups without ever specifying how these people had been "oppressed" and what exactly their oppression had to do with global warming—or global cooling, climate change, climate catastrophe, or whichever jargon the radicals preferred that week.[51]

No matter what the latest "science" is, and however much it may contradict the previous "science," it seems always to require that we breed less, eat less, move less, and dispute less. We must always do the opposite of whatever we have done in the past. The earth may be heating up or cooling down or deceitfully appearing to stay the same, but whatever the weather, the radicals demand we cede more control to experts—provided, of course, that those experts toe the party line.

The sudden popularity of the phrase "scientific consensus" shows how thoroughly political correctness has inverted intellectual life. The phrase rarely if ever appeared in literature, scientific or otherwise, before the 1970s. After a brief dip in popularity during the Reagan era, its use skyrocketed during the 1990s and 2000s.[52] The new phrase reflected a new, politically correct understanding of both politics and science. Politics, once conducted through republican government and consensus, increasingly outsourced rule to purportedly apolitical experts. Meanwhile scientific inquiry, once undertaken by clinical experts, began to rely on popular support for legitimacy.

For decades alarmists have defended their prophecies of earth's imminent destruction by noting that "97 percent of scientists" agree with their doomsday views. NASA makes this claim almost verbatim in the first sentence of an article titled, "Scientific Consensus: Earth's Climate Is Warming." The space agency asserts, "Multiple studies published in peer-reviewed scientific journals show that 97 percent or more of actively publishing climate scientists agree: climate-warming trends over the past century are extremely likely due to human activities."[53]

As the conservative Heartland Institute observed in its 2015 analysis *Why Scientists Disagree about Global Warming*, NASA cited four surveys to arrive at the famous 97 percent figure, but a closer look at those reports reveals that the alleged consensus rests on shaky scientific ground. The space agency cites historian Naomi Oreskes, who in turn cites abstracts of scientific papers, many of which either begin with the premise of catastrophic, man-made global warming or else mention it only in passing.[54]

NASA then cites John Cook, a professor of "cognitive science" better known for his blogs than his scholarly publications, who claims to have discovered 97.1 percent agreement on catastrophic warming among scientists.[55] But a paper published in *Science & Education* debunked that statistic, finding instead that just 1 percent of papers addressing that issue and 0.3 of papers consulted overall endorsed that hypothesis.[56]

A third study, by Maggie Zimmerman, consisted of a two-minute online survey sent to ten thousand random scientists, three thousand of whom responded. Zimmerman ignored responses from scientists whose fields of study might lead them to conclude that the sun, rather than industry, had caused the warming.[57] A fourth study, from William Anderegg presumes that all scientists who had not explicitly refuted the Intergovernmental Panel on Climate Change had thereby endorsed the body's extreme conclusions.[58]

Regardless of how and why the mercury in the thermometer rises or falls, alarmist and skeptic alike must admit the political nature of the debate, which from the beginning has revolved around appeals to popular consensus by governmental bodies, who always seem to reach the same policy conclusions no matter what the data show.

Conservatives have generally attempted to refute their opponents' pseudo-scientific arguments on scientific grounds. When leftists base their power grabs on supposedly catastrophic global warming, conservatives contest the temperature. When the radicals rely on the China virus to justify their political demands, conservatives debate the lethality of the epidemic and the effectiveness of the recommended health measures. But while the Left's dubious scientific claims may indeed merit such skepticism, conservatives give away the game when they quibble over scientific data—an approach that grants their opponents' even more dubious political premises.

When conservatives attack the Green New Deal on the grounds that the earth hasn't really gotten warmer, they tacitly accept the notion that warming would warrant the radical plan. By disparaging coronavirus lockdowns on the grounds that 99.7 percent of people infected with the virus survive, they grant that a lower rate of survival would merit the unprecedented upheaval of our political system.[59]

Even after decades of politically correct chicanery, there remains an alternative to this lose-lose scenario: the defense of the traditional order.

Perhaps warmer weather threatens civilization; perhaps it does not. Maybe the coronavirus poses an unprecedented threat to human life; maybe not. In any event, doctor dictators and expert technocrats have no right to demand that we acquiesce to their every whim.

A free people may welcome the advice of specialists, but we must also consider other, non-"scientific" factors, including the effects of a given policy on the economy, national security, popular culture, civil rights, social relations, and myriad other facets of our republic. Even if "climate change" really could destroy the world by 2031, as Alexandria Ocasio-Cortez claims, or even by 2021, as Britain's Prince Charles has claimed, "science" remains the handmaiden of philosophy, and in a free republic the people must set the nation's course.[60]

The radicals of the 1960s did not demand deference to the proclamations of established experts. On the contrary, they attempted to undermine the authority of the establishment by questioning all received opinion. As the arch-hippy Timothy Leary put it, "Think for yourself, and question authority."[61] From the 1920s to the 1980s, radicals questioned and thereby subverted virtually every established standard in religion, sex, education, behavior, dress, and politics primarily through new standards of speech. During those decades of radical progress, conservatives failed to defend established authority, and many did not even try, preferring the new culture of openness to the old rigidities.

By the 2010s, the new anti-standard of political correctness had pervaded all aspects of life. Even the allegedly apolitical field of scientific research could not resist the new, politically correct rules. Cultural revolutionaries had brought to heel science itself, which they subsequently invoked to legitimize their ideological claims. A movement that undertook the "ruthless criticism of all that exists" had turned even established authority to its own ends. The radicals had not only undermined the old order; they had replaced it.

CHAPTER 15

THE PURGE

On January 7, 2021, the world's most popular social network de-platformed the president of the United States.[1] "We believe the risks of allowing the president to continue to use our service during this period are simply too great," wrote Facebook CEO Mark Zuckerberg, who also suspended the president from Instagram.[2]

Twitter permanently banned the president the following day.[3] Although Twitter boasts just a fraction of Facebook's active monthly users—340 million to 2.7 billion—the smaller social network has proven popular among journalists and politicians, amplifying its power to shape public opinion.[4] President Trump had long relied on Twitter to circumvent hostile news outlets and communicate directly with his supporters through pithy and often eccentric messages, which had the add-on effect of commanding the attention of journalists, who then relayed his remarks verbatim through mainstream media, if only to criticize or marvel at them. The strategy served him well as an instrument both of retail politics and of international diplomacy—that is, until Twitter censored him.[5]

"After close review of recent Tweets from the @realDonaldTrump account and the context around them—specifically how they are being received and interpreted on and off Twitter," the company explained, "we have permanently suspended the account due to the risk of further incitement of violence."[6] At the time of Trump's suspension, Iran's Supreme Leader Ayatollah Khamenei continued to enjoy use of his Twitter account, which he has repeatedly used to call for the genocide of Jews.[7] Twitter has long defended maintaining the Ayatollah's account on the grounds that world leaders constitute a special category and may therefore violate the company's ever-changing speech code. But while the network affords this privilege to genocidal foreign dictators, it would not extend the same courtesy to the sitting U.S. president.

When Twitter stripped the president of his personal account, Trump took to his official White House handle (@POTUS) to protest the company's decision. "As I have been saying for a long time, Twitter has gone further and further in banning free speech, and tonight, Twitter employees have coordinated with the Democrats and the Radical Left in removing my account from their platform to silence me—and YOU," the president tweeted, "the 75,000,000 great patriots who voted for me." Trump went on to explain that Twitter had exploited a legal loophole in Section 230 of the Communications Decency Act, a 1996 law that protected internet service providers from the legal liabilities incurred by traditional publishers. Twitter had claimed to be a neutral technology platform for the purpose of legal protection but behaved like a publisher when it censored politically incorrect views. Trump noted that under the guise of free speech Twitter had established a rigid system for the enforcement of leftist orthodoxy.[8] Within minutes the platform banned his presidential account as well.[9]

Trump next took to his campaign account, which soon met the same fate. Meanwhile, prominent Trump supporters on the platform noticed a significant and steady drop in their followers, with some losing tens of thousands at a clip.[10] The mass censorship prompted many conservatives to open accounts on Parler, a rival platform that distinguished itself as a safe haven for "free speech."[11] But no sooner had many conservatives opened their Parler accounts than Google announced it would ban the new social media platform from its app store, effectively prohibiting access to Parler on the 2.5 billion active Android devices in the world.[12] Apple soon followed suit, demanding that Parler police the speech of its users or else face deletion from the platform, which serves an estimated 1.4 billion iPhones and other devices worldwide.[13]

"We want to be clear that Parler is in fact responsible for all the user generated content present on your service and for ensuring that this content meets App Store requirements for the safety and protection of our users," read Apple's letter to Parler.[14] Ironically, the tech giant insisted on holding Parler to the very standard Apple itself sought to evade by claiming Section 230 protections.

The next day, Apple booted Parler from its App Store, relegating users to accessing the platform through traditional web browsers.[15] Even that accommodation disappeared the following day, when Amazon announced that it would withdraw Parler's web hosting. "Recently, we've seen a steady increase in this violent content on your website, all of which violates our terms," read an email to Parler from the Amazon Web Services "Trust and Safety" team. "It's clear that Parler does not have an effective process to comply with the AWS terms of service."[16] The website was offline within a day.

Meanwhile, the comedienne Kathy Griffin tweeted a photo of herself holding a likeness of President Trump's bloodied, decapitated head.[17] The phrase "Hang Pence," referring to the vice president, trended a few days later.[18] Twitter did not receive any notices from Apple, Google, or anyone else threatening to sever their professional relationship. The platform did not even remove Griffin's graphic tweet, which she had first posted in 2017. The technology giants' tacit policy had become clear: speech would be tolerated or censored according to ideological content.

For years, many self-styled conservatives defended Big Tech censorship on putatively libertarian grounds. They may have considered the technological tyranny foolish or even un-American, but they insisted that "private companies" had the right to censor whomever they pleased. Never mind that Google, Apple, Facebook, and other publicly traded tech giants are some of the largest and most powerful companies in the history of the world.[19] The real threat, insisted conservative defenders of Big Tech, came from the government. It would be foolish, they argued, to wield political power to combat actual leftist censorship of conservatives today because then leftists might theoretically wield that same state power to censor conservatives tomorrow. In the long run it would benefit the cause of free speech, they advised, to leave the tech oligarchs to censor as they pleased. If conservatives objected to the way Jack Dorsey ran his company, they ought to build their own Twitter.

But when conservatives did build their own Twitter, Big Tech banned it—twice. Apple and Google controlled 99 percent of the mobile operating system market.[20] The decision to spike Parler and the earlier Twitter alternative Gab from those platforms all but ensured the social networks' failure.[21] According to the logic of Big Tech's conservative apologists, Apple and Google had every right to remove Parler from their app stores. If conservatives objected to the way those tech giants ran their platforms, the argument followed, they ought simply to make their own operating systems.

But if those operating systems required money, conservatives might run into a snag. As Facebook and Twitter cut off the president's channels of communications, the payment processor Shopify shut down his ability to engage in commerce online. "Based on recent events," declared a Shopify spokesman, "we have determined that the actions by President Donald J. Trump violate our Acceptable Use Policy, which prohibits promotion or support of organizations, platforms, or people that threaten or condone violence to further a cause."[22] PayPal, the world's largest payment processor, also shut down an account indirectly related to the president.[23]

The already implausible suggestion that conservatives "build their own Twitter" proved impossible. Gab, the first attempt at such an undertaking, fizzled when it lost access to its payment processor, blogging platform, e-commerce service, app stores, web host, and even domain registrar.[24] Perhaps Big Tech's apologists expected conservatives to build their own internet. Perhaps they expected them to build their own government.

A group of foolhardy right-wingers seemed to attempt just that on January 6, 2021, when a small number of Trump rally attendees broke away from a peaceful gathering on the National Mall to storm the U.S. Capitol.[25] The riot was less a *coup d'état* than a *cri de coeur*, a directionless mob rather than an insurrection. When the rioters breached the building and forced legislators and staff into hiding, they did not declare a new government and enact new laws. Instead, they posed for photographs while trashing House Speaker Nancy Pelosi's office.[26]

Police officers at the Capitol shot and killed Ashli Babbitt, an Air Force veteran and Trump supporter, as she attempted to enter a secure area of the building. Capitol Police officer Brian Sicknick died the following day, though investigators could not determine even months after the riot whether his death had any connection to the day's events.[27] Although firearms and explosives were later found on the Capitol grounds and at the headquarters of the Republican and Democratic national committees, no one else died from the day's violence.[28] Still, Big Tech quickly used the riot as a pretext for censoring and de-platforming tens of thousands of right-wingers.[29]

Judging by the reaction, one might conclude that the right-wing rioters had introduced violence to American politics. The entire liberal establishment seemed to have forgotten not only that the leftist organizations Black Lives Matter and Antifa had spent much of 2020 burning down cities coast to coast, but also that they had often enjoyed the explicit support of prominent liberals in the media and even elected office.

Leftist rioters killed dozens of people during nationwide attacks that burned countless businesses and sometimes whole neighborhoods to the ground during BLM demonstrations.[30] On CNN, Chris Cuomo justified the violence, demanding, "Please, show me where it says protesters are supposed to be polite and peaceful."[31] Cuomo apparently could not recall the First Amendment to the United States Constitution, which guarantees "the right of the people peaceably to assemble."[32]

Presidential candidate Kamala Harris defended the violence even more forcefully, tweeting a fundraising link encouraging her followers to help bail the leftist rioters out of jail.[33] Many staffers for candidate Joe Biden joined her in supporting the bail fund, which around the same time also helped to secure the release of a man charged with raping an eight-year-old girl.[34] Neither Harris nor the Biden staffers lost access to their accounts on Twitter, which had shortened its own profile biography to the hashtag "Black Lives Matter."[35]

As the BLM riots raged for months, few prominent leftists condemned them and many encouraged the mayhem. As the Capitol riot roiled for hours, every prominent conservative in the country up to and including President Trump condemned it. Then, in the name of public safety and democracy, a handful of Silicon Valley oligarchs censored the duly elected president of the United States.

Had conservative politicians pursued sensible regulation of Big Tech over the course of Trump's presidency, perhaps they could have staved off the great social media purge a while longer. Republican legislators might have stripped the technology giants of their Section 230 protections during their two years of unified government. Even after Democrats took back the House of Representatives, the Trump administration might have pushed to break up the corporations through the Department of Justice and existing antitrust law.

Google claims roughly 90 percent of search engine market share. One company controls the flow of information around the internet, which serves as the modern-day public square.[36] Moreover, many social media platforms attracted a critical mass of users under the fraudulent pretext that they would be able to read and write what they wished, as Attorney General Bill Barr observed during an interview in June of 2020.[37]

Republican legislators dragged tech moguls before public committee hearings and chewed them out for a few hours at a time in pursuit of a video clip or two to use in campaign advertisements. But even the fiercest hearings failed to result in substantive reform, perhaps because those same technology giants donated to the campaigns of the very legislators who vilified them with such gusto on camera. Tired slogans regarding the sacred "free speech" rights of these multinational behemoths mollified conservative voters and protected the tech giants, who expressed their gratitude by unleashing a wave of censorship against conservatives in early 2021.

But the cowardice of Republican legislators to take on their Big Tech benefactors is almost beside the point. Conservatives failed to protect their place in the public square because they remained wedded to an abstract understanding of "free speech" and failed to acknowledge the inevitability of standards in society. Does anyone dispute Instagram's right to ban pornography on its platform?[38] How about if Jdate, a popular Jewish dating app, decided to prohibit Holocaust denial on its service?

Social media platforms have not only a right but also a responsibility to provide their users with a pleasant experience. Google and Apple may have exploited the presence of Nazi rhetoric on Gab as an excuse to ban any even vaguely right-leaning platform from the Internet, but even Gab's executives acknowledged the problem and attempted to minimize the presence of neo-Nazi figures on the website.[39]

This right to define the boundaries of discourse extends not just to the "private sector" of corporations but also to the "public sector" of society as a whole. Before the internet took the public square into the digital realm, politicians fixed the parameters of the literal public square. In the United States, elected officials set the rules for town hall meetings with constituents, a tradition that dates back to seventeenth-century New England.

If ejection from Twitter seems like heavy-handed punishment for falling afoul of the speech police, one can only imagine how the colonist Thomas Morton felt when Governor Bradford banished him from the continent for having composed "sundry rhymes and verses, some tending to lasciviousness." Bradford considered executing Morton but ultimately settled on the more lenient policy of marooning him on a nearby island until an English ship could take him back to Britain.[40]

The Alien Registration Act of 1940, popularly known as the Smith Act, made it illegal to "knowingly or willfully advocate, abet, advise or teach the . . . desirability or propriety of overthrowing the Government of the United States or of any state by force or violence . . . or for anyone to affiliate with any such organization."[41] The government prosecuted hundreds of communists under the law over the ensuing two decades, during which time Hollywood blacklisted countless communist entertainers from the film industry as well.[42] Conservatives during that era understood that the free marketplace of ideas necessarily involves limits.

Even as recently as the Clinton administration, both conservatives and progressives acknowledged the right and responsibility of citizens to police the boundaries of the public square. As the internet grew to take on a larger role in public life, President Bill Clinton signed into law the Child Online Protection Act (COPA) of 1998 with the support of a Republican House and Democrat Senate. The Communications Decency Act itself, now the focus of many efforts to combat Big Tech, attempted to regulate pornography on the internet. But COPA went further. The law sought to restrict minors' access to material that appealed to "prurient interest" as judged by "contemporary community standards," a category more expansive than mere obscenity.[43] Years of litigation stalled implementation of the law until political interest waned, but as recently as the late 1990s both the Right and Left in America recognized that all speech regimes, no matter how free, observe boundaries.[44]

Two decades later, one doubts that either party would support COPA. Popular support on the Left for Drag Queen Story Hour and even "drag kids" dispels any hope that Democrats might support the suppression of prurient material online. Meanwhile, the gradual reduction of conservative political philosophy to slogans such as "free speech absolutism" and "small government" has made laws like COPA unthinkable to many on the Right. But the marriage of right-wing permissiveness and left-wing decadence did not give birth to an idyllic era of "free speech" from the ruins of the old standards. Instead, it simply outsourced the setting of standards to a handful of unaccountable radicals in Silicon Valley.

The de-platforming of the president surprised and worried even some prominent liberals, who recognized for the first time the enormous change in the character of the American regime. "In Pulling Trump's Megaphone, Twitter Shows Where Power Now Lies," the *New York Times* blared.[45] Kevin Roose, the *Times*'s technology columnist, had long cheered Big Tech's creeping censorship of conservatives.[46] But even he worried what the oligarchs' willingness and ability to censor the president meant for American democracy. "Mr. Trump's muzzling provides a clarifying lesson in where power resides in our digital society," wrote Roose, "not just in the precedent of law or the checks and balances of government, but in the ability to deny access to the platforms that shape our public discourse."[47]

The American people never elected Jack Dorsey or Mark Zuckerberg to any office. Their names have never even appeared on a ballot. But, as Roose observes, "they have a kind of authority that no elected official on earth can claim," and "this power appears mostly in subtle and unspoken ways."[48] Even the ironically named American Civil Liberties Union, which once advocated a broad view of free speech but more recently has defended censorship, recognized the dangers posed by Zuckerberg and Dorsey's decision.[49]

"We understand the desire to permanently suspend him now," wrote ACLU lawyer Kate Ruane, "but it should concern everyone when companies like Facebook and Twitter wield unchecked power to remove people from platforms that have become indispensable for the speech of billions—especially when political realities make those decisions easier."[50] Facebook and Twitter, like Amazon, Google, and Apple, are not merely "private companies" entitled to do whatever they please. They are multinational colossi that control public discourse in the United States and around the world. The loss of access to these platforms constitutes high-tech ostracism and the practical removal from public life. And in a republic, whoever controls speech controls politics.

As Big Tech purged some of the most prominent conservatives in the country, the hashtag "1984 is here" trended on Twitter.[51] The president's son, Donald Trump Jr., tweeted, "We are living Orwell's 1984. Free-speech no longer exists in America. It died with big tech and what's left is only there for a chosen few."[52] He reiterated his point the following day, tweeting to his dwindling followers, "Big tech has totally eliminated the notion of free speech in America."[53] But Big Tech had not so much eliminated the notion of free speech in America as it had eliminated the American notion of free speech.

No American in the 1950s could have imagined facing censorship or professional reprisals for supporting the duly elected president, but every American could expect to endure ostracism for harboring communist sympathies, and many did. Today, T-shirts bearing the likeness of the communist revolutionary Che Guevara have so proliferated on college campuses as to become cliché, whereas the possession of "Make America Great Again" hats has gotten conservative students suspended from school.[54]

Is America's speech regime really less "free" today than it was in the past? Communists today may speak more freely than they could in the 1950s under the Smith Act. Dishonest critics of the federal government may speak more freely than they could in the 1790s under the Alien and Sedition Acts. Lechers may speak more freely than their lascivious forebears who endured Governor Bradford's puritanical rule in the 1620s. Leftists, liars, and libertines all enjoy greater freedom of speech today than ever before in our country's history.

Other groups have witnessed an abridgment of their freedom to speak. Conservatives must hold their tongues more often than in years past lest they incur the wrath not of the government, but of the Big Tech tyrants who control the public square. This privatization of speech policing marks a departure from America's traditional method of setting standards through the political process, and conservatives themselves helped to hasten the shift.

When the Second Wave feminists of the 1970s declared that "the personal is the political," they opened up the most intimate aspects of life to public scrutiny while at the same time removing controversial political questions from the realm of legitimate debate, most notably in the Supreme Court's invention of a right to abortion in *Roe v. Wade*. Conservatives responded to this inversion by narrowing the political realm further still through the attacks on "big government" and paeans to the "private sector."

For many conservatives of the late twentieth and early twenty-first centuries, Big Business could do no wrong, and none dared question the "invisible hand" of the "free market."[55] This deference to "the market" as paramount moral arbiter rather than as an instrument conducive to human flourishing has made for the Right its own extra-political idol. Where Barry Goldwater had once enjoined conservatives to "henceforth make war on all monopolies—whether corporate or union" because "the enemy of freedom is unrestrained power," his political descendants saw no danger in shilling for massive corporations so long as it helped to keep the government "small."[56]

"Small government" cannot rule a nation that spans from sea to shining sea and beyond into imperial territories that stretch from Guam to Puerto Rico. The United States operates a military center known as AFRICOM, short for "Africa Command," out of Stuttgart, Germany, despite the lack of U.S. states anywhere in either Europe or Africa.[57] "Small government" cannot support a global empire. But the frivolous dichotomy between "big" and "small" government distracted conservatives from the more important distinction between limited and unlimited government, to which Goldwater referred in his invective against "unrestrained power."[58]

The U.S. Constitution once limited government power through a complex system of checks and balances. James Madison described the difficulty with which he and his fellow framers had constructed that system in *The Federalist*. "You must first enable the government to control the governed," he explained, "and in the next place oblige it to control itself."[59] But progressives of the early twentieth century upended the old system and abolished many of its limits in a concerted effort to unleash the government's ability to effect "progress."[60]

At the same time, radicals recognized that cultural factors such as art, ritual, and language imposed limits on "progress" just as surely as laws and constitutions. So they levied a "war of position" to infiltrate and transform the institutions that shape culture.[61] This "long march through the institutions" required a campaign of "ruthless criticism" to crack the conservative "cultural hegemony" that impeded the progressives' designs.

The cultural revolutionaries promoted a radical skepticism that aimed to "deconstruct" the allegedly oppressive culture of their conservative foes, which they then replaced with ever more rigid speech codes that perverted and more often inverted the old standards that the radicals had overthrown. This new orthodoxy acquired the name "political correctness," an ironic euphemism derived from old-line communists, and politically correct radicals enforced their new code with every bit as much zeal as had the conservative cultural hegemons they supplanted—more so, in fact, as the radicals had cleared away many of the obstacles that had circumscribed their predecessors' power.

After decades of suppressing conservatives' voices in the classroom, the boardroom, Hollywood, Silicon Valley, the bureaucracy, the press, and social media, among other venues, political correctness reached its apotheosis: a handful of radical elites, unfettered from all constraints save their own orthodoxy, left even the duly elected president of the United States speechless.

BACK TO METHUSELAH

"Listen," the Serpent instructed Eve. "I will tell you a great secret. I am very subtle; and I have thought and thought and thought. And I am very wilful, and must have what I want; and I have willed and willed and willed. And I have eaten strange things: stones and apples that you are afraid to eat."[1] President Kennedy never borrowed that diabolical line from George Bernard Shaw's play *Back to Methuselah*, nor did any of the politicians whom Kennedy inspired in the decades that followed. But the socialist playwright's reflection on subtlety, contemplation, and willfulness helps to explain how the Serpent and his own ideological heirs have been able to implement their dream of "things that never were."[2]

Political correctness did not spring into existence all at once, nor did stupid people accidentally foist it upon us. Subtle thinkers have imposed this new speech code upon society over the course of many decades, trading the fruits of our cultural inheritance for the forbidden fruit of its inversion. As we have seen, even scholars sympathetic to political correctness acknowledge that the phrase derives from the rhetoric of communists, who embrace in the words of Whittaker Chambers "the great alternative faith of mankind."[3] The Chinese communist leader Mao Tse-tung popularized the notion of political "correctness" with the official translation of his *Little Red Book* into English in 1966, but Western Marxists had introduced the concepts that came to constitute political correctness decades earlier.

In 1843, Karl Marx called for the "ruthless criticism of all that exists." His most influential disciples understood that political revolution required cultural upheaval, which in turn demanded the disillusionment of the people with the prevailing culture. Georg Lukács advanced this effort through his writings and as culture minister of the short-lived Hungarian Soviet Republic.[4] Herbert Marcuse, Erich Fromm, Max Horkheimer, and other intellectuals of the Frankfurt School contributed to the campaign by developing an entire academic discipline oriented toward critiquing and transforming society rather than merely understanding it.[5] They called this approach, fittingly, Critical Theory.

Preeminent among these thinkers and statesmen was Antonio Gramsci, the Italian Communist Party leader who bequeathed to Western Marxism the concept of "cultural hegemony," the subtle and pervasive mode by which a ruling class controls society. Gramsci proposed two strategies for achieving hegemony: wars of maneuver and wars of position. The former entailed direct confrontation between the revolutionary and the established value systems. The latter involved the subtler strategy of infiltrating the institutions that shape culture.

The first rumblings of this cultural upheaval occurred largely out of public view, but a handful of political prophets sensed the shift, George Orwell and Aldous Huxley most notable among them. Orwell, a democratic socialist, envisioned a dystopian future in which the totalitarian regime controlled its subjects' thoughts through the manipulation of language, historical revision, and outright censorship. When social media platforms censored and de-platformed the sitting president of the United States in January of 2021, Orwell's *Nineteen Eighty-Four* rose once again to the top of the bestseller charts, more than seven decades after it debuted.[6]

Orwell's teacher Aldous Huxley envisioned a different sort of dystopian future, in which the dominant regime ruled not through the suppression of its subjects' desires, but rather through the encouragement of their basest appetites. The World State in *Brave New World* plies its people with drugs and casual sex to keep them placated and submissive.

Sex and drugs took center stage during the cultural upheavals of the 1960s, but behind the scenes two influential thinkers returned to the fray. The long-dead Antonio Gramsci helped to guide the revolution from the grave through student radicals such as Rudi Dutschke, who restyled Gramsci's "war of position" as a "long march through the institutions," which Dutschke believed would provide the radicals with the "cultural hegemony" required to enforce their political vision. At the same time, Herbert Marcuse of the Frankfurt School reemerged as the "father of the New Left" through a series of popular and provocative books and essays. Marcuse's most infamous essay from that period called for a system of "repressive tolerance," according to which right-wing arguments would be censored and leftist ideas encouraged.

Marcuse believed that conservatives' cultural hegemony had endowed the oppressed masses with a "false consciousness" that left them ignorant of their own oppression. True liberation required the destruction of the old moral order, which could only be achieved through the censorship of conservative thought and speech.

As we have seen, the Second Wave feminists of the 1970s attempted to overcome this "false consciousness" by hosting "consciousness-raising" meetings during which previously well-adjusted women discovered new reasons to complain. The women's newfound grievances against their husbands and children might have seemed beyond the reach of politics, but according to these feminists and their leader Carol Hanisch, "The personal is political."[7] Only by opening the most intimate details of their private lives to public scrutiny did these women believe they could effect political change.

Like Marcuse, many of these feminists did not think liberation could be left to chance but rather had to be coerced. The French feminist Simone de Beauvoir, for instance, wanted to prohibit women from staying home and raising their own children.[8] If women had that choice, she believed, they would take it, and domestic life did not conduce to liberation. Beauvoir wanted to force women to be free.

At the same time that Marcuse enthralled aggrieved women on the coasts, the broader Frankfurt School project of Critical Theory began to take over the American university. The radical movement colonized traditional academic disciplines such as history and literature, but it also established new fields of study. "Black Studies," "Women's Studies," and "Queer Studies" departments sprang up on campuses around the country. The literary critic Harold Bloom dubbed these pseudo-disciplines collectively the "School of Resentment," and many conservatives refer to them as "grievance studies."[9]

The academic reformers presented their efforts as a means of making curricula more "inclusive," but they soon revealed their exclusionary agenda, notably when Jesse Jackson led a march down Stanford's campus chanting, "Hey hey! Ho ho! Western Civ has got to go!" In the decades that followed, these intellectual vandals defended their perversions of curricula on the grounds of "academic freedom," a dubious concept that conservatives such as William F. Buckley Jr. once dismissed as a "hoax," though his political heirs came to embrace the notion in a cultural retreat that exemplifies the era.

Once the radicals had conquered the academic side of the university, they turned their attention to the administration, which they accused of tolerating a climate of racial hatred and widespread rape. Bogus statistics gave the reformers' claims a scientific sheen, and a series of high-profile hoaxes kept the narrative in the news. To remedy these contrived evils, the student radicals demanded draconian codes to regulate speech and behavior on campus as well as kangaroo courts to mete out mob justice.

In the spring of 1991, President George H. W. Bush addressed the growing issue of political correctness by name during a commencement speech at the University of Michigan, which had seen its own draconian speech code overturned by a federal court two years earlier.[10] After joking about the mob of leftist students that had gathered to heckle him, Bush declared, "The notion of political correctness has ignited controversy across the land and . . . replaces old prejudice with new ones." But President Bush kept most of his focus overseas on the collapse of the

Soviet Union, the ending of the Cold War, and the development of America's economic and military might. He chose largely to ignore the culture wars that were heating up at home.

Two months later, Bush's nomination of Clarence Thomas to the Supreme Court made political correctness a matter of national political importance after Thomas's former colleague Anita Hill alleged that the judge had "sexually harassed" her over the course of their long working relationship across multiple government agencies. Sex scandals have been the undoing of a great many politicians, but Hill's claims did not involve sex—only speech. Regardless, no one corroborated Hill's charges on the record before the Senate Judiciary Committee, and several former colleagues of Thomas and Hill contradicted her claims. Ultimately Thomas put an end to the "national circus" by turning political correctness against his opponents, whom he accused of perpetrating a "high-tech lynching for uppity blacks who in any way deign to think for themselves."

The attacks on Thomas convinced prominent playwright David Mamet to produce *Oleanna*, the first high-profile work of art to confront political correctness by name. The play depicts the confusion that arises from the rapid transformation of speech and behavior codes as well as the cynical way in which political radicals can exploit those shifting standards.

Contrary to the claims of many conservatives, political correctness did not trade "free speech" for "censorship" so much as it traded one set of standards for another, each with its own taboos. The ancient Israelites prohibited utterance of the Holy Name; politically correct moderns censor Mark Twain's use of "the n-word" in *Huckleberry Finn*.[11] The traditional liturgical calendar dedicates February, March, and June to the Holy Family, St. Joseph, and the Sacred Heart of Jesus, respectively; the liturgical calendar of secular liberalism dedicates those months to "Black History," "Women's History," and "Pride," once considered the deadliest of the seven deadly sins, elevated by political correctness to the paramount virtue.

Political correctness accelerated its incursions on the old standards throughout the 1990s and 2000s, notably through the war on Christmas, an assault on traditional religion that the cultural revolutionaries alternately denied and downplayed. They sued cities to remove Nativity displays and then gaslit conservatives into believing the whole campaign was a figment of their imaginations. When those transformative efforts became impossible to deny, the same radicals insisted that the changes were insignificant, unworthy of conservatives' outrage.

In the second decade of the twenty-first century, politically correct reformers justified their demands that grown men be permitted use of women's bathrooms and changing rooms with the same "no big deal" attitude. But if the rise of transgender ideology did not constitute a major cultural shift, why did leftists expend so much time, effort, and treasure promoting it? Gender dysphoria afflicts only a small number of people, but the thorough liberation that the radicals sought required overcoming not merely the oppressive constraints of culture but even the bounds of nature itself.

The gender ideologues justified their demands with pseudo-scientific jargon, and prominent scientists lent an air of authority to the radicals' political claims. Ironically, as political correctness politicized the most private and intimate aspects of citizens' lives, it simultaneously narrowed the scope of politics by declaring left-wing views "scientific" and therefore beyond the realm of legitimate debate. In the 1970s, "science" had determined that the earth was headed for a new ice age, and therefore we must reorder society and government to avert disaster. When "global cooling" reversed course and became "global warming" over the ensuing decades, "science" demanded the same solutions to avoid the opposite calamity.

Politically correct reformers undermined the old standards by appealing to "free speech" and inveighing against "censorship," but no sooner had the radicals cracked the old moral order than they began to enforce a new standard of speech with all the force and rigidity they once claimed to oppose. Political correctness reached its apotheosis during the early weeks of 2021 when corporate enforcers of the new standards took the liberty of censoring the duly elected president of the United States.

Conservatives have failed to thwart political correctness because they mistake it for a campaign of "censorship" against "free speech" rather than a contest between two competing standards of speech and behavior. But even this description does not do justice to the cleverness of political correctness, which aims less to erect new standards than to destroy the old ones. Political correctness may be understood in this way to be a sort of "anti-standard standard," which succeeds just as surely by persuading people to abandon standards altogether—for instance, in the name of "free speech absolutism"—as it does by impelling acquiescence to its ever-changing dictates.

Politically correct radicals may demand that society redefine marriage on the grounds that sex and desire are innate and immutable, or they may justify their plan on the grounds that sex is socially constructed and there are no such things as "men" or "women." The premises on which the radicals base their demands may contradict one another, but no matter which justification they choose, the traditional conception of marriage must be destroyed. In fact, the insistence on mutually contradictory rationales actually furthers the radicals' ends by rendering people, in George Orwell's words, "unwilling and unable to think too deeply on any subject whatsoever." Orwell called this tactic "doublethink," and he credited it with enabling regimes to "arrest the course of history."[12]

As we have seen, conservatives have mustered two responses, both of which have only accelerated the progress of the radicals' campaign. The most conciliatory conservatives have simply gone along, ceding one piece of the culture after another to political correctness. Their more curmudgeonly brethren have refused to abide by political correctness but nonetheless have effectively tolerated it on broadly liberal grounds. "Free speech absolutists" have refused to acknowledge that liberty entails limits, retreating instead to skeptical platitudes upholding licentiousness, which previous generations of conservatives including the Founding Fathers understood to be the very opposite of liberty. William F. Buckley Jr. denounced this sort of political cowardice in God and Man at Yale when he observed, "Skepticism has utility only when it leads to conviction."[13] Unfortunately since Buckley's time, conservatives have lost their conviction, appealing to a neutral liberal order that never existed. Too many conservatives have become liberals, as Richard Weaver defined the liberal: "someone who doubts his premises even while he is acting on them."[14] In the words of Yeats, "The best lack all conviction, while the worst are full of passionate intensity."[15] The old standards never stood a chance.

Conservatives may perhaps recover some of their squandered cultural inheritance, but any such hope requires changing course. First and foremost, conservatives must ditch the tired slogans that they have parroted for decades. There has never been any such thing as absolute "free speech," and conservatives' delusions to the contrary have afforded radicals the opportunity to dismantle the traditional moral order that conservatives purport to uphold.

Thus far, while I have enjoined conservatives to expend less energy defending the abstract right of free speech and to focus more on using that right to say something substantive, I have intentionally avoided prescribing precisely what we ought to say. That topic deserves its own volume, if not several, and I will not attempt to tack on a new conservative governing philosophy as a coda to this study of political correctness. But so as not to be charged with evading the question entirely, I will offer some general principles.

Any substantive conservative vision must begin with an acknowledgment of moral conscience, which is a judgment of reason whereby we recognize the moral quality of concrete acts. This acknowledgment requires the further recognition that good, evil, virtue, and vice are not mere sentiments or superstitions but eternal realities. We can know this fact through the application of right reason and by the light of revelation, neither of which conservatives can afford to forgo in crafting a political vision, no matter how implausible radicals make both guides to action out to be.

As a prudential matter, conservatives must begin their case against political correctness with the practical tradition of free speech as it has existed in America. Such a defense would require that conservatives admit the necessity of just and prudent censorship. In particular, we would need to restore prohibitions against obscenity, which politically correct radicals have long exploited to arouse the people's base passions and undermine their liberty, just as the Founding Fathers feared.

Vague harangues against "cancel culture" miss the mark because they fail to acknowledge the justice of ostracizing certain people and marginalizing certain ideas. All cultures "cancel." In the 1950s, American society "canceled" communists; in the 2020s, it "cancels" anticommunists. If conservatives hope to recover anything akin to traditional standards, they must not only articulate a moral and political vision but also suppress ideologies and organizations that would subvert that vision.

But what exactly do conservatives hope to defend and restore? Even popular panegyrics to "Western civilization" will not suffice. Both Marxism and Albigensianism arose from within Western civilization, yet one suspects conservatives would rather not reestablish either of those ideologies. The tree of Western civilization includes many divergent branches. An effective campaign to disestablish political correctness must be specific about which aspects of "Western civilization" we hope to reemphasize and restore.

In the spring of 2019, conservative writer Sohrab Ahmari published a controversial op-ed in which he denounced "autonomy-maximizing liberalism" and called for "a public square re-ordered to the common good and ultimately to the Highest Good."[16] If conservatives hope to offer an alternative to the new social standard of political correctness, we must first admit that there is such a thing as the common good, that consequently there must be such a thing as the Highest Good, and that both the common good and the Highest Good have played a significant role in the American political tradition. We must then articulate a plausible vision of both the common and Highest Good.

Contrary to popular and hysterical fears of "theocracy," all regimes necessarily recognize and pursue some conception of the good. Political correctness has promoted various slogans as euphemisms to just such an effect. Most recently it has exalted "diversity, equity, and inclusion," and it has installed deans and vice presidents of "diversity, equity, and inclusion" on campus, in government agencies, and throughout corporate

America to perform the sorts of religious and ethical functions once reserved for chaplains and the episcopacy.

When conservatives eschew any political vision of the good, we do not leave each individual free to pursue his own conscience in the supposedly neutral and value-free playing ground of secular liberalism, as many seem to believe. Instead, we give our ideological foes free rein to define and enforce their opposite vision of the good, to which everyone will ultimately be forced to submit or else face censorship and ostracism, as we see occurring now in real time.

One wonders whether conservatives' reluctance to articulate and enforce a political vision of the good derives from their lack of interest in practicing what they would preach. People who do not go to church have little credibility in encouraging others to practice formal religion. People who have never cracked the spine of *The Iliad* or *The Aeneid* cannot persuasively recommend a return to the classics. As political thinkers from Aristotle to the Founding Fathers well understood, virtue is a habit, and no conservative can hope to conserve what he does not himself practice.

It has become fashionable in recent decades to describe America as "an idea." The United States has a creedal aspect to its character, but it is also a real country with geography, traditions, and people. On the Fourth of July, we celebrate the Declaration of Independence, but we also cook hot dogs and drink beer; we contemplate our rights and liberties, but we also remember the specific people and events that have brought us to our present moment. The performance of cherished, inherited rituals is a sturdier defense against the schemes of cultural revolutionaries than a lifetime of abstract philosophizing.

Political correctness has advanced less through abstract theorizing than through practical politics. Gramsci, the godfather of political correctness, founded and led a political party. His intellectual heirs colonized established institutions, from university campuses to corporate boardrooms. Even the academic Marcuse worked for the precursor to the CIA. When one faddish ideology ceases to suit their practical purposes, the cultural revolutionaries trade it for another, regardless of the contradictions between, for instance, feminism and transgenderism. For all of their theorizing, the politically correct radicals of the past century always seemed to prioritize the exercise of power over philosophical purity.

For too long, conservatives have taken Andrew Breitbart's maxim that "politics is downstream of culture" as an excuse to disengage from the political process and squander the power that voters sometimes give them. Culture does indeed influence politics, as Breitbart observed and this book has detailed at length. But politics likewise influences culture, as even the most ardent disciple of the Breitbart Doctrine will admit if you ask him whether the Great Society programs of the 1960s affected crime and family structure among black Americans.[17]

A cursory look at religion in early twenty-first century Germany highlights the cultural consequences of government policy. According to a 2012 survey, the majority of East Germans are atheists, a proportion that falls to 10.3 percent among their godlier countrymen in West Germany.[18] The regional differences among Germans run deeper than variations in bratwurst. From 1945 until 1990, an officially atheistic, communist government dominated East Germany. The previously Christian culture of that region did not flow downstream to convert the political system and the Soviet puppets who ran it. On the contrary, even after the communists' political regime collapsed, the culture of atheism that their political system had created remained.

A neat and tidy distinction between "politics" and "culture" has never existed and never can exist in practice because each influences the other. Any ideology that pretends to separate the two presupposes a narrow definition of politics—the very definition that has helped political correctness thrive. A people's politics and its culture describe much the same thing: how we all get along together. And that question always requires the articulation and enforcement of standards.

Since censorship of conservative speech appears to be on the rise, it may be prudent to anticipate some objections to the arguments set forth in this book, lest its political incorrectness hasten its "cancelation." I suspect the most frequent criticism this book will inspire is the charge of "illiberalism," which I expect to come more from conservatives than progressives. In recent years conservatives have tended to style themselves "liberal," albeit of the "classical" eighteenth-century variety that they contend progressives have betrayed. Putting aside for a moment the wisdom of a "conservative" movement that values liberalism above all else, the charge of illiberalism falls flat.

My most "illiberal" claim is that all societies necessarily have standards. Even the freest of speech regimes has limits. Has some more "liberal" writer suggested otherwise? John Milton, the most famous defender of free speech in the English language, called for the censorship of Catholics in his most influential apologia for free speech. I have never once suggested muzzling mackerel-snappers, not least of all because then I would not be able to publish this book. If this book is "illiberal," then Milton's *Areopagitica* is downright fascist.

John Locke, the "father of liberalism," argued in his *Letter Concerning Toleration* that "those are not at all to be tolerated who deny the being of a God."[19] As I have demonstrated in this book, all regimes necessarily hold certain religious premises. But nowhere have I advocated the outright censorship of atheists. If my views are "illiberal" or "intolerant," they are nevertheless more liberal and tolerant than the opinions that history's most influential liberal philosopher set forth in his treatise on toleration.

Thus acquitted of "illiberalism," I next expect my critics to charge me with propounding a "conspiracy theory." It is ludicrous, they will argue, to trace gender-neutral bathrooms back to the prison notebooks of some Italian communist or the rantings of some deranged Austrian psychologist and his orgasm box. They will deny that Marxist philosophers ever considered matters of culture, as Wikipedia does when it defines "cultural Marxism" as an anti-Semitic conspiracy theory. They will deny the influence of certain thinkers upon others. They will deny the existence of political correctness itself. I fear that in this book I have, at times, made such extensive use of quotation and citation as to approach pedantry and dullness, and for that I beg the reader's forgiveness. But whatever damage those references have done to readability, they should preclude any credible claim of conspiracy theorizing.

I anticipate a third and final objection from conservatives, particularly those steeped in the platitudinous shallows of late twentieth- and early twenty-first-century political thought. They will complain that the acknowledgment and enforcement of standards would somehow make the Right no different from the Left. One expects this line of attack from the sort of conservative who gets a thrill out of "losing with dignity." Like the critics who lob the first objection we described, these fretful conservatives fear that substantive moral vision will cost the Right its "liberalism," which they cherish above all other political qualities.

Such critics misunderstand not just liberalism, as we have seen, but also politics more broadly, which involves not only form but also substance. The same error presents itself when conservatives refer to members of Antifa as "fascists." It is somewhat ironic that members of an organization that styles itself "anti-fascist" should employ the tactics of fascist Blackshirts. But Antifa militants are not fascists; they are communists and anarchists. The groups may resemble one another in form, but they differ in their substantive visions for politics and government.

The focus on form to the exclusion of substance has given rise to some of the glibbest political arguments, typically involving some superficial observation followed by a reference to Adolf Hitler. Both Jack Dorsey and the Führer may have wielded power to suppress speech they found distasteful, but it does not therefore follow that Dorsey is a Nazi. The content of the speech they suppressed matters. George Washington and Hitler both saluted flags, but the flags they saluted represented different countries with different beliefs. Some future conservative movement that acknowledges the necessity of standards in public life will not thereby become left-wing. Standards are not an end unto themselves. The aim of the standards matters too.

Both men and beasts make sounds. The latter can make only noise, but the former is capable of speech, a distinction that separates and elevates him above the rest of creation. This capacity for speech makes man the political animal. We use language to convey what we understand about the world and how we want to live in it. The process of persuasion and education that ensues from that act of speech constitutes politics. If

we are to master our political future, we must not merely demand the
right to speak; more important, we must have something to say.

ACKNOWLEDGMENTS

I must first thank my wife, Alissa, for her support and advice throughout the composition of this book, as well as my son, Simon, whose due date into this world coincided by a stroke of providence or cosmic sadism with the due date given me by the publisher for this manuscript. Incommodious timing aside, I would like to thank Regnery for having the courage to publish this book, as well as my editors, Harry Crocker and Elizabeth Kantor, for their invaluable help and my agent, Frank Breeden, for his guidance. It is a great honor to publish my first book of words with the nation's leading conservative publisher.

I would like to thank especially my friend Cyprien Sarteau, whose peerless insight helped to shape this book's thesis and arguments, along with many other views I've come to hold over the years. My friends and colleagues at The Daily Wire, including Jeremy Boreing, Andrew Klavan, Ben Shapiro, and Caleb Robison, have given me not only their wisdom but also a platform from which to speak, and I am deeply grateful for both. In this regard, I would also like to thank my friends and colleagues at PragerU, Young America's Foundation, and Verdict, including Jonathan Hay, Chad Abbott, and Senator Ted Cruz.

Last but not least, I would like to thank my wonderful parents, Kim and Tim, and the good Lord above for his endless blessings.

GLOSSARY OF JARGON

affirmative action /əˈfərmədiv ˈakSHən/ *n.*: a system of legal discrimination on the basis of race. *I'm sorry, Mrs. Nguyễn. I understand that you and your husband have worked very hard and saved every penny since emigrating from Vietnam, but I'm afraid your son will have to give his spot at Harvard to someone who has faced disadvantage and hardship. I'm sure you would support affirmative action if only you could check your privilege.*

Antifa /ˈan(t)ēˌfä,ˌanˈtēfə/ *n.*: a militant group of communists and anarchists who commit political violence against "fascists" (see: "fascism"). *The conservative journalist Andy Ngô disputed Joe Biden's claim that "Antifa is an idea, not an organization" after the alleged "idea" gave him a concussion and a brain bleed.*[1]

anti-racism /ˌan(t)ēˈrāˌsizəm,ˌanˌtīˈrāˌsizəm/ *n.*: racism against white people. *"In a racist society, it is not enough to be non-racist, we must be anti-racist," explained the communist terrorist Angela Davis.*[2]

assault weapon /ə'sôlt 'wepən/ *n.*: a scary-looking gun that functions in much the same way as any less-scary-looking gun. *"Assault weapons" have proven much more effective at stopping attackers than "retreat weapons."*

Awoman /ā 'wo͞omən/ *n.*: an exclamation uttered at the end of a politically correct prayer. *"Amen and awoman!" bellowed Representative Emanuel Cleaver II, much to the dismay of the etymologists and hermaphrodites in the audience.*

black body /blak 'bädē/ *n.*: a synonym for "black people" popularized by the left-wing writer Ta-Nehisi Coates, who apparently denies that black people also have souls. *If "the Spirit gives life" and "the flesh is of no avail," then doesn't Ta-Nehisi Coates's exclusive focus on the injustice done to "black bodies" undercut his arguments about "white supremacy"?*

Black Lives Matter /blak lahyvz 'ma-tər/ *n.*: a Marxist organization that set multiple American cities on fire during a series of mostly peaceful protests in 2020. *It is unbelievable that in this day and age there remain so many Americans who don't believe that Black Lives Matter, and that's why every corporation, university, politician, government agency, television host, musician, movie star, and athlete alongside most private citizens have been chanting the phrase for months. Unbelievable, isn't it?*

body positivity /'bädē ˌpäzə'tivədē/ *n.*: a social movement designed to invert traditional health guidelines. *How dare you tell me to eat healthy foods and exercise, Doc? Do you think I come to this office once a year to be insulted? It's called "body positivity"—look it up! Now do your job and tell me I'm perfect.*

cancel /'kansəl/ *vtr.*: to ostracize someone for transgressing politically correct orthodoxy. *Though justice be thy plea, consider this, that, in the course of justice, we would all see cancellation: we do pray for mercy; and that same prayer doth teach us all to render the deeds of mercy.*[3]

cisgender /sis'jendər/ *adj.*: a man who understands that he is a man or woman who understands that she is a woman. *Until we rid society of cisgender normativity, people will persist under the hateful and wrongheaded presumption that men ought to consider themselves men and women should believe themselves to be women.*

climate change /'klīmit CHānj/ *n.*: a catch-all euphemism from the early twenty-first century to account for the apparent halt of global warming after the reversal of global cooling. *Yes, the world did indeed get hot when we said it'd get cold, and it stopped warming for a while when we said it'd get hotter. That's all just part of the unpredictable but always catastrophic nature of "climate change." Try disproving that one, jerk.*

colorblindness /'kələr 'blīndnəs/ *n.*: the refusal to judge a person on the basis of his race, once considered an expression of anti-racism, now considered a form of racism. *"I have a dream that my four little children will one day live in a nation where they will not be judged by the color of their skin but by their character," shrieked Martin Luther King in a cold sweat after waking up from his nightmare of a colorblind dystopia.*

court packing /kôrt 'pakiNG/ *v.*: the replacement by Republicans of deceased and retired judges to a court (archaic: an increase in the number of judges on a court). *"It is right for us to remake the Supreme Court to suit our partisan purposes because Republicans have already engaged in court packing by fulfilling their constitutional obligations," the Democrat egghead explained to Alice in Wonderland.*

credible /'kredəb(ə)l/ *adj.*: spurious (archaic: worthy of belief). *Supreme Court Justice Brett Kavanaugh has been credibly accused of genocide after boofing a few too many 'skis with his high school buddies Mark, P.J., and Slobodan Milošević, according to a recent CNN report.*

cultural appropriation /'kəlCH(ə)rəl ə,prōprē'āSH(ə)n/ *n.*: the politically incorrect adoption by white people of foreign customs. *How dare you serve tacos on Cinco de Mayo? Cultural appropriation is a tool of white supremacy.*

cultural erasure /ˈkəlCH(ə)rəl əˈrāSHər/ *n*.: the politically incorrect refusal of white people to adopt foreign customs. *How come you aren't serving tacos? It's Cinco de Mayo! Cultural erasure is a tool of white supremacy.*

decolonize /dēˈkäləˌnīz/ *v*.: the introduction of an invading force (archaic: the withdrawal of an invading force). *In an effort to decolonize the English Department, we are officially banning the works of Shakespeare, Chaucer, Milton, Keats, Donne, Dickens, and all those other invasive Englishmen.*

Dreamer /ˈdrēmər/ *n*.: foreign children under the age of forty-four who legally reside in the United States illegally. *If we deport the Dreamers, who will babysit their grandkids?*

fake news /fāk n(y)o͞oz/ *n*.: news outlets and articles that tell the truth (archaic: news outlets and articles that spread lies). *Leftists accuse President Trump and his supporters of spreading fake news, a term they reclaimed from Trump, who famously leveled the charge at left-wing news outlets, which first popularized the term in 2016 to slander right-wing news outlets.*

fascism /ˈfaSHˌizəm/ *n*.: anything you don't like. *"The word Fascism has now no meaning except in so far as it signifies 'something not desirable,'" observed George Orwell in words one might expect a fascist to use.*

feminism /ˈfeməˌnizəm/ *n*.: a political movement that holds men and women to be indiscernible rather than complementary. *"Pat Robertson thinks feminism is 'a socialist, anti-family political movement that encourages women to leave their husbands, kill their children, practice witchcraft, destroy capitalism and become lesbians'? We'll show him!" the coven cackled before taking to the skies astride their broomsticks.*

fetus /ˈfēdəs/ *n*.: a non-human, non-living clump of cells, from the Latin word for "offspring." *Fetuses don't have any rights, so it's perfectly fine to kill them, unlike bald eagle eggs, the disturbance of which can land you in prison.*

hacked /hakt/ *adj.*: an excuse used to deny responsibility for humiliating material accidentally posted to the internet. *The guy who hacked into Anthony Weiner's Twitter account looks suspiciously like Anthony Weiner.*

happy holidays /ˈhapē ˈhälə͵dāz/ *n.*: an acceptable Christmastime greeting. *You really shouldn't say "merry Christmas." People might start to think you want to impose your religious views on the militant atheists who impose their religious views on the rest of us. Happy holidays!*

hard work /härd wərk/ *n.*: a tool of white supremacy, according to the Smithsonian (archaic: the virtue of diligence).[4] *You think men of all races are capable of and benefit from hard work? Where's your Klan hood, David Duke?*

hate speech /hāt spēCH/ *n.*: any statement, particularly if true, uttered by a conservative. *Conservatives are a bunch of deplorable, irredeemable, bitter-clinging hicks. But worst of all, they condone hate speech!*

humankind /͵(h)yo͞omənˈkīnd/ *n.*: a politically correct alternative for "mankind" that does not emphasize the role of men, who can hardly claim to be human (also: peoplekind, hudaughterkind). *The King James Bible and Oxford English Dictionary consider "man" a gender-neutral term, but my purple-haired friend's blog says otherwise. "Humankind" it is!*

intersectionality /͵in(t)ərsekSHəˈnalədē/ *n.*: a system of privilege whereby one's value corresponds to the number of alleged victim groups in which one can claim membership. *Buddy, your skin color barely puts you on the intersectionality pyramid. Sheila over there? She's a paraplegic Hindu lesbian—way more oppressed than you. That's why she gets special privileges.*

implicit bias /imˈplisit ˈbīəs/ *n.*: unconscious bigotry. *My sensitivity and anti-racism trainings may be expensive, but it's very important to recognize the implicit biases of which you are unaware. Yes, we take payment up front.*

Islamophobia /izˌlämə'fōbēəˌiˌslämə'fōbēə/ *n.*: criticism of the Islamic religion. *Thank goodness for King Jan Sobieski's Islamophobia at the Battle of Vienna. Without it, Western civilization might have been lost forever!*

justice-involved person /'jəstəs in'välvd 'pərs(ə)n/ *n.*: a criminal who has been arrested. *If you keep committing injustices, Johnny, one of these days you'll wind up a justice-involved person!*

Karen /kə'ren/ *n.*: a socially acceptable slur for white women. *Oh boy, here comes that Karen, probably about to ask for the manager. I hate when people who look like her express their grievances!*

Latinx /ˌla'tēˌneksˌlə'tēˌneks/ *adj.*: an English term for people of South and Central American ancestry that originated in the early twenty-first century as a gender-neutral alternative for the Spanish words "Latino" and "Latina." *I don't care what language you "hablar," Fernando. This is America, and here you're an oppressed Latinx!*

literally Hitler /'lidərəlē hit-ler/ *n.*: a political opponent who is not Adolf Hitler; any effective Republican or conservative officeholder. *I may not know much about language or history, but I know one thing: Donald Trump is literally Hitler.*

man /man/ *n.*: a person who may or may not be a woman (archaic: a person who is not a woman). *You see that man over there? His name's Elliot Page. He was nominated for Best Actress at the 2008 Academy Awards. Don't tell me the patriarchy isn't alive and well.*

mansplaining /'manˌsplāniŋ/ *v.*: the process by which men bring about girl-understanding. *Mansplaining is when I tell you how it is, toots.*

manspreading /'man-ˌspre-diŋ/ *v.*: the politically incorrect act of men sitting. *Unless he's got a biologically male uterus, that fellow is going to have to manspread.*

mask /mask/ *n.*: an indispensable tool for the prevention of viral transmission, according to public health officials (archaic: a useless prop that could never prevent viral transmission, according to public health officials). *"There's no reason to be walking around with a mask. When you're in the middle of an outbreak, wearing a mask might make people feel a little bit better and it might even block a* droplet, *but it's not providing the perfect protection that people think that it is. And, often, there are unintended consequences. People keep fiddling with the mask, and they keep touching their face," Dr. Fauci explained before he made everyone wear masks.*

melanin /ˈmelənɪn/ *n.*: natural pigment that endows black people with superior mental, physical, and spiritual qualities, according to one strain of radical thought. *"Melanin comes with compassion. Melanin comes with soul. White people are actually closer to animals, they are the ones that are actually the true savages," the actor Nick Cannon mused in a rant that mirrored Carol Barnes's racist writing in the* Harvard Crimson.

menstruater /ˈmenstrəˌwātr/ *n.*: a woman who may or may not believe herself to be a man. *Menstruater? I hardly know "her"! Because my pronouns are "he" and "him."*

MeToo /ˈmē-ˈtü/ *vtr.*: To destroy a man's reputation with accusations that may or may not be true. *Remember when Tara Reade #MeToo'd Joe Biden by providing relatively quite a lot of evidence that he assaulted her but then the media buried the story? Me too.*

microaggression /ˌmīkrōəˈgreSHən/ *n.*: an excuse of last resort for those who wish to complain. *People who worry about microaggressions usually have never faced macroaggressions.*

mostly peaceful protest /ˈmōs(t)lē ˈpēsfəl ˈprōˌtest/ *n.*: a riot. *We're happy to report that only four people burned to death at last night's mostly peaceful protest for social justice.*

my truth /mī tro͞oTH/ *n.*: falsehood. *"The truth is, you've got my fingerprints on the murder weapon and a video of me stabbing him. But my truth is, I'm innocent!" yelled the serial killer, persuading the woke jury.*

Nazi /ˈnätsē/ *n.*: a person with whom one disagrees. *The Nazis invaded twenty countries and killed millions of people, which reminds me a lot of my opponent's proposal to cut the corporate tax rate.*

nonbinary /nänˈbīnərē/ *adj.*: the condition of a gender ideologue with commitment issues. *The idea that there are only two sexes is ridiculous. I've been nonbinary since the moment my mother and father conceived me.*

nuclear family /ˈnü-klē-ər ˈfam(ə)lē/ *n.*: an oppressive construct of white supremacy designed to oppress marginalized peoples (archaic: the fundamental political unit singularly conducive to human flourishing). *Black Lives Matter promises on its website to "disrupt the Western-prescribed nuclear family structure," but how do they plan to do it? Will it be with the same Molotov cocktails they use to disrupt police stations and small business?*

partner /ˈpärtnər/ *n.*: a term for a lover or spouse that connotes all the romance of an accounting firm. *My partner Aiden and I have been in a rapturously consensual relationship for six months now, and we're thinking about taking it to the next level by getting matching business cards.*

person of color /ˈpərs(ə)n əv ˈkələr/ *n.*: an acceptable term for certain racial minorities. *Only the vilest racist would call a person of color a "colored person."*

sexual preference /ˈsekSH(o͞o)əl ˈpref(ə)rəns/ *n.*: a homophobic slur to describe one's erotic desires. *Unhinged homophobe Amy Coney Barrett once conflated "sexual orientation" with "sexual preference," as if the two were synonyms.*

Queer /kwir/ *adj.*: a slur for homosexuals that became a term of pride for homosexuals that has once again become a slur for homosexuals, but only when uttered by politically incorrect people. *If you want to major in Queer Studies, the first thing you need to know is that only some of you can ever mention the name of this department.*

racism /ˈrāˌsizəm/ *n.*: the refusal to judge people on the basis of their race (archaic: judging people on the basis of race). *One cannot perpetrate racism against white people, Professor Jeffries explained, because they are savage and spiritually deficient.*

reproductive justice /ˌrēprəˈdəktiv ˈjəstəs/ *n.*: infanticide. *Julian Castro made history during his 2020 presidential run by advocating "reproductive justice" for "trans-women" or, in laymen's terms, the right of men to have abortions.*

reproductive rights /ˌrēprəˈdəktiv rīt/ *n.*: the contrived right to stop reproduction. *James Madison enshrined the reproductive rights of* *women to kill their kids just below the penumbras and to the left of the emanations in the U.S. Constitution.*

riot /'rīət/ *n.*: a mostly peaceful protest. *After Antifa clubbed the third Trump supporter to death, some right-wingers began to fight back, inciting a riot.*

science /'sīəns/ *n.*: the incontestable albeit sometimes self-contradictory proclamations of political correctness (archaic: knowledge; a method of empirical observation). *"Believe science," pleaded Andrew Cuomo as he shipped another busload of coronavirus patients to the nursing home.*

sexism /'seksizəm/ *n.*: the bigoted belief that men and women are different. *If not for sexism, Hillary Clinton would have been elected president—if she were likable and had a record of accomplishment.*

slow the spread /slō THə spred/ *v.*: vanquish germs; formerly a tactic to prevent the overwhelming of hospitals during an epidemic (also: flatten the curve). *"Just fifteen more days to slow the spread," the public health official giggled.*

slut-shame /slət SHām/ *v.*: to discourage promiscuity. *Why won't my conscience stop slut-shaming me?*

social distance /'sōSHəl 'distəns/ *n.*: a contradiction in terms that describes the policy of keeping people apart. *"Social distancing" reminds us that we're "together apart" during this war, which is peace, without our freedom, which is slavery, in our ignorance, which is strength.*

social justice /'sōSHəl 'jəstəs/ *n.*: getting what one does not deserve because one is a member of a favored group. *Timmy has taken a real interest in social justice since going to college. He's fighting for safe, segregated spaces for all POCs, the right of trans-women to win girls' track meets, and an Asian quota to help diversify the campus.*

socialism /'sōSHə,lizəm/ *n.*: an inhuman ideology based on a false anthropology that has bred misery wherever tried but which, its supporters insist, will turn out better next time. *I'm sorry the Castros killed your family, Jorge, but if you just watched Michael Moore's movie, I think you'd appreciate the marvels of Cuba's socialist healthcare system.*

systemic racism /sə'stemik 'rā͵sizəm/ *n.*: the refusal to grant special treatment to people on the basis of race. *Until whites, Asians, and Hispanics pay reparations to Kenyan immigrants, systemic racism will endure.*

they /T͟Hā/ *n.*: the singular pronoun in a schizophrenic culture. *They isn't good at grammar.*

toxic masculinity /'täksik ͵maskyə'linədē/ *n.*: the refusal of some men to behave like women. *My date last night was awful! He insisted on picking me up at my apartment, holding the door, and paying for the entire dinner even after I offered to split the bill. He just oozed toxic masculinity.*

transphobia /͵tranz'fōbēə/ *n.*: the bigoted belief that men are not women. *The transphobic father didn't even applaud when Husky Hank (now Helen) followed his daughter into the changing room at the public pool.*

trunalimunumaprzure /trunalimunumaprzure/ *n.*: a key tenet of Joe Biden's first term agenda. *Thank goodness Joe Biden is going to replace that inarticulate boob Donald Trump. Can you believe we went four years without ever once mobilizing trunalimunumaprzure?*

undocumented American /͵ən'däkyə͵men(t)əd ə'merəkən/ *n.*: a foreign national. *Republicans have paid as little attention to undocumented Americans as they have to unsheltered homeowners and immobile drivers.*

unhoused person /͵ən'houzd 'pərs(ə)n/ *n.*: a bum. *Some hard-hearted people actually call the police on unhoused persons instead of having a little compassion and letting them abuse drugs in their own filth.*

vulva-owner /'vəlvə 'ōnər/ *n.*: a woman, not to be confused with "Volvo-owner." *Vulva-owners have been objectified long enough!*

white supremacy /(h)wīt sə'prem ə si/ *n.*: anything leftists don't like (see also: racism, fascism). *My mandatory anti-racism training session with the world-famous Ibram Kendi taught me so much about the reality of white supremacy.*

woman /ˈwʊmən/ *n.*: a person who may or may not be a man (formerly, a person who is not a man). *Femininity is a social construct, and a woman can dress or act however she pleases, but if a boy picks up a Barbie he's a girl.*

woke /wōk/ *adj.*: a semi-ironic in-term that nonetheless denotes earnest adherence to leftist orthodoxy (see also: political correctness). *"Get woke, go broke" betokens an un-woke bloke. No joke.*

WORKS CITED

"100 Largest Companies in the World by Market Capitalization in 2020," Statista, https://www.statista.com/statistics/263264/top-companies-in-the-world-by-market-capitalization/.

"1940 Statement of Principles on Academic Freedom and Tenure." AAUP. www.aaup.org/report/1940-statement-principles-academic-freedom-and-tenure.

"2020 Report to Congress: Executive Summary and Recommendations." U.S.-China Economic and Security Review Commission, December 2020. https://www.uscc.gov/sites/default/files/2020-12/2020_Executive_Summary.pdf.

ABC News. "Dr. Fauci to Muir: 'Universal Wearing of Masks' Necessary to Combat COVID-19: WNT." August 10, 2020. https://www.youtube.com/watch?v=HAFQknk5nwI&feature=youtu.be&t=152

Abington School District v. Schempp. Supreme Court of the United States, 1963.

Abrams v. United States. Supreme Court of the United States, November 10, 1919.

Ahmari, Sohrab. "Against David French-ism." *First Things*, May 29, 2019. https://www.firstthings.com/web-exclusives/2019/05/against-david-french-ism.

Aitken, Peter. "'Hang Mike Pence' Trends on Twitter After Platform Suspends Trump for Risk of 'Incitement of Violence.'" Fox News, January 9, 2021. https://www.foxnews.com/politics/twitter-trending-hang-mike-pence.

Alfino, Mark. "Another Look at the Derrida-Searle Debate." *Philosophy & Rhetoric* 24, no. 2 (1991): 143–152.

"Alger Hiss." FBI. May 18, 2016. www.fbi.gov/history/famous-cases/alger-hiss.

Allen, Charlotte. "What I Saw at Drag Queen Story Hour," *Wall Street Journal*, October 9, 2019. https://www.wsj.com/articles/what-i-saw-at-drag-queen-story-hour-11570661201.

Allen, Henry. "Thinking Inside the Box." *Wall Street Journal*, June 11, 2011. www.wsj.com/articles/SB10001424052702303657404576361683162870042.

Allen, Irving Lewis. "Earlier Uses of Politically (In)Correct." *American Speech* 70 (1995): 110. doi: 10.2307/455878.

Allen, Jonathan. "New York City Marks 10th Anniversary of Smoking Ban." Reuters, March 28, 2013. www.reuters.com/article/us-usa-smoking-newyork/new-york-city-marks-10th-anniversary-of-smoking-ban-idUSBRE92R0UU20130328.

Allen, Karma. "College Student in Baltimore Hit with Additional Charges over Racist Graffiti." ABC News, December 5, 2018. abcnews.go.com/US/college-student-baltimore-hit-additional-charges-racist-graffiti/story?id=59618395.

Andrew, Scottie. "Boy Scouts Support Black Lives Matter and Will Require Some Scouts to Earn Diversity Badge." CNN, June 17, 2020. www.cnn.com/2020/06/17/us/boy-scouts-black-lives-matter-trnd/index.html.

"Anthony S. Fauci, M.D., NIAID Director." National Institutes of Health. https://www.niaid.nih.gov/about/director.

"Antifa Members Talk Protest Tactics: 'We Don't Depend on Cops.'" NBC News, August 19, 2019. www.youtube.com/watch?v=af50-4eI9PA.

Aptheker, Bettina. *The Morning Breaks: The Trial of Angela* Davis. Cornell University Press, 1997. https://www.jstor.org/stable/10.7591/j.ctt5hhog9.

Aquinas, Thomas. *Summa Theologiae*. www.newadvent.org/summa/3162.htm.

Aristotle. *Politics*. Translated by Benjamin Jowett. The Internet Classics Archive, classics.mit.edu/Aristotle/politics.1.one.html.

———. *Politics*. Translated by William Ellis. Project Gutenberg, June 5, 2009. http://www.gutenberg.org/files/6762/6762-h/6762-h.htm.

Ashcroft v. American Civil Liberties Union. Supreme Court of the United States, 2002.

Associated Press. "Goucher College Student Faces Hate Crime Charges for Racist Graffiti, Baltimore County Police Say." *Baltimore Sun*, December 5, 2018. web.archive.org/web/20181205024254/www.baltimoresun.com/news/maryland/crime/bs-md-co-goucher-hate-crime-charges-20181204-20181204-f3w5n7hccbb6hkdrebflm4uljm-story.html.

Associated Press. "Robertson Letter Attacks Feminists." *New York Times*, August 26, 1992. www.nytimes.com/1992/08/26/us/robertson-letter-attacks-feminists.html.

Aufderheide, Patricia. *Beyond PC: Toward a Politics of Understanding*. Graywolf Press, 1992.

Augustine. *On the Trinity*. Translated by Stephen McKenna. Catholic University of America Press, 1963.

Bailey, Sarah Pulliam, and Michelle Boorstein. "St. John's Episcopal Church, Historic Church next to the White House, Set on Fire during Protests." *Washington Post*, June 8, 2020. www.washingtonpost.com/religion/2020/06/05/st-johns-episcopal-church-historic-church-next-white-house-set-fire-during-protests/.

Bambara, Toni Cade. *The Black Woman: An Anthology*. Washington Square, 2005.

Barrett, Lisa Feldman. "When Is Speech Violence?" *New York Times*, July 15, 2017. www.nytimes.com/2017/07/14/opinion/sunday/when-is-speech-violence.html.

Becket, Lois. "At Least 25 Americans Were Killed during Protests and Political Unrest in 2020." *The Guardian*, October 31, 2020. https://www.theguardian.com/world/2020/oct/31/americans-killed-protests-political-unrest-acled.

"Being Antiracist." National Museum of African American History and Culture, October 9, 2020. nmaahc.si.edu/learn/talking-about-race/topics/being-antiracist.

Bellafiore, Robert. "Summary of the Latest Federal Income Tax Data, 2018 Update." Tax Foundation, September 29, 2020. taxfoundation.org/summary-latest-federal-income-tax-data-2018-update/#:~:text=The%20top%201%20percent%20paid,50%20percent%20(3.7%20percent).

Benedict XVI. *The Spirit of the Liturgy.* Ignatius Press, 2014.

Benjamin, Richard M. "The Bizarre Classroom of Dr. Leonard Jeffries." *The Journal of Blacks in Higher Education* 2 (1993): 91. doi: 10.2307/2962577.

Berkowitz, Bill. "'Cultural Marxism' Catching On." Southern Poverty Law Center, January 1, 1970. www.splcenter.org/fighting-hate/intelligence-report/2003/cultural-marxism-catching.

"*Berkowitz v. President Fellows of Harvard College,*" FindLaw, June 6, 2003. caselaw.findlaw.com/ma-court-of-appeals/1376248.html.

Bernstein, Richard. "In Dispute on Bias, Stanford Is Likely to Alter Western Culture Program." *New York Times*, January 19, 1988. www.nytimes.com/1988/01/19/us/in-dispute-on-bias-stanford-is-likely-to-alter-western-culture-program.html.

"Bernie Sanders in Climate Change 'Population Control' Uproar." BBC, September 5, 2019. https://www.bbc.com/news/world-us-canada-49601678.

Bibien1"U2's Bono & Edge: 'Fucking Brilliant.'" YouTube, June 9, 2007. www.youtube.com/watch?v=COlPQlNguvU.

Bickley, John. "The *New York Times* Dropped Millions on Facebook to Advertise the 1619 Project . . . While Trying to Bully Facebook into Censoring Others." The Daily Wire, July 8, 2020. www.dailywire.com/news/the-new-york-times-dropped-millions-on-facebook-to-advertise-the-1619-projectwhile-trying-to-bully-facebook-into-censoring-others.

Bihan-Colleran, Christèle Le. "Feminist Linguistic Theories and 'Political Correctness': Modifying the Discourse on Women?" University of Poitiers, 2020.

"Biography: Anthony S. Fauci, M.D. NAIAID Director." National Institutes of Health. https://web.archive.org/web/20071030171118/http://www3.niaid.nih.gov/about/directors/biography/.

Bishop, Tricia. "Stores Revert to 'Merry Christmas': Wal-Mart Leads Way, Backing Off from 'Happy Holidays.'" *Chicago Tribune*, November 24, 2006. https://web.archive.org/web/20070312200136/http://www.chicagotribune.com/business/bal-te.bz.christmas24nov24,0,7755319.story

Bloom, Allan. *The Closing of the American Mind.* Simon and Schuster, 1987.

Bleyer, Jennifer. "Five Myths about Hanukkah." *Washington Post*, December 2, 2015. https://www.washingtonpost.com/opinions/five-myths-about-hanukkah/2015/12/02/2ea6fc3c-93ae-11e5-8aa0-5d0946560a97_story.html#:~:text=Hanukkah%20is%20an%20important%20Jewish%20holiday.&text=Unlike%20major%20holidays%20such%20as,light%20candles%20for%20eight%20nights.

Bois, Paul. "WATCH: Nick Cannon: White People Are a Little Less,' 'Closer to Animals,' 'True Savages.'" The Daily Wire, July 15, 2020. www.dailywire.com/news/watch-nick-cannon-white-people-are-a-little-less-closer-to-animals-true-savages.

Boldt, David R. "Colder Winters He[ra]ld Dawn of New Ice Age." *Washington Post*, January 11, 1970. https://web.archive.org/web/20150221224323/http://pqasb.pqarchiver.com/washingtonpost_historical/doc/147902052.html?FMT=ABS&FM

TS=&type=historic&date=washingtonpost+%2C+&author=Wash
ington+Post+Staff+Writer%3B+By+David+R.+Boldt&pub=The+Wa
shington+Post%2C+Times+Herald+%281959-1973%29&desc=Co
lder+Winters+Held+Dawn+of+New+Ice+Age&pqatl=
top_retrieves.

Bonn, Tess. "Conservative Journalist Andy Ngo Says Assault Involving
Antifa Resulted in Brain Injury," *The Hill*, July 25, 2019. https://
thehill.com/hilltv/rising/454712-conservative-journal
ist-andy-ngo-says-antifa-attack-resulted-in-brain-injury.

Bowden, John. "Ocasio-Cortez: 'World Will End in 12 Years' If Climate
Change Not Addressed." *The Hill*, January 22, 2019. thehill.com/
policy/energy-environment/426353-ocasio-cortez-the-world-will-en
d-in-12-years-if-we-dont-address.

Bowers v. Hardwick. Supreme Court of the United States, June 30, 1986.

Bradford, William. *Of Plymouth Plantation, 1620–1647. The Complete
Text*. Knopf, 1963.

———. "The Pestilent Morton and His Merry Mount," Bartleby. https://
www.bartleby.com/400/prose/24.html.

Bradner, Eric, et al. "Biden: 'If You Have a Problem Figuring out Whether
You're for Me or Trump, Then You Ain't Black.'" CNN, May 23,
2020. www.cnn.com/2020/05/22/politics/biden-charlamagne-
tha-god-you-aint-black/index.html.

Brandenburg v. Ohio. Supreme Court of the United States, June 8, 1969.

Brandom, Russell. "There Are Now 2.5 Billion Active Android Devices."
The Verge, May 7, 2019. https://www.theverge.
com/2019/5/7/18528297/google-io-2019-android-devices-play-store-
total-number-statistic-keynote.

"A Breakdown of Who Supports and Opposes George Floyd Protests in
US." TRT World, June 4, 2020. https://www.trtworld.com/magazi
ne/a-breakdown-of-who-supports-and-opposes-george-floyd-
protests-in-the-us-36952.

Breslin, Susannah. "Adult Director Max Hardcore Released from
Prison." *Forbes*, February 19, 2012. www.forbes.com/sites/

susannahbreslin/2011/07/21/adult-director-max-hardcore-released-from-prison-2/#745a3aa343e0.

Brickman, William W. "Academic Freedom: Past and Present." *Journal of Thought* 3, no. 3 (July 1968).

Brooks, Jennifer, and Paul Walsh. "St. Olaf: Report of Racist Note on Black Student's Windshield Was 'Fabricated.'" *Star Tribune*, May 11, 2017. www.startribune.com/st-olaf-report-of-racist-note-on-black-student-s-windshield-was-fabricated/421912763/.

Brown, Nell Porter. "'More As People Than Dating Objects.'" *Harvard Magazine*, March 3, 2014. harvardmagazine.com/2011/11/more-as-people-than-dating-objects.

Brown, Spencer. "'Physically Triggered': Internal Emails Show CSULA Faculty in Hysterics over 'Build the Wall' Activism." Young America's Foundation, September 4, 2019. www.yaf.org/news/physically-triggered-internal-emails-show-csula-faculty-in-hysterics-over-build-the-wall-activism/.

Brown, Zoe, et al. "Charges Filed in Connection to Protest of Conservative Speaker at UMKC." KCTV, April 11, 2019. https://www.kctv5.com/news/charges-filed-in-connection-to-protest-of-conservative-speaker-at-umkc/article_7bc44264-5cc7-11e9-be6d-73d3956e6c78.html.

Buchanan, Patrick. "Culture War Speech: Address to the Republican National Convention (17 August 1992)," Voices of Democracy: The U.S. Oratory Project, March 23, 2016. voicesofdemocracy.umd.edu/buchanan-culture-war-speech-speech-text/.

Buckley, William F. *God and Man at Yale*. Regnery Publishing, 1986.

Buden, Boris. "To Make the Long March Short: A Short Commentary on the Two Long Marches That Have Failed Their Emancipatory Promises." *Crisis and Critique*, November 2018. crisiscritique.org/nov2018/boris.pdf.

Bungaard, Henning, et al. "Effectiveness of Adding a Mask Recommendation to Other Public Health Measures to Prevent SARS-CoV-2 Infection in Danish Mask Wearers." *Annals of Internal*

Medicine, November 18, 2020. https://doi.org/10.7326/M20-6817, https://www.acpjournals.org/doi/10.7326/M20-6817.

Burke, Edmund. *Reflections on the Revolution in France*. Project Gutenberg, 2005. https://www.gutenberg.org/files/15679/15679-h/15679-h.htm.

Burnett, Brigette. "BG Police Say Student Lied about Politically Driven Attack." 13ABC Action News, November 17, 2016. www.13abc.com/content/news/BG-police-say-student-lied-about-politically-driven-attack-401814426.html.

Bush, George H. W. "Bush: "Out of These Troubled Times . . . a New World Order." *Washington Post*, September 12, 1990. www.washingtonpost.com/archive/politics/1990/09/12/bush-out-of-these-troubled-times-a-new-world-order/b93b5cf1-e389-4e6a-84b0-85f71bf4c946/.

———. "Remarks Accepting the Presidential Nomination at the Republican National Convention in Houston." The American Presidency Project, August 20, 1992. www.presidency.ucsb.edu/documents/remarks-accepting-the-presidential-nomination-the-republican-national-convention-houston.

———. "Supreme Court Nomination Announcement," C-SPAN. https://www.c-span.org/video/?18649-1/supreme-court-nomination-announcement.

———. "University of Michigan Commencement Speech." C-Span, May 4, 1991. www.c-span.org/video/?17825-1%2Funiversity-michigan-commencement-speech.

———. "User Clip: George H. W. Bush 1988 Acceptance Speech 'Kinder and Gentler' Clip." C-Span, August 18, 1988. www.c-span.org/video/?c4857525%2Fuser-clip-george-h-w-bush-1988-acceptance-speech-kinder-gentler-clip.

Butter, Michael. "There's a Conspiracy Theory That the CIA Invented the Term 'Conspiracy Theory'—Here's Why." The Conversation, November 25, 2020. theconversation.com/theres-a-conspiracy-theory-that-the-cia-invented-the-term-conspiracy-theory-heres-why-132117.

Byrne, Suzy. "Joy Behar Faces Backlash over Old 'African Woman' Halloween Costume." Yahoo!, February 7, 2019. www.yahoo.com/ lifestyle/joy-behar-faces-backlash-old-african-woman-halloween-costume-143659694.html.

Caesar, Chris. "Perspective: Trump Ran against Political Correctness. Now His Team Is Begging for Politeness." *Washington Post*, March 1, 2019. www.washingtonpost.com/posteverything/wp/2017/05/16/ trump-ran-against-political-correctness-now-his-team-is-begging-for-politeness/.

Caldwell, Christopher. *Age of Entitlement: America Since the Sixties.* Simon & Schuster, 2021.

Cameron, Deborah. "Words, Words, Words." *The War of the Words: The Political Correctness Debate.* Edited by Sarah Dunant. Virago Press, 1994.

"Capitol Riots: Pro-Trump Protesters Storm the US Legislature—in Pictures." BBC, January 6, 2021. https://www.bbc.com/news/ world-us-canada-55568131.

Carroll, Lewis. *Through the Looking Glass.* Project Gutenberg, November 2, 2020. www.gutenberg.org/files/12/12-h/12-h.htm.

Chafuen, Alejandro. "The Sad Decline of The Word 'Capitalism.'" *Forbes*, May 1, 2013. www.forbes.com/sites/ alejandrochafuen/2013/05/01/the-sad-decline-of-the-word-capitalism/?sh=271e8847a712.

Chambers, Whittaker. *Witness.* New York: Random House, 1952.

"Changing Attitudes on Same-Sex Marriage." Pew Research Center's Religion & Public Life Project, Pew Research Center, December 31, 2019. www.pewforum.org/fact-sheet/changing-attitudes-on-gay-marriage/.

Chaplinsky v. New Hampshire. Supreme Court of the United States, March 9, 1942.

Chappell, Bill. "Man Who Posed for Photos Sitting at a Desk in Pelosi's Office Has Been Arrested." NPR, January 8, 2021. https://www.npr.org/sections/congress-electoral-college-tally-live-up

dates/2021/01/08/954940681/man-who-posed-for-photos-sitti ng-at-desk-in-pelosis-office-has-been-arrested.

Chesterton, G. K. *Orthodoxy*. Project Gutenberg, September 26, 2005. www.gutenberg.org/cache/epub/130/pg130.html.

"Christmas." Catholic Answers, www.catholic.com/encyclopedia/ christmas.

Churchill, Winston. "Socialism Is the Philosophy of Failure . . ." The Churchill Project, August 16, 2019. winstonchurchill.hillsdale.edu/ socialism-is-the-philosophy-of-failure-winston-churchill/.

Chiorazzi, Anthony. "Harvard's Religious Past." *Harvard Gazette*, July 26, 2019. news.harvard.edu/gazette/story/2016/10/ harvards-religious-past/.

Chisholm v. Georgia. Supreme Court of the United States, February 18, 1793.

Chiu, Allyson. "'They Were Threatening Me and My Family': Tucker Carlson's Home Targeted by Protesters." *Washington Post*, November 9, 2018. www.washingtonpost.com/nation/ 2018/11/08/they-were-threatening-me-my-family- tucker-carlsons-home-targeted-by-protesters/.

Chow, Kat. "'Politically Correct': The Phrase Has Gone from Wisdom to Weapon." NPR, December 15, 2016. www.npr.org/sections/ codeswitch/2016/12/14/505324427/politically-correct- the-phrase-has-gone-from-wisdom-to-weapon.

Churchill, Winston. "We Shall Fight on the Beaches." The International Churchill Society, April 13, 2017. winstonchurchill.org/resources/ speeches/1940-the-finest-hour/we-shall-fight-on-the-beaches/.

Clausewitz, Carl von. *On War*. Princeton University Press, 1989.

Clayworth, Jason. "Lesbian Attorney Was Biased, Argued the Man Sentenced to 16 Years for Burning Gay Pride Flag." *Des Moines Register*, January 19, 2020. www.desmoinesregister.com/ story/news/investigations/2020/01/15/lesbian-attorney-biased- man-sentenced-16-years-burning-gay-pride-flag-argued/4444888002/.

Coates, Ta-Nehisi. *Between the World and Me*. One World, 2015.

Cochrane, Emily, and Aishvarya Kavi. "Romney Marches with Protesters in Washington." *New York Times*, June 7, 2020. https://www.nytimes.com/2020/06/07/us/politics/mitt-romney-george-floyd-protests.html.

Codevilla, Angelo M. "The Rise of Political Correctness." *Claremont Review of Books*, September 2016. claremontreviewofbooks.com/the-rise-of-political-correctness/.

Coen, Joel, and Ethan Coen, directors. *Hail, Caesar!* Universal Pictures, 2016.

Cohen, Anne. "A Very Brief & Exciting History of the C-Word on Television," Refinery29. www.refinery29.com/en-us/2017/06/156630/cunt-c-word-to-describe-someone-profanity-on-tv.

Colapinto, John. *As Nature Made Him*. HarperCollins, 2001.

———. "The True Story of John/Joan." *Rolling Stone*, December 11, 1997.

"Colorado and Washington: Life after Legalization and Regulation." Marijuana Policy Project. www.mpp.org/issues/legalization/colorado-and-washington-life-after-legalization-and-regulation/.

Colarossi, Natalie. "COVID Lockdowns May Have No Clear Benefit vs. Other Voluntary Measures, International Study Shows." *Newsweek*, January 14, 2021. https://www.newsweek.com/covid-lockdowns-have-no-clear-benefit-vs-other-voluntary-measures-international-study-shows-1561656.

Conger, Kate. "Twitter, in Widening Crackdown, Removes Over 70,000 QAnon Accounts." *New York Times*, January 11, 2021. https://www.nytimes.com/2021/01/11/technology/twitter-removes-70000-qanon-accounts.html.

Cook, John. (@johnfocook). "In our study finding 97.1% consensus on human-caused global warming in abstracts. . . ." Twitter, https://twitter.com/johnfocook/status/1199131486580092928.

Cook, James, and James King. *The Three Voyages of Captain James Cook round the World*. Cambridge University Press, 2015.

"The Cooling World." *Newsweek*, April 28, 1975. https://iseethics.files.wordpress.com/2012/06/the-cooling-world-newsweek-april-28-1975.pdf.

Cooper, Helene. "Ahmadinejad, at Columbia, Parries and Puzzles." *New York Times*, September 25, 2007. www.nytimes.com/2007/09/25/world/middleeast/25iran.html.

Cornelius, Earle. "In 1870, Congress Made Christmas Day a Federal Holiday. But Some Still Question Its Constitutionality." LancasterOnline, December 20, 2019. lancasteronline.com/features/in-1870-congress-made-christmas-day-a-federal-holiday-but-some-still-question-its-constitutionality/article_0d8c3634-22a2-11ea-bf1d-2ba3f3a125db.html.

"Coronavirus Disease (COVID-19): Serology." World Health Organization, June 9, 2020. https://web.archive.org/web/20201023093420/https://www.who.int/news-room/q-a-detail/coronavirus-disease-covid-19-serology.

Corsetti, Renato. "A Mother Tongue Mostly Spoken by Fathers." *Language Problems & Language Planning* 20, no. 3 (1996): 263–73. https://www.ingentaconnect.com/content/jbp/lplp/1996/00000020/00000003/art00004.

Cranley, Ellen. "Twitter Changed Its Profile to Honor Black Lives Matter amid George Floyd Protests." *Business Insider*, May 31, 2020. www.businessinsider.com/twitter-changed-profile-black-lives-matter-2020-5.

Crocker, Lizzie. "Why the New 'One in Four' Campus Rape Statistic Is Misleading." The Daily Beast, September 22, 2015. www.thedailybeast.com/why-the-new-one-in-four-campus-rape-statistic-is-misleading.

Croft, Jay, and Amir Vera. "Thousands of Mourners Visit George Floyd's Casket in Houston to Pay Respects." CNN, June 8, 2020. https://www.cnn.com/2020/06/08/us/george-floyd-houston-visitation/index.html.

Cummings, William. "The World Is Going to End in 12 Years If We Don't Address Climate Change, Ocasio-Cortez Says." *USA Today*, January 22, 2019. https://www.usatoday.com/story/news/politics/onpolitics/2019/01/22/ocasio-cortez-climate-change-alarm/2642481002/.

Cuni-Mertz, Lucas, and Chelsea Engstrom. "One Arrested after Protest at On-Campus Event." U-NEWS, April 11, 2019, https://info.umkc.edu/unews/one-arrested-after-protest-at-on-campus-event.

"Curves Have Their Day in Park; 500 at a 'Fat-In' Call for Obesity." *New York Times*, June 5, 1967. www.nytimes.com/1967/06/05/archives/curves-have-their-day-in-park-500-at-a-fatin-call-for-obesity.html.

The Daily Show with Trevor Noah. "Dr. Anthony Fauci: Getting Politis Out of Public Health: The Daily Social Distancing Show." YouTube, September 22, 2020. https://www.youtube.com/watch?v=5rKt54x6Hpo&feature=youtu.be&t=342.

The Daily Wire. "Babies Are People: Michael Knowles Speaks at the University of Kentucky." YouTube, November 18, 2019. https://www.youtube.com/watch?v=m7stWWsIsFs.

Daniels, Jesse. "On Kwanzaa." Racism Review, December 27, 2009. http://www.racismreview.com/blog/2009/12/27/on-kwanzaa/.

Danner, Chas. "Watch Trump Fondle an American Flag at CPAC." *New York Intelligencer*, March 2020. nymag.com/intelligencer/2020/02/watch-trump-fondle-an-american-flag-at-cpac.html.

Day, Elizabeth. "#BlackLivesMatter: The Birth of a New Civil Rights Movement." *Guardian*, July 19, 2015. www.theguardian.com/world/2015/jul/19/blacklivesmatter-birth-civil-rights-movement.

"Dear Colleague Letter on Transgender Students." U.S. Department of Justice Civil Rights Division and Department of Education Office for Civil Rights, May 13, 2016. https://www.justice.gov/opa/file/850986/download.

Deb, Sopan. "Jimmy Kimmel's 2020 Emmys Monologue: 'You Can't Have a Virus without a Host.'" *New York Times*, September 21, 2020. www.nytimes.com/2020/09/20/arts/television/emmys-kimmel-monologue.html.

"Declaration of Independence: A Transcription." National Archives and Records Administration, www.archives.gov/founding-docs/declaration-transcript.

Dennis v. United States, Supreme Court of the United States, 1951.

Derrida, Jacques. *Of Grammatology*. Johns Hopkins University Press, 2016.

Desmond Is Amazing. "Flackback to NYC Pride 2015. . . ." Facebook, November 10, 2018. https://www.facebook.com/DesmondisAmazing/posts/flashback-to-nyc-pride-2015-and-the-moment-my-life-changed-by-going-viral-the-ne/1080653715429049/.

Dictionary.com, https://www.dictionary.com.

Dostoevsky, Feodor. *Notes from the Underground*." Project Gutenberg, September 13, 2008. www.gutenberg.org/files/600/600-h/600-h.htm.

Downing, Lisa, et al. "Pervert or Sexual Libertarian? Meet John Money, "the Father of F***ology," Salon, January 4, 2015. https://www.salon.com/2015/01/04/pervert_or_sexual_libertarian_meet_john_money_the_father_of_fology/

Douay-Rheims Bible, www.drbo.org.

Dreher, Rod. "Desmond: The *Bacha* of Brooklyn."American Conservative, December 17, 2018. https://www.theamericanconservative.com/dreher/desmond-is-amazing-bacha-brooklyn/.

Drummond, Charles R. "Boston's 'Holiday Tree' Sparks Controversy: Giant Spruce Tree's Name Leads to Local Outcry over Rule of Religion." *Harvard Crimson*, November 28, 2005. https://www.thecrimson.com/article/2005/11/28/bostons-holiday-tree-sparks-controversy-last/.

D'Souza, Dinesh. *Illiberal Education: Political Correctness and the College Experience*. John M. Ashbrook Center for Public Affairs, Ashland University, 1992.

DSM-5, 2013, https://archive.org/details/diagnosticstatis0005unse/page/454.

Dylan, Bob. "Gotta Serve Somebody," *Slow Train Coming*. Columbia, 1975

Ellison, Ralph. *Invisible Man*. W. Ross MacDonald School Resource Services Library, 2018.

Emmons, Libby. "BLM Activists' 'Extortion' Attempt of Local Restaurants Backfires as Cuban Owners Fight Back." The Post Millennial, August 3, 2020. thepostmillennial.com/ cuban-community-refuses-blm-demands.

Edelman, Adam. "Biden Calls for 'Racial Justic"during Emotional George Floyd Funeral Speech," NBC News, June 9, 2020. https:// www.nbcnews.com/politics/2020-election/biden-calls-racial-justice-during-emotional-george-floyd-funeral-speech-n1228566.

Ehrlich, Paul R. The Population Bomb. RiverCity Press, 1975. https:// faculty.washington.edu/jhannah/geog270auto7/readings/population/ Ehrlich%20-%20Population%20Bomb%20Ch1.pdf

Encyclopedia Britannica, https://www.britannica.com.

Encyclopedia.com, https://www.encyclopedia.com.

Engels, Frederick. The Principles of Communism. Translated by Paul Sweezy. Marxists International Archive, February 2005. www. marxists.org/archive/marx/works/1847/11/prin-com.htm.

Engels, Friedrich, and Karl Marx. "The Communist Manifesto." Translated by Allen Lutins with assistance from Jim Tarzia. Project Gutenberg, January 20, 2005. www.gutenberg.org/cache/epub/61/ pg61.html.

Evers, Tony. "Letter to Wisconsin Educators and Students." October 11, 2019. https://content.govdelivery.com/attachments/ WIGOV/2019/11/04/file_attachments/1318304/2019%20 Ornament%20letter.pdf.

Fabbri, Thomas. "Why Is Instagram Deleting the Accounts of Hundreds of Porn Stars?" BBC, November 24, 2019. https://www.bbc.com/ news/blogs-trending-50222380.

"Factcheck: Outdated Video of Fauci Saying 'There's No Reason to Be Walking around with a Mask," Reuters, October 8, 2020. https://www.reuters.com/article/uk-factcheck-fauci-outdated-video-masks/fact-checkoutdated-video-of-fauci-saying-theres-no-reason-to-be-walking-around-with-a-mask-idUSKBN26T2TR.

Farrell, Henry. "Analysis: A Conservative YouTube Star Just Lost His Income Stream for Homophobic Slurs." *Washington Post*, June 6, 2019. www.washingtonpost.com/politics/2019/06/06/conservative-youtube-star-just-lost-his-income-stream-homophobic-slurs-heres-what-happened-why/.

"Fauci on How His Thinking Has Evolved on Masks, Asymptomatic Transmission." *Washington Post*, July 24, 2020. https://www.washingtonpost.com/video/washington-post-live/fauci-on-how-his-thinking-has-evolved-on-masks-asymptomatic-transmission/2020/07/24/799264e2-0f35-4862-aca2-2b4702650a8b_video.html.

F.B. "The Strange Afterlife of Antonio Gramsci's 'Prison Notebooks.'" *Economist*. November 7, 2017. www.economist.com/prospero/2017/11/07/the-strange-afterlife-of-antonio-gramscis-prison-notebooks.

Federer, William J. America's God and Country: Encyclopedia of Quotations, revised edition. Amerisearch, 2000.

Field, Carla. "Report of Rape on Clemson Campus Untrue, Police Say." WYFF, October 9, 2017. www.wyff4.com/article/report-of-rape-on-clemson-campus-untrue-police-say/7146964.

Filmer, Robert. *Patriarcha, or, The Natural Power of Kings*. Edited by Walter Davis, 1983.

Fish, Stanley. *There's No Such Thing as Free Speech . . . and It's A Good Thing Too*. Oxford University Press, 1994.

Fitzsimons, Tim. "Detroit Pastor Charged with Transgender Woman's Murder." NBC News, December 17, 2018. www.nbcnews.com/feature/nbc-out/detroit-pastor-charged-transgender-woman-s-murder-n947236.

Forsloff, Carol. "Kwanzaa Ain't No Good Thing." Digital Journal, December 30, 2008. http://www.digitaljournal.com/article/264192.

Fox, Jesse David, et al. "100 More Jokes That Shaped Modern Comedy." Vulture, February 9, 2017. www.vulture.com/2017/02/100-more-jokes-shaped-modern-comedy-c-v-r.html.

Fox, Margalit. "Shulamith Firestone, Feminist Writer, Dies at 67." *New York Times*, August 31, 2012. www.nytimes.com/2012/08/31/nyregion/shulamith-firestone-feminist-writer-dies-at-67.html.

Franck, Matthew J. "She Omits, You Decide." *National Review*, May 11, 2010. www.nationalreview.com/bench-memos/she-omits-you-decide-matthew-j-franck/.

Free Propaganda. "Nancy Pelosi Pass the Bill to Find out What's in It." YouTube, May 28, 2013. www.youtube.com/watch?v=QV7dDSgbaQo.

French, David. "Intellectual Diversity, Academic Freedom, and the Christian College." *National Review*, May 6, 2010. www.nationalreview.com/phi-beta-cons/intellectual-diversity-academic-freedom-and-christian-college-david-french/.

Fried, Ronald K. "How the Mafia Muscled in and Controlled the Stonewall Inn." The Daily Beast, June 30, 2019. www.thedailybeast.com/how-the-mafia-muscled-in-and-controlled-the-stonewall-inn.

Friedan, Betty. *It Changed My Life: Writings on the Women's Movement.* Harvard University Press, 1998.

Friedman, Shuki. "An Israeli Shabbat." The Israel Democracy Institute, June 23, 2016. en.idi.org.il/articles/2348#:~:text=The%20Ahad%20Ha'am%20once,keep%20and%20maintain%20the%20Shabbat.

Frizell, Sam. "Bernie Sanders Immigration: Why Conservatives Praise Him." *Time*, January 7, 2016. time.com/4170591/bernie-sanders-immigration-conservatives/.

Fukuyama, Francis. "The End of History." *The National Interest*, Summer 1989. www.wright.edu/~christopher.oldstone-moore/fukuyama.htm.

Gaddy, James. "A Recent History of Cursing on Television," *New York*, June 19, 2008. nymag.com/arts/tv/features/47985/.

Galileo Galilei, et al. *Dialogue Concerning the Two Chief World Systems, Ptolemaic and Copernican.* Folio Society, 2013.

Gardner, Laura. "Discovered Manuscript Shows Marcuse's Evolution." BrandeisNOW, October 9, 2013. www.brandeis.edu/now/2013/october/marcuse.html.

Gay, Roxane. "Fifty Years Ago, Protesters Took on the Miss America Pageant and Electrified the Feminist Movement." *Smithsonian Magazine*, January/February 2018. www.smithsonianmag.com/history/fifty-years-ago-protestors-took-on-miss-america-pageant-electrified-feminist-movement-180967504

"George Orwell Review." *Maude's Tavern*, October 9, 2008. maudestavern.com/2008/10/09/george-orwell-review/.

George, Robert. "Liberal Gnosticism." *First Things*, December 2016. https://www.firstthings.com/article/2016/12/gnostic-liberalism.

Gerstmann, Evan. "The Stat That 1 In 5 College Women Are Sexually Assaulted Doesn't Mean What You Think It Means." *Forbes*, January 28, 2019. www.forbes.com/sites/evangerstmann/2019/01/27/the-stat-that-1-in-5-college-women-are-sexually-assaulted-doesnt-mean-what-you-think-it-means/#2d114aab2217.

"Gettysburg College: Hug at Your Own Risk." FIRE, January 17, 2014. www.thefire.org/gettysburg-college-hug-at-your-own-risk/.

Ghanbari, Haraz N. "Decorated Spruce on Capitol Hill Ignites Controversy." *Arizona Daily Star*, December 8, 2005. https://tucson.com/news/national/govt-and-politics/decorated-spruce-on-capitol-hill-ignites-controversy/article_cdf8c405-1afd-5258-94b0-953f9b5cb5d5.html.

Glasser, Susan B. "Donald Trump's 2020 Superspreader Campaign: A Diary." *New Yorker*, November 3, 2020. www.newyorker.com/news/letter-from-trumps-washington/donald-trumps-2020-superspreader-campaign-a-diary.

"The Global Cooling Myth." Real Climate, January 14, 2005. http://www.realclimate.org/index.php/archives/2005/01/the-global-cooling-myth/.

Goldberg, Jonah. "Attacking Diversity of Thought." *National Review*, February 21, 2014. www.nationalreview.com/2014/02/attacking-diversity-thought-jonah-goldberg/.

———. "Feminist Army Aims at Palin." RealClearPolitics, September 13, 2008. www.realclearpolitics.com/articles/2008/09/feminist_army_aims_at_palin.html.

Goldwater, Barry. *The Conscience of a Conservative*. Martino Fine Books, 2011.

Gonshak, Henry. "The Twilight of Common Dreams: Why America Is Wracked by Culture Wars." *Twilight of Common Dreams Review*, mtprof.msun.edu/Win1996/HgonRev.html.

Golshan, Tara, and Ella Nilsen. "Alexandria Ocasio-Cortez's Roll-Out of the Green New Deal, Explained." *Vox*, February 11, 2019. https://www.vox.com/policy-and-politics/2019/2/11/18220163/alexandria-ocasio-cortez-green-new-deal-faq-tucker-carlson.

"Google Suspends 'Free Speech' App Parler." BBC, January 9, 2021. https://www.bbc.com/news/technology-55598887.

Gopalan, Rejani Thudalikunnil. *Developmental Challenges and Societal Issues for Individuals with Intellectual Disabilities*. IGI Global, 2020.

Gordon, Michael, et al., "Understanding HB2: North Carolina's Newest Law Solidifies State's Role in Defining Discrimination." *Charlotte Observer*, March 30, 2017. https://www.charlotteobserver.com/news/politics-government/article68401147.html.

Gore, Al. *Earth in the Balance: Ecology and the Human* Spirit. Houghton Mifflin, 1992.

Graham, David A. "Donald Trump's Case for Tolerance." *The Atlantic*, April 21, 2016, https://www.theatlantic.com/politics/archive/2016/04/trump-transgender-bathroom-north-carolina/479316/.

Graham, Michael. "When It Comes to Charitable Giving, Warren and Sanders Are Millionaires Who Don't 'Pay Their Fair Share.'" InsideSources, January 2, 2020. www.insidesources.com/when-it-comes-to-charitable-giving-warren-and-sanders-are-millionaires-who-dont-pay-their-fair-share-2/.

Gramsci, Antonio. *Prison Notebooks*. Edited by Joseph A. Buttigieg. Columbia University Press, 2011.

"Green New Deal FAQ." Assets Document Cloud, February 7, 2019. https://assets.documentcloud.org/documents/5729035/Green-New-Deal-FAQ.pdf.

Griswold v. Connecticut. Supreme Court of the United States, June 7, 1965.

Griffin, Kathy (@KathyGriffin). "Just resign now. You lost. Its over." Twitter, January 6, 2021. https://web.archive.org/web/20210106231245/https://twitter.com/kathygriffin/status/1346957786517671937.

Gritz, Jennie Rothenberg. "Ranting against Cant." *The Atlantic*, October 15, 2019. www.theatlantic.com/magazine/archive/2003/07/ranting-against-cant/303095/.

Guelzo, Allen C. "Pulitzer Overlooks Egregious Errors to Award Prize to New York Times' Fatally Flawed '1619 Project.'" The Heritage Foundation, May 6, 2020. www.heritage.org/american-founders/commentary/pulitzer-overlooks-egregious-errors-award-prize-new-york-times-fatally.

Guest, Steve (@SteveGuest). "CNN's Christ Cuomo, 'Please. . . ,'" Twitter, June 2, 2020, 9:12 p.m. https://twitter.com/SteveGuest/status/1267987525198585856.

Haines, Lester. "Jane Fonda C-Word Slip Shocks U.S." The Register, February 15, 2008. www.theregister.com/2008/02/15/fonda_slip/.

Hains, Tim. "Inside Edition's Zoe Tur Threatens to Send Breitbart's Ben Shapiro 'Home in an Ambulance' over Jenner Debate." RealClear Politics, July 17, 2015. https://www.realclearpolitics.com/video/2015/07/17/inside_editions_zoe_tur_threatens_to_send_breitbarts_ben_shapiro_home_in_an_ambulance_over_jenner_debate.html.

———. "Ocasio-Cortez: 'The World Is Going to End In 12 Years If We Don't Address Climate Change.'" RealClearPolitics, January 22, 2019. www.realclearpolitics.com/video/2019/01/22/ocasio-cortez_the_world_is_going_to_end_in_12_years_if_we_dont_address_climate_change.html.

Hanby, Kyle, "John Locke: Father of Liberalism," Acton Institute, August 29, 2016. https://blog.acton.org/archives/88741-john-locke-father-of-liberalism.html

Hanisch, Carol. "The Personal Is Political: The Women's Liberation Movement Classic with a New Explanatory Introduction." Women of the World, Unite!, www.carolhanisch.org/CHwritings/PIP.html.

Hannah-Jones, Nikole. "The 1619 Project." *New York Times*, August 14, 2019. www.nytimes.com/interactive/2019/08/14/magazine/1619-america-slavery.html.

Harkov, Lahav. "Twitter Downplays Khamenei Calls for Genocide as Political Speech,"*Jerusalem Post*, July 31, 2020. https://www.jpost.com/middle-east/twitter-downplays-khamenei-calls-for-genocide-as-political-speech-636910.

Harlow, John. "Billionaire Club in Bid to Curb Overpopulation, *Times*, May 24, 2009. https://www.thetimes.co.uk/article/billionaire-club-in-bid-to-curb-overpopulation-d2fl22qhlo2 ; https://www.baltimoresun.com/news/bs-xpm-2009-07-17-0907160033-story.html.

Harrington, Elizabeth. "Pelosi: Obamacare Means 'You Could Be A Photographer or Writer.'" CNS News, March 21, 2013. www.cnsnews.com/news/article/pelosi-obamacare-means-you-could-be-photographer-or-writer.

Harris, Kamala (@KamalaHarris). "If you're able to, chip in now. . . . ." Twitter, June 1, 2020. https://twitter.com/KamalaHarris/status/1267555018128965643.

Harrison, Steve. "Charlotte City Council Approves LGBT Protections in 7–4 Vote." *Charlotte Observer*, February 22, 2016. https://www.charlotteobserver.com/news/politics-government/article61786967.html.

Hartocollis, Anemona. "Yale Lecturer Resigns after Email on Halloween Costumes." *New York Times*, December 8, 2015. www.nytimes.com/2015/12/08/us/yale-lecturer-resigns-after-email-on-halloween-costumes.html.

Hautala, Laura. "Paypal and Shopify Remove Trump-Related Accounts, Citing Policies against Supporting Violence." CNET, January 7, 2021. https://www.cnet.com/news/paypal-and-shopify-remove-trump-related-accounts-citing-policies-against-supporting-violence/.

Hawkins, Derek. "In Portland, Images of Knives, Brass Knuckles, Bricks Show Viciousness of Protests." *Washington Post*, April 29, 2019. www.washingtonpost.com/news/morning-mix/wp/2017/06/05/in-portland-images-of-knives-brass-knuckles-bricks-show-viciousness-of-protests/.

Hawkins, Stephen, et al. "Hidden Tribes: A Study of America's Polarized Landscape." More In Common, October 11, 2018. https://static1.squarespace.com/static/5a70a7c3010027736a22740f/t/5bbcea6b781 7f7bf7342b718/1539107467397/hidden_tribes_report-2.pdf.

Henninger, Daniel. "Opinion: 'You Cannot Be Civil'." *Wall Street Journal*, October 10, 2018. www.wsj.com/articles/you-cannot-be-civil-1539211192.

Hentoff, Nat. "Mugging the Minuteman." *Village Voice*, October 31, 2006. https://web.archive.org/web/20110629121552/http://www.villagevoice.com/2006-10-31/news/mugging-the-minutemen/.

Hervey, Ginger. "Yale Undergraduates Aim to 'Decolonize' the English Department's Curriculum." *USA Today*, June 10, 2016. www.usatoday.com/story/college/2016/06/10/yale-undergraduates-aim-to-decolonize-the-english-departments-curriculum/37418303/.

Hess, Frederick M., and R. J. Martin. "Smithsonian Institution Explains That 'Rationality' & 'Hard Work' Are Racist." RealClearPolicy, July 20, 2020. www.realclearpolicy.com/articles/2020/07/20/smithsonian_institute_explains_that_rationality_and_hard_work_are_racist_499425.html.

Hinderaker, John. "Minnesota's 'Antifascists' Are Fascists." The American Experiment, August 19, 2020. www.americanexperiment.org/2017/06/minnesotas-antifascists-fascists/.

Hines, Alice. "Sashaying Their Way through Youth." *New York Times*, September 8, 2019. https://www.nytimes.com/2019/09/07/style/self-care/drag-kids-desmond-the-amazing.html.

Hitchens, Christopher. "The Fraying of America: A Review of Culture of Complaint: By Robert Hughes." *The War of the Words: The Political Correctness Debate*. Edited by Sarah Dunant. Virago, 1995. 133–44.

Ho, Karen. "George Orwell's "1984" Is Topping Amazon's Best Sellers." Quartz, January 13, 2021. https://qz.com/1956937/george-orwells-1984-is-topping-amazons-best-sellers/.

Hodgson, Geoffrey Martin. *Wrong Turnings: How the Left Got Lost.* The University of Chicago Press, 2018.

Holloway, John. "The Tradition of Scientific Marxism." Marxists Internet Archive, www.marxists.org/subject/marxmyths/john-holloway/article.htm.

Hoonhout, Tobias. "University of Michigan Disbands 'Bias Response Team' n Response to First Amendment Challenge." *National Review,* November 1, 2019. www.nationalreview.com/news/university-of-michigan-disbands-bias-response-team-in-response-to-first-amendment-challenge/.

Hopper, Jessica. "Ted Cruz Says Not Having 'Bathroom Bill' Is 'Opening the Door for Predators.'" ABC News, April 23, 2016. https://abcnews.go.com/Politics/ted-cruz-bathroom-bill-opening-door-predators/story?id=38626340

Horkheimer, Max. *Critical Theory.* Continuum, 1982.

Hosenball, Mark. "Tommy Robinson Fails to Get U.S. Visa." Reuters, November 12, 2018. uk.reuters.com/article/uk-usa-trump-robinson-idUKKCN1NH2M2.

Hosking, Taylor. "Why Do the Boy Scouts Want to Include Girls?" *The Atlantic,* October 13, 2017. www.theatlantic.com/politics/archive/2017/10/why-did-the-boy-scouts-decide-to-accept-girls/542769/.

"How China's One-Child Policy Led to Forced Abortions, 30 Million Bachelors." NPR, February 1, 2016. https://www.npr.org/2016/02/01/465124337/how-chinas-one-child-policy-led-to-forced-abortions-30-million-bachelors.

Howe, Samuel Gridley," *Parallels in Time: A History of Intellectual Disabilities*, Minnesota Department of Administration, mn.gov/mnddc/parallels/four/4b/5.html.

Huangpu, Kate, and Khadija Hussain. "Protesters Disrupt Anti-Immigration Speech by Tommy Robinson at Columbia." *Columbia*

Daily Spectator, October 11, 2017. www.columbiaspectator.com/news/2017/10/11/protesters-disrupt-anti-immigration-speech-by-tommy-robinson-at-columbia/.

Hudson, David L, and Lata Nott. "Hate Speech & Campus Speech Codes." Freedom Forum Institute, March 2017. www.freedomforuminstitute.org/first-amendment-center/topics/freedom-of-speech-2/free-speech-on-public-college-campuses-overview/hate-speech-campus-speech-codes/.

Hughes, Geoffrey. *Political Correctness: A History of Semantics and Culture*. Wiley-Blackwell, 2010.

"Huxley to Orwell: My Hellish Vision of the Future Is Better Than Yours (1949)." Open Culture, March 17, 2015. www.openculture.com/2015/03/huxley-to-orwell-my-hellish-vision-of-the-future-is-better-than-yours.html.

Idso, Craig D., et al. "Why Scientists Disagree about Global Warming: The NIPCC Report on Scientific Consensus." Second edition. The Heartland Institute, 2016. https://www.heartland.org/_template-assets/documents/Books/Why%20Scientists%20Disagree%20Second%20Edition%20with%20covers.pdf.

"'In a Racist Society, It Is Not Enough to Be Non-Racist, We Must Be Anti-Racist,'—Angela Y. Davis," Buffalo Center for Health Equity, https://www.buffalo.edu/content/dam/www/inclusion/docs/Comm%20Health%20Equity.pdf

Inside Edition, "Donald Trump Blasts Latino Kids Curse-Filled Rant: 'They're Stupid People.'" YouTube, November 6, 2015. https://www.youtube.com/watch?v=GdG_uN6DyEo.

Isaac, Mike, and Kate Conger. "Facebook Bars Trump through End of His Term." *New York Times*, January 7, 2021. https://www.nytimes.com/2021/01/07/technology/facebook-trump-ban.html ; https://www.statista.com/statistics/272014/global-social-networks-ranked-by-number-of-users/

Jacobellis v. Ohio. Supreme Court of the United States, June 22, 1964.

Jay, Martin. *The Dialectical Imagination: A History of the Frankfurt School and the Institute of Social Research 1923–1950*. University of California Press, 2008.

Jay, William. *The Life of John Jay*. Harper, 1833.

Jefferson, Margo. "The Thomas–Hill Question, Answered Anew." *New York Times*, November 11, 1994. https://www.nytimes.com/1994/11/11/books/books-of-the-times-the-thomas-hill-question-answered-anew.html?n=Top/Reference/Times%20Topics/Organizations/S/Supreme%20Court.

Jefferson, Thomas. "Draft Reply to the Danbury Baptist Association, [on or before 31 December 1801]." Founders Online, https://founders.archives.gov/?q=danbury%20baptists&s=1111311111&sa=&r=2&sr=.

———. "Thomas Jefferson to Amos J. Cook, 21 January 1816." Founders Online, https://founders.archives.gov/documents/Jefferson/03-09-02-0243.

Jesse Jackson and Students Protest Western Culture Program on Palm Drive, Photograph, 1987." Stanford Stories from the Archives. August 18, 2016. exhibits.stanford.edu/stanford-stories/feature/1980s.

John Doe v. University of Michigan. Supreme Court of the United States, September 22, 1989.

Jones, Collin. "Three Federal Officers May Be Permanently Blinded after Antifa Laser Attack in Portland." The Post Millennial, July 23, 2020. thepostmillennial.com/three-federal-officers-may-be-permanently-blinded-after-antifa-laser-attack-in-portland.

Kaminer, Wendy. "The ACLU Retreats from Free Expression." *Wall Street Journal*, June 20, 2018. https://www.wsj.com/articles/the-aclu-retreats-from-free-expression-1529533065.

Kanik, Hannah. "Here Are the Best Reactions to Twitter Suspending President Trump's Account." *Philly Voice*, January 9, 2021. https://www.phillyvoice.com/twitter-suspends-president-trump-reactions/.

Kapoor, Anjani, et al. "Barriers to Service Provision for Justice-Involved Youth." *Criminal Justice and Behavior* 45, no. 12 (December 1, 2018): 1832–51.

Katz, Sharon. "Incident Prompts Debate on How to Relate Survivor Stories." *Daily Princetonian*, May 22, 1991. www.avoiceformalestudents.com/wp-content/uploads/2013/12/The-Daily-Princetonian.pdf.

Karson, Kendall. "Michigan Gov. Whitmer: Protests 'Undermine'" State's Response to COVID-19 Crisis." ABC News, May 13, 2020. https://abcnews.go.com/Politics/michigan-gov-whitmer-protests-undermine-states-response-covid/story?id=70645516.

Kaufman, David. "How the Pride March Made History." *New York Times*, June 16, 2020. www.nytimes.com/2020/06/16/us/gay-lgbt-pride-march-history.html.

Kellner, Douglas. "Herbert Marcuse." Illuminations, www.uta.edu/huma/illuminations/kell12.htm.

Kengor, Paul. "Cultural Marxism and Its Conspirators: Part 2." *American Spectator*. July 2, 2020. spectator.org/cultural-marxism-and-its-conspirators-part-2/.

———. "Cultural Marxism and Its Conspirators." *American Spectator*. April 3, 2019. spectator.org/cultural-marxism-and-its-conspirators/.

———. *The Devil and Karl Marx: Communism's Long March of Death, Deception, and Infiltration.* Tan Books, 2020.

Kennedy, Lesley. "This Is How FDR Tried to Pack the Supreme Court." History, June 28, 2018. www.history.com/news/franklin-roosevelt-tried-packing-supreme-court.

Kerr, Andrew, and Kyle Hooten. "Bail Fund Promoted by Kamala Harris Helped Man Accused of Sexually Penetrating a Child." Daily Caller, September 16, 2020. https://dailycaller.com/2020/09/16/kamala-harris-minnesota-bail-fund-accused-sexual-assault-child/.

Kimball, Roger. *Tenured Radicals: How Politics Has Corrupted Our Higher Education.* Ivan R. Dee, 2008.

Klein, Christopher. "When Massachusetts Banned Christmas." History, December 22, 2015. www.history.com/news/when-massachusetts-banned-christmas.

Knowles, Elizabeth, and Julia Elliott. *The Oxford Dictionary of New Words.* Second revised edition. Oxford University Press, 1997.

Koblin, John, and Michael M. Grynbaum. "Megyn Kelly's 'Blackface' Remarks Leave Her Future at NBC in Doubt." *New York Times*, October 25, 2018. www.nytimes.com/2018/10/25/business/media/megyn-kelly-skips-today-blackface-nbc.html.

Koop, Chacour. "Smithsonian Museum Apologizes for Saying Hard Work, Rational Thought Is 'White Culture." *Miami Herald*, July 17, 2020. https://www.miamiherald.com/news/nation-world/national/article244309587.html.

Kopan, Tal, and Eugene Scott. "North Carolina Signs Controversial Transgender Bill." CNN, March 24, 2016. https://www.cnn.com/2016/03/23/politics/north-carolina-gender-bathrooms-bill/index.html.

Krastev, Nikola. "Iran's Ahmadinejad Delivers Controversial Speech at U.S. University." RadioFreeEurope/RadioLiberty, February 2, 2012. www.rferl.org/a/1078779.html.

Krebs, Albin, and Robert Mcg. Thomas "Notes on People; Some Disunity Along the United Way." *New York Times*, Septeber 19, 1981. www.nytimes.com/1981/09/19/nyregion/notes-on-people-some-disunity-along-the-united-way.html.

Krisch, Joshua A. "This Shocking Map Shows Republicans' Most Powerful Political Weapon." Fatherly, November 22, 2019. www.fatherly.com/health-science/republicans-have-more-children/.

Kurtz, Stanley. "The Campus Intellectual Diversity Act: A Proposal." *National Review*, February 12, 2019. www.nationalreview.com/corner/the-campus-intellectual-diversity-act-a-proposal/.

Kurtzleben, Danielle. "The Bernie Sanders 'Rape Fantasy' Essay, Explained." NPR, May 29, 2015. www.npr.org/sections/itsallpolitics/2015/05/29/410606045/the-bernie-sanders-rape-fantasy-essay-explained.

Kātz, Barry M. "The Criticism of Arms: The Frankfurt School Goes to War." *The Journal of Modern History* 59, no. 3, (1987): 439–478. doi: 10.1086/243224.

Kirkpatrick, Emily. "J. K. Rowling Proves Her Commitment to Transphobia in Her New Novel." *Vanity Fair*, September 14, 2020.

https://www.vanityfair.com/style/2020/09/jk-rowling-transphobia-new-novel-troubled-blood-controversy.

Lady Gaga. "Lady Gaga—Born This Way (Official Music Video)." Youtube, February 27, 2011. https://www.youtube.com/watch?v=wV1FrqwZyKw

LaPlante, Eve. *American Jezebel: The Uncommon Life of Anne Hutchinson.* HarperOne, 2005.

La Rochefoucauld, François. "Reflections or, Sentences and Moral Maxims." Project Gutenberg, January 25, 2013. www.gutenberg.org/files/9105/9105-h/9105-h.htm.

Lawrence v. Texas. Supreme Court of the United States, June 26, 2003.

Leary, Timothy. *Sound Bites from the Counter Culture* (LP), 1989.

Lee, Dami. "Apple Says There Are 1.4 Billion Active Apple Devices." The Verge, January 29, 2019. https://www.theverge.com/2019/1/29/18202736/apple-devices-ios-earnings-q1-2019#:~:text=Apple%20says%20there%20are%20now, accessories%20like%20AirPods%20aren't.

Lee, MJ, and Eli Watkins. "Cruz, Sanders Face off on Obamacare." CNN, February 8, 2017. www.cnn.com/2017/02/07/politics/obamacare-cruz-sanders-highlights/index.html.

Lee, Timothy B. "Twitter Explains Why It Banned the App for Gab, a Right-Wing Twitter Rival." Ars Technica, August 18, 2017. https://arstechnica.com/tech-policy/2017/08/gab-the-right-wing-twitter-rival-just-got-its-app-banned-by-google/.

Leo XIII. *Quod Apostolici Muneris.* December 27, 1878. www.vatican.va/content/leo-xiii/en/encyclicals/documents/hf_l-xiii_enc_28121878_quod-apostolici-muneris.html.

Leswing, Kif. "Apple Removes Parler from App Store in Wake of U.S. Capitol Riot." CNBC, January 9, 2021. https://www.cnbc.com/2021/01/09/apple-removes-parler-from-app-store-in-wake-of-us-capitol-riot.html.

Levenson, Eric, et al. "What We Know about the Five Deaths in the Pro-Trump Mob That Stormed the Capitol." CNN, January 8, 2021. https://www.cnn.com/2021/01/07/us/capitol-mob-deaths/index.html.

Levine, Martin. "Republicans Give More to Charity Than Democrats, but There's a Bigger Story Here." *Nonprofit Quarterly*, November 5, 2018. nonprofitquarterly.org/republicans-give-more-to-charity-than-democrats-but-theres-a-bigger-story-here/.

Lewis, C. S. "Xmas and Christmas: A Lost Chapter from Herodotus." Khad.com, December 12, 2003. khad.com/post/196009755/xmas-and-christmas-a-lost-chapter-from-herodotus.

Liberto, Daniel. "Voodoo Economics." Investopedia, August 25, 2020. www.investopedia.com/terms/v/voodooeconomics.asp.

Lincoln, Abraham. "Gettysburg Address." Abraham Lincoln Online, November 19, 1863. www.abrahamlincolnonline.org/lincoln/speeches/gettysburg.htm

Lind, Michael. "Buckley vs. Vidal: The Real Story." *Politico*, August 24, 2015. www.politico.com/magazine/story/2015/08/buckley-vs-vidal-the-real-story-121673.

Lipka, Michael. "How Many Jews Are There in the United States?" Pew Research Center, October 2, 2013. https://www.pewresearch.org/fact-tank/2013/10/02/how-many-jews-are-there-in-the-united-states/.

"A Little History of 'Politically Correct.'" *Washington Times*, November 15, 2015. www.washingtontimes.com/news/2015/nov/15/editorial-a-little-history-of-politically-correct/.

Locke, John. *Second Treatise of Civil Government John Locke (1690)*, Marxists Internet Archive, www.marxists.org/reference/subject/politics/locke/ch01.htm.

———. *A Letter Concerning Toleration*, Penn State University's Electronic Classics, 2005. http://self.gutenberg.org/wplbn0000651234-a-letter-concerning-toleration-by-locke-john.aspx?.

Looijen, John. "Edward Kennedy at the Funeral of Robert Kennedy, June 8, 1968." YouTube, October 30, 2014. www.youtube.com/watch?v=rUx2ar-RzVE.

Lopez, Daniel. "The Conversion of Georg Lukács." *Jacobin*, January 24, 2019. https://jacobinmag.com/2019/01/lukacs-hungary-marx-philosophy-consciousness.

Love, Ryan. "University of Oklahoma Launches Mandatory Diversity Training Program for All Campuses." KOKI, August 27, 2020. www.fox23.com/news/local/university-oklahoma-launches-mandatory-diversity-training-program-all-campuses/KGUIZWZD2NHZFBC5TR3ZSNOD7I/.

Lowery, George. "A Campus Takeover That Symbolized an Era of Change." *Cornell Chronicle*, April 16, 2009. news.cornell.edu/stories/2009/04/campus-takeover-symbolized-era-change.

Lukacs, Georg. "Class Consciousness." *History and Class Consciousness*. Translated by Rodney Livingstone. Merlin, 1967.

Lukianoff, Greg. "Campus Speech Codes: Absurd, Tenacious, and Everywhere." FIRE, May 28, 2008. https://www.thefire.org/campus-speech-codes-absurd-tenacious-and-everywhere/.

Lynch v. Donnelly, Supreme Court of the United States, 1984.

Madison, James (writing as Publius). *Federalist 51*, The Avalon Project, avalon.law.yale.edu/18th_century/fed51.asp

Mamet, David. *Oleanna*. London, 2004.

"Manguage." *New York Times*, June 2, 1985. www.nytimes.com/1985/06/02/opinion/manguage.html.

Mann, Charles C. "The Book That Incited a Worldwide Fear of Overpopulation." *Smithsonian Magazine*, January/February 2018. https://www.smithsonianmag.com/innovation/book-incited-worldwide-fear-overpopulation-180967499/.

Manuel, Diane. "Reshaping the Humanities." Stanford Today, 1997. web.stanford.edu/dept/news/stanfordtoday/ed/9705/9705ncf1.html.

Mao Zedong. *Quotations from Chairman Mao*. Universal-Award House, 1971.

Marcuse, Herbert. *One-Dimensional Man*. Routledge, 2002.

———. "Repressive Tolerance (Full Text)." Herbert Marcuse Official Homepage, October 25, 2015. www.marcuse.org/herbert/publications/1960s/1965-repressive-tolerance-fulltext.html.

"Market Share Category: Payment Processing," Datanyze, https://www.datanyze.com/market-share/payment-processing—26.

Marshall, Thurgood. "The Bicentennial Speech." Thurgood Marshall: Supreme Court Justice and Civil Rights Advocate, May 3, 2016,. thurgoodmarshall.com/the-bicentennial-speech/.

Martin, Roland S. "Rep. Maxine Waters Under Scrutiny for Urging Supporters to Confront Trump Officials." YouTube, June 25, 2018. www.youtube.com/watch?v=Tts1q9TgXxg.

Marx, Karl. "Critique of Hegel's Philosophy in General," *Economic and Philosophic Manuscripts of 1844*. Translated by Martin Milligan, 2009. Marxists International Archive, www.marxists.org/archive/marx/works/1844/manuscripts/hegel.htm.

———. "Theses on Feuerbach," Marxists International Archive, www.marxists.org/archive/marx/works/1845/theses/theses.htm.

Mather, Cotton. "Grace Defended. On the Twenty-fifth of December, 1712. Boston-Lecture," Evans Early American Imprint Collection, quod.lib.umich.edu/e/evans/N01303.0001.001/1:2?rgn=div1;view=fulltext.

Matney, Lucas. "President Trump Responds to Twitter Account Ban in Tweet Storm from @POTUS Account." Yahoo!, January 8, 2021. https://finance.yahoo.com/news/president-trump-responds-twitter-account-015555288.html.

Matthews, Dylan. "Bernie Sanders's Fear of Immigrant Labor Is Ugly—and Wrongheaded." *Vox*, July 29 2015. www.vox.com/2015/7/29/9048401/bernie-sanders-open-borders.

McCaskill, Nolan D., and Andrew Desiderio. "Bernie Became a Millionaire in 2016, Records Show." *Politico*, April 15, 2019, www.politico.com/story/2019/04/15/bernie-sanders-millionaire-1276928.

McClelland, Colleen. "Canadian Man Raised as Girl Commits Suicide." *Spokesman-Review*, May 13, 2004. https://www.spokesman.com/stories/2004/may/13/canadian-man-raised-as-girl-commits-suicide/.

McGowan, Andrew. "How December 25 Became Christmas." Biblical Archaeology Society, December 18, 2020. www.biblicalarchaeology.

org/daily/people-cultures-in-the-bible/jesus-historical-jesus/
how-december-25-became-christmas/.

McGreal, Scott. "Are Conservatives Healthier Than Liberals?"
Psychology Today, February 28, 2019. www.psychologytoday.com/
us/blog/unique-everybody-else/201902/are-conservatives-
healthier-liberals.

McHugh, Paul. "Transgender Surgery Isn't the Solution." *Wall Street
Journal*, May 13, 2016. https://www.wsj.com/articles/
paul-mchugh-transgender-surgery-isnt-the-solution-1402615120.

McKay, Tom. "Alt-Right Platform Gab's Management Is Now Blaming
a Leftist Conspiracy for Their Nazi Problem." Gizmodo, June 2,
2018. https://gizmodo.com/alt-right-platform-gabs-
management-is-now-blaming-a-lef-1826510673.

Mcphate, Mike. "California Today: Price Tag to Protect Speech at
Berkeley: $600,000." *New York Times*, September 15, 2017. www.
nytimes.com/2017/09/15/us/california-today-price-tag-to-protect-
speech-at-berkeley-600000.html.

Meads, Timothy. "New Poll Shows Gen Z Is Pretty Confused
About Socialism, Capitalism, And More." Townhall.com, August
19, 2019. townhall.com/tipsheet/timothymeads/
2019/08/19/new-poll-shows-gen-z-is-pretty-confused-about-socialism-
capitalism-and-more-n2551861.

Mencken, Henry Louis. *A Mencken Chrestomathy*. Vintage Books,
1982.

Merriam-Webster Dictionary, www.merriam-webster.com/dictionary.

Mill, John Stuart. *On Liberty*, Project Gutenberg, www.gutenberg.org/
files/34901/34901-h/34901-h.htm.

Miller, Joshua Rhett. "BLM Site Removes Page on 'Nuclear Family
Structure' amid NFL Vet's Criticism." *New York Post*, September
24, 2020. nypost.com/2020/09/24/blm-removes-website-language-
blasting-nuclear-family-structure/.

Miller, Leslie. "The Gap's 'Happy Whatever-You-Wannakuh' Ad
Reignites 'War on Christmas' Debate." *USA Today*, November 23,
2009. http://content.usatoday.com/communities/Religion/

post/2009/11/the-gap-ads—happy-do-whatever-you-wannukah-reignites-war-on-christmas-debate/1?loc=interstitialskip#. X8QY9hNKhZp.

Milton, John. *Areopagitica*, Project Gutenberg, www.gutenberg.org/files/608/608-h/608-h.htm

Miłosz, Czesław, and Jane Zielonko. *The Captive Mind*. Penguin Books, 2001.

"Mobile Operating Systems' Market Share Worldwide from January 1012 to January 2021," Statista, https://www.statista.com/statistics/272698/global-market-share-held-by-mobile-operating-systems-since-2009/.

"Modern Immigration Wave Brings 59 Million to U.S." Pew Research Center, May 30, 2020. www.pewresearch.org/hispanic/2015/09/28/modern-immigration-wave-brings-59-million-to-u-s-driving-population-growth-and-change-through-2065/

Money, John. "The Development of Sexuality and Eroticism in Humankind." *Quarterly Review of Biology* 56, no. 4 (December 1981): 379–404. https://www.jstor.org/stable/2824989?seq=1.

Monroe, Irene. "The Right's Bogus War on Christmas." Dick and Sharon's LA Progressive, https://web.archive.org/web/20130319165707/http://www.laprogressive.com/the-rights-bogus-war-on-christmas/.

"Monthly Harvard-Harris Poll: January 2018 Re-Field." Harvard-Harris Poll, January 2018. harvardharrispoll.com/wp-content/uploads/2018/01/Final_HHP_Jan2018-Refield_RegisteredVoters_XTab.pdf.

"Most Popular Social Networks Worldwide as of January 2021, Ranked by Number of Active Users." Statista, February 9, 2021. https://www.statista.com/statistics/272014/global-social-networks-ranked-by-number-of-users/.

"Mothering; https://www.etymonline.com/Word/Parenting: Search Online Etymology Dictionary." *Index*, www.etymonline.com/search?q=mothering%3B+https%3A%2F%2Fwww.etymonline.com%2Fword%2Fparenting.

Mounk, Yascha. "Americans Strongly Dislike PC Culture." *The Atlantic*, October 30, 2018. www.theatlantic.com/ideas/archive/2018/10/large-majorities-dislike-political-correctness/572581/.

Moyn, Samuel. "The Alt-Right's Favorite Meme Is 100 Years Old." *New York Times*, November 13, 2018. www.nytimes.com/2018/11/13/opinion/cultural-marxism-anti-semitism.html.

Murphy, Tim. "Read Bernie Sanders' 1970s-Era Essays on Sex, Cancer, Revolution, and Fluoride." *Mother Jones*, July 6, 2015. www.motherjones.com/politics/2015/07/bernie-sanders-vermont-freeman-sexual-freedom-fluoride/.

Mussolini, Benito. *The Doctrine of Fascism*. 1936.

Naam, Ramez. "Hunger Is at an All-Time Low. We Can Drive It Even Lower." Ramez Naam, September 9, 2015. https://rameznaam.com/2015/09/09/hunger-is-at-an-all-time-low-we-can-drive-it-even-lower/

Nabokov, Vladimir Vladimirovich. *Nabokov, Bend Sinister*. Severo-Zapad, 1993.

Natter, Ari. "Alexandria Ocasio-Cortez's Green New Deal Could Cost $93 Trillion, Group Says." Bloomberg, February 25, 2019. www.bloomberg.com/news/articles/2019-02-25/group-sees-ocasio-cortez-s-green-new-deal-costing-93-trillion.

Nelson, Steven. "FBI Director Wray Won't Share Officer Brian Sicknick's Cause of Death with Senators." *New York Post*, March 2, 2021,. https://nypost.com/2021/03/02/fbi-director-wray-mum-on-officer-brian-sicknicks-cause-of-death/New International Version." Bible Gateway, www.biblegateway.com/.

"New York Times Corrects the 1619 Project—but It's Still a Giant Lie." *New York Post*, March 15, 2020. nypost.com/2020/03/14/new-york-times-corrects-the-1619-project-but-its-still-a-giant-lie/.

Ngô, Andy. "Inventing Victimhood." *City Journal*, July 1, 2019, www.city-journal.org/campus-hate-crime-hoaxes.

Nicas, Jack. "Parler Pitched Itself as Twitter without Rules. Not Anymore, Apple and Google Said." *New York Times*, January 8, 2021. https://www.nytimes.com/2021/01/08/technology/parler-apple-google.html.

"Nikole Hannah-Jones." Western Michigan University, September 4, 2018. wmich.edu/humanities/nikole-hannah-jones.

Noble, Kenneth B. "Issue of Racism Erupts in Simpson Trial." *New York Times*, January 14, 1995. www.nytimes.com/1995/01/14/us/issue-of-racism-erupts-in-simpson-trial.html.

"No More 'Holiday' Trees at Capitol." *Washington Times*. November 29, 2005. https://www.washingtontimes.com/news/2005/nov/29/20051129-120703-5977r/

Oakeshott, Michael. *Rationalism in Politics and Other Essays*. Liberty Fund, 1991.

"Obama Administration Sues North Carolina over Anti-LGBT Law." BBC News, May 9, 2016. https://www.bbc.com/news/world-us-canada-36252949

Obama, Barack. *Dreams from My Father: A Story of Race and Inheritance*. Canongate, 2016.

Obergefell v. Hodges. Supreme Court of the United States, June 26, 2015.

Ocasio-Cortez, Alexandria (@AOC), "Is anyone archiving these Trump sycophants. . . .," Twitter, November 6, 2020, 3:16 p.m. twitter.com/AOC/status/1324807776510595078.

Ocasio-Cortez, Alexandria (sponsor). "H.Res.109—Recognizing the duty of the Federal Government to Create a Green New Deal." February 12, 2019. https://www.congress.gov/bill/116th-congress/house-resolution/109/text.

O'Connor, Sandra Day. "Liberty, Not Licentiousness," *Liberty*, November/December 1997. libertymagazine.org/article/liberty-not-licentiousness.

Office of the U.S. Surgeon General (@Surgeon_General). "In light of new evidence, @CDC recommends. . . ." Twitter, April 3, 2020, 6:58 p.m. https://twitter.com/Surgeon_General/status/1246210376351592448.

Olson, Tyler. "Coons Says That Confirming Barrett 'Constitutes Court-Packing,' Sasse Responds That's 'Obviously' Incorrect." Fox News, October 11, 2020. www.foxnews.com/politics/fox-news-sunday-ben-sasse-chris-coons-judiciary-committee-barrett.

"Open Letter Advocating for an Anti-Racist Public Health Response to Demonstrations against Systemic Injustice Occurring during the COVID-19 Pandemic." Google Drive, June 5, 2020. https://drive.google.com/file/d/1Jyfn4Wd2i6bRi12ePghMHtX3ysib7K1A/view.

"Origin of That Fish Line." *Duluth News Tribune.* August 17, 2014. www.duluthnewstribune.com/lifestyle/3325954-origin-fish-line.

Orwell, George. *Nineteen Eighty-Four: A Novel.* Penguin Books, 1967.

———. "Politics and the English Language," George Orwell's Library, December 29, 2019. www.orwell.ru/library/essays/politics/english/e_polit.

Ott, Tim. "How George Carlin's 'Seven Words' Changed Legal History." Biography, May 19, 2020. www.biography.com/news/george-carlin-seven-words-supreme-court.

Paczkowski, John, and Ryan Mac, "Amazon Will Suspend Hosting for Pro-Trump Social Network Parler," BuzzFeed News, January 9, 2021. https://www.buzzfeednews.com/article/johnpaczkowski/amazon-parler-aws.

Palmer, Annie. "Facebook Will Block Trump from Posting at Least for the Remainder of His Term." CNBC, January 7, 2021. https://www.cnbc.com/2021/01/07/facebook-will-block-trump-from-posting-for-the-remainder-of-his-term.html.

Park, Jessica. "Is 'Homeless' The Right Word for Those Living on the Street?" Hoodline, October 23, 2020. hoodline.com/2016/12/is-homeless-the-right-word-for-those-living-on-the-street.

Passel, Jeffrey S. "Measuring Illegal Immigration: How Pew Research Center Counts Unauthorized Immigrants in the U.S." Pew Research Center, September 4, 2020. www.pewresearch.org/fact-tank/2019/07/12/how-pew-research-center-counts-unauthorized-immigrants-in-us/.

Patell, Cyrus R. K. "I Face This Challenge." Patell.net, patell.net/2008/06/i-face-this-challenge/.

Payne, Daniel. "UCLA Course Uses Cardi B to Teach about '\'Respectability Politics.'" The College Fix, August 21, 2019. www.

thecollegefix.com/ucla-course-uses-cardi-b-to-teach-about-respectability-politics/.

"Paul Ehrlich." Stanford Profiles, September 15, 2015. https://profiles.stanford.edu/paul-ehrlich.

Pearse, Roger. "The Chronography of 354. Introduction to the Online Edition," 2006. www.tertullian.org/fathers/chronography_of_354_00_eintro.htm.

"Permanent Suspension of @realDonaldTrump," Twitter, January 8, 2021. https://blog.twitter.com/en_us/topics/company/2020/suspension.html.

PoliJAM. "Pelosi: 'We Have to Pass the Bill So That You Can Find Out What Is In It.'" YouTube, March 9, 2010. www.youtube.com/watch?v=hV-05TLiiLU.

Perry, Ruth. "Historically Correct." Women's Review of Books 9, no. 5 (February 1992): 15–16.

Peyser, Andrea. "Far-Left Agitprop for Pre-K Tots: What NYC Schools Have Come To." New York Post, January 27, 2020. https://nypost.com/2020/01/27/far-left-agitprop-for-pre-k-tots-what-nyc-schools-have-come-to/.

Phillips, Amber. "Analysis: They're Rapists.' President Trump's Campaign Launch Speech Two Years Later, Annotated." Washington Post, April 28, 2019. www.washingtonpost.com/news/the-fix/wp/2017/06/16/theyre-rapists-presidents-trump-campaign-launch-speech-two-years-later-annotated/.

Pimlott, J. A. R. "Christmas under the Puritans." History Today 10, no. 12 (December 1960). www.historytoday.com/archive/christmas-under-puritans#:~:text=The%20Puritans%20objected%20to%20the,far%20as%20to%20advocate%20abolition.

Pineda, Paulina. "Perry Lifts Suspension of Student in MAGA Controversy As Conservative Group Steps In." Arizona Republic, March 7, 2019. https://www.azcentral.com/story/news/local/gilbert/2019/03/07/perry-student-back-school-after-maga-controversy/3094372002/.

Pinker, Steven. The Blank Slate: The Modern Denial of Humen Nature. Penguin Books, 2003.

Planas, Roque. "Black Activists Honor Venezuelan President Nicolás Maduro in Harlem." HuffPost, September 29, 2015. www.huffpost.com/entry/black-activists-nicolas-maduro-harlem_n_560a836fe4b0af3706ddc573.

Planned Parenthood v. Casey. Supreme Court of the United States, June 22, 1992.

Plato. Apology, Crito and Phaedo of Socrates. Project Gutenberg, October 12, 2004. www.gutenberg.org/files/13726/13726-h/13726-h.htm.

Ponti, Crystal. "10 Things You May Not Know about the Jamestown Colony." History, August 6, 2019. www.history.com/news/jamestown-colony-settlement-facts.

"The Population Bomb 50 Years Later: a Conversation with Paul Ehrlich." Climate One, May 5, 2018. https://climateone.org/audio/population-bomb-50-years-later-conversation-paul-ehrlich.

President Trump (@POTUS), "As I have been saying for a long time. . . .," Twitter, January 8, 2021, 5:29 p.m. screenshot at Yashar Ali (@yashar), "The president tweeted this. . . .," Twitter, January 8, 2021, 8:35 p.m., https://twitter.com/yashar/status/1347718683351601152.

Prestigiacomo, Amanda. "Actor Says Trans Women Have 'Biologically Female' Penises. And Gets More Graphic from There." The Daily Wire, February 20, 2019. https://www.dailywire.com/news/actor-says-trans-women-have-biologically-female-amanda-prestigiacomo.

Prior, Karen Swallow. "Why Walt Whitman Called America the 'Greatest Poem.'" The Atlantic, July 7, 2020. www.theatlantic.com/entertainment/archive/2016/12/why-walt-whitman-called-the-america-the-greatest-poem/510932/.

"Professor Paul R. Ehrlich." The Royal Society, April 22, 2012. https://web.archive.org/web/20120422185752/https://royalsociety.org/people/paul-ehrlich/.

Prynne, William. Histriomastix: The Player's Scourge, or Actor's Tragedy. Michael Sparke, 1632. Adapted into modern English by the author.

"Queer Studies." Wesleyan University, www.wesleyan.edu/queerstudies/.

"Quran." Towards Understanding the Quran, www.islamicstudies.info,

"Rape and Sexual Assault Victimization among College-Age Females, 1995–2013." Bureau of Justice Statistics (BJS), www.bjs.gov/index. cfm?ty=pbdetail&iid=5176.

Rawls, Philip. "Huck Finn: Controversy over Removing the "N Word" from Mark Twain Novel." *Christian Science Monitor*, January 5, 2011. https://www.csmonitor.com/Books/Latest-News-Wires/2011/0105/Huck-Finn-Controversy-over-removing-the-N-word-from-Mark-Twain-novel.

Rees, Arianna. "A Video of Jimmy Kimmel Dressed in Blackface as Utah Jazz Legend Karl Malone Has Resurfaced. Here's Why." *Deseret News*, February 8, 2019. www.deseret.com/2019/2/8/2066 5327/a-video-of-jimmy-kimmel-dressed-in-blackface-as-utah-jazz-legend-karl-malone-has-resurfaced-here-s-w.

Reich, Wilhelm. *The Function of the Orgasm: Sex-Economic Problems of Biological Energy*. Noonday Press, 1973.

Relman, Eliza. "The Chair of the Democratic Party Just Embraced Progressive Insurgent Alexandria Ocasio-Cortez, Calling Her 'the Future of Our Party.'" *Business Insider*, July 3, 2018. www. businessinsider.com/dnc-tom-perez-alexandria-ocasio-cortez-democratic-socialist-future-2018-7.

"Remember What They Did." The Trump Accountability Project, web. archive.org/web/20201106193255/www.trumpaccountability.net/.

"Report of Sex Assault at APSU Turns out False." *Leaf-Chronicle*, November 15, 2016. www.theleafchronicle.com/story/news/local/clarksville/2016/11/15/report-sex-assault-apsu-turns-out-false/93881490/.

Rewind Me. "Jimmy Kimmel Blackface Oprah Jimfrey the Man Show (2001)." YouTube, August 10, 2018. www.youtube.com/watch?v=E1By6Wj_sAU.

Richardson, Valerie. "Architect of NYT's 1619 Project Draws Distinction between 'Politically Black and Racially Black.'" *Washington Times*, May 22, 2020. www.washingtontimes.com/news/2020/may/22/nikole-hannah-jones-1619-project-draws-distinction/.

Riley, Naomi Schaefer, et al. "'The 1619 Project' Enters American Classrooms." Education Next, December 17 2020. www.educationnext.org/1619-project-enters-american-classrooms-adding-new-sizzle-slavery-significant-cost/.

Robertson, Adi. "Gab Is Back Online After Being Banned by GoDaddy, Paypal, and More." The Verge, November 5, 2018. https://www.theverge.com/2018/11/5/18049132/gab-social-network-online-synagogue-shooting-deplatforming-return-godaddy-paypal-stripe-ban.

Robbins, James S. "Rioting Is Beginnig to Turn People Off to BLM and Protests While Biden Has No Solution." *USA Today*, August 31, 2020. https://www.usatoday.com/story/opinion/2020/08/31/riots-violence-erupting-turning-many-away-blm-and-protests-column/5675343002/.

Robinson, Dana, and Ann Battenfield. "The Worst Outbreaks in U.S. History." Healthline, March 24, 2020. https://www.healthline.com/health/worst-disease-outbreaks-history#measles.

Rodgers, Kayla. "Student Gets into Stanford after Writing #BlackLivesMatter on Application 100 Times." CNN, April 5, 2017. www.cnn.com/2017/04/05/us/stanford-application-black-lives-matter-trnd/index.html.

Roe v. Wade. Supreme Court of the United States, January 22, 1973.

Rogers, Alex. "Barack Obama Stumps for Jon Ossoff in New TV Ad," CNN, December 1, 2020. https://www.cnn.com/2020/12/01/politics/obama-ossoff-ad/index.html.

Roose, Kevin. "In Pulling Trump's Megaphone, Twitter Shows Where Power Now Lies." *New York Times*, January 9, 2021. https://www.nytimes.com/2021/01/09/technology/trump-twitter-ban.html.

———. "On Election Day, Facebook and Twitter Did Better by Making Their Products Worse." *New York Times*, November 5, 2020,. https://www.nytimes.com/2020/11/05/technology/facebook-twitter-election.html.

Rosenberg, Paul. "A User's Guide to 'Cultural Marxism': Anti-Semitic Conspiracy Theory, Reloaded." Salon, May 6, 2019. www.salon.

com/2019/05/05/a-users-guide-to-cultural-marxism-anti-semitic-co
nspiracy-theory-reloaded/.

Russell, Bertrand. *History of Western Philosophy*. Routledge, 2015.

Rutherford, Alexandra. "What the Origins of the '1 in 5' Statistic Teaches
Us about Sexual Assault Policy." *Behavioral Scientist*, February 26,
2020. behavioralscientist.org/what-the-origins-of-the-
1-in-5-statistic-teaches-us-about-sexual-assault-policy/.

Rutler, George W. "Mistaken Predictions." Catholic Education Resource
Center, 2020. www.catholiceducation.org/en/culture/environment/
mistaken-predictions.html.

Saad, Lydia. "What Percentage of Americans Celebrate Christmas?"
Gallup, December 2019. https://news.gallup.com/poll/272357/
percentage-americans-celebrate-christmas.aspx.

Safire, William. "On Language; Linguistically Correct." *New York
Times*, May 5, 1991. timesmachine.nytimes.com/
timesmachine/1991/05/05/846891.html.

Salo, Jackie. "Why You'll No Longer Find 'Convicted Felons' in San
Francisco." *New York Post*, August 22, 2019. nypost.
com/2019/08/22/why-youll-no-longer-find-convicted-
felons-in-san-francisco/.

Sanders, Bernie (@BernieSanders). "Say Bill Gates was actually taxed
$100 billion. . . ." Twitter, November 7, 2019, 11:26 a.m. twitter.
com/berniesanders/status/1192478435693780992.

Sarachild, Kathie. "Consciousness Raising: A Radical Weapon." Rape
Relief Shelter, www.rapereliefshelter.bc.ca/sites/default/files/imce/
Feminist-Revolution-Consciousness-Raising—A-Radical-Weapon-
Kathie-Sarachild.pdf.

"SB-145 Sex Offenders: Registration," (Bill Text). California Legislative
Information, September 14, 2020. leginfo.legislature.ca.gov/faces/
billTextClient.xhtml?bill_id=201920200SB145

Schenck v. United States. Supreme Court of the United States, March 3, 1919.

Scheper, Eric. "Herbert Marcuse: The Ideologue as Paid Agent of U.S.
Imperialism." Marxists Internet Archive, www.marxists.org/history/
erol/ca.firstwave/li-marcuse.htm.

Schmidt, Patrick. "Heckler's Veto." The First Amendment Encyclopedia, https://www.mtsu.edu/first-amendment/article/968/heckler-s-veto.

Schmidt, Samantha. "A Black Student Wrote Those Racist Messages That Shook the Air Force Academy, School Says." *Washington Post*, WP Company, April 29, 2019. www.washingtonpost.com/news/morning-mix/wp/2017/11/08/a-black-student-wrote-those-racist-messages-that -shook-the-air-force-academy/?utm_term=.6ba19098406a.

Schmidt, T. C., et al. *Hippolytus of Rome: Commentary on Daniel and "Chronicon."* Gorgias Press, 2017.

Scholer, J. Lawrence, and the editors of the *Dartmouth Review*. "The Story of Kwanzaa." *Dartmouth Review*, January 15, 2001. http://www.hartford-hwp.com/archives/45a/767.html.

Schow, Ashe. "After Settlement, the Rolling Stone Rape Hoax Saga Is Officially Over." The Federalist, February 13, 2018. thefederalist.com/2018/02/13/settlement-fraternity-rolling-stonerape-hoax-saga-officially/.

"Science: Another Ice Age," *Time*, November 13, 1972, http://content.time.com/time/magazine/article/0,9171,910467,00.html.

"Scientific Consensus: Earth's Climate Is Warming." NASA, https://climate.nasa.gov/scientific-consensus/.

"Scientific Consensus." Google Books Ngram Viewer, https://books.google.com/ngrams/graph?content=%22scientific+consensus%22&year_start=1700&year_end=2015&corpus=15&smoothing=3&direct_url=t1%3B%2C%22%20scientific%20consensus%20%22%3B%2Cco#t1%3B%2C%22%20scientific%20consensus%20%22%3B%2Cco.

Selk, Avi. "Ted Cruz and Wife Are Shouted out of D.C. Restaurant over His Support for Kavanaugh." *Washington Post*, March 28, 2019. www.washingtonpost.com/news/local/wp/2018/09/25/ted-cruz-and-wife-shouted-out-of-d-c-restaurant-over-his-support-for-kavanaugh/.

Serratore, Angela. "Alexander Hamilton's Adultery and Apology." *Smithsonian Magazine*, July 25, 2013. www.smithsonianmag.com/history/alexander-hamiltons-adultery-and-apology-18021947/.

Serwer, Adam. "The Fight over the 1619 Project Is Not about the Facts." *The Atlantic*, December 23, 2019. www.theatlantic.com/ideas/archive/2019/12/historians-clash-1619-project/604093/. ,

Shakespeare, William. *The Merchant of Venice*. Project Gutenberg, March 9, 2019. www.gutenberg.org/files/1515/1515-h/1515-h.htm.

Shakespeare, William. *Hamlet.* Project Gutenberg, September 30, 2019, www.gutenberg.org/files/1524/1524-h/1524-h.htm.

———. *The Tempest.* Project Gutenberg, October 26, 2007. www.gutenberg.org/files/23042/23042-h/23042-h.htm.

Shapiro, Gary. "How Churchill Mobilized the English Language." *New York Sun*, January 18, 2021. www.nysun.com/new-york/how-churchill-mobilized-the-english-language/87862/.

Shaw, George Bernard. *Back to Methuselah: A Metabiological Pentateuch*, Project Gutenberg, August 18, 2018. http://www.gutenberg.org/files/13084/13084-h/13084-h.htm.

Shibley, Robert. "Antioch's Infamous Sexual Assault Policy." FIRE, April 15, 2014. www.thefire.org/antiochs-infamous-sexual-assault-policy/.

Shteyler, Vadim M., et al., "Failed Assignments—Rethinking Sex Designations on Birth Certificates." *New England Journal of Medicine* 383 (2020): 2399–2401. doi: 10.1056/NEJMp2025974, https://www.nejm.org/doi/full/10.1056/NEJMp2025974.

Shugerman, Emily. "How a Student in a Diaper Caused an Eruption in One of America's Biggest Conservative Youth Organisations." *Independent*, June 7, 2018. www.independent.co.uk/news/world/americas/diaper-turning-point-usa-kent-state-student-conservative-youth-republican-kaitlin-bennett-a8230021.html.

Siegel, Lee. "Wrestling with Saul Bellow: A New Biography Renews the Fight over the Authors Reputation." Vulture, March 23, 2015. www.vulture.com/2015/03/saul-bellow-biography.html.

Simon, Mallory. "Over 1,000 Health Professionals Sign a Letter Saying, Don't Shut Down Protests Using Coronavirus Concerns As an Excuse." CNN, June 5, 2020. https://www.cnn.com/2020/06/05/health/health-care-open-letter-protests-coronavirus-trnd/index.html.

Sleeper, Jim. "Allan Bloom and the Conservative Mind." *New York Times*, September 4, 2005. www.nytimes.com/2005/09/04/books/review/allan-bloom-and-the-conservative-mind.html.

Small, Matt. "FBI Offering Up to $50K for Information on DNC and RNC Pipe Bombs." WTOP News, January 8, 2021. https://wtop.com/dc/2021/01/fbi-offering-up-to-50k-for-information-on-dnc-and-rnc-pipe-bombs/.

Smith, Adam. *The Wealth of Nations*. Random House USA, 2020.

———. *An Inquiry into the Nature and Causes of the Wealth of Nations*. "Digression on the Corn Trade." Project Gutenberg, September 7, 2019. http://www.gutenberg.org/ebooks/3300.

Smith, Chris. "Violence against Children Is Al Gore's Cure for Environment." Congressional Record, October 7, 1997. https://www.govinfo.gov/content/pkg/CREC-1997-10-07/html/CREC-1997-10-07-pt1-PgH8566-3.htm.

Smith, Kyle. "Smollett Was 'Clearly Lying,' Says the Comic." *National Review*, August 29, 2019. www.nationalreview.com/corner/dave-chappelle-goes-after-jussie-smollett/.

Smith, Mitch. "Christmas Tree or Holiday Tree? The Frosty Feud Splintering a State." *New York Times*, November 13, 2019. https://www.nytimes.com/2019/11/13/us/wisconsin-christmas-holiday-tree.html.

Soave, Robby. "Study: 80% of Americans Believe Political Correctness Is a Problem." *Reason*, October 11, 2018. reason.com/2018/10/11/political-correctness-americans-vote-maj/.

"*South Park*: It Hits the Fan," IMDb, June 20, 2001. www.imdb.com/title/tt0705935/

"*South Park*: Sponsored Content," IMDb, November 18, 2015. www.imdb.com/title/tt5113842/.

Sowell, Thomas. "Blame the Welfare State, Not Racism, for Poor Blacks' Problems." Penn Live, January 5, 2019. https://www.pennlive.com/opinion/2015/05/poor_blacks_looking_for_someon.html.

Spaeth, Ryu. "The Strange Liberal Backlash to Woke Culture." *The New Republic*, November 25, 2019. newrepublic.com/article/155681/strange-liberal-backlash-woke-culture.

Spangler, Todd. "Netflix Defends *Cuties* as 'Social Commentary' against Sexualization of Young Children." *Variety*, September 14, 2020. variety.com/2020/digital/news/netflix-defends-cuties-against-sexualization-young-girls-1234766347/.

Sparks, Jared, ed. *The Works of Benjamin Franklin*. (C. Tappan, 1844).

SpectricYT. "Offended? It's Called IRONY Bro Are You a Retahrd? Get a Load of This CRINGE NROMIE He Doesn't Get IRONY." Reddit. www.reddit.com/r/okbuddyretard/comments/buhbjc/offended_its_called_irony_bro_are_you_a_retahrd/.

Stanford Dictionary of Philosophy, https://plato.stanford.edu/.

Steinbuch, Yaron. "Black Lives Matter Co-Founder Describes Herself as 'Trained Marxist.'" *New York Post*, June 25, 2020. nypost.com/2020/06/25/blm-co-founder-describes-herself-as-trained-marxist/.

Steinmetz, Katy. "California Legalizes Marijuana: Everything You Need to Know." *Time*, November 9, 2016. time.com/4565438/california-marijuana-faq-rules-prop-64/.

Stern, Michael J. "COVID Has Turned Breathing into a Deadly Event and All of Us into Potential Serial Killers." *USA Today*, November 30, 2020. www.usatoday.com/story/opinion/2020/11/30/covid-turns-everyone-into-potential-killer-by-breathing-column/6455743002/.

"Stonewall Riots." History, May 31, 2017. www.history.com/topics/gay-rights/the-stonewall-riots.

Stubbs, Philip. "The Anatomie of Abuses." Richard Jones, 1583. Adapted into modern English by the author.

Sullivan, Paul. "How Political Ideology Influences Charitable Giving." *New York Times*, November 3, 2018. www.nytimes.com/2018/11/03/your-money/republicans-democrats-charity-philanthropy.html.

Whitney v. California Supreme Court of the United States, May 16, 1927.

Manning, Susan A. "Dance Studies, Gay and Lesbian Studies, and Queer Theory." *Northwestern Scholars*, Cambridge University Press, January 1, 1970. www.scholars.northwestern.edu/en/publications/dance-studies-gay-and-lesbian-studies-and-queer-theory.

Tagawa, Beth. "When Cross-Dressing Was Criminal: Book Details History of Longtime San Francisco Law." SF State News, February 2015. https://news.sfsu.edu/when-cross-dressing-was-criminal-book-documents-history-longtime-san-francisco-law.

Talarico, Lauren. "Houston Public Library Admits Registered Child Sex Offender Read to Kids in Drag Queen Storytime." KHOU 11, March 19, 2019. https://www.khou.com/article/news/local/houston-public-library-admits-registered-child-sex-offender-read-to-kids-in-drag-queen-storytime/285-becf3a0d-56c5-4f3c-96df-add07bbd002a.

Taleb, Nassim Nicholas. Antifragile: Things That Gain from Disorder. Random House, 2016.

Talley, Thomas J. Origins of the Liturgical Year. Liturgical Press.

Tamburin, Adam. "Controversial Professor Carol Swain to Retire from Vanderbilt." The Tennessean, January 23, 2017. www.tennessean.com/story/news/education/2017/01/23/carol-swain-announces-retirement-vanderbilt-university/96959004/.

Tapper, Jake (@jaketapper). "I truly sympathize with those dealing with losing. . . .," Twitter, November 9, 2020. twitter.com/jaketapper/status/1325836769644982273.

Taub, Amanda. "The Truth about 'Political Correctness' Is That It Doesn't Actually Exist." Vox, January 28, 2015. www.vox.com/2015/1/28/7930845/political-correctness-doesnt-exist.

Taylor, John. "Are You Politically Correct?" New York Magazine, January 21, 1991. 32–41.

Texas v. Johnson. Supreme Court of the United States, June 21, 1989.

"Thomas Called 'Absolutely Incapable of the Abuses." Tampa Bay Times, October 14, 2005. www.tampabay.com/archive/1991/10/14/thomas-called-absolutely-incapable-of-the-abuses/.

Thomas, Clarence. "Statement before the Judiciary Committee." American Rhetoric, October 11, 1991. www.americanrhetoric.com/speeches/clarencethomashightechlynching.htm.

Thomas. "George Orwell Review," Maude's Tavern, October 9, 2008, maudestavern.com/2008/10/09/george-orwell-review/.

"Thomas Second Hearing Day 1, Part 1," C-SPAN, https://www.c-span. org/video/?21974-1/thomas-hearing-day-1-part-1.

Thompson, Peter. "Eastern Germany: The Most Godless Place on Earth." *The Guardian*, September 22, 2012. https://www.theguardian.com/ commentisfree/belief/2012/sep/22/atheism-east-germany-godless-place.

Thornton, Stephen P. "Solipsism and the Problem of Other Minds." Internet Encyclopedia, https://iep.utm.edu/solipsis/.

Threatcraft, Torry. "Joe Rogan's Podcast Is Causing Internal Rift at Spotify." Okayplayer, September 17, 2020. www.okayplayer.com/ culture/joe-rogan-podcast-spotify-transphobic-racist.html.

Todd, Bridget. "Clarence Thomas Anita Hill: Never Forget Justice's Sexual Harassment History." Mic, April 4, 2013. www.mic.com/ articles/32733/clarence-thomas-anita-hill-never-forget-justice-s-sexual-harassment-history.

Trent, James W. Inventing the Feeble Mind: A History of Intellectual Disability in the United States. Oxford University Press, 2017.

Troy, Tevi. "Cornell's Straight Flush." *City Journal*, December 13, 2009. www.city-journal.org/html/cornell%E2%80%99s-straight-flush-10659.html.

Trump, Donald Jr. (@DonldJTrumpJr). "It continues . . . Big Tech has totally eliminated. . . ." Twitter. January 9, 2021, 3:41 p.m. https:// twitter.com/DonaldJTrumpJr/status/1348006883861282816.

———. "We are living in Orwell's 1984. . . . ." Twitter, January 8, 2021, 7:10 p.m. https://twitter.com/DonaldJTrumpJr/status/ 1347697226466828288.

"Trump Taints America's Views on Political Correctness." Fairleigh Dickinson University, October 30, 2015. https:// view2.fdu.edu/publicmind/2015/151030/; https://www. pewresearch.org/fact-tank/2016/07/20/in-political-correctness-debate-most-americans-think-too-many-people-are-easily-offended/.

"The Truth About the Religious Right's Phony 'War on Christmas.'" Americans United for Separation of Church and State, www.au.org/

content/the-truth-about-the-religious-rights-phony-war-on-christmas.

Tucker, Sophie. "Fifty Million Frenchmen Can't Be Wrong." *International Lyrics Playground*, lyricsplayground.com/alpha/songs/f/fiftymillionfrenchmencantbewrong.html.

Turner, Christopher. "'Adventures in the Orgasmatron.'" *New York Times*, September 23, 2011. www.nytimes.com/2011/09/23/books/review/adventures-in-the-orgasmatron.html?pagewanted=all.

United States v. Rumely. Supreme Court of the United States, March 9, 1953.

"University of Iowa Hospitals Boasts [sic] 99.7% Coronavirus Survival Rate, amid Financial Woes." *Gazette*, June 4, 2020,. https://www.thegazette.com/subject/news/education/university-of-iowa-hospitals-boasts-997-coronavirus-survival-rate-amid-financial-woes-20200604

Urban Dictionary, www.urbandictionary.com.

"U.S. Religious Landscape Survey: Religious Affiliation: Diverse and Dynamic," Pew Forum on Religion & Public Life, February 2008. https://web.archive.org/web/20150125190643/http://religions.pewforum.org/pdf/report-religious-landscape-study-full.pdf.

U.S. Surgeon General (@Surgeon_General). "Seriously people. . . ." Twitter, February 29, 2020, 4:08 a.m. https://web.archive.org/web/20200302023223if_/https://twitter.com/Surgeon_General/status/1233725785283932160.

Ventresca, Rachel. "Clinton: 'You Cannot Be Civil with a Political Party That Wants to Destroy What You Stand for.'" CNN, October 9, 2018. www.cnn.com/2018/10/09/politics/hillary-clinton-civility-congress-cnntv/index.html.

Verdict with Ted Cruz. "Bill Barr is the Honey Badger. . . . ." Facebook, June 30, 2020. https://www.facebook.com/watch/?v=371801462 1548732.

Veissière, Samuel Paul. "Why Is Transgender Identity on the Rise among Teens?" *Psychology Today*, https://www.psychologytoday.com/us/blog/culture-mind-and-brain/201811/why-is-transgender-identity-the-rise-among-teens.

Vincent, Alice. "Empire Actor Jussie Smollett's 'Faked' Racial Attack: What Really Happened?" *Telegraph*, March 27, 2019. www. telegraph.co.uk/tv/0/jussie-smollett-empire-actor-attack/.

Violas, Paul C. "The Indoctrination Debate and the Great Depression," *History Teacher* 4, no. 4 (May 1971): 25–35.

Virginia Allen "*NY Times* Mum on '1619' Creator Calling '1619 Riots' Moniker an 'Honor.'" The Daily Signal, June 24, 2020. www. dailysignal.com/2020/06/22/new-york-times-mum-on-1619-project-creator-calling-1619-riots-moniker-an-honor/.

Vogue, Ariane de, et al., "Trump Administration Withdraws Federal Protections for Transgender Students," CNN, February 22, 2017,. https://www.cnn.com/2017/02/22/politics/doj-withdraws-federal-protections-on-transgender-bathrooms-in-schools/index.html.

Wallace-Wells, Benjamin. "David French, Sohrab Ahmari, and the Battle for the Future of Conservatism." *New Yorker*, September 12, 2019,. https://web.archive.org/web/20200701055715/https://www. newyorker.com/news/the-political-scene/david-french-sohrab-ahmari-and-the-battle-for-the-future-of-conservatism.

Wagner, Laura. "Journalist Ta-Nehisi Coates among 2015 MacArthur 'Genius' Award Winners." NPR, September 29, 2015. www.npr.org/ sections/thetwo-way/2015/09/29/444221706/journalist-ta-nehisi-coates-among-2015-macarthur-genius-award-winners.

Ward, Karla. "Mitch McConnell Loses Leftovers in Confrontation by Heckler at Louisville Restaurant." *Lexington Herald Leader*, October 20, 2018. www.kentucky.com/news/politics-government/ article220385650.html.

Washington, George. "George Washington: Farewell Address (1796)," U.S. Embassy & Consulate in the Republic of Korea, February 11, 2020. https://kr.usembassy.gov/education-culture/infopedia-usa/ living-documents-american-history-democracy/george-washington-farewell-address-1796/.

"Watching Dr. Jeffries Self-Destruct." *New York Times*, August 25, 1991. www.nytimes.com/1991/08/25/opinion/watching-dr-jeffries-self-destruct.html.

Watson, Alex. "Literally Ok." *Wall Street International*, April 28, 2017. wsimag.com/culture/25065-literally-ok.

"We Respond to the Historians Who Critiqued the 1619 Project." *New York Times*, December 20, 2019. www.nytimes.com/2019/12/20/magazine/we-respond-to-the-historians-who-critiqued-the-1619-project.html.

Weber, Bruce. "Mamet: Hearings Prompted 'Oleana.'" *Chicago Tribune*, September 2, 2018. www.chicagotribune.com/news/ct-xpm-1992-11-12-9204120711-story.html.

Weigel, Moira. "Political Correctness: How the Right Invented a Phantom." *The Guardian*, November 30, 2016. www.theguardian.com/us-news/2016/nov/30/political-correctness-how-the-right-invented-phantom-enemy-donald-trump.

Weis, Kenneth R. "Al Gore: Stabilize Population to Combat Global Warming." *Los Angeles Times*, June 22, 2011. https://latimesblogs.latimes.com/greenspace/2011/06/al-gore-climate-change-population-contraception-fertility.html.

"What's in a Name? Christmas vs. Holiday Tree." NPR, November 30, 2005. https://www.npr.org/transcripts/5032882.

Wheat, Shawn. "Goodyear Responds to Zero-Tolerance Policy Slide Labeled by Employee as Discriminatory." 13 WIBW, August 18, 2020. www.wibw.com/2020/08/18/goodyear-employees-say-new-no-tolerance-policy-is-discriminatory/.

Whitney v. California. Supreme Court of the United States, 1927.

"What We Do," United States Africa Command, January 20, 2013. https://www.africom.mil/what-we-do.

"Why We're Proud of Our Fat Bodies." BBC News, September 22, 2018. www.bbc.co.uk/news/resources/idt-sh/why_we_are_proud_of_our_fat_bodies.

Wikipedia, https://www.wikipedia.org/.

Wilentz, Sean. "A Matter of Facts." *The Atlantic*, January 22, 2020. www.theatlantic.com/ideas/archive/2020/01/1619-project-new-york-times-wilentz/605152/.

Williams, Mara Rose, et al. "'We Cannot Violate the Law': Kansas State Won't Expel Student Who Made Racist Tweets." *Kansas City Star*, July 1, 2020. www.kansascity.com/news/state/kansas/article243925962.html.

Williams, Rob. "'My Dear You Are Ugly, but Tomorrow I Shall Be Sober and You Will Still Be Ugly': Winston Churchill Tops Poll of History's Funniest Insults." *Independent*, October 14, 2013. www.independent.co.uk/news/uk/home-news/my-dear-you-are-ugly-tomorrow-i-shall-be-sober-and-you-will-still-be-ugly-winston-churchill-tops-poll-history-s-funniest-insults-8878622.html.

Wilson, Woodrow. "What Is Progress?" Teaching American History, teachingamericanhistory.org/library/document/what-is-progress/.

Woo, Jaime. "Hot Docs 2019: In Drag Kids, Parents Cheer As Children Slay Gender Norms." April 22, 2019. https://www.theglobeandmail.com/life/parenting/article-in-documentary-drag-kids-parents-cheer-as-children-slay-gender-norms/.

"Words Matter: The Language of Addiction." Partnership to End Addiction. November 17, 2020. drugfree.org/article/shouldnt-use-word-addict/.

"Worldwide Desktop Market Share of Leading Search Engines from January 2010 to January 2021." Statista, https://www.statista.com/statistics/216573/worldwide-market-share-of-search-engines/#:~:text=Ever%20since%20the%20introduction%20of,share%20as%20of%20July%20202

Xiao, Jingyi, et al. "Nonpharmaceutical Measures for Pandemic Influenza in Nonhealthcare Settings—Personal Protective and Environmental Measures." *Centers for Disease Control and Prevention Policy Review* 26, no. 5 (May 2020). https://wwwnc.cdc.gov/eid/article/26/5/19-0994_article.

Yardley, Jonathan. "In New York, a Bigoted Man on Campus." *Washington Post*, August 12, 1991. www.washingtonpost.com/archive/lifestyle/1991/08/12/in-new-york-a-bigoted-man-on-campus/637b6b9e-85b3-4a84-a6b4-d69f48c32fc3/.

York, Byron (@ByronYork). "The National Museum of African American History & Culture. . . ." Twitter. July 15, 2020. https://twitter.com/ByronYork/status/1283372233730203651.

Young Americas Foundation. "Speech Is Not Violence: Knowles Completely Owns Pretentious Professor." YouTube, May 2, 2019. https://www.youtube.com/watch?v=LaERkte8ylA.

Young, Cathy. "Young: Rape Cases and Knee-Jerk Reactions." *Newsday*, March 15, 2016. www.newsday.com/opinion/columnists/cathy-young/10-years-later-the-legacy-of-the-duke-lacrosse-scandal-1.11574704.

NOTES

Preface
1. G. K. Chesterton, *Collected Works of G. K. Chesterton: The Illustrated London News, 1923–1925* (San Francisco, California: Ignatius Press, 1990), 33.

Chapter 1: The West in Wonderland
1. Lewis Carroll, *Through the Looking Glass*, Project Gutenberg, February 25, 2020, www.gutenberg.org/files/12/12-h/12-h.htm.
2. Aristotle, *Politics*, trans. Benjamin Jowett, The Internet Classics Archive, classics.mit.edu/Aristotle/politics.1.one.html.
3. Carl von Clausewitz, *On War*, ed. Michael Howard and trans. Peter Paret (Princeton, New Jersey: Princeton University Press, 1989).
4. Alex Watson, "Literally Ok: A Defense," *Wall Street International*, April 28, 2017, wsimag.com/culture/25065-literally-ok.
5. Anjani Kapoor, et al., "Barriers to Service Provision for Justice-Involved Youth," *Criminal Justice and Behavior* 45, no. 12 (December 1, 2018): 1832–51.
6. Elizabeth Knowles and Julia Elliott, "Political Correctness," *The Oxford Dictionary of New Words*, 2nd rev. ed. (Oxford: Oxford University Press, 1997).

7. George Orwell, *Nineteen Eighty-Four: A Novel.* (London: Penguin Books, 1967).

8. Deborah Cameron, "Words, Words, Words" in *The War of the Words: The Political Correctness Debate*, ed. Sarah Dunant (London: Virago Press, 1994), 31.

9. Stanley Fish, *There's No Such Thing as Free Speech . . . and It's a Good Thing Too* (Oxford: Oxford University Press, 1994).

10. Gary Shapiro, "How Churchill Mobilized the English Language" *New York Sun*, June 12, 2012, www.nysun.com/new-york/how-churchill-mobilized-the-english-language/87862/; Rob Williams, "'My Dear You Are Ugly, but Tomorrow I Shall Be Sober and You Will Still Be Ugly': Winston Churchill Tops Poll of History's Funniest Insults," *Independent*, October 14, 2013, www.independent.co.uk/news/uk/home-news/my-dear-you-are-ugly-tomorrow-i-shall-be-sober-and-you-will-still-be-ugly-winston-churchill-tops-poll-history-s-funniest-insults-8878622.html.

11. Winston Churchill, "We Shall Fight on the Beaches," The International Churchill Society, April 13, 2017, winstonchurchill.org/resources/speeches/1940-the-finest-hour/we-shall-fight-on-the-beaches/.

12. Amber Phillips, "Analysis: 'They're Rapists.' President Trump's Campaign Launch Speech Two Years Later, Annotated," *Washington Post*, April 28, 2019, www.washingtonpost.com/news/the-fix/wp/2017/06/16/theyre-rapists-presidents-trump-campaign-launch-speech-two-years-later-annotated/.

13. Today, we can no longer suppose that ladies even have their own restrooms in which to powder their noses, as we will come to see.

14. "Euphemism," Online Etymology Dictionary, www.etymonline.com/word/euphemism.

15. William Safire, "On Language; Linguistically Correct," *New York Times*, May 5, 1991, timesmachine.nytimes.com/timesmachine/1991/05/05/846891.html.

16. "A Little History of 'Politically Correct': The Soviets Invented It and the University Tolerates It," *Washington Times*, November 15, 2015, www.washingtontimes.com/news/2015/nov/15/editorial-a-little-history-of-politically-correct/.

17. William Shakespeare, *The Tragedy of Hamlet, Prince of Denmark*, Gutenberg Project, November 1998, www.gutenberg.org/files/1524/1524-h/1524-h.htm.

Chapter 2: Redefining Reality

1. Deborah Cameron, "Words, Words, Words" in *The War of the Words: The Political Correctness Debate*, ed. Sarah Dunant (London: Virago Press, 1994); Geoffrey Hughes, *Political Correctness: A History of Semantics and Culture* (Hoboken, New Jersey: Wiley-Blackwell, 2010).

2. Renato Corsetti, "A Mother Tongue Mostly Spoken by Fathers," *Language Problems & Language Planning* 20, no. 3 (1996): 263–73, https://www.ingentaconnect.com/content/jbp/lplp/1996/00000020/00000003/art00004.

3. "Trump Taints America's Views on Political Correctness," Fairleigh Dickinson University, October 30, 2015, https://view2.fdu.edu/publicmind/2015/151030/; Hanna Fingerhut, "In 'Political Correctness' Debate, Most Americans Think Too Many People Are Easily Offended," Pew Research Center, July 20, 2016, https://www.pewresearch.org/fact-tank/2016/07/20/in-political-correctness-debate-most-americans-think-too-many-people-are-easily-offended/.

4. Stephen Hawkins, et al., "Hidden Tribes: A Study of America's Polarized Landscape," More in Common, October 11, 2018, https://static1.squarespace.com/static/5a70a7c3010027736a22740f/t/5bbcea6b7817f7bf7342b718/1539107467397/hidden_tribes_report-2.pdf.

5. Chris Caesar, "Perspective: Trump Ran against Political Correctness. Now His Team Is Begging for Politeness," *Washington Post*, March 1, 2019, www.washingtonpost.com/posteverything/wp/2017/05/16/trump-ran-against-political-correctness-now-his-team-is-begging-for-politeness/.

6. Kat Chow, "'Politically Correct': The Phrase Has Gone from Wisdom to Weapon," NPR, December 15, 2016, www.npr.org/sections/codeswitch/2016/12/14/505324427/politically-correct-the-phrase-has-gone-from-wisdom-to-weapon.

7. Deborah Cameron, "Words, Words, Words," 23.

8. Spencer Brown, "'Physically Triggered': Internal Emails Show CSULA Faculty in Hysterics over 'Build the Wall' Activism," Young America's Foundation, September 4, 2019, www.yaf.org/news/physically-triggered-internal-emails-show-csula-faculty-in-hysterics-over-build-the-wall-activism/.

9. Susan B. Glasser, "Donald Trump's 2020 Superspreader Campaign: A Diary," *New Yorker*, November 3, 2020, www.newyorker.com/news/letter-from-trumps-washington/donald-trumps-2020-superspreader-campaign-a-diary; Michael J. Stern, "COVID Has Turned Breathing into a Deadly Event and All of Us into Potential Serial Killers," *USA*

Today, November 30, 2020, www.usatoday.com/story/opinion/2020/11/30/covid-turns-everyone-into-potential-killer-by-breathing-column/6455743002/.

10. Aaron Greiner, et al., "Open Letter," Google Drive, June 5, 2020, drive.google.com/file/d/1Jyfn4Wd2i6bRi12ePghMHtX3ys1b7K1A/view.

Chapter 3: Cultural Hegemony

1.   Friedrich Engels and Karl Marx, "The Communist Manifesto," trans. Allen Lutins with assistance from Jim Tarzia, Project Gutenberg, January 20, 2005, www.gutenberg.org/cache/epub/61/pg61.html.

2.   Ibid; Karl Marx, "Critique of Hegel's Philosophy in General," *Economic and Philosophic Manuscripts of 1844,* trans. Martin Milligan, 2009, Marxists International Archive, www.marxists.org/archive/marx/works/1844/manuscripts/hegel.htm.

3.   Frederick Engels, *The Principles of Communism,* trans. Paul Sweezy, Marxists International Archive, February 2005, www.marxists.org/archive/marx/works/1847/11/prin-com.htm.

4.   Bill Berkowitz, "'Cultural Marxism' Catching On," Southern Poverty Law Center, August 15, 2003, www.splcenter.org/fighting-hate/intelligence-report/2003/cultural-marxism-catching.

5.   Paul Rosenberg, "A User's Guide to 'Cultural Marxism': Anti-Semitic Conspiracy Theory, Reloaded," Salon, May 6, 2019, www.salon.com/2019/05/05/a-users-guide-to-cultural-marxism-anti-semitic-conspiracy-theory-reloaded/.

6.   "Cultural Marxism Conspiracy Theory," Wikipedia, en.wikipedia.org/wiki/Cultural_Marxism_conspiracy_theory.

7.   Michael Butter, "There's a Conspiracy Theory That the CIA Invented the Term 'Conspiracy Theory'—Here's Why," The Conversation, November 25, 2020, theconversation.com/theres-a-conspiracy-theory-that-the-cia-invented-the-term-conspiracy-theory-heres-why-132117.

8.   Paul Kengor, "Cultural Marxism and Its Conspirators," *American Spectator,* April 3, 2019, spectator.org/cultural-marxism-and-its-conspirators/.

9.   Paul Kengor, "Cultural Marxism and Its Conspirators: Part 2," *American Spectator,* July 2, 2020, spectator.org/cultural-marxism-and-its-conspirators-part-2/.

10. Boris Buden, "To Make the Long March Short: A Short Commentary on the Two Long Marches That Have Failed Their Emancipatory Promises," Crisis & Critique, crisiscritique.org/nov2018/boris.pdf.

11. Samuel Moyn, "The Alt-Right's Favorite Meme Is 100 Years Old," *New York Times*, November 13, 2018, www.nytimes.com/2018/11/13/opinion/cultural-marxism-anti-semitism.html.

12. F.B., "The Strange Afterlife of Antonio Gramsci's 'Prison Notebooks,'" *Economist*, November 7, 2017, www.economist.com/prospero/2017/11/07/the-strange-afterlife-of-antonio-gramscis-prison-notebooks.

13. Antonio Gramsci, *Prison Notebooks*, ed. Joseph A. Buttigieg (New York: Columbia University Press, 2011).

14. Ibid.

15. Ibid.

16. Ibid.

17. Martin Jay, *The Dialectical Imagination: A History of the Frankfurt School and the Institute of Social Research 1923–1950* (Oakland, California: University of California Press, 2008).

18. Ibid.

19. Ibid.

20. Ibid.

21. Paul Kengor and Michael Knowles, *The Devil and Karl Marx: Communism's Long March of Death, Deception, and Infiltration* (Gastonia, North Carolina: TAN Books, 2020).

22. Max Horkheimer, *Critical Theory* (New York: Continuum, 1982).

23. Jay, *The Dialectical Imagination*.

24. Karl Marx, "Theses on Feuerbach," Marxists International Archive, www.marxists.org/archive/marx/works/1845/theses/theses.htm.

25. Christopher Turner, "'Adventures in the Orgasmatron,'" *New York Times*, September 23, 2011, www.nytimes.com/2011/09/23/books/review/adventures-in-the-orgasmatron.html?pagewanted=all.

26. Wilhelm Reich, *The Function of the Orgasm: Sex-Economic Problems of Biological Energy* (New York: Noonday Press, 1973).

27. Henry Allen, "Thinking inside the Box," *Wall Street Journal*, June 11, 2011, www.wsj.com/articles/SB10001424052702303657404576361683162870042.

28. Tim Murphy, "Read Bernie Sanders' 1970s-Era Essays on Sex, Cancer, Revolution, and Fluoride," *Mother Jones*, July 6, 2015, www.

motherjones.com/politics/2015/07/
bernie-sanders-vermont-freeman-sexual-freedom-fluoride/.

29. Danielle Kurtzleben, "The Bernie Sanders 'Rape Fantasy' Essay,
Explained," NPR, May 29, 2015, www.npr.org/sections/
itsallpolitics/2015/05/29/410606045/
the-bernie-sanders-rape-fantasy-essay-explained.

30. Elizabeth Day, "#BlackLivesMatter: The Birth of a New Civil Rights
Movement," *Guardian*, July 19, 2015, www.theguardian.com/
world/2015/jul/19/blacklivesmatter-birth-civil-rights-movement.

31. Torry Threatcraft, "Joe Rogan's Podcast Is Causing Internal Rift at
Spotify," Okayplayer, September 17, 2020, www.okayplayer.com/
culture/joe-rogan-podcast-spotify-transphobic-racist.html.

32. Nolan D. McCaskill and Andrew Desiderio, "Bernie Became a
Millionaire in 2016, Records Show," *Politico*, April 15, 2019, www.
politico.com/story/2019/04/15/bernie-sanders-millionaire-1276928.

33. Sanders, Bernie (@BernieSanders), "Say Bill Gates was actually taxed
$100 Billion. We could end homelessness and provide safe drinking
water to everyone in this country. Bill would still be a multibillionaire.
Our message: the billionaire class cannot have it all when wo many have
so little. Https://T.co/FVlxuIGygf," Twitter, November 7, 2019, 11:26
a.m., twitter.com/berniesanders/status/1192478435693780992.

34. Dylan Matthews, "Bernie Sanders's Fear of Immigrant Labor Is Ugly—
and Wrongheaded," *Vox*, July 29, 2015, www.vox.
com/2015/7/29/9048401/bernie-sanders-open-borders.

35. Sam Frizell, "Bernie Sanders Immigration: Why Conservatives Praise
Him," *Time*, January 7, 2016, time.com/4170591/
bernie-sanders-immigration-conservatives/.

36. Yaron Steinbuch, "Black Lives Matter Co-Founder Describes Herself as
'Trained Marxist,'" *New York Post*, June 25, 2020, nypost.
com/2020/06/25/blm-co-founder-describes-herself-as-trained-marxist/.

37. Roque Planas, "Black Activists Honor Venezuelan President Nicolás
Maduro in Harlem," HuffPost, September 29, 2015, www.huffpost.
com/entry/black-activists-nicolas-maduro-harlem_n_560a836fe4b0af370
6ddc573.

38. Ellen Cranley, "Twitter Changed Its Profile to Honor Black Lives Matter
amid George Floyd Protests," *Business Insider*, May 31, 2020, www.
businessinsider.com/twitter-changed-profile-black-lives-matter-2020-5.

39. Shawn Wheat, "Goodyear Responds to Zero-Tolerance Policy Slide
Labeled by Employee as Discriminatory," wibw.com, www.wibw

.com/2020/08/18/
goodyear-employees-say-new-no-tolerance-policy-is-discriminatory/.

40. Scottie Andrew, "Boy Scouts Support Black Lives Matter and Will Require Some Scouts to Earn Diversity Badge," CNN, June 17, 2020, www.cnn.com/2020/06/17/us/boy-scouts-black-lives-matter-trnd/index. html.

41. Taylor Hosking, "Why Do the Boy Scouts Want to Include Girls?" *The Atlantic*, October 13, 2017, www.theatlantic.com/politics/ archive/2017/10/why-did-the-boy-scouts-decide-to-accept-girls/542769.

42. "Changing Attitudes on Same-Sex Marriage," Pew Research Center's Religion & Public Life Project, Pew Research Center, December 31, 2019, www.pewforum.org/fact-sheet/ changing-attitudes-on-gay-marriage/.

43. Joshua Rhett Miller, "BLM Site Removes Page on 'Nuclear Family Structure' amid NFL Vet's Criticism," *New York Post*, September 24, 2020, nypost.com/2020/09/24/ blm-removes-website-language-blasting-nuclear-family-structure/.

44. Tim Fitzsimons, "Detroit Pastor Charged with Transgender Woman's Murder," NBC News, December 17, 2018, www.nbcnews.com/feature/ nbc-out/detroit-pastor-charged-transgender-woman-s-murder-n947236.

45. "What We Believe," Black Lives Matter, July 20, 2020, www. blacklivesmatter.com/what-we-believe/

46. M. J. Lee and Eli Watkins, "Cruz, Sanders Face Off on Obamacare," CNN, February 8, 2017, www.cnn.com/2017/02/07/politics/obamacare-cruz-sanders-highlights/index.html.

47. John Stuart Mill, *On Liberty*," Project Gutenberg, www.gutenberg.org/ files/34901/34901-h/34901-h.htm; *Whitney v. California*, Supreme Court of the United States, May 16, 1927.

48. Libby Emmons, "BLM Activists' 'Extortion' Attempt of Local Restaurants Backfires as Cuban Owners Fight Back," The Post Millennial, August 3, 2020, thepostmillennial.com/ cuban-community-refuses-blm-demands.

Chapter 4: Standards and Practices

1. George W. Rutler, "Mistaken Predictions," Catholic Education Resource Center, www.catholiceducation.org/en/culture/environment/mistaken-predictions.html.

2. George Orwell, *Nineteen Eighty-Four: A Novel*, (London: Penguin Books, 1967).

3. Sean Wilentz, "A Matter of Facts," *The Atlantic*, January 22, 2020, www.theatlantic.com/ideas/ archive/2020/01/1619-project-new-york-times-wilentz/605152/.

4. Virginia Allen, "*NY Times* Mum on '1619' Creator Calling '1619 Riots' Moniker an 'Honor,'" The Daily Signal, June 24, 2020, www. dailysignal.com/2020/06/22/new-york-times-mum-on-1619-project-creator-calling-1619-riots-moniker-an-honor/.

5. Orwell, *Nineteen Eighty-Four*.

6. Aristotle, *Politics*, trans. Benjamin Jowett, The Internet Classics Archive, classics.mit.edu/Aristotle/politics.1.one.html, 1.1253a

7. George Orwell, "Why I Write," The Orwell Foundation, May 14, 2019, www.orwellfoundation.com/the-orwell-foundation/orwell/essays-and-other-works/why-i-write/.

8. Thomas, "George Orwell Review," Maude's Tavern, October 9, 2008, maudestavern.com/2008/10/09/george-orwell-review/.

9. William Shakespeare, *The Tempest*, October 26, 2007, www.gutenberg.org/files/23042/23042-h/23042-h.htm.

10. "Huxley to Orwell: My Hellish Vision of the Future Is Better Than Yours (1949)," Open Culture, March 17, 2015, www.openculture.com/2015/03/huxley-to-orwell-my-hellish-vision-of-the-future-is-better-than-yours.html.

11. Jessica Park, "Is 'Homeless' the Right Word for Those Living on the Street?" Hoodline, October 23, 2020, hoodline.com/2016/12/is-homeless-the-right-word-for-those-living-on-the-street.

12. "Words Matter: The Language of Addiction," Partnership to End Addiction, November 17, 2020, drugfree.org/article/shouldnt-use-word-addict/.

13. "SB-145 Sex Offenders: Registration," (Bill Text), September 14, 2020, California Legislative Information, leginfo.legislature.ca.gov/faces/billTextClient.xhtml?bill_id=201920200SB145.

14. Todd Spangler, "Netflix Defends 'Cuties' as 'Social Commentary' against Sexualization of Young Children." *Variety*, September 14, 2020, variety.com/2020/digital/news/netflix-defends-cuties-against-sexualization-young-girls-1234766347/.

15. Mike McPhate, "California Today: Price Tag to Protect Speech at Berkeley: $600,000," *New York Times*, September 15, 2017, www.nytimes.com/2017/09/15/us/california-today-price-tag-to-protect-speech-at-berkeley-600000.html.

16. Stanley Fish, *There's No Such Thing as Free Speech . . . and It's a Good Thing Too*, (Oxford: Oxford University Press, 1994).

17. *Chaplinsky v. New Hampshire*, Supreme Court of the United States, March 9, 1942.

18. Susannah Breslin, "Adult Director Max Hardcore Released from Prison," *Forbes*, February 19, 2012, www.forbes.com/sites/ susannahbreslin/2011/07/21/ adult-director-max-hardcore-released-from-prison-2/#745a3aa343e0.

19. John Milton, *Areopagitica*, Project Gutenberg, www.gutenberg.org/ files/608/608-h/608-h.htm. Adapted into modern English by the author.

20. G. K. Chesterton, *Orthodoxy*, Project Gutenberg, September 26, 2005, www.gutenberg.org/cache/epub/130/pg130.html.

21. Fish, *There's No Such Thing as Free Speech.*

Chapter 5: Mao Goes Mainstream

1. *Chisholm v. Georgia*, Supreme Court of the United States, February 18, 1793.

2. Paul C. Violas, "The Indoctrination Debate and the Great Depression," *History Teacher* 4, no. 4 (May 1971): 25–35; Irving Lewis Allen, "Earlier Uses of Politically (In)Correct," *American Speech* 70, no. 1 (1995): 110–12, https://doi.org/10.2307/455878.

3. Ralph Ellison, *Invisible Man*, (Branton, Ontario: W. Ross MacDonald School Resource Services Library, 2018).

4. Ellison, *Invisible Man.*

5. Vladimir Vladimirovich Nabokov, *Nabokov, Bend Sinister* (Saint Petersburg, Russia: Severo-Zapad, 1993).

6. Czesław Miłosz and Jane Zielonko, *The Captive Mind* (New York: Penguin Books, 2001). Lewis, "Earlier Uses of Politically (In)Correct."

7. George Orwell, "Politics and the English Language," George Orwell's Library, December 29, 2019, www.orwell.ru/library/essays/politics/ english/e_polit.

8. Derek Hawkins, "In Portland, Images of Knives, Brass Knuckles, Bricks Show Viciousness of Protests," *Washington Post*, April 29, 2019, www. washingtonpost.com/news/morning-mix/wp/2017/06/05/in-portland-images-of-knives-brass-knuckles-bricks-show-viciousness-of-protests/; NBC News, "Antifa Members Talk Protest Tactics: 'We Don't Depend On Cops,'" YouTube, August 19, 2019, www.youtube.com/ watch?v=af50-4eI9PA; Collin Jones, "Three Federal Officers May Be Permanently Blinded after Antifa Laser Attack in Portland" The Post

Millennial, July 23, 2020, thepostmillennial.com/
three-federal-officers-may-be-permanently-blinded-after-antifa-laser-
attack-in-portland.

9. John Hinderaker, "Minnesota's 'Antifascists' Are Fascists," American
Experiment, August 19, 2020, www.americanexperiment.org/2017/06/
minnesotas-antifascists-fascists/.

10. Orwell, "Politics and the English Language."

11. Benito Mussolini, *The Doctrine of Fascism*, 1936.

12. Nassim Nicholas Taleb, *Antifragile: Things That Gain from Disorder*
(New York: Random House, 2016).

13. Orwell, "Politics and the English Language.".

14. Ruth Perry, "A Short History of the Term *Politically Correct*" in Patricia
Aufderheide, *Beyond PC: Toward a Politics of Understanding*
(Minneapolis, Minnesota: Graywolf Press, 1992).

15. Mao Zedong, *Quotations from Chairman Mao* (Woodbridge, Virginia:
Universal-Award House, 1971).

16. Aufderheide, *Beyond PC*.

17. Mao, *Quotations from Chairman Mao*.

18. Carol Hanisch, "The Personal Is Political: The Women's Liberation
Movement Classic with a New Explanatory Introduction," Women of
the World, Unite!, www.carolhanisch.org/CHwritings/PIP.html.

19. Mao, *Quotations from Chairman Mao*.

20. Ibid.

21. Boris Buden, "To Make the Long March Short: A Short Commentary on
the Two Long Marches That Have Failed Their Emancipatory
Promises," Crisis & Critique, crisiscritique.org/nov2018/boris.pdf.

22. Ibid.

23. Moira Weigel, "Political Correctness: How the Right Invented a
Phantom Enemy," *The Guardian*, November 30, 2016, www.
theguardian.com/us-news/2016/nov/30/political-correctness-how-
the-right-invented-phantom-enemy-donald-trump.

24. Amanda Taub, "The Truth about 'Political Correctness' Is That It
Doesn't Actually Exist," *Vox*, January 28, 2015, www.vox.
com/2015/1/28/7930845/political-correctness-doesnt-exist.

25. Robby Soave, "Study: 80% of Americans Believe Political Correctness Is
a Problem," *Reason*, October 11, 2018, reason.com/2018/10/11/
political-correctness-americans-vote-maj/.

26. Jackie Salo, "Why You'll No Longer Find 'Convicted Felons' in San Francisco," *New York Post*, August 22, 2019, nypost.com/2019/08/2'2/ why-youll-no-longer-find-convicted-felons-in-san-francisco/.

27. Steven Pinker, *The Blank Slate: The Modern Denial of Human Nature*, (New York: Penguin Books, 2003).

28. Rejani Thudalikunnil Gopalan, *Developmental Challenges and Societal Issues for Individuals with Intellectual Disabilities* (Hershey, Pennsylvania: IGI Global, 2020).

29. "Samuel Gridley Howe," *Parallels in Time: A History of Intellectual Disabilities*, Minnesota Department of Administration, mn.gov/mnddc/ parallels/four/4b/5.html.

30. James W. Trent, *Inventing the Feeble Mind: A History of Intellectual Disability in the United States* (Oxford: Oxford University Press, 2017).

31. Pinker, *The Blank Slate*.

32. *Bowers v. Hardwick*, Supreme Court of the United States, June 30, 1986.

33. *Lawrence v. Texas*, Supreme Court of the United States, June 26, 2003.

34. "Queer," Online Etymology Dictionary, www.etymonline.com/word/ queer.

35. Michael Lind, "Buckley vs. Vidal: The Real Story," *Politico*, August 24, 2015, www.politico.com/magazine/story/2015/08/ buckley-vs-vidal-the-real-story-121673.

36. "Queer Studies," Wesleyan University, www.wesleyan.edu/queerstudies/; Henry Farrell, "Analysis: A Conservative YouTube Star Just Lost His Income Stream for Homophobic Slurs," *Washington Post*, June 6, 2019, www.washingtonpost.com/politics/2019/06/06/ conservative-youtube-star-just-lost-his-income-stream-homophobic-slurs-heres-what-happened-why/.

37. Arianna Rees, "A Video of Jimmy Kimmel Dressed in Blackface as Utah Jazz Legend Karl Malone Has Resurfaced. Here's Why," *Deseret News*, February 8, 2019, www.deseret.com/2019/2/8/20665327/a-video-of-jimmy-kimmel-dressed-in-blackface-as-utah-jazz-legend-karl-malone-has-resurfaced-here-s-w; Rewind Me, "Jimmy Kimmel Blackface Oprah Jimfrey The Man Show (2001)," YouTube, August 10, 2018, www. youtube.com/watch?v=E1By6Wj_sAU.

38. Sopan Deb, "Jimmy Kimmel's 2020 Emmys Monologue: 'You Can't Have a Virus without a Host,'" *New York Times*, September 21, 2020, www.nytimes.com/2020/09/20/arts/television/emmys-kimmel-monologue.html.

39. Suzy Byrne, "Joy Behar Faces Backlash over Old 'African Woman' Halloween Costume," Yahoo!, February 7, 2019, www.yahoo.com/lifestyle/joy-behar-faces-backlash-old-african-woman-halloween-costume-143659694.html.

40. John Koblin and Michael M Grynbaum, "Megyn Kelly's 'Blackface' Remarks Leave Her Future at NBC in Doubt," *New York Times*, October 25, Oct. 2018, www.nytimes.com/2018/10/25/business/media/megyn-kelly-skips-today-blackface-nbc.html.

41. Woodrow Wilson, "What Is Progress?," Teaching American History, teachingamericanhistory.org/library/document/what-is-progress/.

42. James Madison, *Federalist* 51, The Avalon Project, avalon.law.yale.edu/18th_century/fed51.asp.

43. Deborah Cameron, "Words, Words, Words" in *The War of the Words: The Political Correctness Debate*, ed. Sarah Dunant (London: Virago Press, 1994).

44. Paul Berman, *Debating P.C.: The Controversy over Political Correctness on College Campuses* (El Dorado, Arkansas: Delta, 1995).

45. Geoffrey Hughes, *Political Correctness: A History of Semantics and Culture* (Hoboken, New Jersey: Wiley-Blackwell, 2010).

46. Sophie Tucker, "Fifty Million Frenchmen Can't Be Wrong," International Lyrics Playground, lyricsplayground.com/alpha/songs/f/fiftymillionfrenchmencantbewrong.html.

47. Ruth Perry, "Historically Correct," *The Women's Review of Books* 9, no. 5 (February 1992): 15–16.

48. SpectricYT, "Offended? It's Called IRONY Bro Are You a Retahrd? Get a Load of This CRINGE NROMIE He Doesn't Get IRONY," Reddit, www.reddit.com/r/okbuddyretard/comments/buhbjc/offended_its_called_irony_bro_are_you_a_retahrd/.

49. "IronyBro," Urban Dictionary, www.urbandictionary.com/define.php?term=IronyBro.

50. Feodor Dostoevsky, *Notes from the Underground*, Project Gutenberg, September 13, 2008, www.gutenberg.org/files/600/600-h/600-h.htm.

51. Jesse David Fox, et al. "100 More Jokes That Shaped Modern Comedy.," Vulture, February 6, 2017, www.vulture.com/2017/02/100-more-jokes-shaped-modern-comedy-c-v-r.html.

Chapter 6: The Tolerant Left

1. Roland S. Martin, "Rep. Maxine Waters under Scrutiny for Urging Supporters to Confront Trump Officials," YouTube, www.youtube.com/watch?v=Tts1q9TgXxg.

2. Karla Ward, "Mitch McConnell Loses Leftovers in Confrontation by Heckler at Louisville Restaurant," *Lexington Herald Leader*, October 20, 2018, www.kentucky.com/news/politics-government/article220385650.html.

3. Avi Selk, "Ted Cruz and Wife Are Shouted Out of D.C. Restaurant over His Support for Kavanaugh," *Washington Post*, March 28, 2019, www.washingtonpost.com/news/local/wp/2018/09/25/ted-cruz-and-wife-shouted-out-of-d-c-restaurant-over-his-support-for-kavanaugh/; Allyson Chiu, "'They Were Threatening Me and My Family': Tucker Carlson's Home Targeted by Protesters," *Washington Post*, November 9, 2018, www.washingtonpost.com/nation/2018/11/08/they-were-threatening-me-my-family-tucker-carlsons-home-targeted-by-protesters/.

4. Daniel Henninger, "Opinion: 'You Cannot Be Civil,'" *Wall Street Journal*, October 10, 2018, www.wsj.com/articles/you-cannot-be-civil-1539211192.

5. "Civility," Online Etymology Dictionary, www.etymonline.com/word/civility.

6. G. K. Chesterton, *Orthodoxy*, Project Gutenberg, September 26, 2005, www.gutenberg.org/cache/epub/130/pg130.html.

7. Douglas Kellner, "Herbert Marcuse" Illuminations, www.uta.edu/huma/illuminations/kell12.htm.

8. Barry M. Kātz, "The Criticism of Arms: The Frankfurt School Goes to War," *Journal of Modern History* 59, no. 3, (1987): 439–78., https://doi.org/10.1086/243224.

9. Eric Scheper, "Herbert Marcuse: The Ideologue as Paid Agent of U.S. Imperialism," Marxists Internet Archive, www.marxists.org/history/erol/ca.firstwave/li-marcuse.htm.

10. "Alger Hiss," Federal Bureau of Investigation, May 18, 2016, www.fbi.gov/history/famous-cases/alger-hiss.

11. Laura Gardner, "Discovered Manuscript Shows Marcuse's Evolution," BrandeisNOW, October 9, 2013, www.brandeis.edu/now/2013/october/marcuse.html.

12. Herbert Marcuse, *One-Dimensional Man* (Abingdon, England: Routledge, 2002).

13. Herbert Marcuse, "Repressive Tolerance (Full Text)," Herbert Marcuse Official Homepage, October 25, 2015, www.marcuse.org/herbert/publications/1960s/1965-repressive-tolerance-fulltext.html.

14. Ibid.

15. "Inform," *Index*, Online Etymology Dictionary, www.etymonline.com/word/inform#etymonline_v_6458; "Indoctrinate," Online Etymology Dictionary, www.etymonline.com/word/indoctrinate.

16. Ibid.

17. Marcuse, "Repressive Tolerance."

18. Ibid.

19. *Hail, Caesar!* directed by Joel Coen and Ethan Coen (Universal City, California: Universal Pictures, 2016).

20. Marcuse, "Repressive Tolerance."

21. Lisa Feldman Barrett, "When Is Speech Violence?" *New York Times*, July 15, 2017, www.nytimes.com/2017/07/14/opinion/sunday/when-is-speech-violence.html.

22. John Holloway, "The Tradition of Scientific Marxism," Marxists Internet Archive, www.marxists.org/subject/marxmyths/john-holloway/article.htm.

23. *Schenck v. U.S.*, Supreme Court of the United States, March 3, 1919.

24. *Abrams v. U.S.*, Supreme Court of the United States, November 10, 1919; *Brandenburg v. Ohio*, Supreme Court of the United States, June 8, 1969.

25. Marcuse, "Repressive Tolerance."

26. John Bowden, "Ocasio-Cortez: 'World Will End in 12 Years' If Climate Change Not Addressed," *The Hill*, January 22, 2019, thehill.com/policy/energy-environment/426353-ocasio-cortez-the-world-will-end-in-12-years-if-we-dont-address.

27. FreePropaganda, "Nancy Pelosi Pass the Bill to Find Out What's in It." YouTube, May 28, 2013, www.youtube.com/watch?v=QV7dDSgbaQo.

28. Marcuse, "Repressive Tolerance."

29. *Texas v. Johnson*, Supreme Court of the United States, June 21, 1989.

30. Jason Clayworth, "Lesbian Attorney Was Biased, Argued the Man Sentenced to 16 Years for Burning Gay Pride Flag," *Des Moines Register*, January 19, 2020, www.desmoinesregister.com/story/news/investigations/2020/01/15/lesbian-attorney-biased-man-sentenced-16-years-burning-gay-pride-flag-argued/4444888002/.

31. Marcuse, Herbert. "Repressive Tolerance."

32. "Declaration of Independence: A Transcription." National Archives and Records Administration, www.archives.gov/founding-docs/declaration-transcript.

33. Danner, Chas. "Watch Trump Fondle an American Flag at CPAC," *Intelligencer*, March 1, 2020, nymag.com/intelligencer/2020/02/watch-trump-fondle-an-american-flag-at-cpac.html.

34. Allen C. Guelzo, "Pulitzer Overlooks Egregious Errors to Award Prize to *New York Times*' Fatally Flawed '1619 Project,'" Heritage Foundation, May 6, 2020, www.heritage.org/american-founders/commentary/pulitzer-overlooks-egregious-errors-award-prize-new-york-times-fatally.

35. Edmund Burke, *Reflections on the Revolution in France*, Project Gutenberg, 2005, https://www.gutenberg.org/files/15679/15679-h/15679-h.htm.

36. Marcuse, "Repressive Tolerance."

37. Lesley Kennedy, "This Is How FDR Tried to Pack the Supreme Court," History, June 28, 2018, www.history.com/news/franklin-roosevelt-tried-packing-supreme-court.

38. Tyler Olson, "Coons Says That Confirming Barrett 'Constitutes Court-Packing,' Sasse Responds That's 'Obviously' Incorrect." Fox News, October 11, 2020, www.foxnews.com/politics/fox-news-sunday-ben-sasse-chris-coons-judiciary-committee-barrett.

39. "Modern Immigration Wave Brings 59 Million to U.S." Pew Research Center, May 30, 2020, www.pewresearch.org/hispanic/2015/09/28/modern-immigration-wave-brings-59-million-to-u-s-driving-population-growth-and-change-through-2065/; Jeffrey S. Passel, "Measuring Illegal Immigration: How Pew Research Center Counts Unauthorized Immigrants in the U.S.," Pew Research Center, September 4, 2020, www.pewresearch.org/fact-tank/2019/07/12/how-pew-research-center-counts-unauthorized-immigrants-in-us/.

40. "Monthly Harvard-Harris Poll: January 2018 Re-Field," January 2018, harvardharrispoll.com/wp-content/uploads/2018/01/Final_HHP_Jan2018-Refield_RegisteredVoters_XTab.pdf.

41. John Locke, *A Letter Concerning Toleration*, Penn State University's Electronic Classics, 2005, http://self.gutenberg.org/wplbn0000651234-a-letter-concerning-toleration-by-locke-john.aspx.

Chapter 7: Nothing Personal

1. Associated Press, "Robertson Letter Attacks Feminists," *New York Times*, August 26, 1992, www.nytimes.com/1992/08/26/us/robertson-letter-attacks-feminists.html.

2. Bertrand Russell, *History of Western Philosophy* (Abingdon, England: Routledge, 2015).

3. Toni Cade Bambara, *The Black Woman: An Anthology* (New York: Washington Square, 2005).

4. Deborah Cameron, "Words, Words, Words" in *The War of the Words: The Political Correctness Debate*, ed. Sarah Dunant (London: Virago Press, 1994).

5. Ibid.

6. Carol Hanisch, "The Personal Is Political: The Women's Liberation Movement Classic with a New Explanatory Introduction," Women of the World, Unite!, www.carolhanisch.org/CHwritings/PIP.html.

7. Roxane Gay, "Fifty Years Ago, Protesters Took on the Miss America Pageant and Electrified the Feminist Movement," *Smithsonian Magazine*, January/February 2018, www.smithsonianmag.com/history/fifty-years-ago-protestors-took-on-miss-america-pageant-electrified-feminist-movement-180967504/.

8. Hanisch, "The Personal Is Political."

9. Kathie Sarachild, "Consciousness Raising: A Radical Weapon," Rape Relief Shelter, www.rapereliefshelter.bc.ca/sites/default/files/imce/Feminist-Revolution-Consciousness-Raising—A-Radical-Weapon-Kathie-Sarachild.pdf.

10. Georg Lukacs, "Class Consciousness," *History and Class Consciousness*, trans. Rodney Livingstone (Decatur, Georgia: Merlin, 1967), available online at Marxists Internet Archive, www.marxists.org/archive/lukacs/works/history/lukacs3.htm.

11. Jonah Goldberg, "Feminist Army Aims at Palin," RealClearPolitics, www.realclearpolitics.com/articles/2008/09/feminist_army_aims_at_palin.html.

12. Valerie Richardson, "Architect of *NYT*'s 1619 Project Draws Distinction between 'Politically Black and Racially Black,'" *Washington Times*, May 22, 2020, www.washingtontimes.com/news/2020/may/22/nikole-hannah-jones-1619-project-draws-distinction/.

13. Eric Bradner, et al., "Biden: 'If You Have a Problem Figuring Out Whether You're for Me or Trump, Then You Ain't Black,'" CNN, May

23, 2020, www.cnn.com/2020/05/22/politics/biden-charlamagne-tha-god-you-aint-black/index.html.

14. Hanisch, "The Personal Is Political."

15. John Locke, *Second Treatise of Civil Government John Locke* (1690), Marxists Internet Archive, www.marxists.org/reference/subject/politics/locke/cho1.htm.

16. Robert Filmer, *Patriarcha, or, The Natural Power of Kings* (Philadelphia, Pennsylvania: Walter Davis, 1983).

17. *Griswold v. Connecticut*, Supreme Court of the United States, June 7, 1965.

18. "Penumbra," Merriam-Webster, www.merriam-webster.com/dictionary/penumbra; "Emanation," Merriam-Webster, www.merriam-webster.com/dictionary/emanation.

19. *Roe v. Wade*, Supreme Court of the United States, January 22, 1973.

20. *Obergefell v. Hodges*, Supreme Court of the United States, June 26, 2015.

21. Hanisch, "The Personal Is Political."

22. "Manguage," *New York Times*, June 2, 1985, www.nytimes.com/1985/06/02/opinion/manguage.html.

23. Genesis 1:27.

24. Cameron, "Words, Words, Words.

25. Christopher Hitchens, "The Fraying of America: A Review of *Culture of Complaint* by Robert Hughes" in *The War of the Words: The Political Correctness Debate*, ed. Sarah Dunant (London: Virago, 1995), 133–44.

26. *United States v. Rumely*, Supreme Court of the United States, March 9, 1953

27. Geoffrey Hughes, *Political Correctness: A History of Semantics and Culture* (Hoboken, New Jersey: Wiley-Blackwell, 2010).

28. "Origin of That Fish Line," *Duluth News Tribune*, August 17, 2014, www.duluthnewstribune.com/lifestyle/3325954-origin-fish-line.

29. Betty Friedan, *It Changed My Life: Writings on the Women's Movement* (Cambridge, Massachusetts: Harvard University Press, 1998).

30. Joshua Rhett Miller, "BLM Site Removes Page on 'Nuclear Family Structure' amid NFL Vet's Criticism," *New York Post*, September 24, 2020, nypost.com/2020/09/24/blm-removes-website-language-blasting-nuclear-family-structure/.

31. "Mothering," Online Etymology Dictionary," www.etymonline.com/sea rch?q=mothering%3B+https%3A%2F%2Fwww.etymonline. com%2Fword%2Fparenting.

32. John Taylor, "Are You Politically Correct?" *New York*, January 21, 1991, 32–41.

33. Ibid.

Chapter 8: The School of Resentment

1. Jennie Rothenberg Gritz, "Ranting against Cant," *The Atlantic*, October 15, 2019, www.theatlantic.com/magazine/archive/2003/07/ ranting-against-cant/303095/.

2. Karen Swallow Prior, "Why Walt Whitman Called America the 'Greatest Poem,'" *The Atlantic*, July 7, 2020, https://www.theatlantic. com/entertainment/archive/2016/12/ why-walt-whitman-called-the-america-the-greatest-poem/510932/.

3. Ginger Hervey, "Yale Undergraduates Aim to 'Decolonize' the English Department's Curriculum," *USA Today*, June 10, 2016, www.usatoday. com/story/college/2016/06/10/ yale-undergraduates-aim-to-decolonize-the-english-departments- curriculum/37418303/.

4. Jacques Derrida, *Of Grammatology* (Baltimore, Maryland: Johns Hopkins University Press, 2016).

5. Mark Alfino, "Another Look at the Derrida-Searle Debate," *Philosophy & Rhetoric* 24, no. 2 (1991):143–52.

6. William Shakespeare, *The Merchant of Venice*, Project Gutenberg, March 19, 2019, www.gutenberg.org/files/1515/1515-h/1515-h.htm.

7. *Abington School District v. Schempp*, Supreme Court of the United States, June 17, 1963.

8. Daniel Payne, "UCLA Course Uses Cardi B to Teach about 'Respectability Politics,'" The College Fix, August 21, 2019, www. thecollegefix.com/ ucla-course-uses-cardi-b-to-teach-about-respectability-politics/.

9. Ryan Love, "University of Oklahoma Launches Mandatory Diversity Training Program for All Campuses," FOX 23 News, August 27, 2020, www.fox23.com/news/local/university-oklahoma-launches-mandatory- diversity-training-program-all-campuses/ KGUIZWZD2NHZFBC5TR3ZSNOD7I/.

10. Payne, "UCLA Course Uses Cardi B to Teach"; Susan A. Manning, "Dance Studies, Gay and Lesbian Studies, and Queer Theory," Dance

Research Journal 34 (2002): 96–105, www.scholars.northwestern.edu/en/publications/dance-studies-gay-and-lesbian-studies-and-queer-theory.

11. "Watching Dr. Jeffries Self-Destruct," *New York Times*, August 25, 1991, www.nytimes.com/1991/08/25/opinion/watching-dr-jeffries-self-destruct.html.

12. Richard M. Benjamin, "The Bizarre Classroom of Dr. Leonard Jeffries," *Journal of Blacks in Higher Education* 2 (Winter 1993–94): 91, https://www.jstor.org/stable/i348950.

13. Paul Bois, "WATCH: Nick Cannon: White People Are 'A Little Less,' 'Closer To Animals,' 'True Savages,'" The Daily Wire, July 15, 2020, www.dailywire.com/news/watch-nick-cannon-white-people-are-a-little-less-closer-to-animals-true-savages.

14. "Watching Dr. Jeffries Self-Destruct"; Jonathan Yardley, "In New York, a Bigoted Man on Campus," *Washington Post*, August 12, 1991, www.washingtonpost.com/archive/lifestyle/1991/08/12/in-new-york-a-bigoted-man-on-campus/637b6b9e-85b3-4a84-a6b4-d69f48c32fc3/.

15. Ibid.

16. "Berkowitz v. President Fellows of Harvard College," FindLaw, June 6, 2003, caselaw.findlaw.com/ma-court-of-appeals/1376248.html; Adam Tamburin, "Controversial Professor Carol Swain to Retire from Vanderbilt," *The Tennessean*, January 23, 2017, www.tennessean.com/story/news/education/2017/01/23/carol-swain-announces-retirement-vanderbilt-university/96959004/; Anemona Hartocollis, "Yale Lecturer Resigns after Email on Halloween Costumes," *New York Times*, December 8, 2015, www.nytimes.com/2015/12/08/us/yale-lecturer-resigns-after-email-on-halloween-costumes.html.

17. Krastev, Nikola, "Iran's Ahmadinejad Delivers Controversial Speech at U.S. University," *RadioFreeEurope/RadioLiberty*, February 24, 2007, www.rferl.org/a/1078779.html.

18. Cooper, Helene. "Ahmadinejad, at Columbia, Parries and Puzzles," *New York Times*, September 25 2007, www.nytimes.com/2007/09/25/world/middleeast/25iran.html.

19. Kate Huangpu and Khadija Hussain, "Protesters Disrupt Anti-Immigration Speech by Tommy Robinson at Columbia," *Columbia Daily Spectator*, www.columbiaspectator.com/news/2017/10/11/protesters-disrupt-anti-immigration-speech-by-tommy-robinson-at-columbia/.

20. Mark Hosenball, "Tommy Robinson Fails to Get U.S. Visa," Reuters, November 12, 2018, uk.reuters.com/article/uk-usa-trump-robinson-idUKKCN1NH2M2.

21. Plato, "Apology, Crito and Phædo of Socrates," Project Gutenberg, October 12, 2004, www.gutenberg.org/files/13726/13726-h/13726-h.htm.

22. It bears noting that Galileo was persecuted more for his impolitic description of the Pope as a "simpleton," and that he was permitted to continue his studies and writing during his "imprisonment" at a well-adorned villa near Florence. Galileo Galilei, et al., *Dialogue Concerning the Two Chief World Systems, Ptolemaic and Copernican* (London: Folio Society, 2013); "Galileo," Encyclopedia.com, www.encyclopedia.com/people/science-and-technology/astronomy-biographies/galileo.

23. William W Brickman, "Academic Freedom: Past and Present," *Journal of Thought* 3, no. 3 (July 1968): 152–58.

24. Anthony Chiorazzi, "Harvard's Religious Past," *Harvard Gazette*, July 26, 2019, news.harvard.edu/gazette/story/2016/10/harvards-religious-past/; Eve LaPlante, *American Jezebel: The Uncommon Life of Anne Hutchinson* (San Francisco, California: HarperOne, 2005).

25. "1940 Statement of Principles on Academic Freedom and Tenure," American Association of University Professors, www.aaup.org/report/1940-statement-principles-academic-freedom-and-tenure.

26. William F. Buckley, *God and Man at Yale* (Washington, D.C.: Regnery Publishing, 1986); Stanley Kurtz, "The Campus Intellectual Diversity Act: A Proposal," *National Review*, February 12, 2019, www.nationalreview.com/corner/the-campus-intellectual-diversity-act-a-proposal/.

27. Jonah Goldberg, "Attacking Diversity of Thought," *National Review*, February 21, 2014, www.nationalreview.com/2014/02/attacking-diversity-thought-jonah-goldberg/; David French, "Intellectual Diversity, Academic Freedom, and the Christian College," *National Review*, May 6, 2010, www.nationalreview.com/phi-beta-cons/intellectual-diversity-academic-freedom-and-christian-college-david-french/.

28. Nikole Hannah-Jones, "The 1619 Project," *New York Times*, August 14, 2019, www.nytimes.com/interactive/2019/08/14/magazine/1619-america-slavery.html.

29. "*New York Times* Corrects the 1619 Project—but It's Still a Giant Lie," *New York Post*, March 15, 2020, nypost.com/2020/03/14/new-york-times-corrects-the-1619-project-but-its-still-a-giant-lie/.

30. "Nikole Hannah-Jones: 'Race and Education in America,'" Western Michigan University, September 4, 2018, wmich.edu/humanities/nikole-hannah-jones#:~:text=Hannah%2DJones%20co%2Dfounded%20the,the%20University%20of%20Notre%20Dame.

31. Adam Serwer, "The Fight over the 1619 Project Is Not about the Facts," *The Atlantic*, January 21, 2020, www.theatlantic.com/ideas/archive/2019/12/historians-clash-1619-project/604093/.

32. "We Respond to the Historians Who Critiqued the 1619 Project," *New York Times*, December 20, 2019, www.nytimes.com/2019/12/20/magazine/we-respond-to-the-historians-who-critiqued-the-1619-project.html.

33. Ibid.

34. "*New York Times* Corrects the 1619 Project."

35. Ibid.

36. Naomi Schaefer Riley, et al., "'The 1619 Project' Enters American Classrooms," Education Next, December 17, 2020, www.educationnext.org/1619-project-enters-american-classrooms-adding-new-sizzle-slavery-significant-cost/.

37. "We Respond to the Historians."

38. Abraham Lincoln, "The Gettysburg Address," Abraham Lincoln Online, November 19, 1863, www.abrahamlincolnonline.org/lincoln/speeches/gettysburg.htm.

39. Christopher Caldwell, *Age of Entitlement: America since the Sixties* (New York: Simon & Schuster, 2021).

40. Crystal Ponti, "10 Things You May Not Know about the Jamestown Colony," History.com, August 6, 2019, www.history.com/news/jamestown-colony-settlement-facts.

41. Edmund Burke, *Reflections on the Revolution in France* (Digireads, 2018).

42. Ryu Spaeth, "The Strange Liberal Backlash to Woke Culture," *New Republic*, November 25, 2019, https://newrepublic.com/article/155681/strange-liberal-backlash-woke-culture.

43. Yascha Mounk, "Americans Strongly Dislike PC Culture," *The Atlantic*, October 30, 2018, www.theatlantic.com/ideas/archive/2018/10/large-majorities-dislike-political-correctness/572581/.

44. Yascha Mounk, "Americans Strongly Dislike PC Culture."

45. Ibid.

Chapter 9: Campus Codes and Coercion

1. George Lowery, "A Campus Takeover That Symbolized an Era of Change," *Cornell Chronicle*, April 16, 2009, news.cornell.edu/stories/2009/04/campus-takeover-symbolized-era-change.

2. Tevi Troy, "Cornell's Straight Flush," *City Journal*, April 12, 2019, www.city-journal.org/html/cornell%E2%80%99s-straight-flush-10659.html.

3. Alice Vincent, "Empire Actor Jussie Smollett's 'Faked' Racial Attack: What Really Happened?" *Telegraph*, March 27, 2019, www.telegraph.co.uk/tv/0/jussie-smollett-empire-actor-attack/.

4. Kyle Smith, "Smollett Was 'Clearly Lying,' Says the Comic," *National Review*, August 29, 2019, www.nationalreview.com/corner/dave-chappelle-goes-after-jussie-smollett/.

5. Andy Ngo, "Inventing Victimhood," *City Journal*, July 1, 2019, www.city-journal.org/campus-hate-crime-hoaxes.

6. Brigette Burnett, "BG Police Say Student Lied about Politically Driven Attack," 13 ABC Action News, November 17, 2016, www.13abc.com/content/news/BG-police-say-student-lied-about-politically-driven-attack-401814426.html.

7. Jennifer Brooks and Paul Walsh. "St. Olaf: Report of Racist Note on Black Student's Windshield Was 'Fabricated,'" *Star Tribune*, May 11, 2017, www.startribune.com/st-olaf-report-of-racist-note-on-black-student-s-windshield-was-fabricated/421912763/.

8. Samantha Schmidt, "A Black Student Wrote Those Racist Messages That Shook the Air Force Academy, School Says," *Washington Post*, April 29, 2019, www.washingtonpost.com/news/morning-mix/wp/2017/11/08/a-black-student-wrote-those-racist-messages-that-shook-the-air-force-academy/?utm_term=.6ba19098406a.

9. "Goucher College Student Faces Hate Crime Charges for Racist Graffiti, Baltimore County Police Say," *Baltimore Sun*, December 5, 2018, web.archive.org/web/20181205024254/www.baltimoresun.com/news/maryland/crime/bs-md-co-goucher-hate-crime-charges-20181204-20181204-f3w5n7hccbb6hkdrebflm4uljm-story.html.

10. Ibid.

11. Karma Allen, "College Student in Baltimore Hit with Additional Charges over Racist Graffiti," ABC News, December 5, 2018, abcnews.go.com/US/college-student-baltimore-hit-additional-charges-racist-graffiti/story?id=59618395.

12. Evan Gerstmann, "The Stat That 1 In 5 College Women Are Sexually Assaulted Doesn't Mean What You Think It Means," *Forbes*, January 28, 2019, www.forbes.com/sites/evangerstmann/2019/01/27/the-stat-that-1-in-5-college-women-are-sexually-assaulted-doesnt-mean-what-you-think-it-means/#2d114aab2217.

13. Lizzie Crocker, "Why the New 'One in Four' Campus Rape Statistic Is Misleading," Daily Beast, September 22, 2015, www.thedailybeast.com/why-the-new-one-in-four-campus-rape-statistic-is-misleading.

14. John Taylor, "Are You Politically Correct?" *New York Magazine*, January 21, 1991, 32–41.

15. Alexandra Rutherford, "What the Origins of the '1 in 5' Statistic Teaches Us About Sexual Assault Policy," *Behavioral Scientist*, February 26, 2020, behavioralscientist.org/what-the-origins-of-the-1-in-5-statistic-teaches-us-about-sexual-assault-policy/.

16. Crocker, "Why the New 'One in Four' Campus Rape Statistic Is Misleading."

17. Ibid.

18. "Rape and Sexual Assault Victimization among College-Age Females, 1995–2013," Bureau of Justice Statistics, www.bjs.gov/index.cfm?ty=pbdetail&iid=5176.

19. Sofi Sinozich and Lynn Langdon, "Rape and Sexual Assault Victimization among College-Age Females, 1995–2013," Bureau of Justice Statistics (BJS), www.bjs.gov/index.cfm?ty=pbdetail&iid=5176.

20. Ibid.

21. Carla Field, "Report of Rape on Clemson Campus Untrue, Police Say," WYFF4, October 9, 2017, www.wyff4.com/article/report-of-rape-on-clemson-campus-untrue-police-say/7146964.

22. Ibid.

23. Ashe Schow, "After Settlement, the *Rolling Stone* Rape Hoax Saga Is Officially Over," The Federalist, February 13, 2018, thefederalist.com/2018/02/13/settlement-fraternity-rolling-stonerape-hoax-saga-officially/.

24. Cathy Young, "Young: Rape Cases and Knee-Jerk Reactions," *Newsday*, March 15, 2016, www.newsday.com/opinion/columnists/cathy-young/10-years-later-the-legacy-of-the-duke-lacrosse-scandal-1.11574704.

25. Sharon Katz, "Incident Prompts Debate on How to Relate Survivor Stories," *Daily Princetonian*, May 22, 1991, www.

avoiceformalestudents.com/wp-content/uploads/2013/12/The-Daily-Princetonian.pdf.

26. "Jesse Jackson and Students Protest Western Culture Program on Palm Drive, Photograph, 1987," Stanford Stories from the Archives, August 18, 2016, exhibits.stanford.edu/stanford-stories/feature/1980s.

27. See, for example, Sarah Pulliam Bailly and Michelle Boorstein, "St. John's Episcopal Church, Historic Church Next to the White House, Set on Fire during Protests," *Washington Post*, June 8, 2020, www.washingtonpost.com/religion/2020/06/05/st-johns-episcopal-church-historic-church-next-white-house-set-fire-during-protests/.

28. Richard Bernstein, "In Dispute on Bias, Stanford Is Likely to Alter Western Culture Program," *New York Times*, January 19, 1988, www.nytimes.com/1988/01/19/us/in-dispute-on-bias-stanford-is-likely-to-alter-western-culture-program.html.

29. Lee Siegel, "Wrestling with Saul Bellow: A New Biography Renews the Fight Over the Author's Reputation," *Vulture*, March 23, 2015, www.vulture.com/2015/03/saul-bellow-biography.html.

30. Ta-Nehisi Coates, *Between the World and Me* (London: One World, 2015).

31. Ibid.

32. Laura Wagner, "Journalist Ta-Nehisi Coates among 2015 MacArthur 'Genius' Award Winners," NPR, September 29, 2015, www.npr.org/sections/thetwo-way/2015/09/29/444221706/journalist-ta-nehisi-coates-among-2015-macarthur-genius-award-winners.

33. Diane Manuel, "Reshaping the Humanities," Stanford Today, 1997, web.stanford.edu/dept/news/stanfordtoday/ed/9705/9705ncf1.html.

34. Bernstein, "In Dispute on Bias, Stanford Is Likely to Alter Western Culture Program."

35. Manuel, "Reshaping the Humanities."

36. Todd Gitlin, "The Twilight of Common Dreams: Why America Is Wracked by Culture Wars" (review), Montana Professor, mtprof.msun.edu/Win1996/HgonRev.html.

37. Jim Sleeper, "Allan Bloom and the Conservative Mind" *New York Times*, September 4, 2005, www.nytimes.com/2005/09/04/books/review/allan-bloom-and-the-conservative-mind.html.

38. Allan Bloom, *The Closing of the American Mind* (New York: Simon and Schuster, 1987).

39. Margalit Fox, "Shulamith Firestone, Feminist Writer, Dies at 67," *New York Times*, August 31, 2012, www.nytimes.com/2012/08/31/nyregion/ shulamith-firestone-feminist-writer-dies-at-67.html.

40. Bloom, *The Closing of the American Mind*.

41. Psalm 8, Douay-Rheims Bible, www.drbo.org/chapter/21008.htm; William Shakespeare, "*Hamlet*, Project Gutenberg, September 30, 2019, www.gutenberg.org/files/1524/1524-h/1524-h.htm.

42. Sandra Day O'Connor, "Liberty, Not Licentiousness," *Liberty*, November/December 1997, libertymagazine.org/article/ liberty-not-licentiousness.

43. George Washington, "George Washington: Farewell Address (1796)," U.S. Embassy & Consulate in the Republic of Korea, February 11, 2020, https://kr.usembassy.gov/education-culture/infopedia-usa/living- documents-american-history-democracy/ george-washington-farewell-address-1796/.

44. Jared Sparks, ed. *The Works of Benjamin Franklin*, (C. Tappan, 1844).

45. Thomas Jefferson, "Thomas Jefferson to Amos J. Cook, 21 January 1816," Founders Online, founders.archives.gov/documents/ Jefferson/03-09-02-0243.

46. Kayla Rodgers, "Student Gets into Stanford after Writing #BlackLivesMatter on Application 100 Times," CNN, April 5, 2017, www.cnn.com/2017/04/05/us/stanford-application-black-lives-matter- trnd/index.html.

47. Mara Rose Williams, et al., "'We Cannot Violate the Law': Kansas State Won't Expel Student Who Made Racist Tweets," *Kansas City Star*, July 1, 2020, www.kansascity.com/news/state/kansas/article243925962.html.

48. David Hudson and Lata Nott, "Hate Speech & Campus Speech Codes," Freedom Forum Institute, March 2017, www.freedomforuminstitute. org/first-amendment-center/topics/freedom-of-speech-2/free-speech-on- public-college-campuses-overview/hate-speech-campus-speech-codes/.

49. *John Doe v. University of Michigan*, U.S. District Court, September 22, 1989.

50. Ibid.

51. Surah An-Nisa 4:16, *Quran*, Towards Understanding the Quran, www. islamicstudies.info/tafheem.php?sura=4; "Surah 4:21, *Quran*, Towards Understanding the Quran, www.islamicstudies.info/tafheem. php?sura=4.

52. *Chaplinsky v. New Hampshire*, Supreme Court of the United States, March 9, 1942.

53. *Jacobellis v. Ohio*, Supreme Court of the United States, June 22, 1964.

54. Tobias Hoonhout, "University of Michigan Disbands 'Bias Response Team' in Response to First Amendment Challenge," *National Review*, November 1, 2019, www.nationalreview.com/news/university-of-michigan-disbands-bias-response-team-in-response-to-first-amendment-challenge/.

55. Nell Porter Brown, "'More as People Than Dating Objects,'" *Harvard Magazine*, November-December 2011, harvardmagazine.com/2011/11/more-as-people-than-dating-objects.

56. Robert Shibley, "Antioch's Infamous Sexual Assault Policy," FIRE, April 15, 2014, www.thefire.org/antiochs-infamous-sexual-assault-policy/.

57. "South Park: Sponsored Content," IMDb, November 18, 2015, www.imdb.com/title/tt5113842/.

58. "Gettysburg College: Hug at Your Own Risk." FIRE, January 17, 2014, www.thefire.org/gettysburg-college-hug-at-your-own-risk/.

Chapter 10: The New Cold War

1. George H. W. Bush, "University of Michigan Commencement Speech," C-SPAN, www.c-span.org/video/?17825-1%2Funiversity-michigan-commencement-speech.

2. Ibid.

3. Ibid.

4. Ibid.

5. Brentdtharp, "User Clip: George H. W. Bush 1988 Acceptance Speech 'Kinder and Gentler' Clip," C-SPAN, February 27, 2020, www.c-span.org/video/?c4857525%2Fuser-clip-george-h-w-bush-1988-acceptance-speech-kinder-gentler-clip.

6. Stanley Fish, *There's No Such Thing as Free Speech . . . and It's A Good Thing Too* (Oxford: Oxford University Press, 1994).

7. Christèle Le Bihan-Collearan, "Feminist Linguistic Theories and 'Political Correctness': Modifying the Discourse on Women?" *The ESSE Messenger* 29, no. 1 (Summer 2020): 120–32, https://essenglish.org/messenger/wp-content/uploads/sites/2/2020/08/29-1-S2020-le-bihan.pdf.

8. Fish, *There's No Such Thing as Free Speech.*

9. Patrick Buchanan, "Culture War Speech: Address to the Republican National Convention (17 August 1992)," Voices of Democracy: The U.S. Oratory Project, March 23, 2016, voicesofdemocracy.umd.edu/buchanan-culture-war-speech-speech-text/.

10. George H. W. Bush, "Remarks Accepting the Presidential Nomination at the Republican National Convention in Houston," The American Presidency Project, August 20, 1992, www.presidency.ucsb.edu/documents/remarks-accepting-the-presidential-nomination-the-republican-national-convention-houston.

11. Ibid.

12. Daniel Liberto, "Voodoo Economics," Investopedia, August 25, 2020, www.investopedia.com/terms/v/voodooeconomics.asp.

13. Ibid.

14. George H. W. Bush, "Bush: "Out of These Troubled Times . . . a New World Order," *Washington Post*, September 12, 1990, www.washingtonpost.com/archive/politics/1990/09/12/bush-out-of-these-troubled-times-a-new-world-order/b93b5cf1-e389-4e6a-84b0-85f71bf4c946/.

15. Francis Fukuyama, "The End of History," *Wright State University*, The National Interest (Summer 1989), www.wright.edu/~christopher.oldstone-moore/fukuyama.htm.

16. David Mamet, *Oleanna* (New York: Vintage Books, 1993).

17. Geoffrey Hughes, *Political Correctness: A History of Semantics and Culture* (Hoboken, New Jersey: Wiley-Blackwell, 2010).

18. Mamet, *Oleanna*.

19. Ibid.

20. Emily Shugerman, "How a Student in a Diaper Caused an Eruption in One of America's Biggest Conservative Youth Organisations," *Independent*, June 7, 2018, www.independent.co.uk/news/world/americas/diaper-turning-point-usa-kent-state-student-conservative-youth-repulican-kaitlin-bennett-a8230021.html.

21. Bruce Weber, "Mamet: Hearings Prompted 'Oleanna,'" *Chicago Tribune*, September 2, 2018, www.chicagotribune.com/news/ct-xpm-1992-11-12-9204120711-story.html.

22. Thurgood Marshall, "The Bicentennial Speech," Speeches, Thurgood Marshall.com, May 3, 2016, thurgoodmarshall.com/the-bicentennial-speech/.

23. Margo Jefferson, "The Thomas-Hill Question, Answered Anew," *New York Times*, November 11, 1994, https://www.nytimes.com/1994/11/11/books/books-of-the-times-the-thomas-hill-question-answered-anew.html?n=Top/Reference/Times%20Topics/Organizations/S/Supreme%20Court.

24. George H. W. Bush, "Supreme Court Nomination Announcement," C-SPAN, https://www.c-span.org/video/?18649-1/supreme-court-nomination-announcement.

25. "Thomas Second Hearing Day 1, Part 1," C-SPAN, October 11, 1991, https://www.c-span.org/video/?21974-1/thomas-hearing-day-1-part-1.

26. Bridget Todd, "Clarence Thomas Anita Hill: Never Forget Justice's Sexual Harassment History," Mic, April 4, 2013, www.mic.com/articles/32733/clarence-thomas-anita-hill-never-forget-justice-s-sexual-harassment-history.

27. "Thomas Called 'Absolutely Incapable of the Abuses,'" *Tampa Bay Times*, October 14, 2005, www.tampabay.com/archive/1991/10/14/thomas-called-absolutely-incapable-of-the-abuses/.

28. Clarence Thomas, "Statement before the Judiciary Committee," American Rhetoric, October 11, 1991, www.americanrhetoric.com/speeches/clarencethomashightechlynching.htm.

29. Ibid.

30. Angela Serratore, "Alexander Hamilton's Adultery and Apology," *Smithsonian Magazine*, July 25, 2013, www.smithsonianmag.com/history/alexander-hamiltons-adultery-and-apology-18021947/.

31. *Planned Parenthood v. Casey*, Supreme Court of the United States, June 22, 1992.

32. Ibid.

33. *Obergefell v. Hodges*, Supreme Court of the United States, June 26, 2015.

Chapter 11: Trading Taboos

1. James Gaddy, "A Recent History of Cursing on Television," *New York Magazine*, June 19, 2008, nymag.com/arts/tv/features/47985/; "South Park: It Hits the Fan," IMDb, June 20, 2001, www.imdb.com/title/tt0705935/.

2. Bibien1, "U2's Bono & Edge: 'Fucking Brilliant,'" YouTube, June 9, 2007, www.youtube.com/watch?v=COlPQlNguvU.

3. Lester Haines, "Jane Fonda C-Word Slip Shocks U.S.," The Register, February 15, 2008, www.theregister.com/2008/02/15/fonda_slip/.

4. Geoffrey Martin Hodgson, *Wrong Turnings: How the Left Got Lost* (Chicago, Illinois: University of Chicago Press, 2018).

5. Inside Edition, "Donald Trump Blasts Latino Kids' Curse-Filled Rant: 'They're Stupid People,'" YouTube, November 6, 2015, https://www.youtube.com/watch?v=GdG_uN6DyEo.

6. Jonathan Allen, "New York City Marks 10th Anniversary of Smoking Ban" Reuters, March 28, 2013, www.reuters.com/article/us-usa-smoking-newyork/new-york-city-marks-10th-anniversary-of-smoking-ban-idUSBRE92R0UU20130328.

7. Katy Steinmetz, "California Legalizes Marijuana: Everything You Need to Know," *Time*, November 9, 2016, time.com/4565438/california-marijuana-faq-rules-prop-64/.

8. "Colorado and Washington: Life after Legalization and Regulation," Marijuana Policy Project, www.mpp.org/issues/legalization/colorado-and-washington-life-after-legalization-and-regulation/.

9. James Cook and James King, *The Three Voyages of Captain James Cook round the World* (Cambridge: Cambridge University Press, 2015).

10. Ibid.

11. Shuki Friedman, "An Israeli Shabbat," Israel Democracy Institute, June 23, 2016, en.idi.org.il/articles/2348#:~:text=The%20Ahad%20Ha'am%20once,keep%20and%20maintain%20the%20Shabbat.

12. Tim Ott, "How George Carlin's 'Seven Words' Changed Legal History," Biography.com, May 19, 2020, www.biography.com/news/george-carlin-seven-words-supreme-court.

13. Anne Cohen, "A Very Brief & Exciting History of the C-Word on Television," Refinery29, www.refinery29.com/en-us/2017/06/156630/cunt-c-word-to-describe-someone-profanity-on-tv.

14. Kenneth B. Noble, "Issue of Racism Erupts in Simpson Trial" *New York Times*, January 14, 1995, www.nytimes.com/1995/01/14/us/issue-of-racism-erupts-in-simpson-trial.html.

15. Ibid.

16. Ibid.

17. Ibid.

18. Ronald K. Fried, "How the Mafia Muscled in and Controlled the Stonewall Inn," Daily Beast, June 30, 2019, www.thedailybeast.com/how-the-mafia-muscled-in-and-controlled-the-stonewall-inn.

19. "Stonewall Riots," History, May 31, 2017, www.history.com/topics/gay-rights/the-stonewall-riots.

20. David Kaufman, David, "How the Pride March Made History," *New York Times*, June 16, 2020, www.nytimes.com/2020/06/16/us/gay-lgbt-pride-march-history.html.

21. Thomas Aquinas, "Question 162. Pride," *Summa Theologiae*, www.newadvent.org/summa/3162.htm.

22. Whittaker Chambers, *Witness* (New York: Random House, 1952).

23. George Bernard Shaw, *Back to Methuselah: A Metabiological Pentateuch*, Project Gutenberg, August 18, 2018, http://www.gutenberg.org/files/13084/13084-h/13084-h.htm.

24. John Looijwn, "Edward Kennedy at the Funeral of Robert Kennedy, June 8, 1968," YouTube, October 30, 2014, www.youtube.com/watch?v=rUx2ar-RzVE.

25. G. K. Chesterton, *Orthodoxy*, Project Gutenberg, September 26, 2005, www.gutenberg.org/cache/epub/130/pg130.html.

26. Cyrus R. K. Patell, "I Face This Challenge," Patell.net, patell.net/2008/06/i-face-this-challenge/.

27. Tim Hains, "Ocasio-Cortez: 'The World Is Going to End in 12 Years If We Don't Address Climate Change,'" RealClearPolitics, www.realclearpolitics.com/video/2019/01/22/ocasio-cortez_the_world_is_going_to_end_in_12_years_if_we_dont_address_climate_change.html; Ari Natter, "Alexandria Ocasio-Cortez's Green New Deal Could Cost $93 Trillion, Group Says," Bloomberg, February 25, 2019, www.bloomberg.com/news/articles/2019-02-25/group-sees-ocasio-cortez-s-green-new-deal-costing-93-trillion.

28. Eliza Relman, "The Chair of the Democratic Party Just Embraced Progressive Insurgent Alexandria Ocasio-Cortez, Calling Her 'the Future of Our Party,'" *Business Insider*, July 3, 2018, www.businessinsider.com/dnc-tom-perez-alexandria-ocasio-cortez-democratic-socialist-future-2018-7.

29. "Utopia," Online Etymology Dictionary, www.etymonline.com/word/utopia.

30. "Eutopia," Dictionary.com, www.dictionary.com/browse/eutopia.

31. Barack Obama, *Dreams from My Father: A Story of Race and Inheritance* (Canongate, 2016).

32. Michael Oakeshott, *Rationalism in Politics and Other Essays* (Liberty Fund, 1991).

33. Winston Churchill, "Socialism Is the Philosophy of Failure," The Churchill Project, August 16, 2019, winstonchurchill.hillsdale.edu/socialism-is-the-philosophy-of-failure-winston-churchill/.

34. Leo XIII, *Quod Apostolici Muneris*, December 27, 1878, www.vatican.va/content/leo-xiii/en/encyclicals/documents/hf_l-xiii_enc_28121878_quod-apostolici-muneris.html.

35. Robert Bellafiore, "Summary of the Latest Federal Income Tax Data, 2018 Update," Tax Foundation, September 29, taxfoundation.org/summary-latest-federal-income-tax-data-2018-update/.

36. Rachel Ventresca, "Clinton: 'You Cannot Be Civil with a Political Party That Wants to Destroy What You Stand For,'" CNN, October 9, 2018, www.cnn.com/2018/10/09/politics/hillary-clinton-civility-congress-cnntv/index.html.

37. Alexandria Ocasio-Cortez (@AOC), "Is anyone archiving these Trump sycophants for when they try to downplay or deny their complicity in the future? I foresee decent probability of many deleted Tweets, writings, photos in the future," Twitter, November 6, 2020, 3:16 p.m., twitter.com/AOC/status/1324807776510595078.

38. Jake Tapper (@jaketapper), "I truly sympathize with those dealing with losing—it's not easy—but at a certain point one has to think not only about what's best for the nation (peaceful transfer of power) but how any future employers might see your character defined during adversity," Twitter, November 9, 11:24 a.m., twitter.com/jaketapper/status/1325836769644982273.

39. "Remember What They Did," Trump Accountability Project, web.archive.org/web/20201106193255/www.trumpaccountability.net/.

40. "Being Antiracist," National Museum of African American History and Culture, October 9, 2020, nmaahc.si.edu/learn/talking-about-race/topics/being-antiracist.

41. Frederick M. Hess and R. J. Martin, "Smithsonian Institution Explains That 'Rationality' & 'Hard Work' Are Racist," RealClearPolicy, 20 July 2020, www.realclearpolicy.com/articles/2020/07/20/smithsonian_institute_explains_that_rationality_and_hard_work_are_racist_499425.html.

42. FreePropaganda, "Nancy Pelosi Pass the Bill to Find out What's in It," YouTube, May 28, 2013, www.youtube.com/watch?v=QV7dDSgbaQo.

43. Elizabeth Harrington, "Pelosi: Obamacare Means 'You Could Be A Photographer or Writer.'" CNSNews.com, March 21, 2013, www.cnsnews.com/news/article/pelosi-obamacare-means-you-could-be-photographer-or-writer.

44. Ibid.

45. Martin Levine, "Republicans Give More to Charity Than Democrats, but There's a Bigger Story Here," *Nonprofit Quarterly*, November 5, 2018, nonprofitquarterly.org/republicans-give-more-to-charity-than-democrats-but-theres-a-bigger-story-here/.

46. Paul Sullivan, "How Political Ideology Influences Charitable Giving," *New York Times*, November 3, 2018, www.nytimes.com/2018/11/03/your-money/republicans-democrats-charity-philanthropy.html.

47. Michael Graham, "When It Comes to Charitable Giving, Warren and Sanders Are Millionaires Who Don't 'Pay Their Fair Share,'" InsideSources, January 2, 2020, www.insidesources.com/when-it-comes-to-charitable-giving-warren-and-sanders-are-millionaires-who-dont-pay-their-fair-share-2/.

48. Albin Krebs and Robert M. Thomas, "Notes on People; Some Disunity along the United Way," *New York Times*, September 19, 1981, www.nytimes.com/1981/09/19/nyregion/notes-on-people-some-disunity-along-the-united-way.html.

49. 1 Corinthians 13, Douay-Rheims Bible, www.drbo.org/chapter/53013.htm.

50. Whittaker Chamber, *Witness* (New York: Random House, 1952).

51. Scott McGreal, "Are Conservatives Healthier Than Liberals?" *Psychology Today*, February 28, 2019, www.psychologytoday.com/us/blog/unique-everybody-else/201902/are-conservatives-healthier-liberals.

52. "Why We're Proud of Our Fat Bodies," BBC News, September 22, 2018, www.bbc.co.uk/news/resources/idt-sh/why_we_are_proud_of_our_fat_bodies.

53. "Curves Have Their Day in Park; 500 at a 'Fat-In' Call for Obesity," *New York Times*, June 5, 1967, www.nytimes.com/1967/06/05/archives/curves-have-their-day-in-park-500-at-a-fatin-call-for-obesity.html.

54. Ibid.

55. Joshua A. Krisch, "This Shocking Map Shows Republicans' Most Powerful Political Weapon," Fatherly, November 22, 2019, www.fatherly.com/health-science/republicans-have-more-children/.

56. François La Rochefoucauld, *Reflections or, Sentences and Moral Maxims*, Project Gutenberg, January 25, 2013, www.gutenberg.org/files/9105/9105-h/9105-h.htm.

Chapter 12: The War on Christmas

1. Henry Louis Mencken, *A Mencken Chrestomathy* (New York: Vintage Books, 1982).

2. William Bradford, *Of Plymouth Plantation, 1620–1647. The Complete Text* (New York: Knopf, 1963). Adapted into modern English by the author.

3. Cotton Mather, "Grace Defended. On the Twenty-fifth of December, 1712. Boston-Lecture," Evans Early American Imprint Collection, quod. lib.umich.edu/e/evans/N01303.0001.001/1:2?rgn=div1;view=fulltext.

4. Christopher Klein, "When Massachusetts Banned Christmas," History, December 22, 2015, www.history.com/news/when-massachusetts-banned-christmas.

5. Earle Cornelius, "In 1870, Congress Made Christmas Day a Federal Holiday. But Some Still Question Its Constitutionality," LancasterOnline, December 20, 2019, lancasteronline.com/features/in-1870-congress-made-christmas-day-a-federal-holiday-but-some-still-question-its-constitutionality/article_0d8c3634-22a2-11ea-bf1d-2ba3f3a125db.html.

6. J. A. R. Pimlott, "Christmas under the Puritans," History Today 10, no. 12 (December 1960), www.historytoday.com/archive/christmas-under-puritans#:~:text=The%20Puritans%20objected%20to%20the,far%20as%20to%20advocate%20abolition.

7. Philip Stubbs, "The Anatomie of Abuses" (Richard Jones, 1583). Adapted into modern English by the author.

8. William Prynne, Histriomastix: The Player's Scourge, or Actor's Tragedy (Michael Sparke, 1632). Adapted into modern English by the author.

9. Roger Pearse, "The Chronography of 354. Introduction to the Online Edition," 2006, www.tertullian.org/fathers/chronography_of_354_00_eintro.htm.

10. Andrew McGowan, "How December 25 Became Christmas," Biblical Archaeology Society, December 18, 2020, www.biblicalarchaeology.org/daily/people-cultures-in-the-bible/jesus-historical-jesus/how-december-25-became-christmas/.

11. Ibid.

12. T. C. Schmidt, et al., Hippolytus of Rome: Commentary on Daniel and "Chronicon" (Piscataway, New Jersey: Gorgias Press, 2017).

13. "Christmas," Catholic Answers, December 16, 2019, www.catholic.com/encyclopedia/christmas.

14. Augustine, On the Trinity, trans. Stephen McKenna (Washington, D.C.: Catholic University of America Press, 1963).

15. Thomas J. Talley, Origins of the Liturgical Year (Collegeville, Minnesota: Liturgical Press, 1991).

16. Benedict XVI, The Spirit of the Liturgy (San Francisco, California: Ignatius Press, 2014).

17. C. S. Lewis, "Xmas and Christmas: A Lost Chapter from Herodotus," Khad.com, December 12, 2003, khad.com/post/196009755/ xmas-and-christmas-a-lost-chapter-from-herodotus.

18. Alejandrao Chafuen, "The Sad Decline of the Word 'Capitalism,'" *Forbes*, May 1, 2013, www.forbes.com/sites/ alejandrochafuen/2013/05/01/the-sad-decline-of-the-word- capitalism/?sh=271e8847a712; Adam Smith, *The Wealth of Nations* (New York: Random House, 2020).

19. "The Truth about the Religious Right's Phony 'War on Christmas,'" Americans United for Separation of Church and State, www.au.org/ content/the-truth-about-the-religious-rights-phony-war-on-christmas.

20. Colbert King, "I Don't Care about 'Merry Christmas,'" *Washington Post*, October 20, 2017, https://web.archive.org/ web/20171106121608if_/https://www.washingtonpost.com/ web/20171106121608if_/https://www.washingtonpost.com/opinions/i- dont-care-about-merry-christmas/2017/10/20/067a47ec-b516-11e7-a908- a3470754bbb9_story.html?utm_term=.00679b4b826f.

21. Ibid.

22. *Lynch v. Donnelly*, Supreme Court of the United States, 1984.

23. Ibid.

24. First Amendment, United States Constitution.

25. Thomas Jefferson, "Draft Reply to the Danbury Baptist Association, [on or before 31 December 1801]." Founders Online, https://founders. archives.gov/?q=danbury%20baptists&s=1111311111&sa=&r=2&sr=.

26. John R. Vile, "Established Churches in Early America," The First Amendment Encyclopedia, 2009, https://mtsu.edu/first-amendment/ article/801/established-churches-in-early-america.

27. Declaration of Independence, July 4, 1776.

28. Bob Seidensticker, "Atheist Monument Critique," Patheos, September 11, 2013, https://www.patheos.com/blogs/crossexamined/2013/09/ atheist-monument-critique-treaty-of-tripoli/.

29. FC

30. Michael B. Oren, "The Middle East and the Making of the United States, 1776 to 1815," Columbia News, November 16, 2005, https://web. archive.org/web/20071214065818/http://www.columbia.edu/cu/ news/05/11/michaelOren.html.

31. Charles Prentiss, *The Life of the Late General Eaton* (Brookfield, Massachusetts: E. Merriam & Company, 1813).

32. William J. Federer, *America's God and Country: Encyclopedia of Quotations*, rev. ed. (Ashtabula, Ohio: Amerisearch, 2000).

33. William Jay, *The Life of John Jay* (New York: J. & J. Harper, 1833).

34. Bob Dylan, "Gotta Serve Somebody" on *Slow Train Coming* (Columbia, 1975).

35. "What's in a Name? Christmas vs. Holiday Tree," NPR, November 30, 2005, https://www.npr.org/transcripts/5032882.

36. Haraz N. Ghanbari, "Decorated Spruce on Capitol Hill Ignites Controversy," *Arizona Daily Star*, December 8, 2005, https://tucson.com/news/national/govt-and-politics/decorated-spruce-on-capitol-hill-ignites-controversy/article_cdf8c405-1afd-5258-94b0-953f9b5cb5d5.html.

37. "No More 'Holiday' Trees at Capitol," *Washington Times*, November 29, 2005, https://www.washingtontimes.com/news/2005/nov/29/20051129-120703-5977r/.

38. Hemal Jhaveri, "Opinionst: D.C. Christmas Tree Controversy," dcist, December 4, 2005, https://dcist.com/story/05/12/04/opinionist-dc-c/.

39. Charles R. Drummond, "Boston's 'Holiday Tree' Sparks Controversy: Giant Spruce Tree's Name Leads to Local Outcry over Rule of Religion," *Harvard Crimson*, November 28, 2005, https://www.thecrimson.com/article/2005/11/28/bostons-holiday-tree-sparks-controversy-last/.

40. Tricia Bishop, "Stores Revert to 'Merry Christmas': WalMart Leads Way, Backing Off from 'Happy Holidays,'" *Chicago Tribune*, November 24, 2006, https://web.archive.org/web/20070312200136/http://www.chicagotribune.com/business/bal-te.bz.christmas24nov24,0,7755319.story.

41. Irene Monroe, "The Right's Bogus War on Christmas," Dick and Sharon's LA Progressive, https://web.archive.org/web/20130319165707/http://www.laprogressive.com/the-rights-bogus-war-on-christmas/.

42. David Mikkelson, "Home for the Holidays: The Home Depot Web Site Includes No Mention of Christmas?," Snopes, December 3, 2008, https://www.snopes.com/fact-check/home-depot-for-the-holidays/; https://thescroogereport.wordpress.com/tag/home-depot/.

43. Leslie Miller, "The Gap's 'Happy Whatever-You-Wannakuh' Ad Reignites 'War on Christmas' Debate," *USA Today*, November 23, 2009, http://content.usatoday.com/communities/Religion/post/2009/11/the-gap-ads—happy-do-whatever-you-wannukah-reignites-war-on-christmas-debate/1?loc=interstitialskip#.X8QY9hNKhZp.

44. Lydia Saad, "What Percentage of Americans Celebrate Christmas?" Gallup, December 2019, https://news.gallup.com/poll/272357/percentage-americans-celebrate-christmas.aspx.

45. Michael Lipka, "How Many Jews Are There in the United States?" Pew Research Center, October 2, 2013, https://www.pewresearch.org/fact-tank/2013/10/02/how-many-jews-are-there-in-the-united-states/.

46. Jennifer Bleyer, "Five Myths about Hanukkah," *Washington Post*, December 2, 2015, https://www.washingtonpost.com/opinions/five-myths-about-hanukkah/2015/12/02/2ea6fc3c-93ae-11e5-8aa0-5d0946560a97_story.html#:~:text=Hanukkah%20is%20an%20important%20Jewish%20holiday.&text=Unlike%20major%20holidays%20such%20as,light%20candles%20for%20eight%20nights.

47. "Kwanzaa," History, December 7, 2020, https://www.history.com/topics/holidays/kwanzaa-history.

48. J. Lawrence Scholer and the editors of the *Dartmouth Review*, "The Story of Kwanzaa," *Dartmouth Review*, January 15, 2001, http://www.hartford-hwp.com/archives/45a/767.html.

49. Jesse Daniels, "On Kwanzaa," Racism Review, December 27, 2009, http://www.racismreview.com/blog/2009/12/27/on-kwanzaa/.

50. Carol Forsloff, "Kwanzaa Ain't No Good Thing," Digital Journal, December 30, 2008, http://www.digitaljournal.com/article/264192.

51. "U.S. Religious Landscape Survey: Religious Affiliation: Diverse and Dynamic," Pew Forum on Religion & Public Life, February 2008, https://web.archive.org/web/20150125190643/http://religions.pewforum.org/pdf/report-religious-landscape-study-full.pdf.

52. Mitch Smith, "Christmas Tree or Holiday Tree? The Frosty Feud Splintering a State," *New York Times*, November 13, 2019, https://www.nytimes.com/2019/11/13/us/wisconsin-christmas-holiday-tree.html.

53. Tony Evers, letter to Wisconsin educators and students, October 11, 2019, https://content.govdelivery.com/attachments/WIGOV/2019/11/04/file_attachments/1318304/2019%20Ornament%20letter.pdf.

54. "Science," Online Etymology Dictionary, https://www.etymonline.com/word/science.

55. "LGBTQ Activists, Gov. Tony Evers Call for State Law Changes," Wisconsin Public Radio, June 17, 2019, https://www.wpr.org/lgbtq-activists-gov-tony-evers-call-state-law-changes; https://madison.com/wsj/news/local/govt-and-politics/democratic-gov-tony-evers-vetoes-four-abortion-bills-passed-by-gop-legislators/article_aad2c431-db56-5df2-91d2-f2f4c0c1725c.html.

Chapter 13: The Battle for the Sexes

1. Lucas Cuni-Mertz and Chelsea Engstrom, "One Arrested after Protest at On-Campus Event," U-NEWS, April 11, 2019, https://info.umkc.edu/unews/one-arrested-after-protest-at-on-campus-event.

2. Young Americas Foundation, "Speech Is Not Violence: Knowles Completely Owns Pretentious Professor," YouTube, May 2, 2019, https://www.youtube.com/watch?v=LaERkte8ylA.

3. Daily Wire, "Babies Are People: Michael Knowles Speaks at the University of Kentucky," YouTube, November 18, 2019, https://www.youtube.com/watch?v=m7stWWsIsFs.

4. Patrick Schmidt, "Heckler's Veto," The First Amendment Encyclopedia, https://www.mtsu.edu/first-amendment/article/968/heckler-s-veto.

5. Nat Hentoff, "Mugging the Minuteman," *Village Voice*, October 31, 2006, https://web.archive.org/web/20110629121552/http://www.villagevoice.com/2006-10-31/news/mugging-the-minutemen/.

6. Zoe Brown, et al., "Charges Filed in Connection to Protest of Conservative Speaker at UMKC," KCTV, April 11, 2019, https://www.kctv5.com/news/charges-filed-in-connection-to-protest-of-conservative-speaker-at-umkc/article_7bc44264-5cc7-11e9-be6d-73d3956e6c78.html.

7. Ibid.

8. Ibid.

9. Tim Hains, "Inside Edition's Zoe Tur Threatens to Send Breitbart's Ben Shapiro 'Home in an Ambulance' over Jenner Debate," RealClearPolitics, July 17, 2015, https://www.realclearpolitics.com/video/2015/07/17/inside_editions_zoe_tur_threatens_to_send_breitbarts_ben_shapiro_home_in_an_ambulance_over_jenner_debate.html.

10. Amanda Prestigiacomo, "Actor Says Trans Women Have 'Biologically Female' Penises. And Gets More Graphic from There," Daily Wire, February 20, 2019, https://www.dailywire.com/news/actor-says-trans-women-have-biologically-female-amanda-prestigiacomo.

11. "Gender," Online Etymology Dictionary, https://www.etymonline.com/word/gender.

12. "Gender," *Oxford English Dictionary Online*, http://dictionary.oed.com/cgi/entry/50093521?query_type=word&queryword=gender&first=1&max_to_show=10&sort_type=alpha&result_place=1&search_id=a4MJ-mHKT13-2771&hilite=50093521

13. Lisa Downing, et al., "Pervert or Sexual Libertarian? Meet John Money, "the Father of F***ology," Salon, January 4, 2015, https://www.salon.com/2015/01/04/pervert_or_sexual_libertarian_meet_john_money_the_father_of_fology/.

14. John Colapinto, *As Nature Made Him* (New York: HarperCollins, 2001).

15. John Money, "The Development of Sexuality and Eroticism in Humankind," *Quarterly Review of Biology* 56, no. 4 (December 1981): 379–404, https://www.jstor.org/stable/2824989?seq=1.

16. Colapinto, *As Nature Made Him*, (New York: HarperCollins, 2000).

17. John Colapinto, "The True Story of John/Joan," *Rolling Stone* (December 11, 1997): 54–97.

18. Colleen McClelland, "Canadian Man Raised as Girl Commits Suicide," *Spokesman-Review*, May 13, 2004, https://www.spokesman.com/stories/2004/may/13/canadian-man-raised-as-girl-commits-suicide/.

19. "Gender Dysphoria," *DSM-5*, 2013, https://archive.org/details/diagnosticstatis0005unse/page/454.

20. Samuel Paul Veissière, "Why Is Transgender Identity on the Rise among Teens?" *Psychology Today*, https://www.psychologytoday.com/us/blog/culture-mind-and-brain/201811/why-is-transgender-identity-the-rise-among-teens.

21. Paul McHugh, "Transgender Surgery Isn't the Solution," *Wall Street Journal*, May 13, 2016, https://www.wsj.com/articles/paul-mchugh-transgender-surgery-isnt-the-solution-1402615120.

22. Ibid.

23. Stephen P. Thornton, "Solipsism and the Problem of Other Minds," Internet Encyclopedia, https://iep.utm.edu/solipsis/.

24. "Manichaeism," *Encyclopedia Britannica*, https://www.britannica.com/topic/Manichaeism; "Albigensian Crusade," *Encyclopedia Britannica*, https://www.britannica.com/event/Albigensian-Crusade.

25. Lady Gaga, "Lady Gaga—Born This Way (Official Music Video)," YouTube, February 27, 2011, https://www.youtube.com/watch?v=wV1FrqwZyKw.

26. Emily Kirkpatrick, "J. K. Rowling Proves Her Commitment to Transphobia in Her New Novel," *Vanity Fair*, September 14, 2020, https://www.vanityfair.com/style/2020/09/jk-rowling-transphobia-new-novel-troubled-blood-controversy.

27. Robert George, "Liberal Gnosticism," *First Things*, December 2016, https://www.firstthings.com/article/2016/12/gnostic-liberalism.

28. "St. Thomas Aquinas," *Stanford Dictionary of Philosophy*, May 24, 2014, https://plato.stanford.edu/entries/aquinas/#:~:text=Thomas%20 is%20frequently%20said%20to,Procrustean%20bed%20of%20 Christian%20doctrine.

29. G. K. Chesterton, *Orthodoxy*, Project Gutenberg, September 26, 2005, www.gutenberg.org/cache/epub/130/pg130.html.

30. Steve Harrison, "Charlotte City Council Approves LGBT Protections in 7–4 Vote," *Charlotte Observer*, February 22, 2016, https://www. charlotteobserver.com/news/politics-government/article61786967.html.

31. Michael Gordon, et al., "Understanding HB2: North Carolina's Newest Law Solidifies State's Role in Defining Discrimination," *Charlotte Observer*, March 30, 2017, https://www.charlotteobserver.com/news/ politics-government/article68401147.html.

32. Tal Kopan and Eugene Scott, "North Carolina Signs Controversial Transgender Bill," CNN, March 24, 2016, https://www.cnn. com/2016/03/23/politics/north-carolina-gender-bathrooms-bill/index. html.

33. "Obama Administration Sues North Carolina over Anti-LGBT Law," BBC News, May 9, 2016, https://www.bbc.com/news/ world-us-canada-36252949.

34. "Dear Colleague Letter on Transgender Students," U.S. Department of Justice Civil Rights Division and Department of Education Office for Civil Rights, May 13, 2016, https://www.justice.gov/opa/file/850986/ download.

35. Ariane de Vogue, et al., "Trump Administration Withdraws Federal Protections for Transgender Students," CNN, February 22, 2017, https:// www.cnn.com/2017/02/22/politics/doj-withdraws-federal-protections- on-transgender-bathrooms-in-schools/index.html.

36. David A. Graham, "Donald Trump's Case for Tolerance," *The Atlantic*, April 21, 2016, https://www.theatlantic.com/politics/archive/2016/04/ trump-transgender-bathroom-north-carolina/479316/.

37. Jessica Hopper, "Ted Cruz Says Not Having 'Bathroom Bill' Is 'Opening the Door for Predators,'" ABC News, April 23, 2016, https://abcnews. go.com/Politics/ted-cruz-bathroom-bill-opening-door-predators/ story?id=38626340.

38. Andrea Peyser, "Far-Left Agitprop for Pre-K Tots: What NYC Schools Have Come To," *New York Post*, January 27, 2020, https://nypost. com/2020/01/27/ far-left-agitprop-for-pre-k-tots-what-nyc-schools-have-come-to/.

39. Charlotte Allen, "What I Saw at Drag Queen Story Hour," *Wall Street Journal*, October 9, 2019, https://www.wsj.com/articles/ what-i-saw-at-drag-queen-story-hour-11570661201.

40. Lauren Talarico, "Houston Public Library Admits Registered Child Sex Offender Read to Kids in Drag Queen Storytime," KHOU 11, March 19, 2019, https://www.khou.com/article/news/local/houston-public- library-admits-registered-child-sex-offender-read-to-kids-in-drag-queen- storytime/285-becf3a0d-56c5-4f3c-96df-add07bbd002a.

41. Benjamin Wallace-Wells, "David French, Sohrab Ahmari, and the Battle for the Future of Conservatism," *New Yorker*, September 12, 2019, https://web.archive.org/web/20200701055715/https://www.newyorker. com/news/the-political-scene/ david-french-sohrab-ahmari-and-the-battle-for-the-future-of- conservatism.

42. Beth Tagawa, "When Cross-Dressing Was Criminal: Book Details History of Longtime San Francisco Law," San Francisco State News, February 2015, https://news.sfsu.edu/ when-cross-dressing-was-criminal-book-documents-history-longtime- san-francisco-law.

43. United States Constitution.

44. James Madison, *Federalist* 51.

45. Chacour Koop, "Smithsonian Museum Apologizes for Saying Hard Work, Rational Thought Is 'White Culture,'" *Miami Herald*, July 17, 2020, https://www.miamiherald.com/news/nation-world/national/ article244309587.html.

46. Alice Hines, "Sashaying Their Way through Youth," *New York Times*, September 8, 2019, https://www.nytimes.com/2019/09/07/style/self-care/ drag-kids-desmond-the-amazing.html.

47. Ibid.

48. Desmond is Amazing, "Flackback to NYC Pride 2015. . . .," Facebook, November 10, 2018, https://www.facebook.com/DesmondisAmazing/ posts/flashback-to-nyc-pride-2015-and-the-moment-my-life- changed-by-going-viral-the-ne/1080653715429049/.

49. Hines, "Sashaying Their Way."

50. Rod Dreher, "Desmond: The *Bacha* of Brooklyn," *American Conservative*, December 17, 2018, https://www. theamericanconservative.com/dreher/ desmond-is-amazing-bacha-brooklyn/.

51. Jaime Woo, "Hot Docs 2019: In Drag Kids, Parents Cheer as Children Slay Gender Norms," April 22, 2019, https://www.theglobeandmail. com/life/parenting/article-in-documentary-drag-kids-parents-cheer-as-children-slay-gender-norms/.

52. Peyser, "Far-Left Agitprop."

53. Genesis 5:2, King James Version.

Chapter 14: Locking Down Dissent

1. Vadim M. Shteyler, et al., "Failed Assignments—Rethinking Sex Designations on Birth Certificates," *New England Journal of Medicine* 383 (December 17, 2020): 2399–401, DOI: 10.1056/NEJMp2025974, https://www.nejm.org/doi/full/10.1056/NEJMp2025974.

2. Natalie Colarossi, "COVID Lockdowns May Have No Clear Benefit vs. Other Voluntary Measures, International Study Shows," *Newsweek*, January 14, 2021, https://www.newsweek.com/ covid-lockdowns-have-no-clear-benefit-vs-other-voluntary-measures-international-study-shows-1561656.

3. "Coronavirus Disease (COVID-19): Serology," World Health Organization, June 9, 2020, https://web.archive.org/ web/20201023093420/https://www.who.int/news-room/q-a-detail/ coronavirus-disease-covid-19-serology.

4. Ibid.

5. Ibid.

6. James S. Robbins, "Rioting Is Beginning to Turn People Off to BLM and Protests while Biden Has No Solution," *USA Today*, August 31, 2020, https://www.usatoday.com/story/opinion/2020/08/31/ riots-violence-erupting-turning-many-away-blm-and-protests-column/5675343002/.

7. Emily Cochrane and Aishvarya Kavi, "Romney Marches with Protesters in Washington," *New York Times*, June 7, 2020, https://www.nytimes. com/2020/06/07/us/politics/mitt-romney-george-floyd-protests.html.

8. Jay Croft and Amir Vera, "Thousands of Mourners Visit George Floyd's Casket in Houston to Pay Respects," CNN, June 8, 2020, https://www. cnn.com/2020/06/08/us/george-floyd-houston-visitation/index.html.

9. Adam Edelman, "Biden Calls for 'Racial Justice during Emotional George Floyd Funeral Speech," NBC News, June 9, 2020, https://www. nbcnews.com/politics/2020-election/biden-calls-racial-justice-during-emotional-george-floyd-funeral-speech-n1228566.

10. Kendall Karson, "Michigan Gov. Whitmer: Protests 'Undermine" State's Response to COVID-19 Crisis," ABC News, May 13, 2020, https://abcnews.go.com/Politics/michigan-gov-whitmer-protests-undermine-states-response-covid/story?id=70645516; "A Breakdown of Who Supports and Opposes George Floyd Protests in US," TRT World, June 4, 2020, https://www.trtworld.com/magazine/a-breakdown-of-who-supports-and-opposes-george-floyd-protests-in-the-us-36952.

11. Mallory Simon, "Over 1,000 Health Professionals Sign a Letter Saying, Don't Shut Down Protests Using Coronavirus Concerns as an Excuse," CNN, June 5, 2020, https://www.cnn.com/2020/06/05/health/health-care-open-letter-protests-coronavirus-trnd/index.html.

12. "Open Letter Advocating for an Anti-Racist Public Health Response to Demonstrations against Systemic Injustice Occurring during the COVID-19 Pandemic," Google Drive, June 5, 2020, https://drive.google.com/file/d/1Jyfn4Wd2i6bRi12ePghMHtX3ys1b7K1A/view.

13. Ibid.

14. "Factcheck: Outdated Video of Fauci Saying 'There's No Reason to Be Walking around with a Mask,'" Reuters, October 8, 2020, https://www.reuters.com/article/uk-factcheck-fauci-outdated-video-masks/fact-checkoutdated-video-of-fauci-saying-theres-no-reason-to-be-walking-around-with-a-mask-idUSKBN26T2TR.

15. "Anthony S. Fauci, M.D., NIAID Director," National Institutes of Health, https://www.niaid.nih.gov/about/director.

16. "Biography: Anthony S. Fauci, M.D., NAIAID Director," National Institutes of Health, https://web.archive.org/web/20071030171118/http://www3.niaid.nih.gov/about/directors/biography/.

17. U.S. Surgeon General (@Surgeon_General), "Seriously people—STOP BUYING MASKS! They are NOT effective in preventing general public from catching #Coronavirus, but if healthcare providers can't get them to care for sick patients, it puts them and our communities at risk!" Twitter, February 29, 2020, 4:08 a.m., https://web.archive.org/web/20200302023223if_/https://twitter.com/Surgeon_General/status/1233725785283932160.

18. Office of the U.S. Surgeon General (@Surgeon_General), "In light of new evidence, @CDC recommends wearing cloth face coverings in public settings where other social distancing measures are difficult to maintain (grocery stores, pharmacies, etc) especially in areas of significant community-based transmission," Twitter, April 3, 2020, 6:58 p.m., https://twitter.com/Surgeon_General/status/1246210376351592448.

19. ABC News, "Dr. Fauci to Muir: 'Universal Wearing of Masks' Necessary to Combat COVID-19: WNT," YouTube, August 10, 2020, https://www.youtube.com/watch?v=HAFQknk5nwI&feature=youtu.be&t=152.

20. Henning Bungaard, et al., "Effectiveness of Adding a Mask Recommendation to Other Public Health Measures to Prevent SARS-CoV-2 Infection in Danish Mask Wearers," *Annals of Internal Medicine*, November 18, 2020, https://doi.org/10.7326/M20-6817, https://www.acpjournals.org/doi/10.7326/M20-6817; Jingyi Xiao, et al., "Nonpharmaceutical Measures for Pandemic Influenza in Nonhealthcare Settings—Personal Protective and Environmental Measures," *Centers for Disease Control and Prevention Policy Review* 26, no. 5 (May 26, 2020), https://wwwnc.cdc.gov/eid/article/26/5/19-0994_article.

21. "Fauci on How His Thinking Has Evolved on Masks, Asymptomatic Transmission," *Washington Post*, July 24, 2020, https://www.washingtonpost.com/video/washington-post-live/fauci-on-how-his-thinking-has-evolved-on-masks-asymptomatic-transmission/2020/07/24/799264e2-0f35-4862-aca2-2b4702650a8b_video.html.

22. The Daily Show with Trevor Noah, "Dr. Anthony Fauci: Getting Politis Out of Public Health: The Daily Social Distancing Show," Youtube, September 22, 2020, https://www.youtube.com/watch?v=5rKt54x6Hp0&feature=youtu.be&t=342.

23. Aristotle, *Politics*, trans. William Ellis, Project Gutenberg, June 5, 2009, http://www.gutenberg.org/files/6762/6762-h/6762-h.htm.

24. Alex Rogers, "Barack Obama Stumps for Jon Ossoff in New TV Ad," CNN, December 1, 2020, https://www.cnn.com/2020/12/01/politics/obama-ossoff-ad/index.html.

25. Ibid.

26. "2020 Report to Congress: Executive Summary and Recommendations," U.S.–China Economic and Security Review Commission, December 2020, https://www.uscc.gov/sites/default/files/2020-12/2020_Executive_Summary.pdf.

27. Dana Robinson and Ann Battenfield, "The Worst Outbreaks in U.S. History," Healthline, March 24, 2020, https://www.healthline.com/health/worst-disease-outbreaks-history#measles.

28. David R. Boldt, "Colder Winters He[ra]ld Dawn of New Ice Age," *Washington Post*, January 11, 1970, https://web.archive.org/web/20150221224323/http://pqasb.pqarchiver.com/

washingtonpost_historical/doc/147902052.html?FMT=ABS&FMTS=&
type=historic&date=washingtonpost+%2C+&author=Washington+Post
+Staff+Writer%3B+By+David+R.+Boldt&pub=The+Washington+Post%
2C+Times+Herald+%281959-1973%29&desc=Colder+Winters+Held+D
awn+of+New+Ice+Age&pqatl=top_retrieves.

29. "Science: Another Ice Age," *Time*, November 13, 1972, http://content.
time.com/time/magazine/article/0,9171,910467,00.html.

30. "The Cooling World," *Newsweek*, April 28, 1975, https://iseethics.files.
wordpress.com/2012/06/the-cooling-world-newsweek-april-28-1975.pdf.

31. "The Global Cooling Myth," Real Climate, January 14, 2005, http://
www.realclimate.org/index.php/archives/2005/01/
the-global-cooling-myth/.

32. "The Cooling World," *Newsweek*.

33. Ramez Naam, "Hunger Is at an All-Time Low. We Can Drive It Even
Lower," Ramez Naam, September 9, 2015, https://rameznaam.
com/2015/09/09/
hunger-is-at-an-all-time-low-we-can-drive-it-even-lower/.

34. "The Cooling World," *Newsweek*.

35. Paul R. Ehrlich, *The Population Bomb* (Rivercity, Massachsetts:
Rivercity Press, 1975), https://faculty.washington.edu/jhannah/
geog270auto7/readings/population/Ehrlich%20-%20Population%20
Bomb%20Ch1.pdf.

36. Charles C. Mann, "The Book That Incited a Worldwide Fear of
Overpopulation," *Smithsonian Magazine*, January/February 2018,
https://www.smithsonianmag.com/innovation/
book-incited-worldwide-fear-overpopulation-180967499/.

37. Ibid.

38. "How China's One-Child Policy Led to Forced Abortions, 30 Million
Bachelors," NPR, February 1, 2016, https://www.npr.
org/2016/02/01/465124337/how-chinas-one-child-policy-led-to-forced-
abortions-30-million-bachelors.

39. Naam, "Hunger Is at an All-Time Low."

40. "Paul Ehrlich," Stanford Profiles, September 15, 2015, https://profiles.
stanford.edu/paul-ehrlich.

41. "Professor Paul R. Ehrlich," The Royal Society, April 22, 2012, https://
web.archive.org/web/20120422185752/https://royalsociety.org/people/
paul-ehrlich/.

42. "The Population Bomb 50 Years Later: A Conversation with Paul Ehrlich," Climate One, May 5, 2018, https://climateone.org/audio/population-bomb-50-years-later-conversation-paul-ehrlich.

43. John Harlow, "Billionaire Club in Bid to Curb Overpopulation, *Times*, May 24, 2009, https://www.thetimes.co.uk/article/billionaire-club-in-bid-to-curb-overpopulation-d2fl22qhlo2; Ron Smith, "The Environmental Problem the World Is Loath to Address," *Baltimore* Sun, July 17, 2009, https://www.baltimoresun.com/news/bs-xpm-2009-07-17-0907160033-story.html.

44. Al Gore, *Earth in the Balance: Ecology and the Human Spirit* (Boston: Houghton Mifflin, 1992).

45. Chris Smith, "Violence against Children Is Al Gore's Cure for Environment," Congressional Record, October 7, 1997, https://www.govinfo.gov/content/pkg/CREC-1997-10-07/html/CREC-1997-10-07-pt1-PgH8566-3.htm.

46. Kenneth R. Weis, "Al Gore: Stabilize Population to Combat Global Warming," *Los Angeles Times*, June 22, 2011, https://latimesblogs.latimes.com/greenspace/2011/06/al-gore-climate-change-population-contraception-fertility.html.

47. "Bernie Sanders in Climate Change 'Population Control' Uproar," BBC, September 5, 2019, https://www.bbc.com/news/world-us-canada-49601678.

48. Ari Natter, "Alexandria Ocasio-Cortez's Green New Deal Could Cost $93 Trillion, Group Says," Bloomberg, February 25, https://www.bloomberg.com/news/articles/2019-02-25/group-sees-ocasio-cortez-s-green-new-deal-costing-93-trillion.

49. "Green New Deal FAQ," February 7, 2019, Assets Document Cloud, https://assets.documentcloud.org/documents/5729035/Green-New-Deal-FAQ.pdf.

50. Tara Golshan and Ella Nilsen, "Alexandria Ocasio-Cortez's Roll-Out of the Green New Deal, Explained," *Vox*, February 11, 2019, https://www.vox.com/policy-and-politics/2019/2/11/18220163/alexandria-ocasio-cortez-green-new-deal-faq-tucker-carlson.

51. Alexandria Ocasio-Cortez (sponsor), "H.Res.109—Recognizing the duty of the Federal Government to Create a Green New Deal," Legislation, Congress.gov, February 12, 2019, https://www.congress.gov/bill/116th-congress/house-resolution/109/text.

52. "Scientific Consensus," Google Books Ngram Viewer, https://books.google.com/ngrams/graph?content=%22scientific+consensus%22&year_start=1700&year_end=2015&corpus=15&smoothing=3&dir

ect_url=t1%3B%2C%22%20scientific%20consensus%20
%22%3B%2Cco#t1%3B%2C%22%20scientific%20consensus%20
%22%3B%2Cco.

53. "Scientific Consensus: Earth's Climate Is Warming," NASA, https://
climate.nasa.gov/scientific-consensus/.

54. Craig D. Idso, et al., "Why Scientists Disagree about Global Warming:
The NIPCC Report on Scientific Consensus," 2nd ed., The Heartland
Institute, 2016, https://www.heartland.org/_template-assets/documents/
Books/Why%20Scientists%20Disagree%20Second%20Edition%20
with%20covers.pdf.

55. John Cook (@johnfocook), "In our study finding 97.1% consensus on
human-caused global warming in abstracts, we addressed this exact
issue by inviting the authors of the papers to categorize their own
research based on the full paper. Result? 97.2% consensus," Twitter,
https://twitter.com/johnfocook/status/1199131486580092928.

56. Idso, et al., "Why Scientists Disagree."

57. Ibid.

58. Ibid.

59. "University of Iowa Hospitals Boasts [*sic*] 99.7% Coronavirus Survival
Rate, amid Financial Woes," *Gazette*, June 4, 2020, https://www.
thegazette.com/subject/news/education/university-of-iowa-hospitals-boasts-
997-coronavirus-survival-rate-amid-financial-woes-20200604.

60. William Cummings, "The World Is Going to End in 12 Years If We
Don't Address Climate Change, Ocasio-Cortez Says," *USA Today*,
January 22, 2019, https://www.usatoday.com/story/news/politics/
onpolitics/2019/01/22/ocasio-cortez-climate-change-alarm/2642481002/;
Matt McGrath, "Climate Change: 12 Years to Save the Planet? Make
That 18 Months," BBC News, July 24, 2019, https://www.bbc.com/
news/science-environment-48964736.

61. Timothy Leary, *Sound Bites from the Counter Culture* (Atlantic, 1989).

Chapter 15: The Purge

1. Mike Isaac and Kate Conger, "Facebook Bars Trump through End of
His Term," *New York Times*, January 7, 2021, https://www.nytimes.
com/2021/01/07/technology/facebook-trump-ban.html; "Most Popular
Social Networks Worldwide as of January 2021, Ranked by Number of
Active Users," Statista, February 9, 2021, https://www.statista.com/
statistics/272014/global-social-networks-ranked-by-number-of-users/.

2. Annie Palmer, "Facebook Will Block Trump from Posting at Least for the Remainder of His Term," CNBC, January 7, 2021, https://www.cnbc.com/2021/01/07/facebook-will-block-trump-from-posting-for-the-remainder-of-his-term.html.

3. "Permanent Suspension of @realDonaldTrump," Twitter, January 8, 2021, https://blog.twitter.com/en_us/topics/company/2020/suspension.html.

4. "Most Popular Social Networks," Statista.

5. Jessica Guynn, "Trump Permanently Banned from Twitter over Risk He Could Incite Violence," *USA Today*, January 8, 2021, https://www.usatoday.com/story/tech/2021/01/08/twitter-permanently-bans-president-trump/6603578002/.

6. "Permanent Suspension of @realDonaldTrump," Twitter.

7. Lahav Harkov, "Twitter Downplays Khamenei Calls for Genocide as Political Speech," *Jerusalem Post*, July 31, 2020, https://www.jpost.com/middle-east/twitter-downplays-khamenei-calls-for-genocide-as-political-speech-636910.

8. President Trump (@POTUS), "As I have been saying for a long time, Twitter has gone further and further in banning free speech, and tonight, Twitter employees have coordinated with the Democrats and the Radical Left in removing my account from their platform … " Twitter, January 8, 2021, 5:29 p.m., screenshot by Yashar Ali (@yashar), "The president tweeted this from the @POTUS account but the tweets have already been taken down by Twitter," Twitter, January 8, 2021, 8:35 p.m., https://twitter.com/yashar/status/1347718683351601152.

9. Lucas Matney, "President Trump Responds to Twitter Account Ban in Tweet Storm from @POTUS Account," Yahoo!, January 8, 2021, https://finance.yahoo.com/news/president-trump-responds-twitter-account-015555288.html.

10. It happened to me!

11. "Google Suspends 'Free Speech' App Parler," BBC, January 9, 2021, https://www.bbc.com/news/technology-55598887.

12. Russell Brandom, "There Are Now 2.5 Billion Active Android Devices," The Verge, May 7, 2019, https://www.theverge.com/2019/5/7/18528297/google-io-2019-android-devices-play-store-total-number-statistic-keynote.

13. Jack Nicas, "Parler Pitched Itself as Twitter without Rules. Not Anymore, Apple and Google Said," *New York Times*, January 8, 2021, https://www.nytimes.com/2021/01/08/technology/parler-apple-google.

html; Dami Lee, "Apple Says There Are 1.4 Billion Active Apple Devices," The Verge, January 29, 2019, https://www.theverge.com/2019/1/29/18202736/apple-devices-ios-earnings-q1-2019#:~:text=Apple%20says%20there%20are%20now,accessories%20like%20AirPods%20aren't.

14. Nicas, "Parler Pitched Itself as Twitter without Rules."

15. Kif Leswing, "Apple Removes Parler from App Store in Wake of U.S. Capitol Riot," CNBC, January 9, 2021, https://www.cnbc.com/2021/01/09/apple-removes-parler-from-app-store-in-wake-of-us-capitol-riot.html.

16. John Paczkowski and Ryan Mac, "Amazon Will Suspend Hosting for Pro-Trump Social Network Parler," BuzzFeed News, January 9, 2021, https://www.buzzfeednews.com/article/johnpaczkowski/amazon-parler-aws.

17. Kathy Griffin (@KathyGriffin), "Just resign now. You lost. Its over," Twitter, January 6, 2021, https://web.archive.org/web/20210106231245/https://twitter.com/kathygriffin/status/1346957786517671937.

18. Peter Aitken, "'Hang Mike Pence' Trends on Twitter after Platform Suspends Trump for Risk of 'Incitement of Violence,'" Fox News, January 9, 2021, https://www.foxnews.com/politics/twitter-trending-hang-mike-pence.

19. "The 100 Largest Companies in the World by Market Capitalization in 2020," Statista, https://www.statista.com/statistics/263264/top-companies-in-the-world-by-market-capitalization/.

20. "Mobile Operating Systems' Market Share Worldwide from January 1012 to January 2021," Statista, https://www.statista.com/statistics/272698/global-market-share-held-by-mobile-operating-systems-since-2009/#:~:text=Android%20maintained%20its%20position%20as,of%20the%20global%20market%20share.

21. Timothy B. Lee, "Twitter Explains Why It Banned the App for Gab, a Right-Wing Twitter Rival," Ars Technica, August 18, 2017, https://arstechnica.com/tech-policy/2017/08/gab-the-right-wing-twitter-rival-just-got-its-app-banned-by-google/.

22. Laura Hautala, "Paypal and Shopify Remove Trump-Related Accounts, Citing Policies against Supporting Violence," CNET, January 7, 2021, https://www.cnet.com/news/paypal-and-shopify-remove-trump-related-accounts-citing-policies-against-supporting-violence/.

23. "Market Share Category: Payment Processing," Datanyze, https://www.datanyze.com/market-share/payment-processing—26; Hautala, "Paypal and Shopify Remove Trump-Related Accounts."

24. Adi Robertson, "Gab Is Back Online after Being Banned by GoDaddy, Paypal, and More," The Verge, November 5, 2018, https://www. theverge.com/2018/11/5/18049132/gab-social-network-online-synagogue-shooting-deplatforming-return-godaddy-paypal-stripe-ban.

25. "Capitol Riots: Pro-Trump Protesters Storm the U.S. Legislature—in Pictures," BBC, January 6, 2021, https://www.bbc.com/news/world-us-canada-55568131.

26. Bill Chappell, "Man Who Posed for Photos Sitting at a Desk in Pelosi's Office Has Been Arrested," NPR, January 8, 2021, https://www.npr.org/sections/congress-electoral-college-tally-live-updates/2021/01/08/954940681/man-who-posed-for-photos-sitting-at-desk-in-pelosis-office-has-been-arrested.

27. Steven Nelson, "FBI Director Wray Won't Share Officer Brian Sicknick's Cause of Death with Senators ," New York Post, March 2, 2021, https://nypost.com/2021/03/02/fbi-director-wray-mum-on-officer-brian-sicknicks-cause-of-death/; Eric Levenson, et al., "What We Know about the Five Deaths in the Pro-Trump Mob That Stormed the Capitol," CNN, January 8, 2021, https://www.cnn.com/2021/01/07/us/capitol-mob-deaths/index.html.

28. Matt Small, "FBI Offering Up to $50K for Information on DNC and RNC Pipe Bombs," WTOP News, January 8, 2021, https://wtop.com/dc/2021/01/fbi-offering-up-to-50k-for-information-on-dnc-and-rnc-pipe-bombs/.

29. Kate Conger, "Twitter, in Widening Crackdown, Removes Over 70,000 QAnon Accounts," New York Times, January 11, 2021, https://www.nytimes.com/2021/01/11/technology/twitter-removes-70000-qanon-accounts.html.

30. Lois Becket, "At Least 25 Americans Were Killed during Protests and Political Unrest in 2020," The Guardian, October 31, 2020, https://www.theguardian.com/world/2020/oct/31/americans-killed-protests-political-unrest-acled.

31. Steve Guest (@SteveGuest), "CNN's Chris Cuomo: 'Please, show me where it says protesters are supposed to be polite and peaceful.' As riots and looting have broken out in cities across the country, this is the message the brother of New York governor Andrew Cuomo shares at the top of his show," Twitter, June 2, 2020, 9:12 p.m., https://twitter.com/SteveGuest/status/1267987525198585856; Steve Guest (@SteveGuest), "1 Amd: "Congress shall make no law respecting an establishment of religion, or prohibiting the free exercise thereof; or abridging the freedom of speech, or of the press; or the right of the people PEACEABLY to

assemble, & to petition the Government for a redress of grievances," Twitter, June 2, 2020, 9:33 p.m., https://twitter.com/SteveGuest/status/1267987525198585856.

32. Ibid.

33. Kamala Harris (@KamalaHarris), "If you're able to, chip in now to the @MNFreedomFund to help post bail for those protesting on the ground in Minnesota," Twitter, June 1, 2020, 4:34 p.m., https://twitter.com/KamalaHarris/status/1267555018128965643.

34. Andrew Kerr and Kyle Hooten, "Bail Fund Promoted by Kamala Harris Helped Man Accused of Sexually Penetrating a Child," Daily Caller, September 16, 2020, https://dailycaller.com/2020/09/16/kamala-harris-minnesota-bail-fund-accused-sexual-assault-child/.

35. Ellen Cranley, "Twitter Changed Its Profile to Honor Black Lives Matter amid George Floyd Riots," *Business Insider*, May 31, 2020, https://www.businessinsider.com/twitter-changed-profile-black-lives-matter-2020-5.

36. "Worldwide Desktop Market Share of Leading Search Engines from January 2010 to January 2021," Statista, https://www.statista.com/statistics/216573/worldwide-market-share-of-search-engines/.

37. Verdict with Ted Cruz, "Bill Barr is the Honey Badger ft. Attorney General Bill Barr, Ep. 34" Facebook, June 30, 2020, https://www.facebook.com/watch/?v=3718014621548732.

38. Thomas Fabbri, "Why Is Instagram Deleting the Accounts of Hundreds of Porn Stars?" BBC, November 24, 2019, https://www.bbc.com/news/blogs-trending-50222380.

39. Tom McKay, "Alt-Right Platform Gab's Management Is Now Blaming a Leftist Conspiracy for Their Nazi Problem," Gizmodo, June 2, 2018, https://gizmodo.com/alt-right-platform-gabs-management-is-now-blaming-a-lef-1826510673.

40. William Bradford, "The Pestilent Morton and His Merry Mount," Bartleby, https://www.bartleby.com/400/prose/24.html.

41. Alien Registration Act.

42. *Dennis v. United States*, Supreme Court of the United States, 1951.

43. Child Online Protection Act.

44. *Ashcroft v. American Civil Liberties Union*, Supreme Court of the United States, 2002.

45. Kevin Roose, "In Pulling Trump's Megaphone, Twitter Shows Where Power Now Lies," *New York Times*, January 9, 2021, https://www.nytimes.com/2021/01/09/technology/trump-twitter-ban.html.

46. Kevin Roose, "On Election Day, Facebook and Twitter Did Better by Making Their Products Worse," *New York Times*, November 5, 2020, https://www.nytimes.com/2020/11/05/technology/facebook-twitter-election.html.

47. Roose, "In Pulling Trump's Megaphone."

48. Ibid.

49. Wendy Kaminer, "The ACLU Retreats from Free Expression," *Wall Street Journal*, June 20, 2018, https://www.wsj.com/articles/the-aclu-retreats-from-free-expression-1529533065.

50. Roose, "In Pulling Trump's Megaphone."

51. Hannah Kanik, "Here Are the Best Reactions to Twitter Suspending President Trump's Account," *Philly Voice*, January 9, 2021, https://www.phillyvoice.com/twitter-suspends-president-trump-reactions/.

52. Donald Trump Jr. (@DonldJTrumpJr), "We are living in Orwell's 1984. . . .," Twitter, January 8, 2021, 7:10 p.m., https://twitter.com/DonaldJTrumpJr/status/1347697226466828288.

53. Donald Trump Jr. (@DonldJTrumpJr), "it continues . . . Big Tech has totally eliminated. . . .," Twitter, January 9, 2021, 3:41 p.m., https://twitter.com/DonaldJTrumpJr/status/1348006883861282816.

54. Paulina Pineda, "Perry Lifts Suspension of Student in MAGA Controversy as Conservative Group Steps In," *Arizona Republic*, March 7, 2019, https://www.azcentral.com/story/news/local/gilbert/2019/03/07/perry-student-back-school-after-maga-controversy/3094372002/.

55. Adam Smith, *An Inquiry into the Nature and Causes of the Wealth of Nations*, Project Gutenberg, September 7, 2019, book 4, chapter 5, "Digression on the Corn Trade," http://www.gutenberg.org/ebooks/3300.

56. Barry Goldwater, *The Conscience of a Conservative* (Boonsboro, Maryland: Martino Fine Books, 2011).

57. "What We Do," United States Africa Command, January 20, 2013, https://www.africom.mil/what-we-do.

58. Goldwater, *The Conscience of a Conservative*.

59. James Madison, *Federalist* 51.

60. Woodrow Wilson, "What Is Progress," Teaching American History, 1913, https://teachingamericanhistory.org/library/document/what-is-progress/.

61. Antonio Gramsci, *Prison Notebooks*, ed. Joseph A. Buttigieg (New York: Columbia University Press, 2011).

Conclusion: Back to Methuselah

1. George Bernard Shaw, *Back to Methuselah: A Metabiological Pentateuch*, Project Gutenberg, August 18, 2018, http://www.gutenberg.org/files/13084/13084-h/13084-h.htm.

2. Ibid.

3. Deborah Cameron, "Words, Words, Words" in *The War of the Words: The Political Correctness Debate*, ed. Sarah Dunant (London: Virago Press, 1994); Whittaker Chambers, *Witness* (New York: Random House, 1952).

4. Daniel Lopez, "The Conversion of Georg Lukács," *Jacobin*, January 24, 2019, https://jacobinmag.com/2019/01/lukacs-hungary-marx-philosophy-consciousness.

5. Max Horkheimer, *Critical Theory* (New York: Continuum, 1982).

6. Karen Ho, "George Orwell's '1984' Is Topping Amazon's Best Sellers," Quartz, January 13, 2021, https://qz.com/1956937/george-orwells-1984-is-topping-amazons-best-sellers/.

7. Hanisch, "The Personal Is Political."

8. Friedan, *It Changed My Life: Writings on the Women's Movement.*

9. Jennie Rothenberg Gritz, "Ranting against Cant," *The Atlantic*, July 2003, https://www.theatlantic.com/magazine/archive/2003/07/ranting-against-cant/303095/.

10. Greg Lukianoff, "Campus Speech Codes: Absurd, Tenacious, and Everywhere," Foundation for Individual Rights in Education, May 28, 2008, https://www.thefire.org/campus-speech-codes-absurd-tenacious-and-everywhere/.

11. Phillip Rawls, "Huck Finn: Controversy over Removing the "N Word" from Mark Twain Novel," *Christian Science Monitor*, January 5, 2011, https://www.csmonitor.com/Books/Latest-News-Wires/2011/0105/Huck-Finn-Controversy-over-removing-the-N-word-from-Mark-Twain-novel.

12. George Orwell, *Nineteen Eighty-Four: A Novel*, (London: Penguin Books, 1967).

13. William F. Buckley Jr., *God and Man at Yale* (Washington, D.C.: Regnery Publishing, 1986).

14. Ibid.

15. William Butler Yeats, "The Second Coming," September 2, 2017, https://www.poetryfoundation.org/poems/43290/the-second-coming.

16. Sohrab Ahmari, "Against David French-ism," *First Things*, May 29, 2019, https://www.firstthings.com/web-exclusives/2019/05/against-david-french-ism.

17. Thomas Sowell, "Blame the Welfare State, Not Racism, for Poor Blacks' Problems," Penn Live, January 5, 2019, https://www.pennlive.com/opinion/2015/05/poor_blacks_looking_for_someon.html.

18. Peter Thompson, "Eastern Germany: The Most Godless Place on Earth, *The Guardian*, September 22, 2012, https://www.theguardian.com/commentisfree/belief/2012/sep/22/atheism-east-germany-godless-place.

19. Kyle Hanby, "John Locke: Father of Liberalism," Acton Institute, August 29, 2016, https://blog.acton.org/archives/88741-john-locke-father-of-liberalism.html; John Locke, *A Letter Concerning Toleration*, Penn State University's Electronic Classics, 2005, http://self.gutenberg.org/wplbn0000651234-a-letter-concerning-toleration-by-locke-john.aspx.

Appendix: Glossary of Jargon

1. Tess Bonn, "Conservative Journalist Andy Ngo Says Assault involving Antifa Resulted in Brain Injury," *The Hill*, July 25, 2019, https://thehill.com/hilltv/rising/454712-conservative-journalist-andy-ngo-says-antifa-attack-resulted-in-brain-injury.

2. "'In a Racist Society, It Is Not Enough to Be Non-Racist, We Must Be Anti-Racist,'—Angela Y. Davis," Buffalo Center for Health Equity, https://www.buffalo.edu/content/dam/www/inclusion/docs/Comm%20Health%20Equity.pdf; Bettina Aptheker, *The Morning Breaks: The Trial of Angela Davis* (Ithaca, New York: Cornell University Press, 1997), https://www.jstor.org/stable/10.7591/j.ctt5hhog9.

3. William Shakespeare, *The Merchant of Venice* IV.1, Project Gutenberg, March 9, 2019, https://www.gutenberg.org/files/1515/1515-h/1515-h.htm, adapted to cancel culture.

4. Byron York (@ByronYork), "The National Museum of African American History & Culture wants to make you aware of certain signs of whiteness: Individualism, hard work, objectivity, the nuclear family, progress, respect for authority, delayed gratification, more. (via @RpwWilliams)" Twitter, July 15, 2020, 8:05 a.m., https://twitter.com/ByronYork/status/1283372233730203651.

INDEX